URBAN MOBILITY AND SOCIAL EQUITY IN LATIN AMERICA

EDITORIAL ADVISORY BOARD

Lucy Budd, De Montfort University, UK
Michela Le Pira, University of Catania, Italy
Becky Loo, University of Hong Kong, Hong Kong
Corinne Mulley, University of Sydney, Australia
John Nelson, University of Sydney, Australia
Joachim Scheiner, Technical University of Dortmund, Germany

TRANSPORT AND SUSTAINABILITY

Series Editors   Stephen Ison, John Shaw and Maria Attard

Recent Volumes:

Volume 1:   Cycling and Sustainability
Volume 2:   Transport and Climate Change
Volume 3:   Sustainable Transport for Chinese Cities
Volume 4:   Sustainable Aviation Futures
Volume 5:   Parking: Issues and Policies
Volume 6:   Sustainable Logistics
Volume 7:   Sustainable Urban Transport
Volume 8:   Paratransit: Shaping the Flexible Transport Future
Volume 9:   Walking: Connecting Sustainable Transport with Health
Volume 10: Transport, Travel and Later Life
Volume 11: Safe Mobility: Challenges, Methodology and Solutions

TRANSPORT AND SUSTAINABILITY
VOLUME 12

URBAN MOBILITY AND SOCIAL EQUITY IN LATIN AMERICA: EVIDENCE, CONCEPTS, METHODS

DR DANIEL OVIEDO
University College London, UK

DR NATALIA VILLAMIZAR DUARTE
Universidad Nacional de Colombia, Colombia

DR ANA MARCELA ARDILA PINTO
Universidade Federal de Minas Gerais, Brazil

United Kingdom – North America – Japan
India – Malaysia – China

Emerald Publishing Limited
Howard House, Wagon Lane, Bingley BD16 1WA, UK

First edition 2021

Copyright © 2021 Emerald Publishing Limited

Reprints and permissions service
Contact: permissions@emeraldinsight.com

No part of this book may be reproduced, stored in a retrieval system, transmitted in any form or by any means electronic, mechanical, photocopying, recording or otherwise without either the prior written permission of the publisher or a licence permitting restricted copying issued in the UK by The Copyright Licensing Agency and in the USA by The Copyright Clearance Center. Any opinions expressed in the chapters are those of the authors. Whilst Emerald makes every effort to ensure the quality and accuracy of its content, Emerald makes no representation implied or otherwise, as to the chapters' suitability and application and disclaims any warranties, express or implied, to their use.

British Library Cataloguing in Publication Data
A catalogue record for this book is available from the British Library

ISBN: 978-1-78769-010-3 (Print)
ISBN: 978-1-78769-009-7 (Online)
ISBN: 978-1-78769-011-0 (Epub)

ISSN: 2044-9941 (Series)

Printed and bound by CPI Group (UK) Ltd, Croydon, CR0 4YY

ISOQAR certified Management System, awarded to Emerald for adherence to Environmental standard ISO 14001:2004.

Certificate Number 1985
ISO 14001

INVESTOR IN PEOPLE

CONTENTS

List of Figures and Tables — ix

List of Contributors — xiii

Editor Biographies — xv

Contributor Biographies — xvii

Prologue — xxi
Karen Lucas

Acknowledgements — xxiii

Urban Mobility and Social Equity: An Introduction
Natalia Villamizar Duarte, Daniel Oviedo and
Ana Marcela Ardila Pinto — 1

Chapter 1   Should Urban Transport Become a Social Policy? Interrogating the Role of Accessibility in Social Equity and Urban Development in Bogotá, Colombia
Daniel Oviedo and Luis Ángel Guzmán — 11

Chapter 2   Mobility and Gender Equity in Latin America: Different Mobile Burdens and Contributions in Montevideo (Uruguay)
Diego Hernández and Daniela de los Santos — 33

Chapter 3   Children and Urban Mobility: Care Dynamics on Family Mobility Patterns
Gabriela Cicci Faria — 59

Chapter 4   'Like Sardines in a Can'. Gender, Stratification and Mobility in the Lives of Female Household Employees in Bogotá, Colombia
Friederike Fleischer and Ivette S. Sepúlveda Sanabria — 85

Chapter 5 Sustainable Transport and Gender Equity: Insights from Santiago, Chile
Lake Sagaris and Ignacio Tiznado-Aitken   *103*

Chapter 6 Gendered Exploration of Emotive and Instrumental Well-Being for Cyclist Woman in Latin America
Beatriz Mella Lira   *135*

Chapter 7 Active Commute to School, Physical Activity and Health of Hispanic High School Students in the United States
Ivis García and Keuntae Kim   *149*

Chapter 8 Children's Mobility and Playability in the Neighbourhood of Río Piedras: Perspectives from Children and Adults
Norma I. Peña-Rivera and Enery López-Navarrete   *169*

Chapter 9 Mobility and Equity: The Problem of Access to City Spaces by Individuals Submitted to Psychiatric Hospitalisation
Luiza Morena Alves Lopes   *191*

Chapter 10 Urban Accessibility in Belo Horizonte, Brazil: A Case Study of Mobility Practices and Demands of People with Disabilities in the Mobility Systems
Ana Marcela Ardila Pinto, Marcos Fontoura De Oliveira, Bruna Barradas Cordeiro and Laíse Lorene Hasz Souza e Oliveira   *209*

Epilogue
Julio D. Dávila   *235*

Index   *239*

LIST OF FIGURES AND TABLES

FIGURES

Fig. 1.1.	Boundaries and Configuration of Bogotá Region.	18
Fig. 1.2.	Income Distribution and Average Motorised Travel Times in Bogotá.	20
Fig. 1.3.	Generated and Attracted Non-Mandatory Walking Daily Trips.	22
Fig. 1.4.	Potential Accessibility to Employment and Education Opportunities by Transport Mode.	23
Fig. 1.5.	Differences in Potential Accessibility to Employment and Education by Transport Mode.	24
Fig. 1.6.	Average Generalised Travel Cost for Non-Mandatory Activities by Mode.	25
Fig. 2.1.	Conceptual Framework.	37
Fig. 2.2.	Immobility (Including Constrained Mobility) by Gender and Other Sociodemographic Indicators (Percentages).	39
Fig. 2.3.	Average Travel Time and Distance by Gender.	40
Fig. 2.4.	Travel Mode by Gender (Percentages).	41
Fig. 2.5.	Access to Mobility Resources by Gender (Percentages).	41
Fig. 2.6.	Purpose of the Trip (Excluding Trips to Home) by Gender (Percentages).	42
Fig. 2.7.	Trips Related to Domestic/Care Activities, by Mode and Gender (Population Older than 18 Years).	43
Fig. 2.8.	Female Contributions to Care and Work-oriented Trips by Transport Mode; Population Older than 18 Years (Percentages).	43
Fig. 2.9.	Female Contribution to the Amount of Minutes Allocated to Care-oriented Trips; Population Older than 18 Years (Percentages).	44
Fig. 2.10.	Itinerary: Home–Work–Home; Population between the Ages of 18 and 64 (32% of Men and 26% of Women).	45
Fig. 2.11.	Itinerary: Home–Care Activity–Home; Population between the Ages of 18 and 64 (4% of Men and 8% of Women).	46
Fig. 2.12.	Itinerary: Home–Activity 1–Activity 2–Home; Population between the Ages of 18 and 64 (9% of Men and 13% of Women).	47
Fig. 2.13.	Itinerary: Home–Work–Activity–Home; Population between The Ages of 18 and 64 (5% of Men and 8% of Women).	48

Fig. 2.14.	Itinerary: Home–Activity 1–Activity 2–Activity 3–Home; Population between the Ages of 18 and 64 (22% of Men and 23% of Women).	50
Fig. 2.15.	Itinerary: Home–Work–Activity 2–Activity 3–Home; Population between the Ages of 18 and 64 (11% of Men and 9% of Women).	51
Fig. 2.16.	Itinerary: Home–Activity 1–Activity 2–Work–Home; Population between the Ages of 18 and 64 (7% of Men and 4% of Women).	52
Fig. 3.1.	Route Motivation of Men of RMBH.	67
Fig. 3.2.	Route Motivation of Women of RMBH.	68
Fig. 3.3.	Route Motivations of Men Responsible for the Household.	68
Fig. 3.4.	Route Motivations of Women Responsible for The Household.	69
Fig. 3.5.	Influence of the Age of Cohabiting Children on the Mobility of the Care of Adults in Charge of Household.	71
Fig. 3.6.	Influence of the Educational Level and Age of Cohabiting Children in the Mobility of Care.	73
Fig. 3.7.	Modes – General Population.	73
Fig. 3.8.	Modes – Household Heads.	74
Fig. 3.9.	Influence of Cohabiting Children in Non-motorised Mode.	75
Fig. 3.10.	Influence of Cohabiting Children in Collective Mode.	75
Fig. 3.11.	Influence of Cohabiting Children in Motorised Individual Mode.	75
Fig. 3.12.	Influence of the Level of Education in Transport Mode.	76
Fig. 3.13.	Influence of the Age of Cohabiting Children and Level of Education in Non-motorised Use.	77
Fig. 3.14.	Influence of the Age of Cohabiting Children and Level of Education in Non-motorised Use.	77
Fig. 3.15.	Influence of the Age of Cohabiting Children and Level of Education in Motorised Individual Use.	78
Fig. 4.1.	Interlocutors' Residence-Work Journeys and Modes of Transportation.	91
Fig. 5.1.	Three Different Views of 'Equality' and 'Equity' Illustrate the Wicked Problem Behind Terms Many People Take for Granted. In Transportation, Walking and Walkability are Often Neglected in Both Planning and Research, Despite Their Crucial Interactions with Gender, Equity, Health, Road Safety and Urban Security Issues.	107
Fig. 5.2.	Spatial Distribution and Population of the Comunas, with the Poorest Spread Through Most of the City, with the Jurisdictions in the Centre (SAN = Santiago Centre; PRO = Providencia) Having More Mixed Incomes, and Four Towards the City's Eastern Edge (LB = Lo Barnechea, VI = Vitacura, LCO = Las Condes and LR = LaReina) Posting Very High Incomes.	110

Fig. 5.3.	Distribution of Walking Trips in General (Above) and Walking Trips Made Mainly by Women (Below), Revealing the High Dependence on Walking as a Major Transport Mode in Low-Income Comunas. Moreover, Women Account for a Disproportionately High Percentage of Those Trips.	113
Fig. 5.4.	Sexual Harassment Reported by Women is Remarkably Consistent Across Modes, Including Walking Trips (Access/Egress) Related to Public Transit. Metro is the Only Part of the Travel Chain Covered by a Security System.	119
Fig. 8.1.	Conditions That Create Playability Poverty.	172
Fig. 8.2.	Photo Shooting Tour. Capetillo, San Juan, Puerto Rico, 2016.	178
Fig. 8.3.	Children Drawing on Map of Their Community and Final Map. Capetillo, San Juan, Puerto Rico, 2016.	178
Fig. 8.4.	Drawing with Chalks on the Sidewalk and Street, Capetillo, San Juan, Puerto Rico, 2016.	179
Fig. 8.5.	Río Piedras Neighbourhood and its Eight Sub-Barrios, San Juan, Puerto Rico 2015 [Map]. 1:7,500.	179
Fig. 8.6.	Map of Capetillo Sub-Barrio and Critical Sites for Play in Capetillo from the Perspective of Children. San Juan, Puerto Rico, 2015.	180
Fig. 8.7.	Children Forming Barriers for Traffic Calming on the North and South Sides Corners of the Street. Capetillo, San Juan, Puerto Rico 2016.	182
Fig. 9.1.	Mobility at the Transitory Hospital.	198
Fig. 10.1.	Percentage Distribution of Persons With and Without Disabilities by Age in the City of Belo Horizonte.	220
Fig. 10.2.	Percentage Distribution of Per Capita Income in Minimum Wages of People with Disabilities.	221
Fig. 10.3.	Number of Trips per Day per Person in Belo Horizonte According to the Disability Type.	222
Fig. 10.4.	Percentage Distribution of Modes of Transport of People with Disabilities in Belo Horizonte.	223
Fig. 10.5.	Percentage Distribution of the Demands of the Participants of the Focus Group Regarding the Mobility for People with Disabilities in Belo Horizonte, by Thematic Axes.	225

TABLES

Table 1.1.	Percentage of All Trips by Trip Purpose and Modal Share 2011.	21
Table 3.1.	Percentage of Persons Responsible for Children in the Immobility Sample.	66
Table 3.2.	Influence of the Age of Cohabiting Children on the Motivations of Adult Caregivers.	70
Table 3.3.	Motivation of Trips by Level of Education.	72
Table 3.4.	Ratio of Trips Per Journey.	78
Table 5.1.	Modal Share in Santiago: Soaring Automobility in Recent Decades.	110
Table 5.2.	Public Investment* in Transportation in Recent Years, Millions USD.	111
Table 5.3.	Poverty in Santiago Comunas (Ranked by No. of Persons and Percentage of Population).	112
Table 5.4.	Overall Sustainability (%).	114
Table 5.5.	Where Do Women Travel Most, by Each Mode?	115
Table 5.6.	Gender, Age and Trip Purpose (%).	117
Table 5.7.	Trip Purpose Ranked Using 'Care' Criteria (Women are Majority Realising These Trips).	118
Table A1.	Gender and Transport in Santiago: An Overview.	128
Table 7.1.	Demographic Characteristics and Physical Activity Behaviours in NYPANS Survey Data Sample ($n = 7,398$).	158
Table 7.2.	Complex Survey Data Quasi-Poisson Regression Results: Race/Ethnicity Effects.	160
Table 9.1.	Methodological Strategies to Data Collection and Analysis.	196
Table 9.2.	Transportation Use Difficulties.	200
Table 9.3.	Resident's Profile.	201
Table 9.4.	Residential Therapeutics Service Mobility Profile.	202
Table 10.1.	Percentage Distribution of Reasons for Travelling in Belo Horizonte According to the Disability Type.	222

LIST OF CONTRIBUTORS

Ana Marcela Ardila Pinto, Federal University of Minas Gerais, UFMG, Brazil

Bruna Barradas Cordeiro, Federal University of Minas Gerais, UFMG, Brazil

Julio D. Dávila, University College London, UK

Daniela de los Santos, Universidad Católica del Uruguay, Uruguay

Gabriela Cicci Faria, Federal University of Minas Gerais, UFMG, Brazil

Friederike Fleischer, Universidad de Los Andes, Colombia

Marcos Fontoura de Oliveira, Transport and Transit Company of Belo Horizonte, BH-TRANS., Brazil

Ivis García, University of Utah, USA

Luis Ángel Guzmán, Universidad de Los Andes, Colombia

Laíse Lorene Hasz Souza e Oliveira, Federal University of Minas Gerais, UFMG, Brazil

Diego Hernández, Universidad Católica del Uruguay, Uruguay

Keuntae Kim, University of Utah, USA

Luiza Morena Alves Lopes, Federal University of Minas Gerais, UFMG, Brazil

Enery López-Navarrete, University of Puerto Rico, Puerto Rico

Karen Lucas, University of Manchester, UK

Beatriz Mella Lira, Pontificia Universidad Católica de Chile, Chile

Daniel Oviedo, University College London, UK

Norma I. Peña-Rivera, University of Puerto Rico, Puerto Rico

Lake Sagaris, Pontificia Universidad Católica de Chile, Chile

Ivette S. Sepúlveda Sanabria, Fundación Universitaria San Alfonso, Colombia

Ignacio Tiznado-Aitken, Pontificia Universidad Católica de Chile, Chile

Natalia Villamizar Duarte, Universidad Nacional de Colombia, Colombia

EDITOR BIOGRAPHIES

Daniel Oviedo is an Assistant Professor at the Development Planning Unit of University College London. He is a Civil Engineer and Urban Development Planner with over 10 years of experience in urban transport in Global South cities. His research focusses on accessibility, inequality, social exclusion, informal transport and sustainability. He leads INTALInC in Latin America.

Natalia Villamizar Duarte is an Associate Professor in the School of Architecture and Urbanism at the Universidad Nacional de Colombia. She has worked in urban design, urban planning and policymaking for over 15 years. Her work focusses on processes and practices of governing, public space and urban mobility, planning of urban borders and community–university partnerships.

Ana Marcela Ardila Pinto is an Associate Professor of Sociology at the Federal University of Minas Gerais. She is a sociologist with over 20 years of experience in urban sociology, urban planning and mobility. Her work focusses on public space, sociability and urban mobility policy in Bogotá, Rio de Janeiro and Belo Horizonte.

CONTRIBUTOR BIOGRAPHIES

Bruna Barradas Cordeiro holds a Master's in Sociology from Participatory Planning Geographical Information System (PPGIS)/Federal University of Minas Gerais (UFMG in the research field of Urban Sociology, and a Bachelor's in Social Sciences from the same university. Currently, she is a Researcher at the Center of Urban Studies at UFMG, working with urban mobility, hawkers and informal economy in mobility spaces.

Julio D. Dávila is a Professor of Urban Policy and International Development, and a Director of the Development Planning Unit, University College London. He is a civil engineer and urban development planner with 30 years' international experience in research and consultancy. His research focusses on local government and social and political transformations, and governance of urban infrastructure.

Daniela de los Santos is a Sociologist. She is a Researcher at the Interdisciplinary Centre for Development Studies-Uruguay (CIEDUR), Universidad Católica del Uruguay, Uruguay and a Research Assistant at the Catholic University of Uruguay. Her fields of interest are gender and economic inequalities, public policy, social science methodology and urban studies.

Gabriela Cicci Faria holds a Master's in Urban Sociology from the Federal University of Minas Gerais and is a Social Psychologist graduated from the same institution. Her main themes of interest in research are urban mobility, gender, space and subjectivity.

Friederike Fleischer is an Associate Professor at the Department of Anthropology, Universidad de los Andes, Colombia. Her books include *Suburban Beijing* (2010) and *Soup, Love, and a Helping Hand* (2018). She recently published 'Atravesando la Ciudad ....' (EURE, 2019) and 'The Normalization of Bogota Social Housing Residents ...' (City & Society, forthcoming).

Marcos Fontoura De Oliveira is a Civil Engineer and an Urbanist in the Federal University of Minas Gerais. He has a Master's in Public Administration from the João Pinheiro Foundation and a Doctorate in Social Sciences from PUC-Minas. He is an advisor to the Presidency of the Empresa de Transportes e Trânsito de Belo Horizonte, BH-TRANS.

Dr Ivis García is originally from Puerto Rico. She is an Assistant Professor of City and Metropolitan Planning at the University of Utah. She is a National Institute for Transportation and Communities Researcher. Her work has been published in *Urban Studies, Journal of the American Planning Association, Journal of Planning Education and Research*, among other urban planning journals.

Luis Ángel Guzmán is an Associate Professor at the School of Engineering at Universidad de los Andes. His research interests include urban mobility, transport and land-use interaction and social and economic analysis of inequalities related to urban transport and policy evaluation.

Laíse Lorene Hasz Souza e Oliveira holds Master's in Sociology from PPGS/ Federal University of Minas Gerais (UFMG) in the research field of Urban Sociology and Bachelor's in Social Sciences from the same university. Presently, she is a Researcher at the Center of Urban Studies at UFMG, working with urban mobility and waiting spaces.

Diego Hernández is an Associate Professor, at the Department of Social Sciences, Universidad Católica del Uruguay. He develops research on transport, mobility, social exclusion and equity, including topics like spatial accessibility, affordability and gender. He has published his research work in scientific journals and has worked as a consultant for national and international institutions.

Keuntae Kim is a PhD student at the Department of City and Metropolitan Planning and holds a Master's degree in City Planning from Seoul National University, and another Master's degree in Urban Design from School of City and Regional Planning at the Georgia Institute of Technology.

Luiza Morena Alves Lopes completed her graduation in Occupational Therapy (2012) and MSc in Sociology (2018) at the Federal University of Minas Gerais. Since 2012, she works as Occupational Therapist at the Universal Health System with mentally suffering individuals, including participating in the closing process of the last Psychiatric Hospital of Belo Horizonte.

Enery López-Navarrete is an Early Childhood Specialist with studies in Urban Planning from Graduate School of Planning, UPR. Her work focusses on weaving children's play into communities. Her favourite places to do research include sidewalks, streets and unused spaces to visibilize children in open public spaces.

Karen Lucas is a Professor of Transport and Social Analysis at the Institute of Transport Studies, University of Leeds and a Deputy Director of the Leeds Social Sciences Institute. She has 20 years of experience in social research in transport. She is a world-leading expert in the area of transport-related social exclusion. She is also the Director of INTALInC.

Beatriz Mella Lira is Postdoctoral Researcher at the BRT+ Centre of Excellence, Pontificia Universidad Católica de Chile, and a former PhD Researcher at the Bartlett School of Planning, University College London. She has recently co-edited the book *A Companion to Transport, Space and Equity* (Edward Elgar Publishing).

Norma I. Peña-Rivera, PhD, is a Professor and a Director of the Graduate School of Planning at the University of Puerto Rico, Río Piedras. Her research areas include transportation and land-use planning, spatial decision support systems and social exclusion by mobility.

Lake Sagaris is an Associate Professor in the Department of Transport Engineering and Logistics, Pontificia Universidad Católica de Chile, Centre for Sustainable Urban Development CEDEUS, BRT+ Centre of Excellence. She holds a PhD in Planning and Geography. She specialises in collaborative governance, transport justice and walk–bike–bus sustainability trio from a gender and equity perspective.

Ivette S. Sepúlveda Sanabria is a Professor of Social Work at Fundación Universitaria San Alfonso, Colombia. Her research is about care policies and the care economy. Her publications include 'Políticas sobre el cuidado en Bogotá…' (Trabajo Social, 2017) and Se nos va el cuidado, se nos va la vida… (2018).

Ignacio Tiznado-Aitken is Postdoctoral Researcher at the Centre for Sustainable Urban Development, CEDEUS, Pontificia Universidad Católica de Chile. He holds a PhD in Transport Engineering from Pontificia Universidad Católica de Chile and he was a Visiting Postgraduate Researcher at the Institute for Transport Studies at the University of Leeds. His main research interests are accessibility, affordability, equity, poverty and transport justice.

PROLOGUE

URBAN MOBILITY AND SOCIAL EQUITY IN LATIN AMERICAN CITIES: EVIDENCE, CONCEPTS AND METHODS FOR MORE INCLUSIVE CITIES

Karen Lucas

I have been researching and writing about transport inequities and their punitive social consequences for the affected individuals and communities for more than 20 years now and in numerous geographical contexts. I am pleased to say that over this time more and more academics from around the world are becoming interested in researching this topic, as well as trying to influence policymakers, planners and the funders of transport projects to think more about social equity in the design and operation of urban transport systems. It is an important issue in all geographical contexts, whether in the Global North or South, in urban, suburban or rural contexts, and everywhere in between, for all forms of transport, as well as for urban planning and for how we shape our cities and their rural hinterlands.

Inequality in all its dangerous and pernicious forms infuriates me, especially when the people who experience it have no control over the power structures that create it and no opportunities to fight against it. The mobility and accessibility inequalities caused by exclusionary transport and land-use systems are particularly insidious because almost all countries have overlooked them within their social development and welfare agendas. However, lack of access to transport resources can have hugely negative social outcomes over a person's life course, denying them participation in many activities and opportunities, and can even destroy the well-being of whole communities. In the main, these inequalities are not something that individuals can themselves resolve, although they may invent highly creative strategies to cope with them on a daily basis. Nevertheless, a fundamental overhaul of the power structures that plan and finance urban transport systems as well as dedicated evidence-based policies, integrated planning and sustained project interventions are needed to change the current trajectory, so that cities can become inclusive places for all.

Latin America is a vast subcontinent and so we are often talking about very different physical conditions, political economies and human capabilities across the different countries under consideration, as well between the urban conurbations within them. What all its countries demonstrate, in common with the rest of the world, is that mobility resources are almost always distributed unevenly (and often unfairly) and in line with traditional social divisions, so that usually lower income groups get to have much less of them, as do women, children, older people, people with disabilities and other socially disadvantaged groups. It is unsurprising that they undertake most of their trips by walking or walk long distances to access the limited transit services that are available to them. This in turn reduces their opportunities to access employment and other key activities within the rapidly expanding urban realm.

These problems can be particularly acute for low-income women, who not only have to travel to far-flung places outside their areas of residence to take up domiciliary employment in the middle-class areas of the city, but must also combine this travel with the still highly gendered responsibilities of caring for children and elderly relatives and managing the home. The high demands placed on low-income women to travel away from the home to secure a living in the far-flung and often gated communities of the middle-class households in many Latin American cities can also have severe knock-on consequences for their children and family relationships. As such, as the case studies identify, mobility poverty is a social problem from the point of view of social participation and inclusion, and one that needs full integration with other welfare policies, such as housing, employment, healthcare and education provision, in order to address a much broad set of Sustainable Development Goals for Latin American cities.

It is for this reason that the texts that Oviedo, Villamizar and Ardila have brought together in this edited collection are so important. They provide the underpinning theories, concepts and evidence base that has been missing for so long within the discourses surrounding the provision of sustainable *and equitable* mobility in developing cities. Not only do these Latin American case studies serve to highlight the negative consequences of having inadequate mobility resources for people's lives and livelihoods, but they also demonstrate how person-centric designed and context-specific projects can successfully provide inclusive accessibility for all within cities. That the authors are themselves from Latin American origins also lends a certain sense of passion and integrity to the work. That many of them are early career researchers offers the old hands, like myself, hope for the continuance of teaching, research and policy action addressing the intersectionalities between mobility inequalities and social well-being.

It is, thus, my hope that this book will receive the attention it deserves from the people who can make a real difference on the ground in these domains, and so, to recognise the important role of urban mobility in the achievement of greater social equity at every level of Latin American society.

Professor Karen Lucas
School of Environment, Education and Development
University of Manchester

ACKNOWLEDGEMENTS

The culmination of this publication is the result of a collective effort of a wide network of academics, citizens and professionals concerned with understanding the links between urban mobility and social equity. Such network is the result of the collaboration of researchers, universities and research centres, development agencies, public and private institutions, non-governmental organisations and citizens of countries across Latin America and beyond. By committing research, financial, logistical support, translation, editorial and affective support, each one of these individuals and organisations has made this book possible. We express our sincere thanks to each and all of them.

We also want to thank researchers, friends and colleagues of the Latin American Branch of the International Network for Transport and Accessibility in Low Income Communities, INTALInC LAC. This network has offered us, the editors and contributors, a space for voicing debates and exploring the implications for transport planning and urban mobility and their interaction with other dimensions of planning. We thank the members of the network who actively engaged in the production of this book. We also express our gratitude to the editorial and logistic team at Emerald for their undying support in editing and publishing the final product, with a great interest in contributing to the production of knowledge in Latin America. Finally, to our readers, thank you for the opportunity to share our research with you and for continuing expanding the interest in social research in urban mobility in Latin America and the Global South.

URBAN MOBILITY AND SOCIAL EQUITY: AN INTRODUCTION

Natalia Villamizar Duarte, Daniel Oviedo and Ana Marcela Ardila Pinto

URBAN MOBILITY AND SOCIAL EQUITY: AN INTRODUCTION

Urban mobility plays a significant role in shaping urban form and people's experiences in and of the city. Such a role is largely determined by both infrastructures and services for urban mobility, as well as the interactions between social actors while using them. How these infrastructures, services and interactions materialise has an impact on people's accessibility to urban services, amenities and opportunities.

Rapid demographic growth and urbanisation processes have outpaced the capacity of governments to respond to increasing mobility demands and needs of the urban population. This lack of capacity manifests in an unequal distribution of benefits and negative externalities of transport that tend to disproportionately affect already vulnerable population groups (Jones & Lucas, 2012; Oviedo & Titheridge, 2016). As such, manifested inequality is an undeniable part of our urban realities in understanding distributional issues in urban mobility that becomes a central concern in research agendas particularly in contexts facing large social inequity. This edited volume examines how spatial and social mobilities are deeply intertwined in the reproduction of both spatial and social inequities in Latin American cities. The book focuses on Latin America as a unique setting for the critical examination of the links between urban mobility and social equity. However, recognising that these links can be underpinned by similar cultural and social drivers not tied to a fixed geography, the volume includes a chapter examining experiences of Hispanic population in the United States.

The emphasis in Latin American cities gives scale and dimension to current urban challenges associated with urban mobility in the region. Latin America is at present the most urbanised region in the planet, with very high shares of urban population that are above 60% even in countries with lower comparative urban population rates such as Colombia and Peru. Such reality, along with continued demographic growth and increased urbanisation, poses considerable challenges for accommodating urban societies in an efficient and equitable manner (McGranahan, 2015). Available responses to such challenges are largely dependent on changing dynamics associated with urban mobility and on our understanding of the multiplicity of mobility needs and practices in different Latin American cities.

Inequalities in the distribution of costs and benefits of mobility infrastructure and services contribute to the reproduction of social inequalities and levels of exclusion in cities (Manderscheid, 2009). Low income, women, children and people with various forms of disability, among other socially vulnerable populations, endure most negative effects of poor-quality infrastructure and inefficient transport systems (Lucas, Mattioli, Verlinghieri, & Guzman, 2016; Titheridge, Christie, Mackett, Oviedo, & Ye, 2014). Most vulnerable populations not only have to tolerate longer journey times, increased exposure to pollution, increased risk of traffic and insecurity but also experience sharp differences in their ability to access opportunities, services and relations in the city (de Vasconcellos, 2001; Jirón & Zunino, 2017; Jones & Lucas, 2012; Oviedo & Titheridge, 2016).

Traditional conceptual and empirical approaches for the study of urban mobility build on functional and economic principles focussing on variables such as distance, demographics, urban functions, land uses, etc.. Under this perspective, people have been understood as abstract agents whose mobility decisions are rational and predictable (Chorley & Haggett, 2014). These traditional planning approaches see urban mobility primary as a transport problem and focus on demand and efficiency, often overlooking social or spatial equity considerations (Keeling, 2008). Furthermore, the toolkit for mainstream transport planning rarely incorporates specific indicators to measure the contribution of mobility and transport to accessibility, equity and social development (Geurs & van Wee, 2004; Jones & Lucas, 2012; van Wee, 2016). Even less do they consider the different agents involved in the construction of diverse forms of mobility in their everyday practices (Cresswell, 2011).

The multiplicity of mobility needs and practices is still a relatively understudied issue in Latin American cities, despite many local transport and mobility plans and regulations incorporating social inclusion and equity as central objectives (Scholl, 2016). To advance in this area, it is critical to look at different social dimensions that can help explaining uneven outcomes of transport planning and urban mobility. Effective evidence-based communication of the social consequences of urban transport and mobility will contribute to improve people's ability to fully participate and be included in society. This book provides methodological, conceptual and policy insights from different contexts in the region to further explore the relationships between the state, civil society and private sector and the provision of more socially just mobility in Latin American cities.

It is essential to reflect on the intersecting social relations of class, gender, race, age and physical/mental ability in access to the city, its services and infrastructure to advance debates on social equity. Jones and Lucas (2012) proposed five categories that are central to understanding social impacts and distributional effects of transport systems and decision-making: accessibility, movement and activities, health, financial and community. These five categories have helped define conceptual and methodological frameworks that incorporate individuals' characteristics, perspectives and experiences in urban mobility studies. Researches about differential accessibility (Oviedo & Titheridge, 2016), gender inequality in transport (Campaña, Giménez-Nadal, & Molina, 2018; Cass, Shove, & Urry, 2005; Manderscheid, 2014; Uteng & Cresswell, 2008), active travel and well-being, the role of travelling experiences, rhythms and representations of the urban agents (Cresswell & Merriman, 2011; Schonferder & Axhausen, 2016) and scales of accessibility (Jones & Lucas, 2012) have demonstrated the importance of social dimensions of movement for understanding inequality in urban mobility and transport systems.

The contributions in this volume expand on these debates by providing rigorous evidence of the social impacts of urban mobility and transport policies in Latin America. Works in this volume also discuss concepts and methods for explaining the distributional effects of transport policies and for exploring alternatives to ensure equity and non-discrimination in access for more inclusive cities. Recognising the deep relationship between accessibility, equity and inclusion, we have organised the 10 contributions in this book in three sections: *structural dimensions of accessibility, active travel and local accessibility and accessibility of emerging mobilities*. These themes are detailed enough to help us provide an overarching structure for the entire book but also are broad enough to admit very different perspectives to their debates about accessibility.

Contributions in our first section: *structural dimensions of accessibility* focus on the role of mobility and transport on the opportunity to access urban services and activities. The contributions in our second section: *active travel and local accessibility* emphasise on the intersection between sustainable forms of transport, equity, health and well-being generally. The third and final section: *accessibility of emerging mobilities* spotlights on understanding the needs and demands of very specific groups of population whose vulnerable condition represents a challenge for social equity in mobility and transport policymaking.

Structural Dimensions of Accessibility

Questions on accessibility have been central to the study of social impacts mobility and transport. Accessibility is a concept that not only has shifted the understanding of urban mobility but that is also a measure of segregation and different forms of exclusion. When access to the city becomes a desirable goal, the means for access (i.e. mobility) become indicators of attainment of such goal. Traditional accessibility studies focus on the relationship between transport and land-use based on generalised understanding of the needs and desires of travellers (Banister, Watson, & Wood, 1997; Bergmann & Sager, 2008; Cresswell, 2011). This generalisation does not necessarily account for the complexity of needs and desires of different groups of individuals. The four chapters in this section offer a remarkable analysis of equity implications of accessibility from a socioeconomic and gender perspectives.

In the first chapter, Oviedo and Guzmán examine the role of transport as an enabler of opportunities that contribute to human development and well-being. Using the case of Bogotá Metropolitan Region in Colombia, the authors discuss accessibility metrics from an equity perspective. Using income to represent social and economic differences, this work assesses imbalances in accessibility and the implications of equity for different areas of the region. Their findings show that for mandatory accessibility, the imbalance between the population and accessibility is higher for the most vulnerable populations. For non-mandatory accessibility,[1] these figures are similar, suggesting higher costs of access for peripheral areas where low income and vulnerable population are located. Based on their findings, this chapter provides important reflections for policy and practice, stressing the role of mobility and transport as a mechanism to reduce the gap in access across social groups to promote equity and social development.

In the second chapter, Hernández and de los Santos present a descriptive analysis of patterns of mobility behaviour in Montevideo, Uruguay. Significant in this work is the methodological choice of carrying out the analysis from three different approaches: mainstream mobility indicators, care mobility indicators and tour-based analysis. While different results are presented for each approach, this work demonstrates persistent gender inequality in different levels of accessibility to services and other types of urban opportunities. Findings show that this gap is closely related to two aspects: the level of heterogeneity in daily itineraries of men and women, and access to different means of transport, particularly private transport. The study suggests that women devote more of their time to *care mobility*, largely characterised by shorter distances, more trips and more dependence on public transportation and active modes. Access to private modes of transport is an important variable in mobility patterns, posing yet another challenge for women, who generally have more limited access to motorised vehicles. Finally, these indicators of inequality increase among women in the low-income population segment.

In Chapter 3, Faria continues with an analysis of care dynamics and mobility patterns in Belo Horizonte, Brazil. This chapter also uses a gender perspective to analyse how the presence of children in a household impacts the mobility of the family members responsible for the household. As in the previous chapter, findings demonstrate a persistent gender inequality with women taking more trips associated with childcare. However, such levels of inequality vary depending on the children's level of schooling and age. Besides these findings, this work offers an important discussion about the difference between the concepts of *accessibility* and *access* where the latter incorporates not only physical but also social dimensions of mobility such as access to network, to information, to economic means and even to autonomous use of time.

In the last chapter of this section, Fleischer and Sepúlveda Sanabria offer a qualitative analysis of household employees' motility. This concept, first proposed by Kaufmann, Bergman, and Joye (2004), refers to people's capacity to be mobile and the effect of their subjective experience of mobility. Using this framework, the work demonstrates how the intersection between local labour regimes, gender and transport has unequal effects on women's mobility in Bogotá, Colombia. The authors illustrate how a negative experience of the daily commute in public transport systems highly influences household employees desire to travel for purposes other than work. In the end, these subjective decisions are effectively limiting women access to urban space and opportunities.

Active Travel and Local Accessibility

Active travel, mainly walking and cycling, are a central issue in current transport studies. Whether related to sustainable transport (David Banister, 2007; Parkin, 2012; Pucher & Buehler, 2017), health and well-being (Delbosc, 2012), and local mobility practices and accessibility (Dávila, 2013; Jirón, 2010), these studies illustrate the intersection between active travel and social equity. While there is evidence that walking and biking have a positive impact in environmental sustainability, as well as individual health and well-being, there is also proof that these benefits are not evenly distributed among different population groups. Even more concerning is that these forms of active transport are not always a choice, but the result of larger inequalities in accessibility (Jones & Lucas, 2012). The three chapters in this section identify important equity implications of active travel from gender and racial perspectives.

In Chapter 5, the first one in this section, Sagaris and Tiznado-Aitken discuss the equity implications of women's travel patterns and sustainable transport in Santiago, Chile. Using the perspective of transport justice, the authors explore forms of discrimination based on cultural gender roles and mobility barriers for women. Their findings highlight the importance of considering non-work-related trips when assessing women's mobility patterns. Like the works of Hernández and de los Santos (Chapter 2) and Faria (Chapter 3), this work demonstrates women's higher participation in care mobilities and in walking trips, with a major impact on women in the low-income segments of population. Particular to this chapter is the complementary analysis of the effect of gender violence[2] on women's mobility, which demonstrates important changes in women's travel behaviours translating into significant inequalities in access to urban opportunities.

In Chapter 6, Mella Lira explores the relations between transport, accessibility and well-being through the analysis of emotional, instrumental and social reasons of female cyclists in four different Latin American cities: Santiago, Bogotá, Buenos Aires and Mexico City. While the instrumental reasons account for more traditional utilitarian evaluation of travel, emotional factors serve to complement the understanding of how travel decisions are made. As other chapters in this volume (see Chapters 2, 3 and 5) that focussed on a gender perspective, the author identifies that among instrumental reasons, care mobility is relevant, together with access to labour markets and strengthening of social relationships. In line with findings about changes in women's travel behaviours due to gender violence, presented in the previous chapter, Mella Lira identifies security and sexual harassment as one factor why many women chose not to bike, while others expressed feeling more secure on a bike compared to walking. However, in both cases, this specific topic affects negatively women's well-being which translated into limited accessibility.

In Chapter 7, García and Kim analyse whether ethnicity and other sociocultural characteristics influence active commute of high school Hispanic students in the USA. The authors found that compared with non-Hispanic groups, walking is the most predominant physical activity. Beyond the active commute to and from school, this study found an important relationship between engaging in active travel, for reasons different than commuting, and distances to public parks and other recreational public spaces. The authors also found that while perceptions of safety influence choosing active travel – particularly walking, it does not influence Hispanics and African Americans physical activity. Age also has an impact on choosing active commute, with students more likely to walk or bike between 10th grade, when they are old enough, and 12th grade when they or their peers start owning a car. Overall, this chapter recognises that a close relationship between urban planning and health can be mediated by a better understanding of active travel patterns and behaviours.

Challenging Accessibilities

To account for the complexity of dimensions that interfere in the use of urban goods and services, recent accessibility studies have examined mobility needs and demands of diverse groups of people from their own perspective An increased interest in examining the intersections between accessibility and gender, race and class has taken place in subfield. However, more distinct population groups, such as children, the elderly and people with disabilities, are not as visible in the policy arena. This final section contains three chapters that explore precisely the mobility needs and demand of children, individuals on psychiatric hospitalisation and people with disabilities.

We have called this section 'challenging accessibilities' because it compiles works that examine the experiences groups that are just emerging within the accessibility debate in academia as well as the policy arena. Making these agents visible is central for advancing accessibility studies as they challenge our understanding of normality and of the average individual. Recognising the mobility needs of these groups forces us to think about more diverse forms of accessibility and movement (Boys, 2014; Hamraie, 2017; Hine & Mitchell, 2001; Imrie, 2000). Furthermore, appreciating their practices, experiences, perspectives and, above all, their rights opens an opportunity to move towards a more accessible and inclusive city. A city conceived to ensure the accessibility of children, elderly, people with physical and mental disabilities, etc., will potentially be able to include everyone. In the end, these less visible populations can become society's measure of (in)accessibility.

In Chapter 8, Peña-Rivera and López-Navarrete study children's geographies to gain insights into their needs related to mobility and their opportunity to access urban space. Framed on Lucas (2012) concept of mobility poverty, the authors analyse the participation of children in city dynamics in San Juan, Puerto Rico, particularly focussing on their access to free, active play. This work reminds us how distinct children mobility can be, and its intrinsic relation with playing, which is the way in which children comprehend and experience the world. Thus, the authors of this chapter call for some specific considerations: first, to recognise play as an integral part of children accessibility; second, to keep in mind the multiple micro- and mesoscales at stake in children's mobility; and third, to remember that children's capacity to move primarily depends on their access to safe walking spaces. Findings from this work demonstrate that crime, adults' perception of security and the presence of motorised vehicles limit children's access to urban space. Also, this work illustrates how different perspectives can either limit or promote children's access to urban space. While an adult's perspective is that playability depends on access to playgrounds, children recurrently appropriated streets as their place to play.

In Chapter 9, Lopes presents an in-depth qualitative assessment of the effect that the Brazilian psychiatric reform had on the accessibility of individuals on psychiatric hospitalisation in Belo Horizonte, Brazil. The shift from long psychiatric hospitalisation to residential therapeutic services substantially transformed the ways in which these individuals use, access and appropriate urban space. Findings from this work illustrate that the mobility of individuals with mental disability is characterised by proximity, and most trips are done walking. The use of transport systems poses limitations because the buses are overcrowded, and physical accessibility is difficult. Notable in this work are, first, identifying that people with mental disabilities have distinct and unique ways of accessing the city, and second, revealing that mobility has a direct effect on the autonomy of these individuals. In the end, this work stresses the need to further advance in our understanding of the relations between accessibility, mobility and mental disabilities.

In the last chapter in this section and this volume, Ardila Pinto, Fontoura De Oliveira, Barradas Cordeiro and Hasz Souza e Oliveira examine the accessibility of people with disabilities to urban transport systems. The authors point out that while the objective of urban policies includes universal accessibility, the city and its policymakers still do not comprehend multiple needs and demands of this population. While the analysis uses descriptive statistical analysis to compare mobility patterns between people with and without disability, this is complemented with a qualitative analysis of perceptions of people with disabilities. Results of this analysis show higher levels of immobility and greater challenges to access public transportation. The higher levels of immobility translate an uneven access to the city's goods and services, especially those related to health, education and work. As for the challenges, it is noteworthy that they do not only relate to service operation and infrastructure but also to attitudes and behaviours of service providers and other citizens. A final, yet significant, finding is the role of public spaces as key transition between the city's goods and services and the transport system. Inadequate conditions of public space in terms of surfaces, levels, doors or other accesses as well as information systems jeopardise the access to people with disabilities.

General Contributions

Contributions to this volume have been concerned with understanding and measuring inequalities from the perspective of urban agents that are exposed to multiple situations of inequality. Diverse approaches to assessing accessibility are included in this book. An equity perspective was introduced in one of the chapters (Chapter 1). The gender perspective was addressed by five of the chapters (Chapters 2–6), while inequalities related to race was addressed directly only in one of the chapters (Chapter 7). Three of the chapters focussed on segments of population traditionally overlooked in transport studies (Chapters 8–10), which offers new theoretical, methodological and political challenges to accessibility studies as well as to mobility and transport planning and policy.

The publication is a unique contribution to the international literature as it encompasses a collection of experiences, knowledge and empirical evidence, specific from Latin American cities. It will allow the reader to learn about the urban reality and mobility experiences in five different Latin American cities. In each of the eight chapters presenting a single case study, the reader will be able to identify the territorial, economic, political and social particularities of each place as well as local visions of agents that produce the urban space. The remaining two chapters offer a comparative perspective by introducing a multicity analysis: one of them including four different cities in Latin America and the other examining the active travel experiences of young Hispanics in the USA.

Works in this volume use both qualitative and quantitative methods to understand the relationship between objective and subjective aspects of accessibility and inequality. Four of the chapters carry our quantitative analysis, of which two directly discuss accessibility metrics and propose ways to improve them (Chapters 1 and 2). Four chapters draw upon diverse qualitative techniques such as ethnographic observations, interviews, workshops and focus groups (Chapters 4, 6, 8 and 10). And two contributions decided to use mix methods (Chapters 5 and 10). While findings are diverse across the different chapters, four themes emerge as central to debates in accessibility: first, the implications of the dynamics of care in accessibility; second, the not so visible conditions of immobility that result from limited accessibility; third, the importance of rethinking methods and techniques that measure accessibility; and four, the potential to learn from the mobility practices and experiences of understudied population groups.

Taken together, the different works in this volume offer a broad presentation of case studies across various Latin American cities, methodological, conceptual and policy insights from different contexts in the region in relation to social equity and transport, a largely overlooked topic in international research on the region. Chapters in this book also offer a novel reflection on intersecting social relations of class, gender, ethnicity, religion, race, age and physical/mental ability in access to the city, and its services and infrastructure in various Latin American cities. Overall, this is an original contribution to further understand issues of accessibility, equity and social development in the study of mobilities and transport planning in cities of the Global South.

This volume was possible thanks to the collaboration of researchers who are part of the Latin American Branch of the International Network for Transport and Accessibility in Low Income Communities, INTALInC LAC. This network has offered us, the editors and contributors, a space for voicing debates and exploring the implications for transport planning and urban mobility and their interaction with other dimensions of planning. This book is the first outcome of this collective effort of co-production of knowledge and policies recommendations, which recognises the diversity of each city and different groups while striving for the social construction of shared solutions. In the end, we hope this book contributes with methodological, conceptual and policy insights from different contexts in the region to further explore the relationships between the state, civil society and private sector and the provision of more socially just mobility in Latin American cities.

NOTES

1. Trips related to accessing healthcare services, shopping, leisure, job hunting, personal business, meeting someone and drop off or pick up someone/something.
2. Measured through safety perception and experiences of sexual harassment.

REFERENCES

Banister, D. (2007). Sustainable transport: Challenges and opportunities. *Transportmetrica*, *3*(2), 91–106. https://doi.org/10.1080/18128600708685668

Banister, D., Watson, S., & Wood, C. (1997). Sustainable cities: Transport, energy, and urban form. *Environment and Planning B: Planning and Design*, *24*(1), 125–143. https://doi.org/10.1068/b240125

Bergmann, S., & Sager, T. (Eds.). (2008). *The ethics of mobilities: Rethinking place, exclusion, freedom and environment*. London: Ashgate.

Boys, J. (2014). *Doing disability differently: An alternative handbook on architecture, dis/ability and designing for everyday life*. Abingdon: Routledge.

Campaña, J. C., Giménez-Nadal, J. I., & Molina, J. A. (2018). Gender norms and the gendered distribution of total work in Latin American households. *Feminist Economics*, *24*(1), 35–62. https://doi.org/10.1080/13545701.2017.1390320

Cass, N., Shove, E., & Urry, J. (2005). Social exclusion, mobility and access. *The Sociological Review*, *53*(3), 539–555. https://doi.org/10.1111/j.1467-954X.2005.00565.x

Chorley, R. J., & Haggett, P. (2014). *Socio-economic models in geography* (1st ed. 1967). London: Routledge.

Cresswell, T. (2011). Mobilities I: Catching up. *Progress in Human Geography*, *35*(4), 550–558. https://doi.org/10.1177/0309132510383348

Cresswell, T., & Merriman, P. (Eds.). (2011). *Geographies of mobilities: Practices, spaces, subjects*. London: Ashgate.

Dávila, J. D. (Ed.). (2013). *Urban mobility & poverty: Lessons from Medellín and Soacha, Colombia*. London: University College London, Development Planning Unit, Universidad Nacional de Colombia, & Facultad de Arquitectura.

de Vasconcellos, E. A. (2001). *Urban transport, environment, and equity: The case for developing countries*. London: Earthscan.

Delbosc, A. (2012). The role of well-being in transport policy. *Transport Policy*, *23*, 25–33. https://doi.org/10.1016/j.tranpol.2012.06.005

Geurs, K. T., & van Wee, B. (2004). Accessibility evaluation of land-use and transport strategies: Review and research directions. *Journal of Transport Geography*, *12*(2), 127–140. https://doi.org/10.1016/j.jtrangeo.2003.10.005

Hamraie, A. (2017). *Building access: Universal design and the politics of disability*. Minneapolis, MN: University of Minnesota Press.

Hine, J., & Mitchell, F. (2001). Better for everyone? Travel experiences and transport exclusion. *Urban Studies*, *38*(2), 319–332. https://doi.org/10.1080/00420980020018619

Imrie, R. (2000). Disabling environments and the geography of access policies and practices. *Disability & Society*, *15*(1), 5–24. https://doi.org/10.1080/09687590025748

Jirón, P. (2010). Mobile borders in urban daily mobility practices in Santiago de Chile. *International Political Sociology*, *4*(1), 66–79. https://doi.org/10.1111/j.1749-5687.2009.00092.x

Jones, P., & Lucas, K. (2012). The social consequences of transport decision-making: Clarifying concepts, synthesising knowledge and assessing implications. *Journal of Transport Geography*, *21*, 4–16. https://doi.org/10.1016/j.jtrangeo.2012.01.012

Jirón, P., & Zunino, D. (2017). Dossier. Movilidad Urbana y Género: Experiencias latinoamericanas. *Revista Transporte y Territorio*, *16*, 1–8.

Kaufmann, V., Bergman, M. M., & Joye, D. (2004). Motility: Mobility as capital. *International Journal of Urban and Regional Research*, *28*(4), 745–756. https://doi.org/10.1111/j.0309-1317.2004.00549.x

Keeling, D. J. (2008). Latin America's transportation conundrum. *Journal of Latin American Geography*, *7*(2), 133–154. https://doi.org/10.1353/lag.0.0005

Lucas, K. (2012). Transport and social exclusion: Where are we now? *Transport Policy, 20*, 105–113. https://doi.org/10.1016/j.tranpol.2012.01.013

Lucas, K., Mattioli, G., Verlinghieri, E., & Guzman, A. (2016). Transport poverty and its adverse social consequences. *Proceedings of the Institution of Civil Engineers – Transport, 169*(6), 353–365. https://doi.org/10.1680/jtran.15.00073

Manderscheid, K. (2009). Unequal mobilities. In T. Ohnmacht, H. Maksim, & M. M. Bergman (Eds.), *Mobilities and inequality* (pp. 27–50). Surrey: Ashgate Publishing Company.

Manderscheid, K. (2014). Criticising the solitary mobile subject: Researching relational mobilities and reflecting on mobile methods. *Mobilities, 9*(2), 188–219. https://doi.org/10.1080/17450101.2013.830406

McGranahan, G. (2015). Urbanization. In J. D. Wright (Ed.), *International encyclopedia of the social & behavioral sciences* (pp. 958–964). Amsterdam: Elsevier. https://doi.org/10.1016/B978-0-08-097086-8.72120-9

Oviedo, D., & Titheridge, H. (2016). Mobilities of the periphery: Informality, access and social exclusion in the urban fringe in Colombia. *Journal of Transport Geography, 55*, 152–164. https://doi.org/10.1016/j.jtrangeo.2015.12.004

Parkin, J. (Ed.). (2012). *Cycling and sustainability*. Bingley: Emerald.

Pucher, J., & Buehler, R. (2017). Cycling towards a more sustainable transport future. *Transport Reviews, 37*(6), 689–694. https://doi.org/10.1080/01441647.2017.1340234

Scholl, L. (2016). *Urban transport and poverty: Mobility and accessibility effects of IDB-supported BRT systems in Cali and Lima*. Washington, DC: Inter-American Development Bank. https://doi.org/10.18235/0000328

Schonferder, S., & Axhausen, K. W. (2016). *Urban rhythms and travel behaviour: Spatial and temporal phenomena of daily travel*. London: Routledge.

Titheridge, H., Christie, N., Mackett, R., Oviedo, D., & Ye, R. (2014). *Transport and poverty: A review of the evidence*. London: UCL. https://www.ucl.ac.uk/transport/sites/transport/files/transport-poverty.pdf

Uteng, T. P., & Cresswell, T. (Eds.). (2008). *Gendered mobilities*. Aldershot: Ashgate.

van Wee, B. (2016). Accessible accessibility research challenges. *Journal of Transport Geography, 51*, 9–16. https://doi.org/10.1016/j.jtrangeo.2015.10.018

CHAPTER 1

SHOULD URBAN TRANSPORT BECOME A SOCIAL POLICY? INTERROGATING THE ROLE OF ACCESSIBILITY IN SOCIAL EQUITY AND URBAN DEVELOPMENT IN BOGOTÁ, COLOMBIA

Daniel Oviedo and Luis Ángel Guzmán

ABSTRACT

This chapter presents a critical examination of the interaction between concepts such as equity and accessibility in a framework of sustainable and inclusive urban development. The analysis compiles a series of reflections that build on previous research that focusses on the role of transport as enabler of opportunities for material and social capital, healthcare and leisure, which contribute to human development and well-being. The research discusses accessibility metrics for mandatory and non-mandatory travel in the context of current global agendas for social and development policies. It also introduces methodological reflections in relation to the analysis of accessibility indices from an equity perspective highlighting the role of equity metrics such as the Palma ratio and Lorenz curves. The authors link accessibility and urban development seeking to inform current approaches for policy development and assessment in a context of high manifested inequity. The research is set in the context of the Bogotá Metropolitan Region, a paradigmatic case of transport development and policy in the Global South. The findings seek to contribute to present transport policy and practice, providing relevant insights to support actions that redistribute accessibility to opportunities and questioning some of the paradigms of mainstream transport planning in cities like Bogotá, suggesting a more relevant role of transport policy as a potential engine of equity and social development.

Keywords: Equity; accessibility; transport; well-being; urban development; transport policy

1. INTRODUCTION

Mainstream transport planning in cities of the Global South tends to follow the principles of efficiency, resource maximisation and pursue economic growth via infrastructure investments resulting from a long-standing tradition of planning adopted mainly from North America and Europe. During the second part of the twentieth century, large-scale funding for infrastructure development took place globally, targeting improving speed and capacity for vehicle volumes under the assumption of a direct link between transport and economic growth. Such principles have governed the way in which most cities in Latin America have developed over five decades, following the introduction of the *urban transport planning process* in the 1960s and 1970s (Dimitriou & Gakenheimer, 2011). The critique to traditional principles of urban transport planning and the call for more interdisciplinary approaches to the planning, distribution and delivery of infrastructure and services for urban mobility have been extensively covered in the international literature (see Levy, 2013; Lucas & Jones, 2012; Martens, 2018). However, such critique has been almost entirely produced from scholars in the Global North, often overlooking the complexities inherent to urban development processes in emerging economies with higher rates of urbanisation and population growth than their more industrialised counterparts. Furthermore, traditional approaches to design, construction and operation of public transport systems in cities in regions such as Latin America, Africa and South East Asia still respond to planning criteria and regimes grounded in behavioural economics and on aggregated data sources that focus on the average user (Levy, 2013).

In contexts where historical infrastructure deficits and urban development regimes marked by informality, segregation and inequality have led to an unequal distribution of connectivity in cities (Oviedo & Dávila, 2016), the re-examination of traditional tenets of urban transport planning and delivery becomes an urgent issue of debate for urban researchers and practitioners. The relationships between social identity, transport and planning in the context of urban development in Latin America require critical reflections on the intersecting social relations of class, gender, ethnicity, religion, race, age and physical/mental ability in processes of urban development. Similarly, researchers and practitioners in modern urban transport planning, research and decision-making need examining how spatial and social mobilities intertwine in the reproduction of both spatial and social inequalities in cities. This chapter introduces accessibility and equity as alternative forms of interpretation of the current social consequences of transport policy and planning and inputs for reflection in relation to their potential implications for sustainable and inclusive development. The chapter focusses on differences by income, which despite not being representative of different social identities is an accepted proxy for social and economic differences which can lay the foundation for more in-depth analysis at more disaggregated scales.

One of the main limitations of mainstream approaches to transport planning adopted not only in the Global South but also in industrialised contexts is that these approaches tend to homogenise users based on dominant demographics, periods and areas of high travel demand, assuming observable mobility patterns as a reflection of the travel needs of the general population. The resulting standardisation of features of the population and its mobility needs lead to systems designed for very specific users: men of working age, with average purchasing power and with full physical and cognitive skills (Gössling, Schröder, Späth, & Freytag, 2016). This 'normalisation' and generalisation of users limits access to opportunities, goods and services offered by cities to socially vulnerable groups such as women, the elderly, children and people with reduced mobility. Not recognising that not all city dwellers are in the same social position to take advantage of available transport systems, forms of urban transport planning in most rapidly growing cities end up generating social exclusion effects on specific groups differentiated by the intersection of social identities of race, gender, age, class and physical and cognitive abilities.

Reflections about the limitations of traditional approaches to urban transport planning are essential in the context of global development agendas that increasingly recognise the social implications for transport planning and its interaction with other kinds of planning. The United Nations' Sustainable Development Goals (SDGs) encompass such recognition of the role of cities and their transport systems in achieving more inclusive and sustainable societies. Of course, one of the most relevant contributions of the SDGs is that cities are acknowledged as engines of development, which suggest a global commitment to transform cities into inclusive, accessible, safe, resilient and sustainable places.

The concept of accessibility, defined as 'the extent to which land-use and transport systems enable individuals or group of individuals to reach activities or destinations by means of (a combination of) transport modes' (Geurs & van Wee, 2004, p. 128), is suggested in this chapter and previous research as a way to understand the links between mobility and land use, and it has the potential to inform decision-making for more sustainable and just cities (Cheng & Bertolini, 2013). Accessibility incorporates dimensions beyond that of simply physical movement, going beyond the interpretation of mobility as travel. Accessibility is a well-known concept mostly that has been increasingly applied in research and practice, particularly in the Global North. Moreover, recent research suggests that if integrated into transport policies and practice, accessibility planning can reduce the gaps associated with socioeconomic, environmental and spatial inequalities in cities (Benevenuto & Caulfield, 2019; Levy, 2013; Levy & Dávila, 2017; Lucas, 2011; Vasconcellos, 2014).

Latin America is the most urbanised region on the planet, where about 80% of its population lives in cities (Roberts et al., 2017). Its rapid economic and demographic growth, paired with development, accompanied by a rapid increase in motorisation for private use (cars and motorcycles), contribute to low-quality urban expansion processes and socio-spatial inequities intimately connected with urban mobility. The steady increase in fleets of private vehicles has led to higher use of fossil fuels, leading to environmental degradation and adverse health effects. Despite such trends, Latin American cities still depend largely on public transport services, often operating informally, to address most travel needs for the population, suggesting a central role of public transport in urban mobility in the region (Hidalgo & Huizenga, 2013).

The added advantage of incorporating an accessibility approach to the analysis of urban mobility issues in Latin American cities is that it helps researchers and practitioners accounting for the inequalities in the spatial distribution of opportunities. Although most wealth and economic output of developing countries concentrate in cities, opportunities for employment, education and social development are concentrated in a handful of areas within urban environments, which boast comparatively greater connectivity and high land prices. In contrast, urban peripheries tend to act as focal points of concentration of extreme poverty, which creates huge inequalities between socioeconomic groups. According to a recent Global Monitoring Report (World Bank & International Monetary Fund, 2016), access and mobility are not distributed fairly in Latin America.

The urban form resulting from this inequitable urban model has a direct and negative impact on the well-being of the inhabitants of the region. A quick look at this situation reveals a worrying reality: large differences in access to opportunities and services for different socioeconomic groups. The consequences of high levels of socio-spatial segregation and urban inequalities translate into thousands of hours lost in traffic, growth in road accident levels, inefficiency in the provision of urban services and disproportionate levels of risk and exclusion of most vulnerable populations.

Transport deficiency can translate into difficulties in accessing social life, education, health and economic opportunities (Gwilliam, 2010). Likewise, inequalities in access have implications within households and generate high levels of accumulated marginalisation in their most vulnerable members (children, elderly and people with reduced mobility), or transferring costs disproportionately to others, because of their social position (e.g. women who are responsible for care and mobility of other household members) (Oviedo & Titheridge, 2016). In other words, the large costs of trips related to productive activities and urban settings that privilege such types of trips have negative implications in terms of access and inclusion of people who perform other functions, such as care travel, shopping, errands and other activities considered not mandatory.

This chapter also has policy relevance beyond the context of Bogotá and its surrounding municipalities as it showcases relevant concepts and methods for addressing the UN's SDGs, particularly SDG 11 of sustainable and inclusive communities and cities. The research engages directly and indirectly with the target of achieving efficient and inclusive urban transport systems that serve as catalysts for positive changes in environmental, social and economic development. This chapter addresses mobility and planning of transport systems as means that mitigate problems of segregation and social, spatial and economic exclusion as recurring problems in cities from the Global South. In Section 2, the chapter provides an overview of conceptual approaches to accessibility and its intrinsic relationship with equity and inclusion. Building on such conceptual debates, in Section 3, we analyse the case of Bogotá, Colombia, focussing on the distribution of accessibility and equity. In Sections 4 and 5, the chapter stresses the relevance of targeted interventions to reduce access gaps, the recognition of the diversity of social actors and their identities, and the need to design transport systems for socially vulnerable populations.

2. ACCESSIBILITY AS A MEASURE OF URBAN (IN)EQUALITY

In the late 1960s and beginnings of 1970s, the concept of social justice began to capture some attention within the world of urban planning. Harvey (2009) argued that to pursue social justice, it is necessary to achieve a fair distribution of resources and processes of development (pp. 116–117). Fraser (1998) built on such ideas to add that in societies with a certain degree of urban development, there is a need for redistribution and recognition, which are necessary conditions for social justice and equity.

The standard focus on efficiency and minimisation of travel costs underpinning mainstream transport planning is a desirable yet insufficient objective in relation to the equitable and just distribution of access in the city (Deka, 2004, p. 353). Different scholars have advocated about the need to move from travel behaviour analysis focussed on trip-based travel choices and activity-based studies to the planning of transport from an accessibility-based perspective (Lyons, 2003). Deka (2004) argues that transport services enable access to opportunities such as work, healthcare, retail and recreation (p. 336). However, the unequal distribution of land uses and transport services become potential instruments for the production and reproduction of social and spatial inequalities (Oviedo & Dávila, 2016). In other words, transport networks 'either moderate or aggravate social inequalities by enhancing or restricting accessibility' (Manderscheid, 2009).

Since the 1990s, the accessibility approach has reinterpreted mobility from a desirable end, to a means to achieve access to opportunities, turning access into a primary social good (Martens, Golub, & Robinson, 2012; van Wee & Geurs, 2011) and mobility into an intermediate good. This marked an increased relevance of the social value of transport as a precondition to exercise the right to the city and perceive the benefits of living in an urban area (Lowe, Stanley, & Stanley, 2018).

In Latin America, differentiated provision of transport networks has contributed to the phenomenon of splintering urbanism (Graham & Marvin, 2001), which helps explaining biases and inequalities in transport planning and the spatial gaps associated with rapid urban growth and the consolidation of premium spaces in urban areas. Such phenomenon leads to wealthier groups locating in well-connected spaces that enable better access to information, social interactions and conditions for the accumulation of capital. By the same token, lower income and less attractive zones of the city become increasingly disconnected (Oviedo & Dávila, 2016). There is an urgent need to consider social justice in the transport planning process to reduce gaps in access and mobility across social groups and identities (Jones & Lucas, 2012, p. 13)

Accessibility allows researchers and practitioners to link transport and land use. The definition of accessibility involves linking transport and land use with desired destinations. However, what can be desired or needed involves a high degree of complexity as there is a broad range of human activities that can be accessed (Cass, Shove, & Urry, 2005). Modern approaches to accessibility need developing a deeper understanding not only of where people go but also where they want to go, why they want to go and what constraints they have for using transport and accessing land use (Cass et al., 2005).

Accessibility also needs to be understood in the different scales that it takes place. Jones and Lucas (2012) ague that individuals need to experience good levels of accessibility at the micro, macro and strategic level in order to take advantage of the opportunities offered by urban environments (p. 6). At the microscale, accessibility refers to the ability of individuals from all social groups – specifically those with physical or cognitive disabilities – to use transport systems and navigate urban spaces. This encompasses the design of vehicles and motorised modes, as well as the features of the built environment that enable mobility of all users (Jones & Lucas, 2012, p. 6).

The mesoscale of accessibility refers to the ability to move at the neighbourhood level, which includes considerations of the connectivity and permeability of urban networks both by walking and when using different motorised and non-motorised transport systems. At the mesoscale, accessibility is influenced by aspects of walkability and cycle ability, and the features of the built environment that enable access to different social groups. This scale also considers qualitative and subjective variables such as perceptions of safety, community cohesion and social interaction (Jones & Lucas, 2012).

Finally, the strategic scale of accessibility – one of the most frequently analysed in the academic literature in Latin America – focusses on the ability to travel from one area of the city to another, or between cities to participate in a desired activity (Jones & Lucas, 2012). This scale of accessibility considers the spatial and temporal distribution of opportunities and population, as well as the configuration of transport and infrastructure networks that connect the demand of travel with the supply of opportunities for employment, education, health, culture and social interactions.

These scales shift the focus towards the individual experience, capabilities and societal processes enhancing further conceptualisations as the one proposed by Jones and Lucas (2012) in which accessibility 'provides measures of the degree to which people can reach the goods and services that society considers are necessary for them to live their daily lives, but with an emphasis on potential/capability rather than actual behaviour' (p. 6); hence, a person-based interest of accessibility raises differing from the activity- or location-based (Martens, 2012). Seemingly, acknowledging the characteristics of our society as a network, Cass, Shove, and Urry propose that access is the 'ability to negotiate space and time so as to accomplish practices and maintain relations that people take to be necessary for normal social participation. People need to "access" networks if they are to participate in a complex, multiply networked society' (Cass et al., 2005, p. 543). For Cass et al. (2005), access is influenced by the nature of the transport system, but also by the time-space organisation of households and of facilities and opportunities which individuals seek to access. In this sense, the temporal component and household dynamics appear as a relevant element within the accessibility framework. The authors bring to the front that access has four key dimensions: financial in terms of the required economic resources to travel, physical as the distribution of physical constraints, organisational as the way in which services and facilities are organised, and temporal in terms of the required time and personal coordination of time (Cass et al., 2005).

The intersection between different scales of accessibility is essential in processes of transport and land-use integration and coordination (Cervero, 2001, 2002; Litman, 2010; Suzuki, Cervero, & Iuchi, 2013). Such processes involve the development of strategies of mixed land use and the integration of different transport modes, mediated by characteristics of policy and the built environment. Strategies of transport and land-use integration are essential in redressing social and spatial inequalities associated with urban mobility and can respond to accessibility imbalances at all scales via neighbourhood development, transit-oriented development, location efficiency, improvement of jobs-housing balance, reduction of spatial mismatch and support of transport concurrency (Steiner in Wagner & Caves, 2012). Accessibility has also been linked with wider notions of well-being such as liveability, which, according to Appleyard, Ferrell, Carroll, and Taecker (2014), is 'the accessibility people have to opportunities in and around the public realm (for commuting, work, education, rest, rejuvenation, etc.) to improve or maintain their desired quality of life' (p. 68).

3. BOGOTÁ AND THE UNEQUAL DISTRIBUTION OF ACCESSIBILITY

Bogotá, the capital of Colombia and one of the cities with the largest population in Latin America, has become a paradigmatic case in terms of transport planning thanks in part to the successful implementation of its rapid bus system (bus rapid transit – BRT), called Transmilenio. In the last decades, a considerable number of studies in the areas of urban studies and transport have examined Bogotá from the perspective of accessibility, emphasising the multiple social and spatial imbalances that the urban and transport structures of the city have left consequently (Bocarejo, Escobar, Hernandez, & Galarza, 2016; Bocarejo & Oviedo, 2012; Guzman & Oviedo, 2018; Guzman, Oviedo, & Bocarejo, 2016; Guzman, Oviedo, & Rivera, 2017; Munoz-Raskin, 2010; Rodriguez & Targa, 2004).

For years, the city has developed along well-defined transport corridors, which have been consolidated as a result of investments in mass public transport and the brokers with the highest demand for travel. These dynamics have contributed to phenomena of high spatial concentration opportunities and unidirectional travel from residential areas in the peripheries to the expanded city centre, which concentrates the greatest number of opportunities for the inhabitants of the city, manifest in key economic nodes, cultural, educational activity and socialisation spaces of the inhabitants.

The concentration of activities and the increases of land value in central areas of the cities, accompanied by dynamics of internal migration from rural zones, have contributed to an increase of population of low income in the urban peripheries. Most peripheral informal and low-income settlements are characterised by high densities, little urban planning and limited to none access to urban services and amenities, and limited availability of public spaces and formal public transport. Despite long-term processes of neighbourhood upgrading in many neighbourhoods of informal origin, the organisation of the territory in Bogotá separates most clusters of opportunities such as work, study and leisure from places of residence of low-income residents, which contributes to the increase in travel distances and the dependence of public transport to guarantee such displacements.

Bogotá exhibits common characteristics in Latin American cities in relation to its socioeconomic and productive structure. The city has expanded from its historic centre along transport corridors that connect it with the main transport hubs of goods to logistics centres – historically in the country's ports – and emerging infrastructure focussed on public transport, first by rail and after the early 2000s in high-capacity Transmilenio services. This trend was replicated for decades leading to the expansion of urban sprawl and conurbation (both regulated and organic) with other municipalities that have been shaping the functional and unofficial area of Metropolitan Bogotá (see Guzman et al., 2017). This functional integration is shown descriptively in Fig. 1.1 in the form of work-related

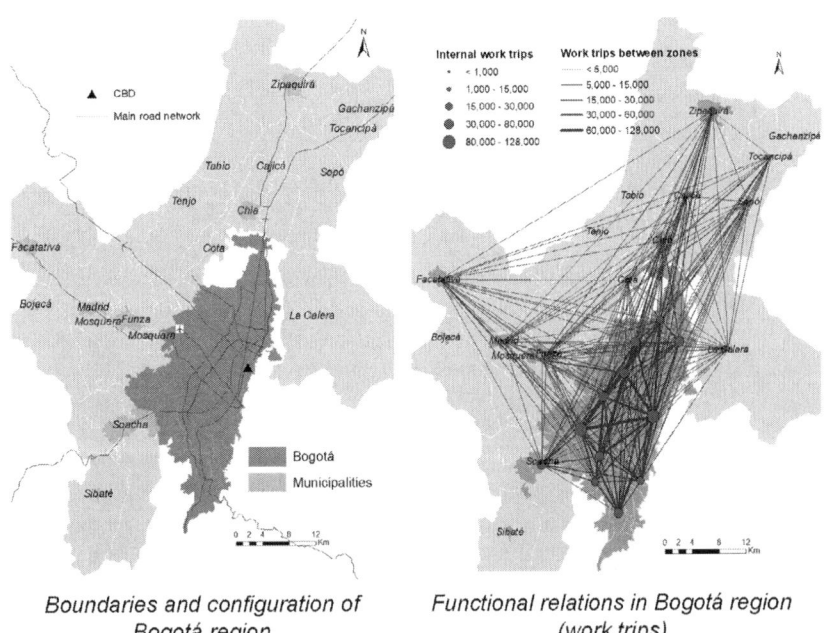

Fig. 1.1. Boundaries and Configuration of Bogotá Region. *Source*: Own elaboration based on Guzman et al. (2017).

trips per day. The points indicate the intensity of the internal relations of large areas in the city (intrazonal work trips). The lines represent the quantity of trips between different areas and municipalities.

Although conurbation and suburbanisation of neighbouring municipalities with Bogotá is not new, improvement and expansion of infrastructure in the region and a growing vision of metropolitan development have led to dynamics of access to transport and employment in the city that have surpassed the administrative limits of the city of Bogotá (see Oviedo & Dávila, 2016; Guzman et al., 2017).

Due to this historical pattern of development, most of the productive activities have been concentrated in proximity to the historic centre, generating an expanded centre (CBD in Fig. 1.1) in the centre-east transport corridors and the road to the airport. The concentration of economic activities in the expanded centre of the city has led to a greater density of investments in infrastructure and connectivity in and to areas of greater attractiveness in terms of job opportunities, as well as in the concentration of commercial and social opportunities and essential infrastructure as educational institutions, health and public space (Guzman et al., 2017).

These tendencies in the planning of the city have as a consequence the phenomenon of 'Splintering Urbanism' (Graham & Marvin, 2001), which involves investments in connectivity of zones with greater attractiveness by means of both public developments and the privatisation of infrastructure while simultaneously it overlooks more remote areas, with less attractiveness and, generally, in those with lower incomes, reducing its accessibility to the rest of the city (Oviedo & Dávila, 2016). A notable exception to this is the expansion of public transport systems to areas characterised by concentrating low- and middle-low-income households, particularly through investments on Bogotá's BRT system Transmilenio to the peripheries and neighbouring municipality Soacha. However, lack of sufficient supply of both services and infrastructure at the local level, especially in areas of informal origin and challenging topography, have maintained a comparative disconnection of more socially vulnerable households in the Bogotá region (Oviedo & Dávila, 2016).

As a result, the greater attractiveness and accessibility in central areas has direct effects on the land values and the real estate market. The urban and economic consolidation of the central areas of Bogotá have been accompanied by accelerated increases in land values in the proximity of the areas of concentration of opportunities and the gradual displacement of social groups of low-middle and low income to the peripheries, as well as in neighbouring municipalities. This pattern has been repeated since the birth of the city (Guzman et al., 2017). The above factors have defined this cycle of constant segregation and differences in access to the goods and services of the city, which persists despite investments in public transport and is reflected in Fig. 1.2, whose first consequence measured in terms of transport is the average high travel time motorised from peripheral areas.

The primary data source for the analyses in this chapter is the Bogotá mobility survey (Secretaría Distrital de Movilidad (SDM), 2011), which includes socioeconomic data and travel data for a typical workday. Table 1.1 indicates the distribution of the 17.49 million trips by all modes of transport in Bogotá and its immediate surroundings in 2011,

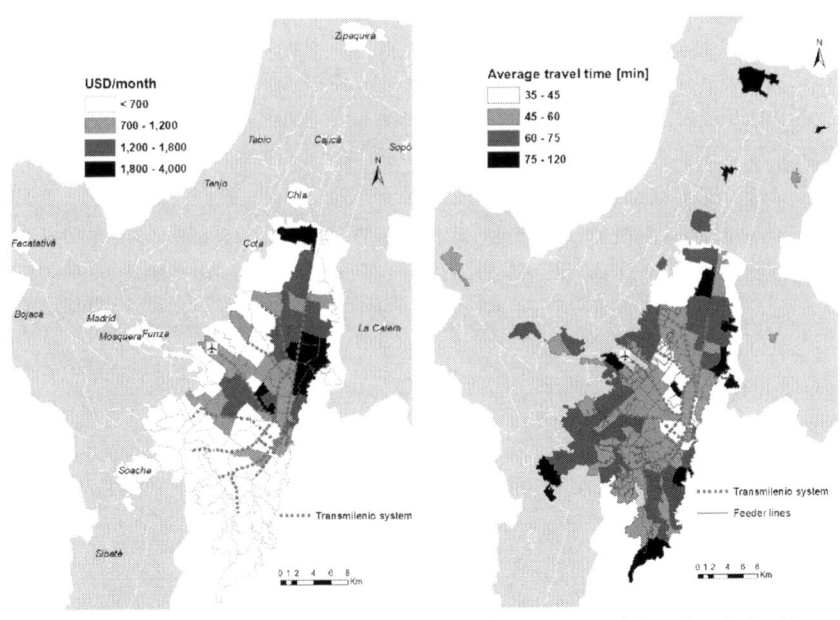

Fig. 1.2. Income Distribution and Average Motorised Travel Times in Bogotá.
Source: Guzman, Oviedo, and Rivera (2016).

categorised by trip type and specific trip purpose. The results show that 'return to home' generates more individual trips (45.3%) than the rest of the trips. However, if we ignore this trip purpose and focus on trips home based, the purpose going 'to work' (13.1%) is the travel purpose that generates more home-based trips. If we added 'work-related business' (2.6%) and 'school' purposes (11.2%) to commuting travel, mandatory travel accounts for around 26.9% of total daily trips. This marked (*) travel purposes are considered as mandatory activities. This implies that non-mandatory activities comprise 27.7% of the daily trips, illustrating the relevance of detailed analysis of access to opportunities other than those associated with commuting trips, supporting both an accessibility-oriented analysis of the conditions in Bogotá and the limitations of mainstream approaches to transport planning mentioned in Sections 1 and 2.

Non-work related activities tend to have flexible locations and schedules (i.e. a traveller has more than one possible choice of destination for each activity, depending on his location and travel budget), which also makes their inclusion in mainstream transport planning more complex (van Wee, 2012). Table 1.1 also reflects the multiplicity of mode choices involved in non-mandatory access by showing transport modes used for trips according to trip purpose. The striking result here is that slow modes (walk and bike, non-motorised) are the transport mode used by a large margin in Bogotá region. This is especially true for 'take/pick up someone' and 'shopping' activities, which probably reflects the convenience of walking/biking from home to nearby neighbourhood services that offers these activities. Public transport (including Transmilenio, traditional buses and inter-municipal buses) is the second most common choice of mode followed by cars as the third most popular choice (Guzman et al., 2017).

Table 1.1 shows the great importance of non-motorised trips to non-work activities. However, when measuring accessibility by travel time (there is no monetary costs), accessibility reflects the attractiveness of opportunities weighted by the time needed to travel from the origin to the destination. This type of accessibility is not homogeneous in terms of the travel time threshold, which ranges from 5 to 30 min (Vale et al., 2016), and is not possible to make valid comparisons with other transport modes. In this case, the average walking travel time is around 15 min, with extreme values between 3 and 50 min. This average travel time suggests an approximate 1.5 km of travel distance. These data suggest that a high percentage of these trips generated by each zone (UPZ)[1] have the same zone as its destination. As seen in Fig. 1.3, some particular (marked) zones located in the urban periphery concentrate around 45% of both generated and attracted non-mandatory walking trips. This suggests a high degree of dependency on walking to access most opportunities, sometimes involving disproportionately long walking times as well as exposures to road safety risks and pollution as pedestrian facilities are often limited poorly signalised.

The spatial, economic, social and transport supply distribution in the city of Bogotá has effects on the distribution of potential accessibility to job opportunities and the access of different users to jobs. As opportunities are spatially centralised and located far from most lower income areas, disposable time and income for accessing other relevant opportunities are limited, which is compounded by constrained local availability of opportunities that can be accessed walking. This

Table 1.1. Percentage of All Trips by Trip Purpose and Modal Share 2011.

Trip Purpose	Non-Motorised (%)	Public Transport (%)	Car (%)	Taxi (%)	Motorcycle (%)	Others (%)	Total (%)
To work*	5.7	23.1	16.9	12.8	29.5	10.1	13.1
Work-related business*	1.3	3.1	6.7	4.0	6.2	1.6	2.6
School*	13.9	8.0	3.5	3.6	3.7	32.6	11.2
Healthcare	0.9	4.2	3.2	9.9	0.6	1.0	2.4
Visit friends/relatives	3.0	2.8	3.5	3.6	1.2	1.5	2.9
Return to home	46.9	44.7	40.5	43.6	42.6	46.7	45.3
Take/pick up someone	9.9	1.9	8.7	4.8	5.2	1.4	6.7
Take/pick up something	1.0	0.7	1.5	0.8	0.7	0.5	0.9
Out to eat/drink	1.2	0.2	1.4	0.8	0.6	0.1	0.8
Shopping	7.6	2.1	3.8	3.4	1.3	0.5	4.9
Personal business	3.1	6.0	5.6	6.5	5.3	1.5	4.3
Social/recreational	3.4	0.9	1.8	2.5	0.8	0.8	2.3
Job search	0.1	0.4	0.0	0.0	0.1	0.0	0.2
Other	2.1	2.0	2.9	3.6	2.1	1.5	2.2
Total	49.6	30.1	10.3	3.5	2.3	4.1	100

Source: Own elaboration based on Mobility Survey (2011).
*Commuting trips.

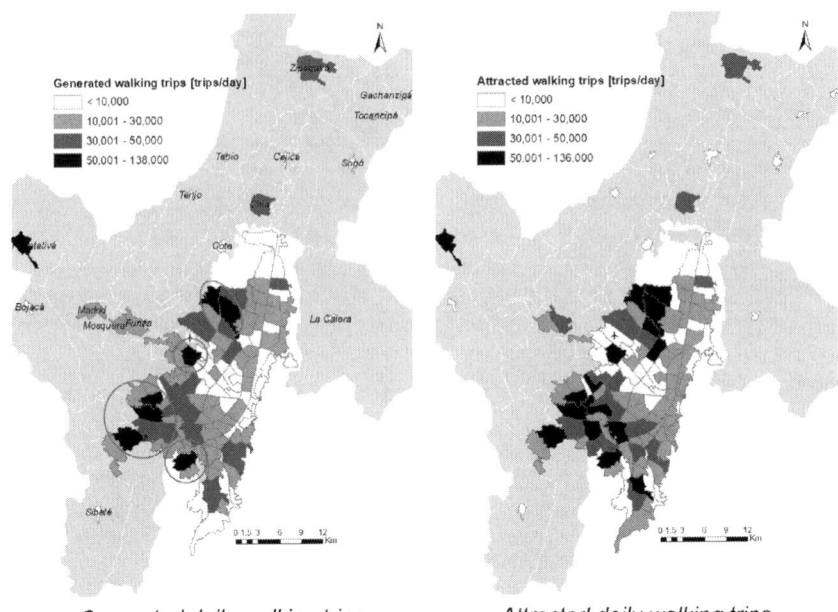

Fig. 1.3. Generated and Attracted Non-Mandatory Walking Daily Trips.
Source: Own elaboration based on Mobility Survey (2011).

requires a more detailed exploration of the accessibility by motorised means, especially public transport, which is the most common motorised alternative for low-income residents. An approach to explore accessibility is summarised by Equation 1, which has been used in several investigations since the beginning of the decade of 2010 for the study of accessibility to jobs in the city of Bogotá (Bocarejo & Oviedo, 2012). This accessibility metric considers the dimension of land use and job offer in the city (O_j) and a decay function that depends on a parameter (β_i) associated with the characteristics of each area of origin and costs (C_{ij}) associated with travelling between origins and destinations by mode of transport. Accessibility (A_i) calculated with this method is expressed by estimating the total of potentially accessible opportunities from each area of the city from which work trips originate. This metric of potential accessibility at the origin has allowed several studies (Bocarejo. & Oviedo, 2012; Guzman et al., 2017) to estimate the imbalances of accessibility and the implications of equity for different areas of the city.

Equation 1: Potential accessibility considering times and travel costs

$$A_i^m = \sum_j O_j \exp(-\beta_i^m \cdot C_{ij}^m) \qquad C_{ij}^m = t_{ij}^m + C_{ij}^m / v_{OT}$$

Source: Guzman et al. (2017).

The results of applying Equation 1 show the number of work and study opportunities that can be accessed from each area of the city. In all cases, studies have found similar patterns of accessibility in the city: lower levels of accessibility in conventional public transport, as in the recently implemented integrated transport system (SITP), evidencing that in the peripheries and low-income areas, there are the greatest positive effects of potential accessibility in the feeding areas of the BRT system and the central areas with the greatest concentration of opportunities (Guzman & Oviedo, 2018; Guzman et al., 2017). The results also suggest a positive effect of Transmilenio for areas farther away from the expanded centre of the city. An interesting result shown in Fig. 1.4 is the highest comparative value of per capita accessibility (number of accessible work and study opportunities divided by the population of each area) on public transport compared to the private vehicle. Given the higher travel costs and lower motorisation, especially in lower income areas, the values of accessibility in automobile are lower than the other modes, although their distribution is more uniform throughout the city.

Now, if accessibility is understood as a quantity of opportunities, 50% of the population of the Bogotá region access only 32% of the opportunities offered by the city (for car users). Comparing the levels of accessibility for a mode of transport with the density of places of residence, employment and study, the distribution of accessibility of the car is less equitable (-8%), while a better relationship is observed in the distribution of accessibility of public transport ($+6\%$). The high-income group has a uniform distribution, that is, when observing the 50th percentile of the population, half of the population experienced approximately the same levels of average accessibility in the region. This only occurs in higher income groups, while the most vulnerable populations present an inequitable distribution of accessibility.

These results are summarised in Fig. 1.5, which expresses the georeferenced accessibility index for the city of Bogotá for different modes of transport (Guzman et al., 2017). Consequently, the differences between the proportion of accessibility and the proportion of population in each area, presented in Fig. 1.5, make it possible to identify the accessibility imbalances in the city more clearly.

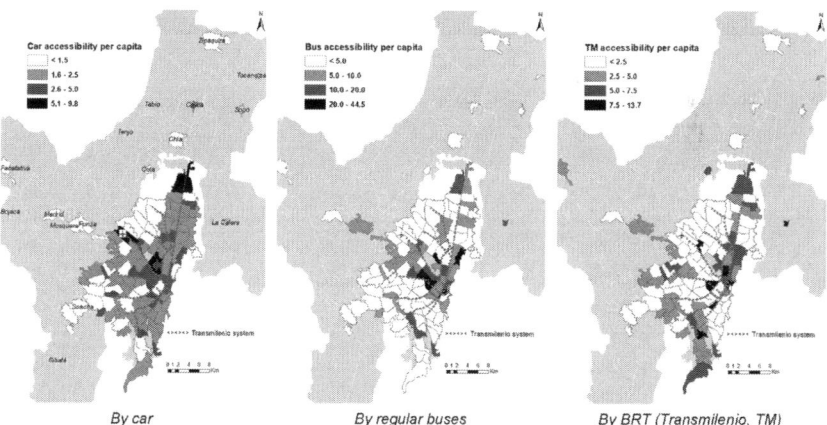

Fig. 1.4. Potential Accessibility to Employment and Education Opportunities by Transport Mode. *Source*: Own elaboration based on Guzman et al. (2016).

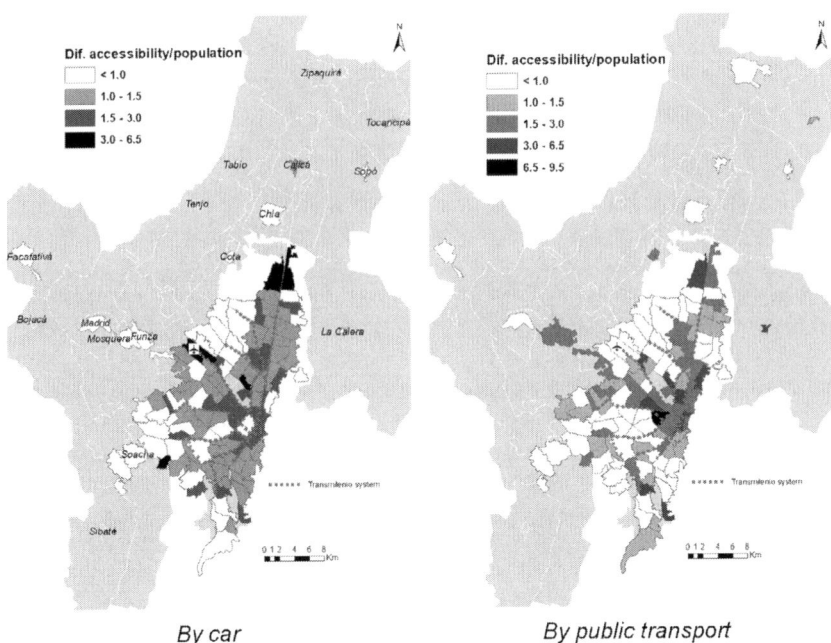

By car   By public transport

Fig. 1.5. Differences in Potential Accessibility to Employment and Education by Transport Mode. *Source*: Own elaboration based on Guzman et al. (2016).

The areas in which this indicator is less than 1 reflect an imbalance between the population and accessibility, that is, there are more residents than accessibility. This has clear implications for equity because it implies that there are areas of the city where the characteristics of the transport supply and the conditions of demand for mobility services do not allow residents to have a potential of at least one job opportunity per inhabitant.

The relationship between travel behaviour (transport system) and land use (activities system) allows us to estimate potential opportunities for interaction (Geurs & Ritsema van Eck, 2001). Non-mandatory accessibility is approached in the same fashion as mandatory accessibility shown earlier. In this case, the measure of attractiveness was related with the travel purposes of accessing healthcare services, shopping, leisure, job hunting, personal business, meeting someone and drop off or pick up someone/something (see Table 1.1). These opportunities were selected as they contribute to building social capital, physical and mental health, as well as relating to networks of support and obligation that contribute to a full life (Sen, 1993). This measure incorporates both land use and transport systems in the form of a sum of potential destinations, for example, hospitals, shops, malls, parks, etc.. The expected results show the opportunities weighted according to their generalised travel cost functions by transport mode.

The estimations of generalised travel costs for non-mandatory activities show high travel expenditure to access non-mandatory activities in the peripheries of

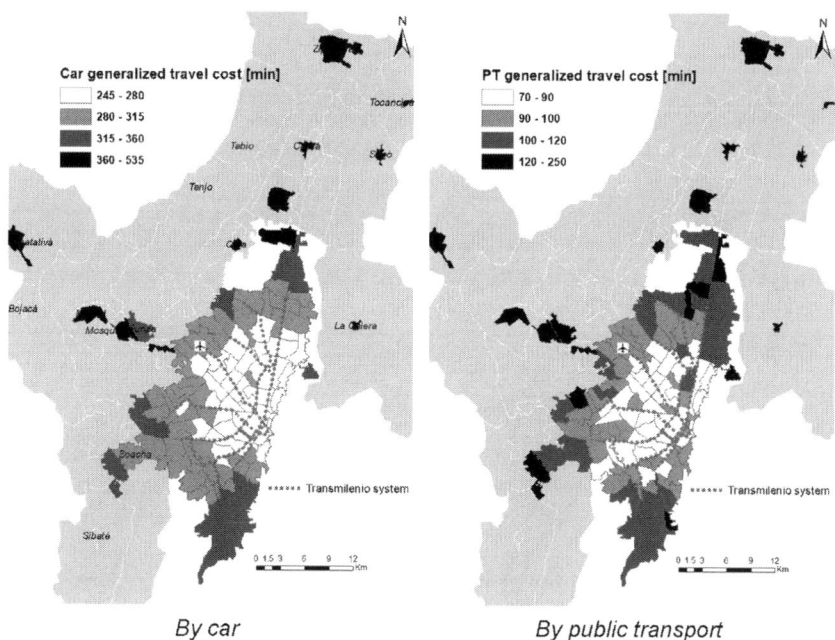

Fig. 1.6. Average Generalised Travel Cost for Non-Mandatory Activities by Mode.
Source: Own elaboration.

Bogotá, as well as the municipalities forming the Bogotá region. Costs used for the estimation of accessibility shown in Fig. 1.6 vary by trip purpose and travel mode and pair of origin–destination; however, these have been aggregated as a single non-mandatory purpose. These data provide an easily comparable representation of accessibility to activities not often measured in a context such as Bogotá. Although, Figs. 1.3 and 1.4 suggest a more decentralised structure of the city in terms of the spatial distribution of non-mandatory opportunities and urban facilities, the travel expenditure estimates suggest considerably higher costs of access for peripheral areas, similar to results obtained for mandatory activities in a previous study (Guzman et al., 2017).

The calculation of non-mandatory accessibility required data on the attractiveness of no-job/study-related activity and the impedance between ij zones (generalised travel cost). For this analysis, we employ a similar formulation developed previously by some of the authors (Guzman et al., 2017). Our calculation of the potential estimates the accessibility of the opportunities in a zone (i) to all other areas (j), given that fewer or more distant opportunities will be less attractive or more difficult to reach as specified in Equation 1.

Accessibility results show relevant contrasts between areas of the city closer to the city centre and the periphery, which are closely related with differences in income groups. Non-mandatory normalised accessibility values suggest higher accessibility (via both private and public transport) in the areas with lower income in the southern part of the city and the middle-income areas in the north-west of Bogotá. The results were compared with the population in the different Urban Planning Zones in order to compare the effective accessibility in different zones. Per capita accessibility by private vehicle is higher in areas of the bottom 40%, despite income and motorisation figures suggesting much lower access to this transport alternative in such areas. The estimation of per capita accessibility allows for a comparable indicator of the number of potential opportunities accessible as a ratio of the potential demand for such opportunities. The higher the per capita accessibility, the higher the potential of an individual in a given zone to access valuable opportunities not related to work or education. By contrast, there is higher accessibility to non-mandatory opportunities by public transport in more central and higher income areas, which are better located in relation to the distribution of opportunities presented in Fig. 1.3. These results contrast to the results found by other studies (Kawabata & Shen, 2007; Lovett, Haynes, Sünnenberg, & Gale, 2002; Van Vugt, Meertens, & Van Lange, 1995), which usually find accessibility levels to be higher by car. Here, our results are consistent mainly because of the two basic assumptions: using the car is much more expensive than public transport, because we are including the operation cost per kilometre (which includes insurances, maintenance, parking costs and fuel), and also, because the car ownership index for the bottom 40 population is in average, 52 veh/1,000 inhab, while for top 10 population, the index is 480 veh/1,000 inhab.

One of the main limitations of the estimations is that information for non-motorised travel is of comparatively lower quality and scale than that for motorised travel, which constrains the estimation of non-motorised accessibility indices. However, public transport accessibility can be a good proxy for local accessibility indices, which may suggest higher access in the areas with lower travel expenditure via walking and cycling.

4. REFLECTIONS FOR POLICY AND PRACTICE IN LATIN AMERICA

Findings in Section 3 provide context-specific evidence to support that marked spatial inequalities, socioeconomic segregation and informality present in most Latin American cities could be partially mitigated with an inclusive, accessible and affordable urban transport that is integrated into the urban space. Our findings suggest that the contribution of public transport, particularly mass transit such as Bogotá's BRT, increases the ability of low-income populations to access employment opportunities located in the city centre. The analyses of both the spatial distribution of opportunities in Bogotá and its surrounding municipalities, and the location of different income groups across the urban space of the city reflect the clear role of transport infrastructure and services in integrating and connecting citizens with the opportunities and the various degrees of inequality in access across the population. The accessibility approach was adopted in this chapter as a way of supporting evidence-based distributional debates that can contribute to developing an urban transport policy with a social focus. Evaluating the performance of transport projects from accessibility can be transformative. By deploying an easily understandable concept that can measure whether mobility investments improve access to jobs, services and opportunities, it is possible to differentiate the levels of access in various zones of the city, as well as making visible the inequalities in transport expenditure for both mandatory and non-mandatory opportunities such as those shown in Figs. 1.2 and 1.6. Such high travel costs in the lower income and peripheral neighbourhoods that contrast with the better-connected high-income households closer to the city centre are a reflection of a long-standing tradition of focussing on goals deeply rooted in mainstream policy and practices such as increasing travel speeds, minimising delays and maximising passenger volumes.

To consider accessibility as a structuring axis in the discussion about transport policy (i.e. accessible mobility) can enable integral planning and evaluation of urban transport systems. This is possible as accessibility forces planners, practitioners and decision makers to consider the interaction between its different components, and it makes visible conditions of vulnerability and inequality within the territory, as is shown in Section 3, where access inequalities throughout the Bogotá region were demonstrated. The use of measures such as the Palma ratio makes it evident that the minority in the top-income tiers concentrate higher potential access to jobs than the bottom 40% of the income distribution. An accessibility approach facilitates the implementation of specific measures to reduce such inequalities. Furthermore, an integral vision of accessibility in its different scales and temporal dynamism can contribute to account for the side effects of urban transport policies. For instance, if accessibility is greatly improved throughout the city, incentives for urban expansion may be generated in the long term, leading to a potential imbalance in urban development.

People and their mobility needs should be at the centre of urban policies, which needs to rethink the criteria used for planning and operation of urban transport systems in particular, and mobility in general in cities such as Bogotá. The differentials of accessibility a sustainable city must provide its citizens with an accessible system that allows them to achieve the largest amount of opportunities offered by the city in an efficient, reliable manner and at reasonable costs and times. Public transport subsidies have been suggested as a progressive measure, which as mentioned have been picked up by decision makers (Guzman & Oviedo, 2018). Since the benefit in terms of increased accessibility may be the missing support for advances in social policy, the development of baseline accessibility analysis such as the one presented in this chapter can serve to assess effects of urban transport policies seeking to redress social inequalities by targeting specific determinants of accessibility. Such determinants include the redistribution of opportunities, reduction of travel costs via, for example, subsidies, and the improvement in travel conditions that entail lower travel times. In this regard, beyond improving and developing new infrastructure and increasing the supply of transport, it is necessary to take into account its distribution in the territory and the costs of access across socioeconomic groups. This would increase the possibility of having positive impacts in reducing inequalities and in increasing well-being.

To design transport policies that point to a new culture of mobility that combines activities, connects urban centres and gives priority to alternative modes of transport, it will not be enough to design and apply isolated measures. A global strategy that includes real mobility alternatives in all modes, including walking and cycling, is necessary. This has become a clear gap in both research and practice, as there is little to no explicit research about micro and meso accessibility, which is illustrated by the concentration of non-motorised and walking trips shown in Table 1.1 and Fig. 1.3, which are largely similar in most contexts in Colombia and Latin America. Moreover, it is necessary to recognise the need for intersectoral planning and a common understanding that a public transport system of high quality is not only an alternative to the private vehicle in many territorial areas, but it is also an incentive to make more efficient use of the territory, promoting other forms of accessibility.

5. CONCLUSIONS

The notions of accessibility, access and equity allow us to examine and make explicit differences in the capacity of social groups and individuals in specific areas to take advantage of the opportunities offered by cities. The analysis of accessibility and the marked inequalities around it across social and economic groups contribute to critically study the role of transport as an intermediate good in the process of capital accumulation in urban contexts and to recognise the complex interaction between provision of infrastructure and transport services, economic development, land use and demographic change. Such processes are essential in the context of economic systems of production, consumption and distribution.

Likewise, by studying aspects such as equity and access at different scales, it is possible to understand the power relations that underpin the social construction of space – including public transport. This also enables us to examine the exclusionary experience of different social groups in public spaces created and shaped by modes and urban transport alternatives. Urban transport systems and their integration with land-use systems can enable or hinder access to opportunities, goods and services that help build human, financial and social capital. Such a feature makes transport a direct contributor to social mobility and inclusive economic development. Transport facilitates conditions for the production and reproduction of inequalities in relation to access to key opportunities for social, cultural and economic development by means of different modes of transport both motorised and non-motorised. This goes beyond the concerns of transport planning as it can also underpin modern concerns in urban planning such as health, inclusive mobility and environmental quality.

Accessibility studies allow us to examine the distribution of material benefits and burdens associated with urban mobility in the context of environmental sustainability. One of the main objectives of urban policy in terms of accessibility is equal access to activities in the city, which ensures a dignified life in a sustainable local and global environment. Therefore, it must be recognised that sustainable mobility also implies enabling citizens to exercise freedom of movement without social control or under restrictions imposed by the natural environment or the built environment that result from the provision for specific social groups. The illustrated accessibility analyses for cities such as Bogotá allow to inform the 'reciprocal recognition' (Levy, 2013) of those transport users excluded by virtue of their social position, in this case highlighted by the difference by income, and communities negatively affected by the operation of transport systems. As concepts and metrics are relatively simple to interpret by both specialists and non-specialists, the analysis of access and its implications for equity can inform parity political participation in the decision-making of all transport users, suppliers and those affected by it.

The accessibility study also provides arguments for the abandonment of mainstream and trend planning ('predict and provide') and contributes to the potential of building future development scenarios, making comparisons between social and economic areas and groups and the development of studies of social effects of transport in contexts with limited data availability. In this vein, accessibility analysis can inform prioritisation studies of urban transport policies and projects with specific objectives to close access gaps between social groups. By reinterpreting urban mobility in terms of potential and effective accessibility to fundamental opportunities for social and economic development, it is possible to rethink the objectives and impacts of urban transport beyond traditional measures of travel time savings and cost-benefit evaluations.

Finally, it is necessary to develop better ways of communicating the social consequences of transport to decision makers both within and outside the transport sector. This chapter builds on evidence of a paradigmatic case of urban transport development to illustrate how valuable evidence can draw attention to the need for addressing poverty and lack of accessibility as potential drivers of social exclusion. The production of socially oriented information for policy and planning such as accessibility indices, Gini indices and Palma ratios can also contribute to close the gaps between planning, designing and implementing new transport policies and the needs and preferences of urban dwellers affected by such policies. To reduce urban inequalities in contexts such as Bogotá and many other cities in Latin America, it is necessary to adopt a broader perspective of transport as a social policy. Accessibility can be the first step in setting such a perspective.

NOTE

1. Zonal planning units, 112 urban UPZ in Bogotá and 17 municipalities.

REFERENCES

Appleyard, B., Ferrell, C. E., Carroll, M. A., & Taecker, M. (2014). Toward livability ethics. *Transportation Research Record*, *2403*(1), 62–71. https://doi.org/10.3141/2403-08

Benevenuto, R., & Caulfield, B. (2019). Poverty and transport in the global south: An overview. *Transport Policy*, *79*, 115–124. https://doi.org/10.1016/j.tranpol.2019.04.018

Bocarejo, J. P., & Oviedo, D. R. (2012). Transport accessibility and social inequities: A tool for identification of mobility needs and evaluation of transport investments. *Journal of Transport Geography*, *24*, 142–154. https://doi.org/10.1016/j.jtrangeo.2011.12.004

Bocarejo, J. P., Escobar, D., Hernandez, D. O., & Galarza, D. (2016). Accessibility analysis of the integrated transit system of Bogotá. *International Journal of Sustainable Transportation*, *10*(4), 308–320. https://doi.org/10.1080/15568318.2014.926435

Cass, N., Shove, E., & Urry, J. (2005). Social exclusion, mobility and access. *Sociological Review*, *53*(3), 539–555. https://doi.org/10.1111/j.1467-954X.2005.00565.x

Cervero, R. (2001). Walk-and-ride: Factors influencing pedestrian access to transit. *Journal of Public Transportation*, *3*(4), 1–23. https://doi.org/10.5038/2375-0901.3.4.1

Cervero, R. (2002). Built environments and mode choice: Toward a normative framework. *Transportation Research Part D: Transport and Environment*, *7*(4), 265–284. https://doi.org/10.1016/S1361-9209(01)00024-4

Cheng, J., & Bertolini, L. (2013). Measuring urban job accessibility with distance decay, competition and diversity. *Journal of Transport Geography*, *30*, 100–109. https://doi.org/10.1016/j.jtrangeo.2013.03.005

Deka, D. (2004). Social and environmental justice issues in urban transportation. In S. Hanson & G. Giuliano (Eds.), *The geography of urban transportation* (pp. 332–355). New York, NY: The Guilford Press.

Dimitriou, H., & Gakenheimer, R. (2011). *Urban transport in the developing world: A handbook of policy and practice*. Cheltenham: Edward Elgar. Retrieved from https://books.google.co.uk/books?hl=en&lr=&id=09kM2SfGTwsC&oi=fnd&pg=PR1&dq=xavier+Godard,+2011+transportation+urban&ots=CwBhTBCQig&sig=u_xnvfhNO4-071q0i9tFIfi-5BQ

Fraser, N. (1998). Social justice in the age of identity politics: Redistribution, recognition, and participation. In L. Ray & A. Sayer (Eds.), *Culture and economy after the cultural turn* (pp. 25–52). London: SAGE Publications.

Geurs, K. T., & Ritsema van Eck, J. R. (2001). Accessibility measures: Review and applications. Evaluation of accessibility impacts of land-use transportation scenarios, and related social and economic impact. *RIVM Report*, *787*, 1–265. Retrieved from https://rivm.openrepository.com/rivm/handle/10029/9487

Geurs, K. T., & van Wee, B. (2004). Accessibility evaluation of land-use and transport strategies: Review and research directions. *Journal of Transport Geography*, *12*(2), 127–140. https://doi.org/10.1016/j.jtrangeo.2003.10.005

Gössling, S., Schröder, M., Späth, P., & Freytag, T. (2016). Urban space distribution and sustainable transport. *Transport Reviews*, *36*(5), 1–21. https://doi.org/10.1080/01441647.2016.1147101

Graham, S., & Marvin, S. (2001). *Splintering urbanism: Networked infrastructures, technological mobilities and the urban condition*. New York, NY: Psychology Press. Retrieved from https://books.google.co.uk/books?hl=en&lr=&id=JA9dNAR5evEC&oi=fnd&pg=PA1&dq=graham+and+marvin+splintering+urbanism&ots=f3L8baPogl&sig=Rx1mXN2wmhRsYNX-XU3sRset96w

Guzman, L. A., & Oviedo, D. (2018). Accessibility, affordability and equity: Assessing 'pro-poor' public transport subsidies in Bogotá. *Transport Policy*, *68*, 37–51. https://doi.org/10.1016/j.tranpol.2018.04.012

Guzman, L. A., Oviedo, D., & Bocarejo, J. P. J. P. (2016). City profile: The Bogotá metropolitan area that never was. *Cities*, *60*(Part A), 202–215. https://doi.org/http://dx.doi.org/10.1016/j.cities.2016.09.004

Guzman, L. A., Oviedo, D., & Rivera, C. (2017). Assessing equity in transport accessibility to work and study: The Bogotá region. *Journal of Transport Geography*, *58*, 236–246. https://doi.org/10.1016/j.jtrangeo.2016.12.016

Gwilliam, K. (2010). Transport: More than the sum of its parts. Retrieved from https://trid.trb.org/view.aspx?id=1163850

Harvey, D. (2009). *Social justice and the city. Interventions 086*. Athens, GA: University of Georgia Press.

Hidalgo, D., & Huizenga, C. (2013). Implementation of sustainable urban transport in Latin America. *Research in Transportation Economics*, *40*(1), 66–77. https://doi.org/10.1016/j.retrec.2012.06.034

Jones, P., & Lucas, K. (2012). The social consequences of transport decision-making: Clarifying concepts, synthesising knowledge and assessing implications. *Journal of Transport Geography, 21*, 4–16. https://doi.org/10.1016/j.jtrangeo.2012.01.012

Kawabata, M., & Shen, Q. (2007). Commuting inequality between cars and public transit: The case of the San Francisco Bay Area, 1990–2000. *Urban Studies, 44*(9), 1759–1780. https://doi.org/10.1080/00420980701426616

Levy, C. (2013). Travel choice reframed: "Deep distribution" and gender in urban transport. *Environment and Urbanization, 25*(1), 47–63. https://doi.org/10.1177/0956247813477810

Levy, C., & Dávila, J. D. (2017). Planning for mobility and socio-environmental justice: The case of Medellín, Colombia. In A. Allen, L. Griffin, & C. Johnson (Eds.), *Environmental justice and urban resilience in the Global South* (pp. 37–56). New York, NY: Palgrave Macmillan. https://doi.org/10.1057/978-1-137-47354-7_3

Litman, T. (2010). Evaluating public transit benefits and costs: Best Practices Guidebook. *World Transit Research*. Retrieved from https://www.worldtransitresearch.info/research/2707. Accessed on July 15, 2020.

Lovett, A., Haynes, R., Sünnenberg, G., & Gale, S. (2002). Car travel time and accessibility by bus to general practitioner services: A study using patient registers and GIS. *Social Science and Medicine, 55*(1), 97–111. https://doi.org/10.1016/S0277-9536(01)00212-X

Lowe, C., Stanley, J., & Stanley, J. (2018). A broader perspective on social outcomes in transport. *Research in Transportation Economics, 69*, 482–488. https://doi.org/10.1016/j.retrec.2018.03.006

Lucas, K. (2011). Making the connections between transport disadvantage and the social exclusion of low income populations in the Tshwane Region of South Africa. *Journal of Transport Geography, 19*(6), 1320–1334. https://doi.org/10.1016/j.jtrangeo.2011.02.007

Lucas, K., & Jones, P. (2012). Social impacts and equity issues in transport: An introduction. *Journal of Transport Geography, 21*, 1–3. https://doi.org/10.1016/j.jtrangeo.2012.01.032

Lyons, G. (2003). The introduction of social exclusion into the field of travel behaviour. *Transport Policy, 10*(4), 339–342. https://doi.org/10.1016/j.tranpol.2003.09.001

Manderscheid, K. (2009). Unequal mobilities. In T. Ohnmacht, H. Maksim, & M. M. Bergman (Eds.), *Mobilities and inequality* (pp. 27–50). Surrey: Ashgate. Retrieved from https://books.google.co.uk/books?hl=en&lr=&id=fikHDAAAQBAJ&oi=fnd&pg=PA27&dq=manderscheid+2009+mobilities&ots=TWSr1pbJRr&sig=NzmE3tGbmq3GvUF8uQwkW9TpG-c

Martens, K. (2018). Ageing, impairments and travel: Priority setting for an inclusive transport system. *Transport Policy, 63*, 122–130. https://doi.org/10.1016/j.tranpol.2017.12.001

Martens, K., Golub, A., & Robinson, G. (2012). A justice-theoretic approach to the distribution of transportation benefits: Implications for transportation planning practice in the United States. *Transportation Research Part A – Policy and Practice, 46*(4), 684–695. https://doi.org/10.1016/j.tra.2012.01.004

Munoz-Raskin, R. (2010). Walking accessibility to bus rapid transit: Does it affect property values? The case of Bogotá, Colombia. *Transport Policy, 17*(2), 72–84. https://doi.org/10.1016/j.tranpol.2009.11.002

Oviedo, D., & Dávila, J. D. (2016). Transport, urban development and the peripheral poor in Colombia. *Journal of Transport Geography, 51*, 180–192.

Oviedo, D., & Titheridge, H. (2016). Mobilities of the periphery: Informality, access and social exclusion in the urban fringe in Colombia. *Journal of Transport Geography, 55*, 152–164. https://doi.org/10.1016/j.jtrangeo.2015.12.004

Roberts, M., Blankespoor, B., Deuskar, C., & Stewart, B. (2017). *Urbanization and development: is Latin America and the Caribbean different from the rest of the world?* Policy Research working paper. Washington, D.C.: World Bank Group.

Rodriguez, D., & Targa, F. (2004). Value of accessibility to Bogotá's bus rapid transit system. *Transport Reviews, 24*(5), 587–610. https://doi.org/10.1080/0144164042000195081

Secretaría Distrital de Movilidad (SDM). (2011). Encuesta de Movilidad 2011, Informe de indicadores: encuesta de movilidad de Bogotá. Bogotá, Colombia.

Sen, A. (1993). Capability and well-being. In M. Nussbaum & A. Sen (Eds.), *The quality of life* (p. 30). Oxford: Clarendon Press.

Suzuki, H., Cervero, R., & Iuchi, K. (2013). *Transforming cities with transit: Transit and land-use integration for sustainable urban development*. Washington, DC: World Bank Publications. https://doi.org/10.1596/978-0-8213-9745-9

Vale, D. S., Saraiva, M., & Pereira, M. (2016). Active accessibility. *Journal of Transport and Land Use*, 9(1), 209–235. Retrieved from http://www.jstor.org/stable/26203215

Van Vugt, M., Meertens, R. M., & Van Lange, P. A. M. (1995). Car versus public transportation? The role of social value orientations in a real-life social dilemma. *Journal of Applied Social Psychology*, 25(3), 258–278. https://doi.org/10.1111/j.1559-1816.1995.tb01594.x

van Wee, B. (2012). How suitable is CBA for the ex-ante evaluation of transport projects and policies? A discussion from the perspective of ethics, Transport Policy. *Pergamon*, 19(1), 1–7. doi: 10.1016/j.tranpol.2011.07.001

van Wee, B., & Geurs, K. (2011). Discussing equity and social exclusion in accessibility evaluations. *European Journal of Transport and Infrastructure Research*, 11(4), 350–367. https://doi.org/10.18757/ejtir.2011.11.4.2940

Vasconcellos, E. (2014). *Urban transport environment and equity: The case for developing countries*. New York, NY: Routledge. Retrieved from https://books.google.co.uk/books?hl=en&lr=&id=O2B9AwAAQBAJ&oi=fnd&pg=PP1&dq=Urban+Transport,+Environment+and+Equity:+the+case+for+developing+countries+by+Eduardo+A+Vasconcellos&ots=qMUbomAfS-&sig=t8uSScMxwNA66avWjoLpcZWCtgw

Wagner, F., & Caves, R. W. (2012). *Community livability: Issues and approaches to sustaining the well-being of people and communities*. New York, NY: Routledge.

World Bank, & International Monetary Fund. (2016). *Global monitoring report 2015/2016: Development goals in an era of demographic change*. Washington, DC: World Bank.

CHAPTER 2

MOBILITY AND GENDER EQUITY IN LATIN AMERICA: DIFFERENT MOBILE BURDENS AND CONTRIBUTIONS IN MONTEVIDEO (URUGUAY)

Diego Hernández and Daniela de los Santos

ABSTRACT

This chapter describes gender differences in Montevideo through the study of daily mobility. Generally, mobility studies do not account for gender differences more than in a superficial way, distinguishing basic travel patterns by sex. However, different patterns and mobility behaviours can obscure situations of deeply entrenched gender inequality that have direct consequences on the opportunities that men and women are able to reach. To disentangle these inequalities, this work addresses some mainstream mobility indicators classified by gender but also some specific indicators, with special attention to care mobility as a factor that can restrain women's ability to move. Moreover, a tour-based analysis is performed to shed light on gendered schedules and mobility patterns. Results show that women's mode share comprises a larger proportion of transit trips, they travel shorter distances – investing more time – and they contribute in a greater proportion than men to care mobility, especially among the lower quintiles of income. While men's commuting patterns have a defined 'home-based work' profile, women have a higher level of heterogeneity in their daily itineraries. Access to private motorised means of transport is a key variable in explaining the configuration of mobility patterns, and there is a persistent gender gap in this matter. The chapter concludes that, as several authors have reported, gender is a marker in terms of mobility. It sets specific conditions for urban life in general and mobility in particular that, in turn, may be the cause of further inequality.

Keywords: Care mobility; gender; travel behaviour; daily mobility; everyday life; Montevideo; Uruguay

1. INTRODUCTION

Latin America has a long tradition on gender studies, focussing, for instance, on socially constructed roles, women's participation in the labour market, occupational segregation, family dynamics and sexual division of labour (see, for instance, Amarante & Rossel, 2018; Campaña, Giménez-Nadal, & Molina, 2018; Esquivel, Budlender, Folbre, & Hirway, 2008). However, even when it is embedded in the general problem, discussion of gendered mobilities is novel. Indeed, the bulk of literature on this topic comes from industrialised countries, and there is no robust regional accumulation on this matter.

The objective of this chapter is to describe gender differences in Montevideo through the study of daily mobility. Generally, mobility studies do not account for gender differences more than in a superficial way, distinguishing basic travel patterns by sex. However, different patterns and mobility behaviours can obscure situations of deeply entrenched gender inequality that have direct consequences on the opportunities that men and women are able to reach. The chapter builds on the notion that different mobility patterns may shed light to elucidate urban inequalities between men and women (Alcaino, Domarchi, & López Carrasco 2009; Hjorthol, 2008; Jiron, 2017; Roberts, 2013; Sanchez de Madariaga, 2013).

Socially constructed gender roles that bind women to a reproductive role and men to the productive world affect urban spaces, roles and dynamics of flow and fixity in dissimilar ways (Buckingham, 2013). As a result, patterns of activities and schedules are different between men and women. There are marked differences in travel purposes and distances, mode share and other aspects of travel behaviour. In this sense, care mobility, that is, mobility with a purpose related to familial maintenance activities, is a typically feminised type of mobility and, eventually, restricts women's possibilities of movement. Thus, to understand urban gender-based potential inequality, it is necessary to assess this type of mobility. It also calls attention to the analysis of itineraries and not only separate trips, as care tasks demand strong reconciliation efforts.

The chapter aims to address this research question: how the relation between gender and mobility works in the case of Montevideo in terms of social and urban equity?

This chapter constitutes a contribution to daily mobility and everyday life studies from a 'transport and society' perspective. In the same vein, it also contributes to gender studies since mobility can be considered as a field in which gender inequality unfolds. Thus, its relevance is ascribed in the 2030 Agenda for Sustainable Development, in the New Urban Agenda, and more especially in the Gender Agenda, considering both global (Sustainable Development Goals,[1] Convention on the Elimination of All Forms of Discrimination Against Women) and regional frameworks (e.g. Montevideo Strategy for Implementation of the Regional Gender Agenda).

This chapter is structured as follows. The next section presents a conceptual discussion of gender and mobility. Afterwards, the chapter describes basic features of Montevideo, technical specifications of the most important data source, a mobility survey of the Montevideo Metropolitan Region (MMR) and the methodology applied. Empirical findings are deployed in the next section, and the chapter closes with concluding remarks.

2. CONCEPTUAL FRAMEWORK

The discussion on gendered mobilities is embedded in a broader one on gender inequality. One of the main topics of this discussion pertains to socially constructed gender roles that bind women to reproductive roles and men to the productive world. Given this sexual division of labour, women have traditionally been ascribed to reproductive tasks related to household subsistence. These tasks have only recently been considered as work that requires abilities, time and dedication regardless of the fact that they occur in the domestic sphere (Sanchez de Madariaga, 2013). Meanwhile, men are supposed to play the role of the household breadwinner related to income-earning activities. As care or reproductive work is considered domestic, to some extent families have been regarded as the only responsible institution to provide care, without the active participation of the state and the market.

Female labour participation rates have grown significantly over the past few decades. However, the sexual division of paid and domestic labour is not changing at the same pace and men's participation in domestic care work remains far from that of women's. These elements, in addition to the ageing of the population, comprise what it is known as the 'care crisis' (ECLAC, 2010). There is an increase in the number of dependent people due to demographic factors and, simultaneously, a lack of redistribution of care responsibilities between genders inside the household as women enter the labour force, as well as very few reconciliation measures promoted by the states and markets. In other words, the previous model of distribution of domestic and care responsibilities has been destabilised, but its redistribution and reorganisation are still in dispute (Pérez Orozco, 2009). Regarding paid work, in the context of a highly segmented labour market, women face higher rates of informality, lower wages, occupational segregation (ECLAC, 2016) and greater elasticity in their labour (Espino, Isabella, Leites, & Machado, 2017).

From an empirical perspective, the phenomenon of sexual division of labour has been widely documented through the application of time-use surveys (Amarante & Rossel, 2018; Campaña et al., 2018; Esquivel et al., 2008). This tool tends to focus on static time division without considering the depth of the organisation and order of the activities as well as their spatial localisation. However, socially constructed gender roles affect how people relate to urban spaces and structures and mould the dynamics of space-time flow and fixity[2] in dissimilar ways (Buckingham, 2013; Cresswell & Uteng, 2008; Kwan, 1999; Naess, 2008; Schwanen, Kwan, & Ren, 2008). As a result, activity patterns and schedules differ between men and women who must struggle to reconcile quotidian activities that may include work, dependent care and even leisure (Buckingham, 2013).

Time geography has contributed a great deal of the literature to elucidate the joint effect of space and time regarding everyday life. From this perspective, it is possible to identify a set of space-time constraints (Hägerstrand, 1970). These constraints result in different levels of accessibility to services and other types of urban opportunities (Ellegård & Svedin, 2012; Ellegård, 1999; Hernandez & Rossel, 2015; Kwan, 1999; McQuoid & Dijst, 2012; Neutens, 2012, 2015; Neutens, Delafontaine, Scott, & De Maeyer, 2012; Neutens, Schwanen, & Witlox, 2011; Schwanen et al., 2008).

Thus, there is interplay relationship between the city, household activities and needs that can increase or reduce obstacles in everyday life. This discussion is far from gender neutral. On the contrary, women carry the burden of most unpaid work even as they participate in income-earning activities. City planning, however, tends to prioritise areas related to more valued activities, that is, the areas in which 'productive' activities take place. The same is true for transport and infrastructure planning, leaving infrastructure and resources for other types of activities as secondary (Buckingham, 2013; Naess, 2008; see Sanchez de Madariaga, 2013).

In this vein, Levy (2013) argues that even though more than two decades have expired since researchers began to highlight the importance of gender relations in urban transport, there is still a gap in the transport planning literature when it comes to exploring and understanding the 'deep distributional' dimensions of 'travel choice'. The author emphasises the importance of the gender and right to the city (see Lefebvre, 1968) perspective in order to gain a critical understanding of transport needs and barriers, as well as to improve policy-planning capacities for transport planners.

Regarding mobility-specific discussion, the literature has extensively shown different activity and mobility patterns for men and women in terms of the number and distance of trips, purposes, chain trips and transport modes, among other aspects (Alcaino, Domarchi, & López Carrasco, 2010; Bernard, Seguin, Bussiere, & Polacchini, 1996; Emond, Tang, & Handy, 2009; Herbel et al., 2010; Hernández, 2012; McQuaid & Chen, 2012; Naess, 2008; Peralta Quiros, Mehndiratta, & Ochoa, 2014; Sanchez de Madariaga, 2013; Scheiner & Holz-Rau, 2012). Since mobility also plays a role in the opportunities and capacity to fulfil some needs and desires, these differential patterns could also reinforce original inequalities or even gendered social roles. Thus, gender and mobility present a bidirectional relationship. On the one hand, mobility constrains female daily life because of particular movement patterns. On the other hand, gender roles represent actual barriers to women's mobility in the form of space-time constraints or imposed immobility for care purposes. Murray (2008) posits an example of motherhood practices that are increasingly mobile and demand 'management' efforts given the multiplicity of destinations, activities, schedules, critical time points and other factors. In addition, social expectations of "good" mothering could result in unsustainable mobility for mothers. According to Murray (2008), 'Mobility can therefore represent significant constraints on mothers' lives, just as gender roles can represent barriers to mobility' (p. 56). Fig. 2.1 synthesises the conceptual framework of the chapter.

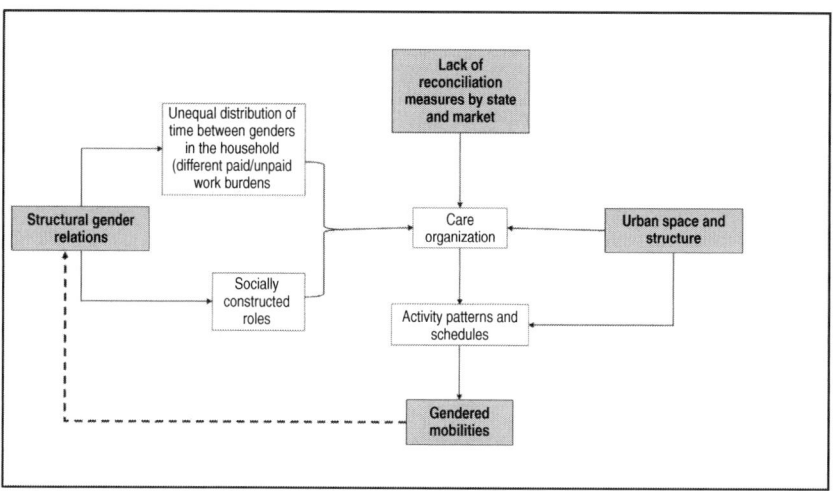

Fig. 2.1. Conceptual Framework. *Source*: Elaborated by the Authors.

3. CASE STUDY

Montevideo has 1.3 million inhabitants living in approximately 450,000 households. The entire metropolitan area encompasses 1.8 million inhabitants. It is the capital of Uruguay and the smallest jurisdiction, nevertheless concentrating approximately 40% of the entire country's population as well as the political, economic and strategic management centres. Since the 1990s, Montevideo's demographic growth has been moderate, with a slight decrease in the first decade of the 2000s as a result of a process of migration towards suburban centres within the metropolitan region by middle-income population.

Regarding basic mobility data, in the MMR approximately one in five individuals over four years old is immobile (no trip records during the mobility survey reference day). On average, 4.2 million trips take place in the MMR on a workday, resulting in 2.44 trips per person. Each trip has an average duration of 24.3 minutes, and the most important purpose is work (31% after excluding home as a destination). Two-thirds of the trips are motorised, and the rest are mostly short walks (up to 10 blocks).

4. DATA AND METHODS

The data source for this study is the 2016 Household Mobility Survey applied in the MMR. This face-to-face survey gathered information from 2,230 households, from which 5,946 individuals and 12,546 trips were surveyed – this is representative for the MMR. The metropolitan region was split into eight sociogeographic strata with an expected sample size of 150 cases for each. Variable estimation of the basic mobility indicators is representative at the sample stratum level. The data were collected during September and October 2016 by specially trained interviewers directed by a field general coordinator and regional supervisors (see Mauttone & Hernandez, 2017).

In terms of methodology, to understand the problem of gendered mobilities, it is insufficient to simply consider different travel patterns from a purely mainstream perspective. To consider a gender perspective, this chapter adopts two specific mobility issues: care mobility and individual itineraries based on a tour-based analysis.

The first issue consists of the assessment of indicators that describe activities related to the subsistence of the household and the care of its members. In the literature, this set of activities is identified as mobility of care (Sanchez de Madariaga, 2013) or dual consumption (Alcaino et al., 2009, 2010) as it satisfies the needs not only of the person who moves, but includes another member(s) of the household. It includes those activities traditionally classifiable as unpaid work but that require leaving the home to accomplish, for example, shopping or taking a child to school. Several studies refer to this type of mobility (Alcaino et al., 2009; Hernández, 2012; Sanchez de Madariaga, 2013; Zucchini, 2015). In many cases, not considering them as a single type of activity results in losing visibility in the observed patterns of mobility, so grouping them as a purpose in itself is part of a necessary conceptual and operational mechanism to understand gender cleavage (Sanchez de Madariaga, 2013). Specifically, we define 'care mobility' as the one whose purpose relates to shopping/running errands for the household, picking up/dropping off kids from school, picking up/dropping off or accompanying somebody.

The second specific concept to be considered in this chapter transcends individual trips and refers to the set of movements as a person's single attribute. While considering trips as a unit is central, understanding how they combine for a person is equally relevant. Two people may make two identical trips between two points in the city, but if one of them does it in the context of other previous or subsequent trips, their mobility conditions are different, in the same way as if this is done in the morning or afternoon hours during peak or off-peak times. This position is intimately linked to the notion of reconciliation between activities. In effect, households do not solve and plan their activities in isolation; they do so in relation to a shared agenda. Therefore, it is very likely that this approach will reveal inequalities between genders that would be invisible from a trip-based perspective.

To construct people's itineraries, the duration and distance[3] relative to each trip are taken into account, as well as the departure and arrival time from and to each activity. The trip purposes are recoded as activities. The duration of each activity is computed from the arrival and departure times. It must be considered that we construct stylised itineraries based on mean data for all variables (duration, distance, arrival and departure time), which can lead to errors in certain cases. Each itinerary defines a set of persons, for instance, the one that carried out two trips during the day. For each one, we indicate the percentage of the population from the mobility survey that this subset represents.

5. RESULTS

To present the research findings, the empirical evidence is organised according to three main approaches posed in the conceptual discussion. The first pertains to basic mainstream mobility indicators discriminated by sex. The second presents data on specific care mobility indicators; specifically, female and male contributions to this type of mobility are discussed. Finally, a tour-based data analysis is performed.

5.1 Gendered Mobility Patterns

One of the first dimensions to analyse pertains to people's immobility, that is, when a person declares that she did not take any trips in the reference period of a mobility survey. In surveys such as the MMR mobility survey, all types of trips were recorded without a minimum threshold, so if a person took a trip that required her to walk three blocks one way and three blocks back, he was not considered immobile. Nevertheless, there is a specific group of people that travel only within a nearby territory. In operative terms, these locally anchored patterns consist of trips taken entirely by walking and that do not exceed 10 blocks.

To date, the literature on immobility has not reached a unique interpretation for the 'immobile' person. However, the absence of displacements or a locally anchored pattern is in itself a relevant fact. In Montevideo, women have higher rates of immobility than men: 22% of women did not leave the house the day before the survey, versus 18% of men. In addition, women also surpass men in locally anchored trips (19% vs 15%). When considering the sum of these categories, it is possible to observe that 4 in 10 women (41%) are immobile or do not travel beyond their neighbourhood, while among men this proportion decreases to 3 in 10 (33%).[4]

To analyse these figures using socioeconomic configurations, both categories are considered together (Fig. 2.2). Women have higher levels of immobility/local

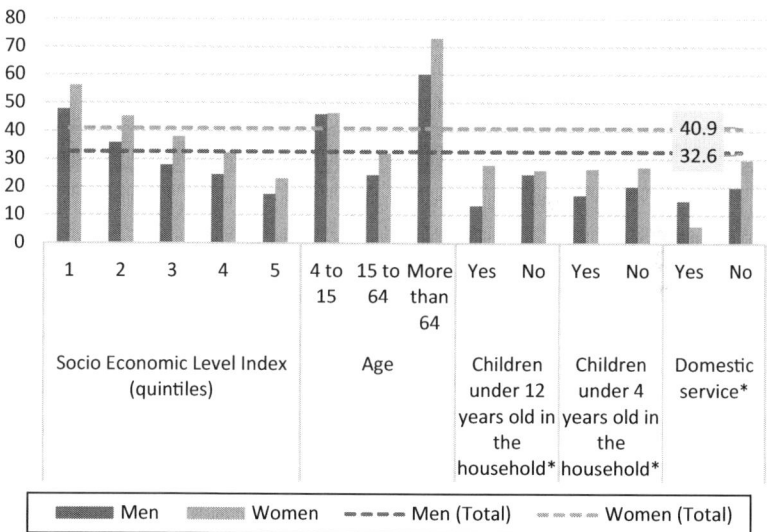

Fig. 2.2. Immobility (Including Constrained Mobility) by Gender and Other Sociodemographic Indicators (Percentages). *Source*: Elaborated by the Authors Based on MMR Mobility Survey Data.
*Population between the Ages of 25 and 49 Years Old.

trips regardless of socioeconomic status[5] and age (leaving aside children younger than 15 years old). Moreover, the gender gap in mobility for adults (between the ages of 25 and 49) widens when children under 12 years old are present in the household. Women in households that hire domestic help are even more mobile than men. One plausible explanation may relate to dual-earner households in which women have to simultaneously afford time and travel burdens for both productive and reproductive activities.

Regarding basic travel behaviour, men and women have similar trip rates (2.4 for men vs 2.3 for women). On average, Montevidean women travel shorter distances than men, but their trips are more time consuming (Fig. 2.3).

Among the respondents who took at least one trip during the day, regardless of distance or duration, the women's mode share had a greater proportion of transit trips and short walking trips. Meanwhile, the men travelled mostly by private motorised vehicles (car or motorcycle) (Fig. 2.4). These patterns are closely related to actual access to different means of transport. Generally, it is considered that a person has access to a car if there is one available in the household. However, the existence of this resource does not guarantee that it is equally distributed between the household members.

Fig. 2.5 shows that women's access to private mobility resources is much lower than men's. For instance, as much as 67% of women over 18 years old do not have a driver's license. This figure drops to 31% for men. Furthermore, women living in households with at least one car or motorcycle have less access to it than their male counterparts do: 1 in 5 claims never to have access to the vehicle, versus less than 1 in 10 men. Conversely, while 59% of men claim to always have access to a vehicle, only 32% of women say they do. Moreover, 90% of men who travelled using a private motorised vehicle the day of the survey did it as a driver, but only 62% of women said the same.

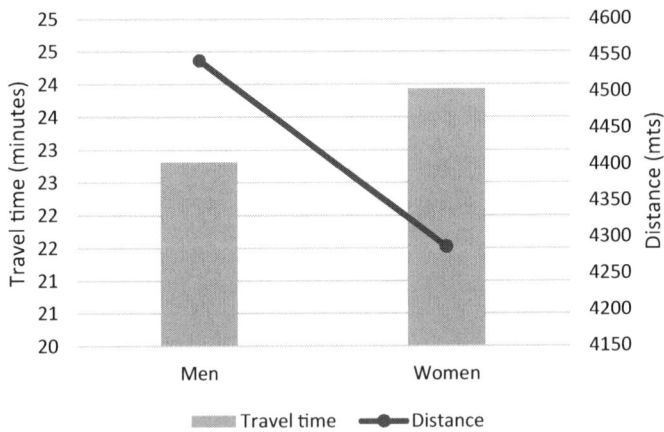

Fig. 2.3. Average Travel Time and Distance by Gender. *Source*: Elaborated by the Authors Based on MMR Mobility Survey Data.

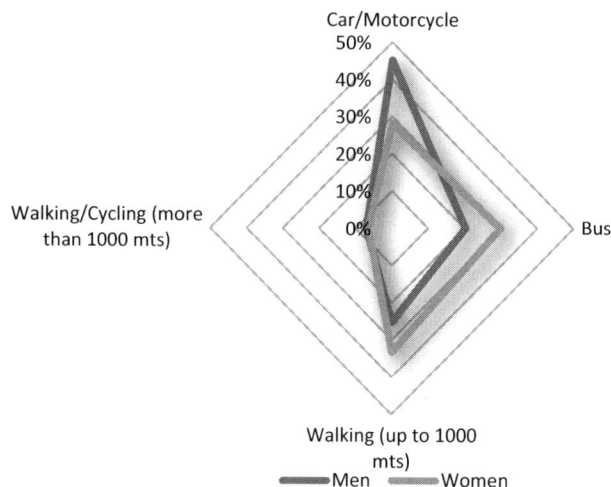

Fig. 2.4. Travel Mode by Gender (Percentages). *Source*: Elaborated by the Authors Based on MMR Mobility Survey Data.

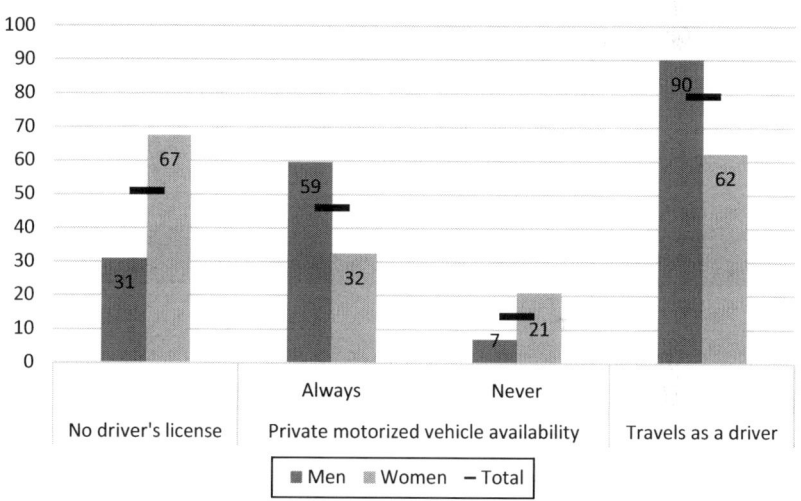

Fig. 2.5. Access to Mobility Resources by Gender (Percentages).
Source: Elaborated by the Authors Based on MMR Mobility Survey Data.
Note: All three indicators are calculated for populations over 18 years old. Private motorised vehicle availability is calculated for populations over 18 years old who live in households with at least one car or motorcycle. In the survey, the question of vehicle availability allows for intermediate answers (rarely, regularly and frequently) but only extreme values are displayed. In the case of 'Travels as a driver', it corresponds to trips made by people over 18 years old via private transport modes.

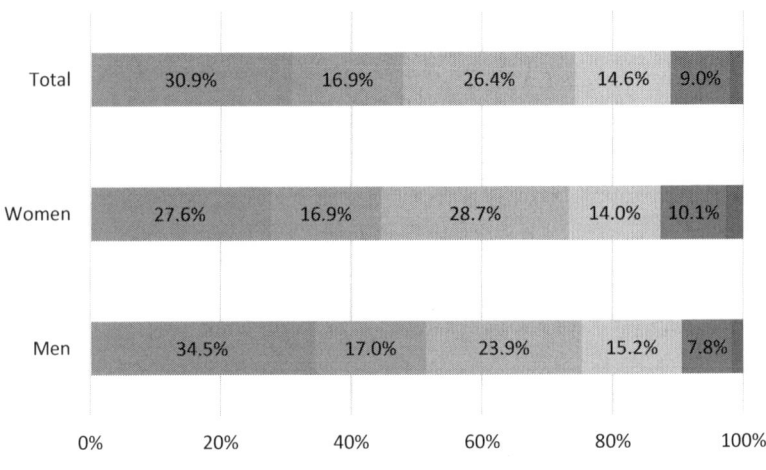

Fig. 2.6. Purpose of the Trip (Excluding Trips to Home) by Gender (Percentages). *Source*: Elaborated by the Authors Based on MMR Mobility Survey Data.

When analysing the purpose of the trips (Fig. 2.6), men seem to have a greater proportion destined to work (35% vs 28% in the case of women), whereas women allocate a larger share of their trips to domestic or care-oriented activities (29% vs 24% in the case of men).[6] Although these differences are not overwhelming, they constitute a mobility pattern that, when complemented with the information presented in the following sections, reinforces the concept of gendered mobility.

5.2 Care Mobility

As previously noted, we define care mobility as a set of trips related to activities that are typically considered unpaid work or that belong to the reproductive sphere. At the operational level, the trips were considered care oriented when they had one of the following purposes: 'shopping for home', 'drop/pick up children', 'drop/pick up somebody' and 'accompany somebody'.

To define this category, contribution to care mobility can be measured in terms of the number of trips and a percentage of the total amount of minutes allocated to care-oriented trips. Considering the first criterion, women account for 6 in 10 of all trips that are care oriented. In fact, as shown in Fig. 2.7, 29% of all care-oriented trips are performed by women walking short distances (10 blocks or less), which means a relevant portion of care mobility is female and locally anchored. Regarding care-related trips performed in private motorised vehicles, men account for the highest share (23%), although women also have a high participation rate (18%). Except for private motorised mobility, women contribute to a higher extent than men to care mobility in all other transport modes.

Fig. 2.8 compares female contributions to care-oriented trips and work-oriented trips. First, women have a greater weight in care-oriented mobility than

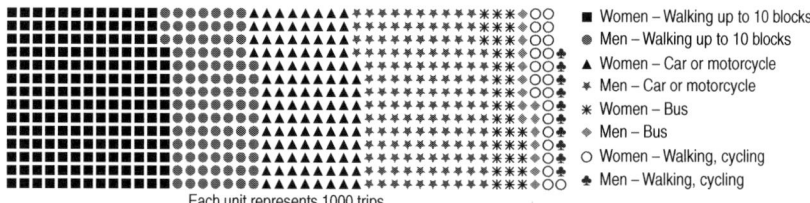

Fig. 2.7. Trips Related to Domestic/Care Activities, by Mode and Gender (Population Older Than 18 Years). *Source*: Elaborated by the Authors Based on MMR Mobility Survey Data.

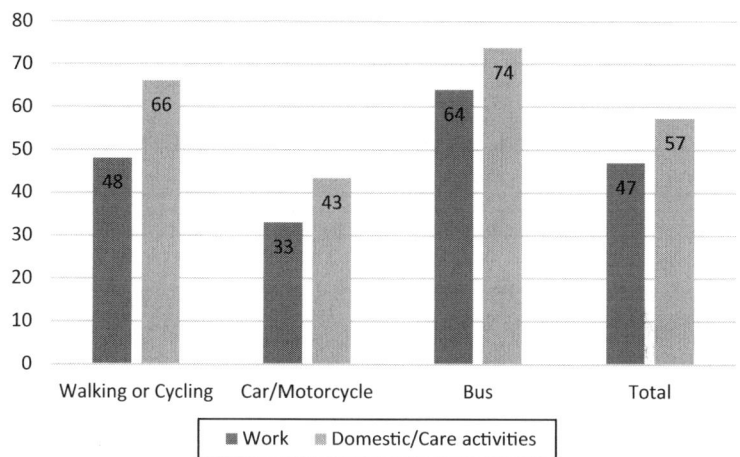

Fig. 2.8. Female Contributions to Care and Work-oriented Trips by Transport Mode; Population Older Than 18 Years (Percentages). *Source*: Elaborated by the Authors Based on MMR Mobility Survey Data.

in work-oriented mobility regardless of the transport mode. Second, as previously noted, female contribution to care mobility rises when travelling by bus and active modes: 7 of 10 of these types of trips are taken by females.

One could argue that even when it is true that women contribute the largest portion of care trips, a relevant share consists of short distances and durations. For this reason, it is useful to analyse the contribution in terms of the time devoted to care mobility. Women account for 59% of the minutes that are globally dedicated to care-oriented trips. It is interesting to note that the time allocated to care mobility is not only unequally distributed by gender but also by socioeconomic level. Poorer women (the first quintile) contribute 77% of the time dedicated to care-oriented trips compared to men in the same socioeconomic situation (Fig. 2.9). Meanwhile, men and women with higher incomes distribute this time more equally.[7] Most likely, better access to motorised vehicles in the higher quintiles improves male participation in this type of mobility; in the lowest quintiles, where most care mobility is done by walking short distances, women are the protagonists.

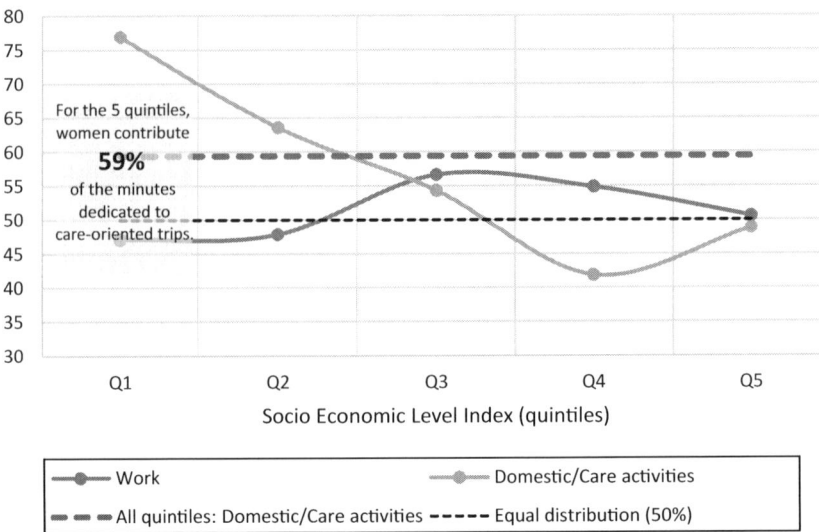

Fig. 2.9. Female Contribution to the Amount of Minutes Allocated to Care-oriented Trips; Population Older Than 18 Years (Percentages).
Source: Elaborated by the Authors Based on MMR Mobility Survey Data.

5.3 Activity-Based Approach: Men and Women's Differential Itineraries

The previous sections presented a trip-based analysis of gendered mobility patterns including both mainstream and gender-specific indicators. This section adopts an activity-based approach that focusses on each person's daily itinerary in terms of trips and activities. In contrast to trip-based analysis, this approach enables the synthesis of mobility-based personal attributes. As stated in the conceptual section, this perspective reveals several aspects of time-space constraints such as schedules, spatial patterns and reconciliation difficulties that cannot be grasped through the analysis of isolated trips.

It seems that a simple two-way pattern (home–activity–home) is the most common kind of mobility for both men and women: 55% of men and 54% of women follow this type of pattern among the population that moved during the day. Furthermore, approximately 20% of the mobile respondents (21% of men and 20% of women) follow an itinerary that involves four trips, and approximately 10% (8% of men and 12% of women) follow an itinerary that involves three trips. Only approximately 13% of people (14% of men and 12% of women) take more than four trips per day, and a residual percentage take only one trip.

The charts to follow represent some of Montevideo's most typical itineraries for active persons aged 18–64. Information is aggregated by the number of trips carried out by the person. In particular, this chapter considers three groups that comprise almost 9 of 10 persons in the survey: two, three and four trips corresponding to one, two and three out-of-home activities held during the day. Every tour comprises persons who started and finished their day at home. Note that in each figure's title it is possible to find the percentage of men and women that carry out each itinerary.

Figs. 2.10 and 2.11 represent two-trip itineraries: home-based work trips (the most frequent, 26% of female intineraries and 32% of male itineraries) and home-based care trips. Fig. 2.10 shows that men who make two trips per day and whose activity is going to work, tend to leave the house earlier than women; they remain longer at work and return slightly earlier. This is strongly associated with the weight that 'home-based work' profiles have in this simple mobility pattern. On average, men leave their home at approximately 8 a.m., remain at work for approximately 9 hours and return home at approximately 6 p.m. They travel on average 8.5 km in 36–39 minutes. In contrast, the average woman's departure time is 8.45 a.m.; they remain at work for approximately 8 hours and return at approximately 6 p.m. They travel on average 7.5 km in 41–45 minutes. These are typical mobility patterns for full-time workers but are structured by differential access by gender to mobility resources.

Fig. 2.11 shows a two-trip itinerary in which the main activity relates to care. It represents 8% of female itineraries and 4% of male itineraries. In this case, the duration of the activity is much shorter but still follows a gendered pattern: women spend approximately an hour in the activity, while men spend only 36 minutes. Moreover, women travel longer distances (2.4 km) and for twice as many minutes (19–20 minutes) than men (1.4 km in 11 minutes). Approximately 19% of women travel to their care activities by bus versus less than 5% of men. Private motorised

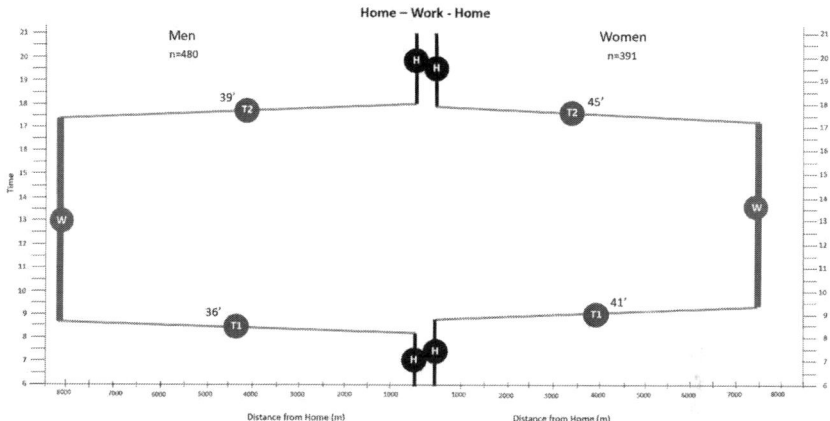

Fig. 2.10. Itinerary: Home–Work–Home; Population between the Ages of 18 and 64 (32% of Men and 26% of Women). *Source*: Elaborated by the Authors Based on MMR Mobility Survey Data.

	Starting Point: Home		Men	Women
Trip 1	Duration (')/distance from home (m)		36/8493	41/7448
	Mode	Car/motorcycle	48.2%	24.4%
		Bus	36.1%	57.7%
		Walking/cycling	13.5%	16.2%
Work	Duration (hours)		8.7	7.8
Trip 2	Duration (')/distance from home (m)		39/0	45/0
	Mode	Car/motorcycle	48.8%	23.3%
		Bus	33.5%	57.7%
		Walking/cycling	15.2%	18.2%

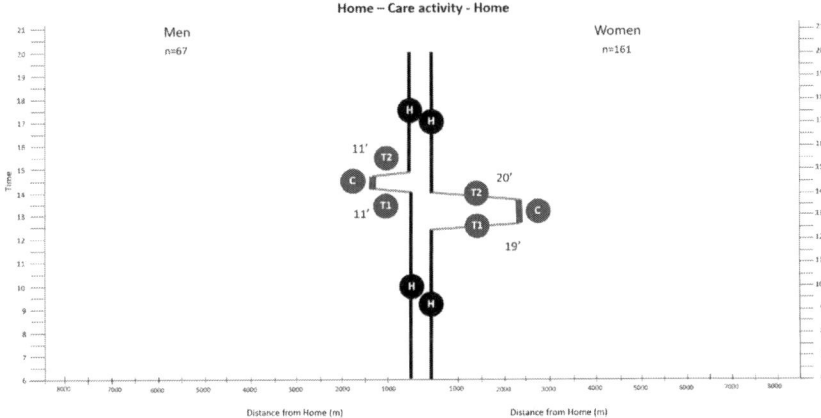

Fig. 2.11. Itinerary: Home–Care Activity–Home; Population between the Ages of 18 and 64 (4% of Men and 8% of Women). *Source*: Elaborated by the Authors Based on MMR Mobility Survey Data.

	Starting Point: Home		Men	Women
Trip 1	Duration (')/distance from home (m)		11/1490	19/2405
	Mode	Car/motorcycle	18.6%	15.9%
		Bus	4.6%	18.6%
		Walking/cycling	76.8%	63.8%
Care activity	Duration (hours)		0.6	1.0
Trip 2	Duration (')/distance from home (m)		11/0	20/0
	Mode	Car/motorcycle	18.6%	16.1%
		Bus	4.6%	18.4%
		Walking/cycling	76.8%	63.8%

mobility has a lower relevance in this particular itinerary, and active modes increase the importance. It must be noted that the average arrival and departure time that frames the activity in the early afternoon is actually strongly influenced by a distribution concentrated in three time points during the day: early morning trips, noon trips and late afternoon trips. In fact, the time frame that appears in the chart is, in reality, one of the least common to harbour two-way care mobility but constitutes the arithmetic mean of the trimodal distribution previously mentioned.

Figs. 2.12 and 2.13 describe somewhat more complex itineraries consisting of three trips and two activities. The first is a generic itinerary containing some relevant information. Some gendered patterns are again present: women's average travel time is higher, they leave the house a little later than men and return at the end of the day at approximately the same time, and the duration of at least one of the two activities is significantly shorter. In this particular case, however, there are no relevant differences in the distances travelled. Interestingly, in this more complex itinerary, private motorised vehicles play a predominant role and increase by 20 percentage points for both men and women (reaching approximately 60% and 40%, respectively) compared to a basic two-trip itinerary.

Regarding purpose, approximately 6 in 10 people who make three trips a day start by commuting to work. In parallel, 18% of women and 16% of men start

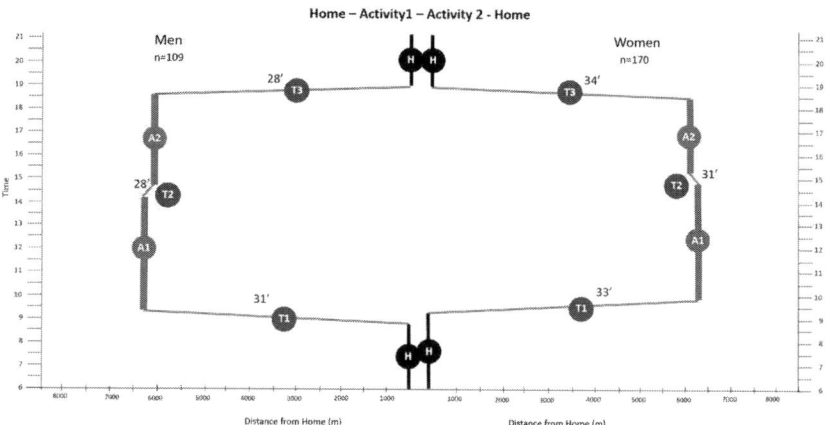

Fig. 2.12. Itinerary: Home–Activity 1–Activity 2–Home; Population between the Ages of 18 and 64 (9% of Men and 13% of Women). *Source*: Elaborated by the Authors Based on MMR Mobility Survey Data.

	Starting Point: Home		Men	Women
Trip 1	Duration (')/distance from home (m)		30.6/6246	32.9/6336
	Mode	Car/motorcycle	62.9%	40.6%
		Bus	22.1%	43.1%
		Walking/cycling	13.5%	15.7%
Activity 1	Activity	Work	59.8%	62.6%
		Study	8.4%	5.6%
		Care	18.4%	16.5%
		Leisure	1.7%	5.5%
		Other	10.9%	9.9%
	Duration (hours)		4.9	5.0
Trip 2	Duration (')/distance from home (m)		27.5/6216	30.5/6141
	Mode	Car/motorcycle	57.3%	37.3%
		Bus	24.2%	45.4%
		Walking/cycling	16.9%	16.7%
Activity 2	Activity	Work	38.1%	31.9%
		Study	10.2%	14.5%
		Care	16.1%	24.2%
		Leisure	24.7%	16.6%
		Other	11.0%	12.9%
	Duration (hours)		4.0	3.3
Trip 3	Duration (')/distance from home (m)		28/0	34/0
	Mode	Car/motorcycle	61.2%	39.4%
		Bus	22.8%	41.3%
		Walking/cycling	12.8%	16.9%

by performing care-related activities. On average, they remain approximately 5 hours in the first activity, and between 2 p.m. and 3 p.m. travel for half an hour (28 minutes for men and 31 minutes for women) to the second activity, which is located a similar distance from the household as the first one. In many cases, the second activity is work-related (38% for men and 32% for women), but it can also be related to care (more strongly among women), leisure (more strongly among men) or study (more strongly among women) (see the attached table).

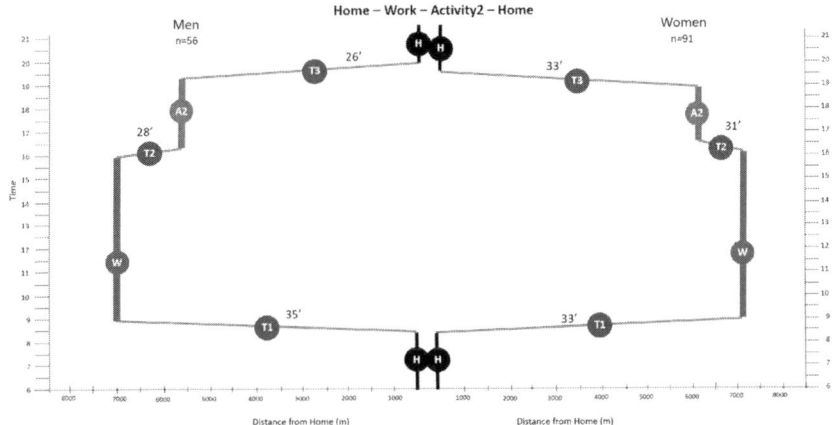

Fig. 2.13. Itinerary: Home–Work–Activity–Home; Population between the Ages of 18 and 64 (5% of Men and 8% of Women). *Source*: Elaborated by the Authors Based on MMR Mobility Survey Data.

	Starting Point: Home		Men	Women
Trip 1	Duration (')/distance from home (m)		35/7008	37/7352
	Mode	Car/motorcycle	57.7%	40.9%
		Bus	28.2%	49.7%
		Walking/cycling	11.5%	8.4%
Work	Duration (hours)		6.9	7.2
Trip 2	Duration (')/distance from home (m)		28/5595	31/6145
	Mode	Car/motorcycle	52.0%	39.3%
		Bus	30.5%	48.6%
		Walking/cycling	17.5%	11.1%
Activity 2	Activity	Work	37.8%	26.3%
		Study	14.9%	18.1%
		Care	19.0%	25.1%
		Leisure	20.2%	18.3%
		Other	8.1%	12.2%
	Duration (hours)		3.2	2.4
Trip 3	Duration (')/distance from home (m)		26/0	33/0
	Mode	Car/motorcycle	60.7%	45.0%
		Bus	26.5%	38.7%
		Walking/cycling	12.8%	12.5%

Taking into account that work is the most common first activity in a three-trip itinerary, Fig. 2.13 considers it a fixed activity at the beginning of the day. This time, both men and women leave the house at approximately the same time, travel similar distances and remain at work for approximately 7 hours. The share of people who travel by active modes and transit decreases compared to the two-trip 'home-based work' profile. The second activity for 38% of men and 26% of women is another work-related activity. Nevertheless, for one in four women, it relates to care or domestic responsibilities, a ratio that decreases to one in five pertaining to men. Undoubtedly, these differences in purposes explain that men stay on average 48 minutes more in the second activity: work-related activities tend to be longer than care-related activities.

Finally, Figs. 2.14–2.16 show itineraries constituting four trips and three activities. Again, the first is generic for all people from 18 to 64 years old who register this type of itinerary. Some distinctive patterns can be observed. For instance, both distances and travel times are significantly smaller than in the previous itineraries. Also, in most cases, people return home for their 'second activity' (82–83% of the cases). It can be hypothesised that the distance they need to travel for the first activity is not very substantial, enabling them to return home before engaging in another activity later in the day.

Men leave on average half an hour earlier than women for their first activity (at 8.30 a.m.) and travel over 5 km for 25 minutes. Meanwhile, women leave at approximately 9 a.m. and only travel 3 km, which takes them on average 22 minutes. Men stay for an hour longer than women in the first activity. They both return home in the early afternoon, stay there for two and a half to three hours, and leave again after 4 p.m. On average, the third activity tends to be slightly closer to home than the first activity (especially in the case of men) and implies 20 minutes of travelling for both sexes. It lasts two to two and a half hours.

In general terms, 53% of men and 42% of women that make four trips travel to work for their first activity, whereas 26% of men and 37% of women travel to perform care-related tasks. Thus, while women show no clear predominance between work and care at the beginning of the day, men clearly show more a work-related profile. For their third activity, men are more divided between work (32%) and care-related tasks (31%). In contrast, only 20% of women mark work as their third activity versus 40% who register a care-related activity. Another relevant activity that occurs during the late afternoon pertains to leisure (25% for men and 20% for women).

Regarding mode, half of the men perform all four trips by car or motorcycle. This figure oscillates between 25% and 30% in the case of women whose access to these resources increases for trips that happen later in the day (numbers 3 and 4). In addition, the use of active modes increases in the third and fourth trip for both sexes. In the case of transit, women's share drops from 30% in the first two trips to 20% in trips 3 and 4, though it barely oscillates between 21% and 17% in the case of men.

Fig. 2.15 fixes work as the first activity. The time of departure changes to half an hour earlier for men and one hour earlier for women. Distance, travel time and activity duration increase for the first one (work), maintaining the observed differences by gender. Activity 2 is also predominantly at home, and activity 3 adopts a very similar pattern to the activity described in the generic chart (see the attached table). In this scheme, nevertheless, both the second and third activities are shorter than in the generic chart. The share of women who travel to work by bus to and from the first activity rises to 40%, and the share of women who walk or cycle drops compared to the generic chart. Men's modal choice, on the contrary, does not change in a dramatic way, except that private motorised mobility increases by a few points.

Finally, Fig. 2.16 fixes work as the last of the three activities. Interestingly, the purpose of the first trip is work-related for most people: 53% of men and 45% of women. In addition, 30% of men and 37% of women conduct out-of-home

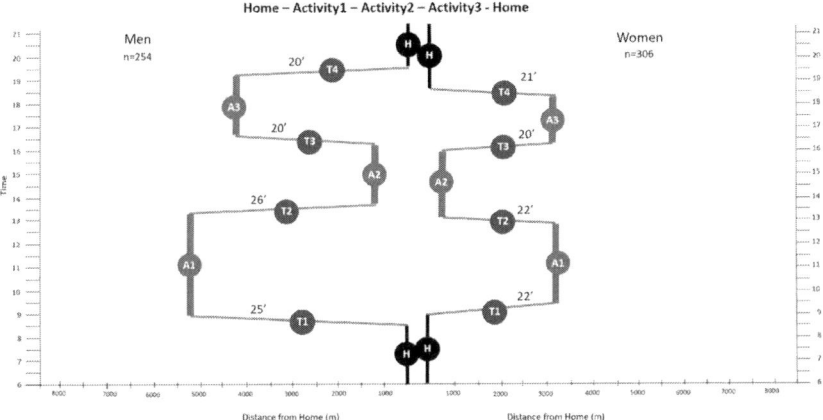

Fig. 2.14. Itinerary: Home–Activity 1–Activity 2–Activity 3–Home; Population between the Ages of 18 and 64 (22% of Men and 23% of Women).
Source: Elaborated by the Authors Based on MMR Mobility Survey Data.

	Starting Point: Home		Men	Women
Trip 1	Duration (')/distance from home (m)		25/5208	22/3263
	Mode	Car/motorcycle	49.6%	26.5%
		Bus	20.8%	32.1%
		Walking/cycling	27.1%	40.8%
Activity 1	Activity	Work	53.0%	42.2%
		Study	9.4%	4.7%
		Care	25.6%	36.7%
		Leisure	2.1%	6.3%
		Other	9.0%	10.0%
	Duration (hours)		4.4	3.3
Trip 2	Duration (')/distance from home (m)		26/1157	22/671
	Mode	Car/motorcycle	50.8%	24.6%
		Bus	16.8%	30.5%
		Walking/cycling	30.1%	44.4%
Activity 2	Activity	Home	82.8%	81.8%
		Work	6.6%	5.7%
		Study	0.4%	1.8%
		Care	1.8%	4.6%
		Leisure	3.0%	3.5%
		Other	5.1%	2.6%
	Duration (hours)		2.6	2.9
Trip 3	Duration (')/distance from home (m)		20/4219	20/3146
	Mode	Car/motorcycle	51.7%	27.5%
		Bus	17.4%	21.4%
		Walking/cycling	29.5%	50.9%
Activity 3	Activity	Home	0.1%	0.2%
		Work	31.6%	19.8%
		Study	3.7%	7.0%
		Care	31.0%	40.2%
		Leisure	24.8%	20.0%
		Other	8.9%	12.8%
	Duration (hours)		2.5	2.1
Trip 4	Duration (')/distance from home (m)		22/0	21/0
	Mode	Car/motorcycle	53.2%	29.5%
		Bus	16.8%	19.4%
		Walking/cycling	28.6%	48.8%

Mobility and Gender Equity in Latin America

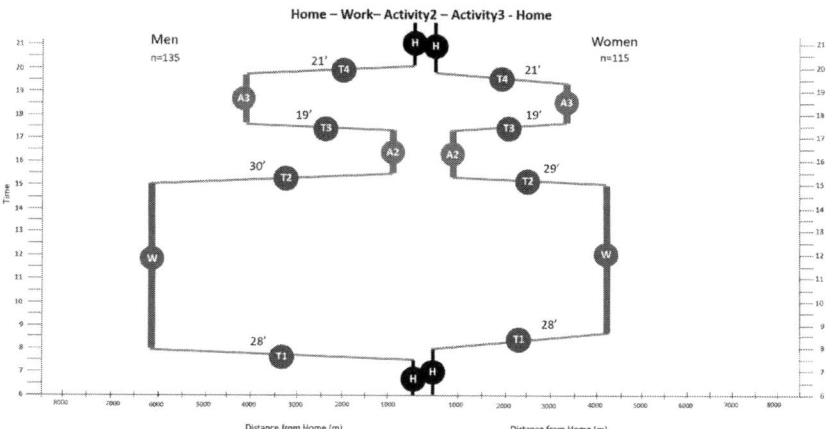

Fig. 2.15. Itinerary: Home–Work–Activity 2–Activity 3–Home; Population between the Ages of 18 and 64 (11% of Men and 9% of Women). *Source*: Elaborated by the Authors Based on MMR Mobility Survey Data.

	Starting Point: Home		Men	Women
Trip 1	Duration (')/distance from home (m)		28/6275	28/4243
	Mode	Car/motorcycle	54.9%	31.5%
		Bus	19.0%	44.1%
		Walking/cycling	23.9%	23.5%
Work	Duration (hours)		7.1	6.3
Trip 2	Duration (')/distance from home (m)		30/950	29/741
	Mode	Car/motorcycle	55.9%	28.1%
		Bus	14.0%	40.8%
		Walking/cycling	27.8%	30.2%
Activity 2	Activity	Home	85.4%	81.6%
		Work	5.3%	6.0%
		Study		0.2%
		Care	1.8%	3.0%
		Leisure	3.3%	7.4%
		Other	4.2%	1.8%
	Duration (hours)		1.8	2.0
Trip 3	Duration (')/distance from home (m)		19/4275	19/3330
	Mode	Car/motorcycle	51.4%	31.2%
		Bus	13.9%	20.9%
		Walking/cycling	34.7%	47.7%
Activity 3	Activity	Work	31.3%	21.0%
		Study	6.8%	8.3%
		Care	28.4%	40.1%
		Leisure	26.3%	20.8%
		Other	7.3%	9.8%
	Duration (hours)		2.1	1.9
Trip 4	Duration (')/distance from home (m)		21/0	21/0
	Mode	Car/motorcycle	53.6%	33.7%
		Bus	14.1%	17.8%
		Walking/cycling	32.3%	45.0%

care-related activities when they start the day. This first activity is on average shorter than the fixed one (the third) and lasts approximately 3 hours for men and slightly more than 2 hours for women. For activity number 2, the percentage

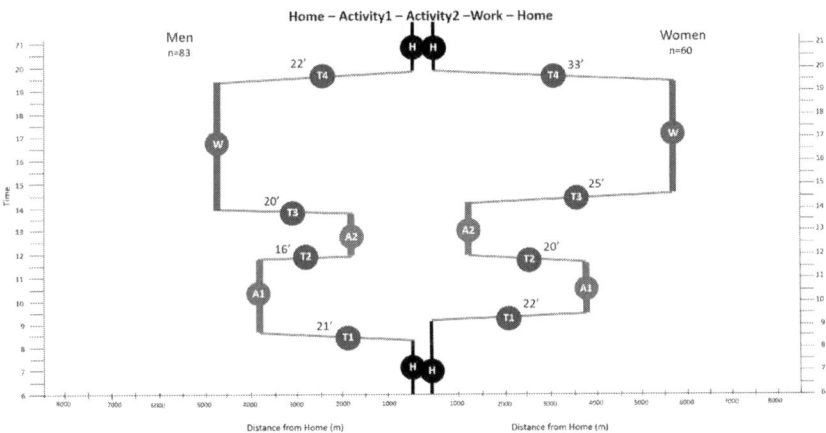

Fig. 2.16. Itinerary: Home–Activity 1–Activity 2–Work–Home; Population between the Ages of 18 and 64 (7% of Men and 4% of Women). *Source*: Elaborated by the Authors Based on MMR Mobility Survey Data.

	Starting Point: Home		Men	Women
Trip 1	Duration (')/distance from home (m)		21/3870	22/3751
	Mode	Car/motorcycle	63.9%	24.0%
		Bus	14.8%	31.3%
		Walking/cycling	21.3%	44.7%
Activity 1	Activity	Home	2.1%	0.4%
		Work	52.6%	44.7%
		Study	7.7%	1.4%
		Care	29.4%	36.7%
		Leisure	1.7%	5.3%
		Other	6.6%	11.5%
	Duration (hours)		3.1	2.2
Trip 2	Duration (')/distance from home (m)		16/1703	20/1213
	Mode	Car/motorcycle	61.0%	23.6%
		Bus	12.5%	26.9%
		Walking/cycling	26.5%	49.5%
Activity 2	Activity	Home	75.9%	72.2%
		Work	4.1%	9.0%
		Study	0.8%	
		Care	5.1%	10.8%
		Leisure	7.0%	5.0%
		Other	7.0%	3.1%
	Duration (hours)		1.7	2.3
Trip 3	Duration (')/distance from home (m)		20/4741	25/5652
	Mode	Car/motorcycle	63.3%	39.9%
		Bus	12.5%	35.4%
		Walking/cycling	10.9%	5.5%
Work	Duration (hours)		5.4	4.8
Trip 4	Duration (')/distance from home (m)		22/0	33/0
	Mode	Car/motorcycle	67.8%	37.5%
		Bus	9.9%	40.0%
		Walking/cycling	10.9%	8.1%

of people who return home is lower than in the itineraries previously described. Although 76% of men and 72% of women go home in the middle of the day (and stay approximately 2 hours), a significant 11% of women dedicate that time to care-related activities outside of the home (vs 5% of men). When they finally go to work in the early afternoon, women stay on average under 5 hours, and men over 5 hours. They return home at approximately 8 p.m.

Regarding the trips themselves, in this last itinerary, there is a greater predominance of private motorised mobility. Among men, it reaches the largest percentage in the last trip (approximately 70%). It also increases among women, reaching a maximum of approximately 40% in the third and fourth trips. In this case, active modes have a greater relevance for the first two trips, especially among women (45–50%), but they significantly decrease for trips 3 and 4: only 6–8% of women walk or cycle to work when it is fixed as a third activity in the day versus 11% of men. The change in the ratio may pertain to preventive safety measures taken by women when they plan to return home late. However, it is also relevant that women travel further than men in this instance (5.7 km vs 4.7 km), which can reduce their preference for active modes of transportation.

6. CONCLUSIONS

In general, the descriptive analysis herein confirms the expected gendered mobility patterns presented by previous studies. Women's mode share comprises a larger proportion of transit trips, they travel shorter distances and they contribute in a greater proportion than men to care mobility. In this vein, women account for 6 in 10 of all trips that are care oriented. This contribution varies according to the transport mode: when travelling by car, it decreases to 4 in 10. However, travelling by bus and active modes (walking or cycling) increases women's contribution to approximately 7 in 10 trips. If time spent travelling is introduced into the equation, women account for 59% of the minutes that are globally dedicated to care-oriented trips. Moreover, poorer women contribute 77% of the time dedicated to care-oriented trips compared to men in the same socioeconomic situation.

Regarding the activity-based approach applied in this study, it is apparent that a simple two-way pattern (home–activity–home) is the most common type of mobility for both men and women. While men's commuting patterns have a defined 'home-based work' profile, women have a higher level of heterogeneity in their daily itineraries. Two-way mobility related to care is much more relevant for women than men.

Regardless of the number of trips, a tour-based analysis shows some distinctive patterns: women's average travel time is higher than men's, even when distances are shorter. Women leave home slightly later than men and return at the end of the day at approximately the same time. In general, the duration of at least one of the two activities is significantly shorter. One salient exception includes those with a home–care activity–home itinerary, in which women spend more time than men.

Furthermore, access to private motorised means of transport is a key variable in explaining the configuration of mobility patterns, and there is a persistent gender gap in this matter. Approximately two-thirds of men living in the MMR reported regular access to a car in the household. Meanwhile, only one-third of women reported such access. The fact that men travel longer distances in shorter times is directly related to their access to these resources. The activity-based analysis suggests that as daily schedules become more complex, both men and women increase their access to private means of transport, but the gender gap remains.

This chapter calls attention to the need to overcome a limited perspective on transport equity that does not consider gender-based inequality. From a gendered mobilities framework and by incorporating space-time elements into the discussion, it is possible to reveal a set of elements that are either the cause or an indicator of gender inequality. As a matter of fact, average numbers of mainstream indicators obscure part of that inequality. For that reason, it is necessary to develop a profound study of care mobility and activity-based itineraries. When complemented with a detailed view of travel conditions under a specific 'gendered prism', the analysis of core mobility indicators takes on a new meaning, and it is possible to expose hidden inequalities among men and women. Aggregated statistics and averages are not sufficient to accomplish this task.

In addition, as feminist literature and mobility studies indicate, there are vulnerability compounds that enhance gender inequality. Specifically, income is a crucial variable for understanding the mechanisms of women's vulnerability in several fields, such as urban mobility. To some extent, it does not suffice to consider the existence of differences between men and women but it is also necessary to assess differences within women. This is a relevant finding to reflect on a regional-specific framework on gendered mobility. As shown with the evidence from Montevideo, women in the Global South have several obstacles due to the mobility conditions. These conditions are grounded in broader social inequities. Meanwhile, in the Global North, it seems to be more frequent that women find obstacles derived from hyper-mobility requirements. It is relevant in the future to assess more accurately the combination of gender and socioeconomic status. To do so, it is necessary to reach a comparative agenda on this topic.

Finally, the case of Montevideo constitutes empirical evidence in line with literature on gendered mobilities and gender-sensitive urban planning. Indeed, as several authors have reported, gender is a marker in terms of mobility. It sets specific conditions for urban life in general and mobility in particular that, in turn, may be the cause of further inequality. In short, to adopt this gender perspective is beneficial for understanding general mobility inequality in Latin America and the differential access between social groups to urban opportunities under contexts of social inequality and exclusion. It is also possible to argue that mobility is a valid case for the study of gender relations and inequalities, and that it should be included among the repertoire of more traditional analytic tools that are limited to a somewhat static view of time and space such as time-use analysis.

Moreover, the results of this chapter may be useful inputs for transport and urban planners in Latin America. It calls the attention to the need of a gendered perspective for planning. The absence of this perspective may boost gender inequality that, as it was mentioned before, is related to socioeconomic inequality.

NOTES

1. In particular, the 5th SDG aims to achieve gender equality and empower all women and girls.
2. By fixity we refer to those activities in people's daily life that are fixed in time and space. They must be carried out in the same place and at the same time. Therefore, these activities 'anchor a space–time *prism* in an individual's daily activity schedule, which represents the person's opportunity to participate in activities and travel in space–time' (Shen, Chai, & Kwan, 2015, p. 1). Fixity and flow of daily activities are useful notions to study how mobility is shaped by space–time constraints.
3. The survey enables the assessment of the census tract of the respondent's household as well as those that correspond to each destination he or she travels to during the day.
4. Chi-square test shows statistically significant association at 0.000 level for gendered and the described variables.
5. The socioeconomic level index is calculated as a proxy for income (see Mauttone & Hernandez, 2017).
6. Chi-square test shows statistically significant association at 0.000 level for gendered and the described variables.
7. In fact, the fourth quintile shows a particular distribution when men's contribution to care mobility surpasses women's by approximately 8 percentage points.

REFERENCES

Alcaino, P., Domarchi, C., & López Carrasco, S. (2009, January). Gender differences in time use and mobility: Time poverty and dual consumption. Paper presented at the First Workshop of the Time Use Observatory (TUO), Santiago de Chile.

Alcaino, P., Domarchi, C., & López Carrasco, S. (2010). *Time, poverty and transport: An exploration into mobility patterns contribution to poverty measurements.* Paper presented at the Second Workshop of the Time Use Observatory Workshop, San Felipe, Chile..

Amarante, V., & Rossel, C. (2018). Unfolding patterns of unpaid household work in Latin America. *Feminist Economics, 24*(1), 1–34. https://doi.org/10.1080/13545701.2017.1344776

Bernard, A., Seguin, A.-M., Bussiere, Y., & Polacchini, A. (1996). Household structure and mobility patterns of women in O–D surveys: Methods and results based on the case studies of Montreal and Paris. Paper presented at Trabajo Presentado en la Women's Travel Issues Second National Conference, October.

Buckingham, S. (2013). Gender, sustainability and the urban environment. In I. Sanchez de Madariaga & M. Roberts (Eds.), *Fair shared cities. The impact of gender planning in Europe.* London: Routledge.

Campaña, J. C., Giménez-Nadal, J. I., & Molina, J. A. (2018). Gender norms and the gendered distribution of total work in Latin American households. *Feminist Economics, 24*(1), 35–62. https://doi.org/10.1080/13545701.2017.1390320

Cresswell, T., & Uteng, T. P. (2008). Gendered mobilities: Towards an holistic understanding. In T. P. Uteng & T. Cresswell (Eds.), *Gendered mobilities* (pp. 1–12). Hampshire: Ashgate Pub.

ECLAC. (2010). Social panorama of Latin America 2009. Santiago de Chile: ECLAC. Retrieved from https://www.cepal.org/en/publications/1249-social-panorama-latin-america-2009

ECLAC. (2016). *Social panorama of Latin America 2015.* Santiago de Chile: ECLAC.

Ellegård, K. (1999). A time-geographical approach to the study of everyday life of individuals – A challenge of complexity. *Geojournal, 48*(3), 167–175.

Ellegård, K., & Svedin, U. (2012). Torsten Hägerstrand's time-geography as the cradle of the activity approach in transport geography. *Journal of Transport Geography, 23*, 17–25.

Emond, C., Tang, W., & Handy, S. (2009). Explaining gender difference in bicycling behavior. *Transportation Research Record: Journal of the Transportation Research Board, 2125*, 16–25. https://doi.org/10.3141/2125-03

Espino, A., Isabella, F., Leites, M., & Machado, A. (2017). Do women have different labor supply behaviors? Evidence based on educational groups in Uruguay. *Feminist Economics, 23*(4), 143–169. https://doi.org/10.1080/13545701.2016.1241415

Esquivel, V., Budlender, D., Folbre, N., & Hirway, I. (2008). Explorations: Time-use surveys in the south. *Feminist Economics*, *14*(3), 107–152. https://doi.org/10.1080/13545700802075135

Hägerstrand, T. (1970). What about people in regional science? *Papers of the Regional Science Association*, *24*(1), 6–21. https://doi.org/10.1007/BF01936872

Herbel, S., Gaines, D., National Research Council (U.S.), Transportation Research Board, Cambridge Systematics, & United States Federal Highway Administration. (2010). *Women's issues in transportation: Summary of the 4th international conference. Volume 1: Conference overview and plenary papers*. Washington, DC: Transportation Research Board.

Hernández, D. (2012). Políticas de tiempo, movilidad y transporte público: Rasgos básicos, equidad social y de género. PNUD Uruguay, Intendencia de Montevideo.

Hernandez, D., & Rossel, C. (2015). Inequality and access to social services in Latin America: Space–time constraints of child health checkups and prenatal care in Montevideo. *Journal of Transport Geography*, *44*, 24–32. https://doi.org/10.1016/j.jtrangeo.2015.02.007

Hjorthol, R. (2008). Daily mobility of men and women – A barometer of gender equality? In T. Uteng & T. Cresswell (Eds.), *Gendered mobilities* (pp. 193–212). Hampshire: Ashgate Pub.

Jiron, P. (2017). Planificación urbana y del transporte a partir de relaciones de interdependencia y movilidad del cuidado. In M. N. Rico & O. Segovia (Eds.), *¿Quién cuida en la ciudad?: Aportes para políticas urbanas de igualdad* (pp. 405–432). CEPAL.

Kwan, M.-P. (1999). Gender and individual access to urban opportunities: A study using space–time measures. *The Professional Geographer*, *51*(2), 211–227. https://doi.org/10.1111/0033-0124.00158

Lefebvre, H. (1968). *Le Droit à la ville*. Paris: Anthropos.

Levy, C. (2013). Travel choice reframed: "deep distribution" and gender in urban transport. *Environment & Urbanization*, *25*(1), 47–63. https://doi.org/10.1177/0956247813477810

Mauttone, A., & Hernandez, D. (2017). Encuesta de Movilidad del Área Metropolitana de Montevideo. Principales resultados e indicadores. Intendecias de Montevideo, Canelones y San José, Ministerio de Transporte y Obras Públicas, CAF, PNUD Uruguay y UDELAR.

McQuaid, R. W., & Chen, T. (2012). Commuting times – The role of gender, children and part-time work. *Research in Transportation Economics*, *34*(1), 66–73. https://doi.org/10.1016/j.retrec.2011.12.001

McQuoid, J., & Dijst, M. (2012). Bringing emotions to time geography: The case of mobilities of poverty. *Journal of Transport Geography*, *23*, 26–34.

Murray, L. (2008). Motherhood, risk and everyday mobilities. In T. Uteng & T. Cresswell (Eds.), *Gendered mobilities* (pp. 47–63). Hampshire: Ashgate Pub.

Naess, P. (2008). Gender differences in the influences of urban structure on daily travel. In T. Uteng & T. Cresswell (Eds.), *Gendered mobilities* (pp. 173–192). Hampshire: Ashgate Pub.

Neutens, T. (2012). Accessibility to public service delivery: A combination of different indicators. In K. T. Geurs, K. J. Krizek, & A. Reggiani (Eds.), *Accessibility analysis and transport planning*, (pp. 118–132). Cheltenham: Edward Elgar Publishing.

Neutens, T. (2015). Accessibility, equity and health care: Review and research directions for transport geographers. *Journal of Transport Geography*, *43*, 14–27. https://doi.org/10.1016/j.jtrangeo.2014.12.006

Neutens, T., Delafontaine, M., Scott, D. M., & De Maeyer, P. (2012). An analysis of day-to-day variations in individual space–time accessibility. *Journal of Transport Geography*, *23*, 81–91.

Neutens, T., Schwanen, T., & Witlox, F. (2011). The prism of everyday life: Towards a new research agenda for time geography. *Transport Reviews*, *31*, 25–47.

Peralta Quiros, T., Mehndiratta, S., & Ochoa, C. (2014). *Gender, travel and job access: Evidence from Buenos Aires*. Buenos Aires: Banco Mundial.

Pérez Orozco, A. (2009). *Global perspectives on the social organization of care in times of crisis: Assessing the situation*. Gender, Migration and Development Series, Working Paper 5, United Nations International Research and Training Institute for the Advancement of Women (UN-INSTRAW).

Roberts, M. (2013). Introduction: Concepts, themes and issues in a gendered approach to planning. In I. Sanchez de Madariaga & M. Roberts (Eds.), *Fair shared cities. The impact of gender planning in Europe* (pp. 1–18). London: Routledge.

Sanchez de Madariaga, I. (2013). The mobility of care: A new concept in urban transportation. In I. Sanchez de Madariaga & M. Roberts (Eds.), *Fair share cities: The impact of gender planning in Europe* (pp. 33–48). Farnham: Ashgate.

Scheiner, J., & Holz-Rau, C. (2012). Gender structures in car availability in car deficient households. *Research in Transportation Economics*, *34*(1), 16–26. https://doi.org/10.1016/j.retrec.2011.12.006

Schwanen, T., Kwan, M.-P., & Ren, F. (2008). How fixed is fixed? Gendered rigidity of space–time constraints and geographies of everyday activities. *Geoforum*, *39*(6), 2109–2121. https://doi.org/10.1016/j.geoforum.2008.09.002

Shen, Y., Chai, Y., & Kwan, M. (2015). Space–time fixity and flexibility of daily activities and the built environment: A case study of different types of communities in Beijing suburbs. *Journal of Transport Geography*, *47*, 90–99. https://doi.org/10.1016/j.jtrangeo.2015.06.014

Zucchini, E. (2015). *Género y transporte: Análisis de la movilidad del cuidado como punto de partida para construir una base de conocimiento más amplia de los patrones de movilidad*. El caso de Madrid, Tesis doctoral, Universidad Politécnica de Madrid.

CHAPTER 3

CHILDREN AND URBAN MOBILITY: CARE DYNAMICS ON FAMILY MOBILITY PATTERNS

Gabriela Cicci Faria

ABSTRACT

Access can be understood as the spatial dimension of social inclusion and exclusion. It is from this understanding that the authors incorporate the gender perspective when analysing the possibilities of mobility in the city. This research focusses on a specific moment in the life cycle of men and women: childbirth and the presence of children in the household. The aim is to elucidate how much the presence of children in the household impacts the urban mobility of the people responsible for the household, comparing data of men and women responsible for households with or without cohabiting children. The authors used descriptive statistics and correlation analysis based on data from the Origin–Destination Survey 2012 of Belo Horizonte, Brazil. The authors analysed the travel motivations, the ratio of journeys by trips and the means of transportation used, in addition to some indicators of immobility. The results of the research show the impact of the presence of children in an unequal way considering the gender of those responsible for the household, with women in all scenarios carrying out a greater frequency of trips associated with care, but in a specific way according to their degree of schooling and their children's ages.

Keywords: Urban mobility; access; gender; children; care mobility; travel motivations

1. INTRODUCTION

The theme of access and accessibility has occupied part of a scientific field concerned with the production of more egalitarian cities and societies. By combining gender studies with those of urban sociology, the concept of access began to be present based on reflections related to the possibilities of women's mobility in the city. The purpose of this research is to find out how much the presence of children at home impacts the daily urban mobility of the heads of household, comparing data between men and women. Do children in their different ages have any influence on the patterns of displacement of those who are responsible for them? How cohabiting with children at home affects the possibilities of moving?

These questions will be answered based on an analysis of family mobility practices that had the data obtained by the Origin–Destination (O–D) Survey of the Metropolitan Area of Belo Horizonte, Brazil as source. Belo Horizonte is a city located in the south-eastern part of the country, capital of the state of Minas Gerais, with an approximate population of 4.8 million distributed in 34 municipalities. It is a metropolitan region that highly concentrates opportunities of services, jobs and distribution of transport. Almost 85% of the region's gross domestic product (GDP) is concentrated in only three municipalities, with the capital accounting for 45% of the total.[1] The economic inequality scenario is also seen in the scale of the city of Belo Horizonte, also centralising its services, employment opportunities and transportation supply, with its GDP distributed unevenly among central neighbourhoods, the periphery and the favelas.

The capital is home to approximately half of the inhabitants of the metropolitan area (RMBH), presenting a demographic density of 7,167 inhabitants per km^2.[2] It is a city with a high rate of motorisation, in which 36.6% of the daily trips are carried out in motorised individual mode, 34.8% are carried out on foot and 28.1% in collective mode. Longitudinal analysis of Origin-Source Surveys shows a strong increase in the rate of motorisation since the 1990s, when the percentage of trips made in automobiles and motorcycles added was close to 20%.[3]

When regarding fertility rates, Belo Horizonte presented in 2018 an average of 1.3 children per woman, in a decreasing trend that has been diminishing from 2.0 in 1991 to 1.7 in 2000.[4] Overall, this trend has been seen in Brazil since the 1960s, when the fertility rate was of six children per woman, and in 2018, it reached an average of 1.89.[5] Recent data concerning income presented an average of 3.6 minimum wages per month in the city.[6] Furthermore, these data come aside with a Gini index of 0.60, one that has remained stable since 1991 according to data from the Atlas of Human Development. One last piece of information that we would like about the city when considering mobility patterns is its uneven topography, with an average declivity rate of 8.25%.[7]

In order to interpret the data of the different populations within the cities and their travelling profiles, an analysis will be carried out based on the sex of those responsible for the household, their education level and the age of the children cohabiting in their home. We will use the motivation of the trips, the means of transport used and the ratio of trips per journey to make our analysis in relation to the different situations encountered. It is important to highlight that this O–D Survey considers only the variables 'Man' and 'Woman' when dealing with the interviewees' gender, and it is not possible to analyse specific profiles of people who may not identify themselves in this binary division of gender identity. Also, the survey does not contain a variable related to race or ethnicity.

The organisation of this work consists of first presenting a brief review of the literature on the matters of access, mobility and gender, and how they relate. Then, presenting the methodology used, followed by the results. Finally, discussing the data obtained and presenting the conclusions.

2. MOBILITY, ACCESS AND GENDER

Urban and transportation planners have always been concerned with issues related to access and accessibility. However, in the technical or in the scientific field, these terms may still appear somewhat nebulous. Geurs and Van Wee (2004) emphasise how the concept of accessibility was often misunderstood, poorly defined or poorly measured due to its complexity. Also, they point out that the concept of accessibility often found in academic productions is treated in a way equivalent to the one of access. In order to facilitate the work of technicians and researchers, accessibility as a construct has usually been reduced to more easily interpreted measures such as travel speed (Geurs & Van Wee, 2004) or the adaptation of the geographic space to a standard infrastructure (Castillo, 2017).

For this work, it is necessary to mark the difference between the concepts of accessibility and access. The former was described by Geurs and Van Wee (2004, p. 218) as '(...) the extent to which land-use and transport systems enable (groups of) individuals to reach activities or destinations by means of a (combination of) transport mode(s)'. However, this study is situated within a theoretical and epistemological framework that encompasses urban mobility beyond the transport system (Sheller & Urry, 2006), as a social and procedural network of mobile people, goods, ideas and narratives. From this point, our understanding of accessibility does not necessarily go into modes of transportation, once it can also be accomplished in a virtual or symbolic way, for example, and we prefer to conceptualise it as the relative ease with which a person can reach potential destinations, according to Neutens et al. (2010, with Schwanen et al., 2015).

The perspective of Cass, Shove, and Urry (2005) will be used to guide the concept of access, which suggests its understanding as the spatial (and mobile) dimension of social inclusion or exclusion. This concept is also aligned with the view of mobilities according to Sheller and Urry (2006), once Cass et al. (2005) understand that access-related barriers are found not only in the physical sphere of the transport space or system but also in the access to networks of services, work, information, *family networks* or influence networks, for example. Their concept includes four dimensions of access, roughly being: (a) financial, considering the possibility of being able to pay for public transport, a private car or mobile data for online mobility; (b) physical, concerning physical or cognitive abilities for mobility; (c) organisational that includes the ways in which public transport is organised in its schedules and distribution in the city, as well as the organisation and availability of information for mobility; and (d) temporal, which observes the possibilities of sovereignty over one's own time (Breedveld, 1998 with Cass et al., 2005).

When looking at the production that combines the themes of mobility, access and gender, one frequently realises that the latter often appears in analysis that measures different capacities of socially vulnerable groups to move through geographic space, being either women, peripheral groups or people with disabilities (Geurs & Van Wee, 2004; Pereira, 2018; Schwanen et al., 2015). Also, descriptive studies of patterns and experiences of women in their everyday urban mobility, using both quantitative and qualitative methodologies, are frequent (Best & Lanzendorf, 2005; Jirón, 2007; Kwan, 2000; Tanzarn, 2008, among others). These studies, with their differences and potentialities, provided this study with a rich amount of data on female mobility and gender relations in the mobility that guided our question about the impact of children on the family mobility of those responsible. Besides the studies of Madariaga (2013) and Manderscheid (2014), which led our research question, we identified a lack of studies that combined gender analysis with family mobility and the presence of children in the household.

Regarding the differences in mobility patterns, it is shown that there are inequalities between men and women regarding the use of means of transport, use and availability of time, possibilities of choosing the paths, motivations of the routes and the structure of the routes taken. Let us look into them in the following paragraphs.

As for inequalities in the use of means of transport, studies carried out in African (Tanzarn, 2008), Latin American (Brevis, 2016; Jirón, 2007; Prefeitura De de São Paulo, 2016; Rosa, 2018) and European and North American contexts (Best & Lanzendorf, 2005; Hjorthol, 2008) have shown that women travel more by public transport and on foot than men, who mostly use individual motorised transportation. In situations where the car access is disputed or negotiated by residents, studies in European contexts (Hjorthol, 2008; Scheiner & Holz-Rau, 2012; Schwanen, 2007) and Central Asia (Schwanen et al., 2015) show that men are the ones who have priority in its use, even if women are the ones who have been investing in social networks that ensure access to vehicles from neighbours, for example (Schwanen et al., 2015).

Space–time constraints were described by Kwan (2000) in the North American context and also mentioned by Best and Lanzendorf (2005) in the European context. Their data evidence patterns of female trips which are closer to their homes and less flexible in scheduling when compared to the trips performed by men. Limitations concerning space are also described in South and North American contexts. Valentine (1989) and Siqueira (2015) focus on the circumscription of women to certain spaces due to their greater sense of fear or insecurity in the public spaces of the city, reporting a decrease in the possible map of their circulation. Elvir (2016), regarding the Brazilian context, evidences the reality of women in situations of high vulnerability who, without enough income to access public or informal transportation, have their paths limited to their bodily capacity of walking. In addition, studies that associate female mobility with harassment experiences have also shown limitations in their journeys and evidenced differences in the perception of public transport safety between men and women (De Lima, Monteiro, & Maia, 2017).

It is noted that studies describing mobility patterns are sometimes located in the differences between men and women, and sometimes explore other aspects related to them, bringing different nuances to the analysis. Some of these studies use the gender perspective within the framework of the differences between men and women, while others are closer to the feminist readings that extrapolate the description of practices or patterns to make a critical reading of the inequalities found.

Madariaga (2013) is one of the authors that finds herself on the critical framework and retakes the literature on the sexual division of labour and care work when thinking about mobility and gender, conceptualising the mobility of care. By making it visible that this fundamental work of reproduction of life – the care for the household and the children – has very often been in the hands of women in Western societies, this author proposes a different reading from the one usually made of the patterns of mobility found in O–D surveys. By separating care-related activities – shopping, escorting (accompanying children, the elderly or other people in need) and health-related routes – the percentages of trips made with these motivations appear fragmented and very small when compared to trips motivated by work or study. Her proposal, then, is that we do a joint analysis of such ways of mobility, comprising them as ways of mobility related to care work. Thus, at the same time that we visualise this care work, we can have a more accurate understanding of the dynamics of mobility and gender relations that might affect them.

The gender perspective applied to mobility also allowed the analysis of mobility from a familiar, relational perspective, denying the analysis of a neutral or completely autonomous mobile subject (Manderscheid, 2014). Analysis under this aspect enabled us to identify multitasking patterns in people's mobility, but very often they were associated with women's and mothers' journeys. (Jirón, 2007; Lyra, 2016; Madariaga, 2013; Svab, 2016). Multitasking or chained journeys are those where different tasks and stops are incorporated into a trip that has a main motivation, for example, dropping off a child at school or stopping to buy breakfast on one's way to work. Madariaga (2013) points out how the presence of young children at home increases the number of multitasking trips performed by mothers, but does not increase those of fathers.

Upon the information that has already been proposed, the influence of the presence of children on the mobility of those responsible for the household will be investigated more deeply. It will be done based on the analysis and interpretation of the data from the O–D Survey held in 2012 in the city of Belo Horizonte, as explained in the following text.

3. METHODOLOGY

In order to analyse the mobility of the families, we have used the data provided by the O–D Survey held in Belo Horizonte, Brazil, in 2012 – its most recent version. The O–D Survey, as it is called, collects information about the trips of the RMBH interviewing people at their homes and at strategic points of the city's transportation system in order to collect information from a sample representative of the population. It is nowadays the main instrument used by the public sector for mobility planning policies due to its large volume and scope of information.

According to the O–D Survey Manual (Bhtrans, 2016a), in 2012, 100,656 people were interviewed in 44,126 households in the city. The areas of the metropolitan region were divided into 1,289 homogeneous areas, these being the adequate collection units to establish minimum samples in socioeconomic surveys developed for the RMBH (Bhtrans, 2016a). The sample definition was made for a maximum error of 5% and a 95% confidence level (Bhtrans, 2016b). With this structure, two types of information were collected in the field: the socioeconomic characteristics of the different regions of the study area and the profile of the trips made on the previous day by all the residents of the household. Data were collected through surveys in households as well as at transport terminals, at the contour line of the region and at crossing lines between municipalities. Because of its diversity, scope and relevance, the household-based survey was chosen as the data source, which has the largest volume of information and the possibility of expanding the results for the rest of the population. Interviews were made aiming to collect details about all the journeys made by all the family members of the household, using as a reference the day before the interview. When necessary, family members would respond about the journey of those who were not present at the moment, leading to uncertainties on the data that cannot be measured. Also, the choice of analysing only the day before the interview diminishes the opportunity of accessing routes related to leisure (on weekends) or to shift work patterns, for example. Other limitations concerning the database are the lack of variables of race and ethnicity, as well as the reduced importance given to short journeys performed by foot or inside the neighbourhood – which are crucial for mobilities motivated by care work, as it will be discussed ahead. Furthermore, when analysing the trip motivations, a more detailed division of motifs would provide a deeper understanding of mobility behaviour. A final general comment on the limitations of this survey relates to a highly individual perspective of mobility, which we aim to stress from Manderscheid's (2014) perspective.

While making a first superficial analysis of the data, it was noticed that the methodology of the O–D 2012 Survey makes an important differentiation with respect to the concepts of trips and journeys. A trip is defined as a 'partial displacement of a person in a particular stretch, by a certain mode of transport' (Bhtrans, 2016a, p. 15), while journeys, being the basic transportation data of an O–D Survey, is understood as 'the displacement between two specific points, with defined purpose, using one or more means of transport' (Bhtrans, 2016a, p. 15). Also, according to the O–D Survey Manual 2012 (Bhtrans, 2016a), the internal travel table was assembled from the trips' table, since it groups the partial displacements of a journey with a defined purpose. Simply put, a journey is made up of one or more trips.

In order to analyse and compare the mobility of men and women in the RMBH, it seemed more appropriate to work on the trips table, since it encompasses a greater detail of the journeys. Taking into account the existing literature on women's mobility and care mobility (Jirón, 2007; Madariaga, 2013; Manderscheid, 2014), it is necessary to stress the complexity of multitasking trips, which could be lost if we used the internal travel table.

Descriptive statistics of the population characteristics of the RMBH and their displacement patterns were produced. With the help of the Stata software, the sociodemographic data of the sample of the population that did not report any travel on the previous day were first analysed, in order to find patterns of constraint on the family mobility associated with the presence of children at home. We then proceeded to analyse the mobility patterns found among people who report routes, considering the general population, displacements of persons in charge of the household (and their partners) and the displacement of persons in charge of the household who reported living with children at different ages (1–17 years old). A gender variable was used to compare the impact of the presence of children on the routes of men and women in these strata. A cut was made on the level of education of the interviewees, in order to compare different family dynamics in unequal socioeconomic contexts. For this analysis, the income of the individual was not considered due to a large number of women without any income in different educational strata, which could bias our reading. The following were considered for the descriptive statistics: the motivations of the route, the mode of transport used and the ratio of trips per journey, namely, how many trips are carried for each journey – again, taking into account the existing bibliography about the mobility of care and multitasking trips (Jirón, 2007; Madariaga, 2013).

4. RESULTS

4.1. Immobility

The exploratory analysis of the 2012 O–D Survey showed that approximately 40% of the population interviewed had not taken any routes on the day before the survey (reference day used for data collection). Such a high number motivated us to also direct our analysis to immobility. The choice to devote some research time to this sample stratum, however, is confronted with some specific limitations. In the O–D Survey, the expansion factor is calculated by two components, the first being the population expansion factor: the ratio between the number of households according to the census and the number of households surveyed in each homogeneous area of territorial division. The second component is the travel calibration factor, which represents the number of trips that a given response represents in the RMBH. What limits the analysis is the fact that the 2012 O–D Survey presents only the final expansion factor of the trips, formed by the multiplication of the population factor with the calibration factor (Bhtrans, 2016). This means that those people who did not travel the day before – the stratum here analysed – do not have the expansion factor, making it impossible to infer the results obtained with this sample for the rest of the RMBH universe. It is therefore necessary to clarify that in this part of the analysis, the results are of a *sample*, not the population. Thus, it will be called *immobility sample*.

The data from this stratum show a significantly higher number of people with permanent or temporary disabilities, very advanced age (over 65 years old) or very young (up to 4 years old), as well as people who are unemployed or whose income is below minimum wage, endorsing results already found in other studies and reports (Mauttone & Hernandez, 2017; Tanzarn, 2008). The aim, however, was to find out how much of this population lived with young children at home, and it was found an amount almost 10 times higher in the immobility sample than the value for people living with children under five than in the total population interviewed. When describing how multitasking trips increase among mothers cohabiting with their children, but not among fathers, Madariaga (2013) uses 5-year-old children as a reference age. Using such reference, it was found that 26.23% of the immobility sample consisted of adults living with children aged five or under – the value found in the total population was of only 2.68%.

This information was used to analyse how much the age of the children influenced the presence of people responsible for them in the sample.[8] The result can be seen in Table 3.1.

One can see that the older the children,[9] the lower the percentage of persons without mobility the previous day. The high values found pointed to a disturbing immobility of people who have small children – who need care and often need to be accompanied for their displacements – in their households. Some factors have already been pointed out as crucial to increasing or decreasing urban mobility, such as income, physical abilities of the person, place of dwell, organisation of transport systems or even their availability, among others, in a multidimensional dynamics (Cass et al., 2005; Toledo, 2019). The data found suggest that family organisation should also be a factor taken into account when thinking about people's mobility and motility through space, as conceptualised by Kaufmann, Bergman, and Joye (2004), meaning the capacity of people to be mobile in the geographic or social space.

4.2. Mobility

For the analysis of mobility, three main aspects in different population groups were taken into account: (1) the motivation of the trips; (2) the modes of transport used; and (3) the ratio of trips per journey (how many trips are made for each

Table 3.1. Percentage of Persons Responsible for Children in the Immobility Sample.

Age of Cohabiting Children (y.o.)	Responsible in the Sample (%)	Cumulative (%)
1	6.51	6.51
2	6.44	12.95
3	5.48	18.43
4	4.46	22.89
5	3.34	26.23
6	2.13	28.36
7	1.29	29.65
8	1.06	30.71
9	0.72	31.43
10	0.51	31.94
11	0.58	32.52
12	0.51	33.03

Source: Own elaboration.

journey). Also, the following population groups were considered: (a) the population in general, dividing the results for men and women; (b) men and women who declared themselves to be responsible for the household (and their partner); and (c) men and women who declared themselves responsible for the household and were cohabiting with children or adolescents from 1 to 17 years old.[10] The data of heads of household were also analysed according to their level of education.

4.2.1. Motivation

The objective in analysing the motivations of the trips of the mentioned populations is to verify if and how much the presence of the children in the domestic environment influences the number of trips realised for the purpose of taking care of the household and the family. It will also be able to check what other purposes diminish to the detriment of care mobility.

For the analysis of the motivations, the ones referring to the return to the house and the scales performed in the trips were suppressed. As mobility of care, the motivations of health, purchasing and escorting were grouped, according to the previously mentioned proposal of Madariaga (2013). The O–D Survey conducted at RMBH does not allow one to divide the purchasing motivation between what is bought for oneself or for the home/family, as it has already been done in other mobility studies (Mauttone & Hernandez, 2017). It is necessary to emphasise that for this analysis, as well as for the following ones, the expansion factor was considered, and it was possible to expand the results for the RMBH population. Taking the population in general, then, regardless of the responsibility for the household, the presence of children or the level of schooling, it is possible to observe the following (Figs. 3.1 and 3.2).

It was noticed that the main differences in the motivation of the trips are found in the values referring to the percentages of trips performed for work, care and leisure. While the men of this population have 46.96% of their trips destined for work, this figure is 34.82% for women. Contrarily, 18.76% of women's trips are

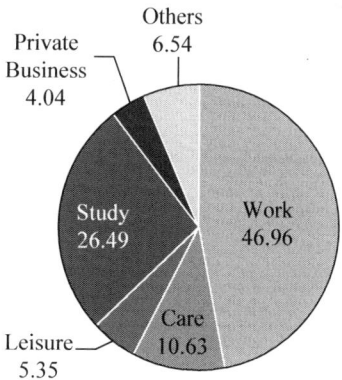

Fig. 3.1. Route Motivation of Men of RMBH. *Source*: Own elaboration

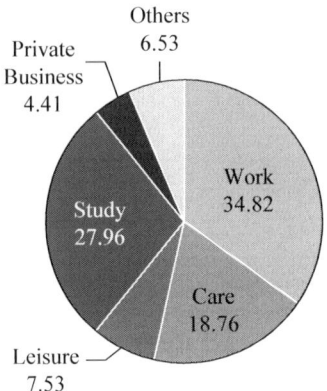

Fig. 3.2. Route Motivation of Women of RMBH. *Source*: Own elaboration.

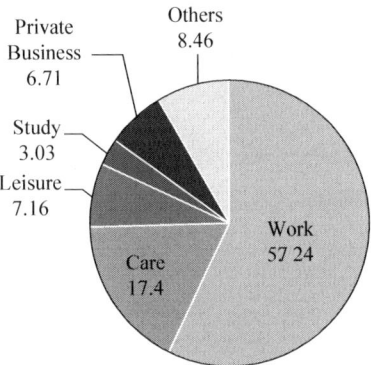

Fig. 3.3. Route Motivations of Men Responsible for the Household. *Source*: Own elaboration.

associated with care, compared to only 10.63% of men. A small difference is recorded in terms of leisure time, where women have 2.18% more trips for this purpose when compared to men.

If one observes the standards of the men and women who declared themselves responsible for their household, there is a similar scenario, but with more accentuated differences. Work and care mobility increases for both genders, while for study purposes, the values are very low. Although work-related mobility remains relatively close to that of the general population (from 46.96% to 57.24% for men and from 34.82% to 37.52% for women), the increase that is seen in the mobility of care in the case of women in charge of the household (from 18.76% to 30.54%) shows that, in this situation, almost a third of all the mobility performed by them was related to care work – a value 13.14% higher than what is found in the case of men in the same situation (Figs. 3.3 and 3.4).

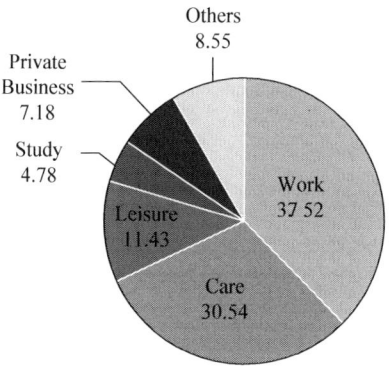

Fig. 3.4. Route Motivations of Women Responsible for the Household.
Source: Own elaboration.

When considering the presence of children in the household, it was noticed how their age influences the motivations of adults in specific ways according to the gender of the one responsible for the household. Table 3.2 and Fig. 3.5 show how. As we track the frequency of trips engaged by motivations of care, work and others trough sex, a clear pattern appears. We have chosen to highlight it by showing the percentage difference between men and women concerning trips of work and care – those who appeared with most singular differences. The percentage difference values (gray column) were calculated from the difference between women and men. That is, when cohabiting with a 1-year-old children, men presented 69.85% of work-motivated journeys and women had 35%; this means that the value of the journeys made by women for this purpose was 99.57% lower (−99.57) than that presented by men. Contrarily, in the mobility of care, only 8.74% of the journeys made by men had this purpose, against 28.57% of those made by women. Thus, we had that the frequency of care trips performed by women in this context was 69.40% higher than men.

Clearly, as it has been seen in the general chart for home caregivers, the mobility of care is unevenly distributed and always shows higher values for the women responsible for the household (or spouses of the caregiver). It is relevant to highlight, however, how the increase–decrease dynamics of the care mobility according to the children's age occur. It is possible to see inverted tendencies of increase–decrease in the number of trips destined for care in the curve of men and women, as on the initial years of the child, the mobility destined to care grows among the male population, but from the fourth year of age on, one can notice a continuous crescent in care mobility of responsible women until the age of seven – the highest value for care trips, for both women and men.

As to the trips destined to work, it is perceived that again there is a difference that is sustained in values, always superior in the case of the men. The greatest inequality found reaches 42.95% in a scenario with 6-year-old children at home,

Table 3.2. Influence of the Age of Cohabiting Children on the Motivations of Adult Caregivers.

Motivation of Routes (%)

	Work			Care			Leisure		Study		Priv. Business		Others	
	Men	Women	Difference	Men	Women	Difference	Men	Women	Men	Women	Men	Women	Men	Women
Age of Cohabiting Children (y.o.) 1	69.85	35	−99.57	8.74	28.56	69.40	4.69	15.6	3.24	3.08	4.53	10.06	8.96	7.7
2	68.83	34.62	−98.82	15.29	25.92	41.01	2.2	10.05	3.68	5.62	1.86	18.85	8.13	4.94
3	75.97	45.01	−68.78	7.4	32.29	77.08	2.37	7.27	3.69	4.12	4.12	4.88	6.45	6.44
4	65.7	48.87	−34.44	15.34	29.96	48.80	5.33	4.72	4.63	3.29	1.99	3.06	7.01	10.1
5	63.24	36.8	−71.85	16.08	33.8	52.43	4.25	6.51	4.38	5.26	2.85	6.76	9.21	10.87
6	71.63	28.68	−149.76	14.61	39.38	62.90	2.1	5.47	2.5	2.69	2.77	11.81	6.39	11.97
7	61.9	28.16	−119.82	16.12	45.33	64.44	2.54	6.13	3.4	6.91	5.04	2.58	11	10.89
8	59.32	31.23	−89.95	20.39	40.38	49.50	7.26	6.6	2.77	4.34	2.92	3.88	7.35	13.57
9	62.02	31.52	−96.76	19.34	40.09	51.76	3.44	6.63	6.15	4.71	1.84	7.35	7.21	9.71
10	63.07	33.26	−89.63	13.47	41.82	67.79	6.34	7.64	3.52	2.91	4.14	5.23	9.46	9.15
11	64.96	33.97	−91.23	15.63	38.41	59.31	3.57	6.09	2.73	7.3	3.51	3.33	9.6	10.88
12	63.4	38.91	−62.94	18.3	31.85	42.54	4.23	7.36	2.11	3.54	4.54	6.3	7.41	12.04
13	69.22	45.1	−53.48	15.76	31.62	50.16	4.17	8.35	2.31	4.21	2.71	3.66	5.84	7.07
14	66.96	46.44	−44.19	14.56	31.76	54.16	3.93	4.93	2.69	5.57	3.82	4.37	8.05	6.93
15	67.7	46.34	−46.09	14.45	26.89	46.26	2.97	8.61	2.89	5.45	3.89	5.66	8.1	7.04
16	68.64	47.81	−43.57	11.15	22.77	51.03	7.86	8.23	2.8	7.07	2.55	7	7	7.13
17	68.59	49.57	−38.37	11.61	21.43	45.82	4.64	7.55	1.87	5.35	3.97	6.5	9.32	9.61

Source: Own elaboration.

Children and Urban Mobility 71

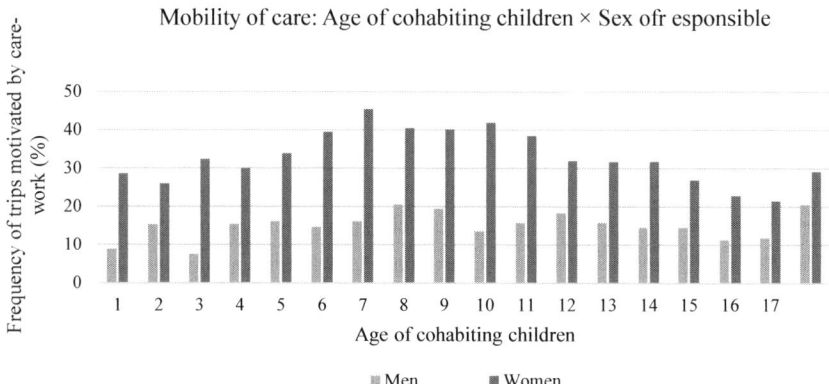

Fig. 3.5. Influence of the Age of Cohabiting Children on the Mobility of the Care of Adults in Charge of Household. *Source*: Own elaboration.

where work mobility occupies 71.63% of the male trips and only 28.68% of the female ones. In regard to leisure mobility, there is high percentage found in the case of women with 1-year-old infants at home – values that decrease systematically up to 4 years and then oscillate between 6% and 8%. One consideration that can be made with regard to this observation is about the sense of leisure: caring, and thus, rides made with infants or with small children are generally interpreted as pleasurable activities for mothers and fathers with children, but may also be interpreted as care *work* (Hirata, 2002), being experienced by those responsible for the household in an ambiguous way, sometimes there are feelings of pleasure and joy, but also anguish, stress and sadness (Molinier, 2012).

When analysing the motivations of care under the perspective of the degree of education, one perceives nuances that remain invisible when we focus on the gender of the responsible for the household (Table 3.3).

It is perceived specific dynamics considering this indirect indicator of class, strata of low, medium and high schooling, regarding both the trips destined to work and care. We recall that the data refer to men and women who declare themselves responsible for households, and thus, there are those with only preschool education performing fewer work-related courses than any other stratum analysed – both men and women. Contrarily, they are the ones that present the highest values related to the mobility of care and leisure – although the inequality between the values presented by men and women remains.

It is also noticeable that the differences between men and women decrease with the increase in schooling – both for work and care trips. In the case of care, we can relate this pattern to factors such as the outsourcing of care (Hirata & Kergoat, 2007; Molinier, 2012), in which people with higher incomes, associated with high schooling, have more ways to outsource home and child care tasks. Among the examples of outsourcing are the hiring of maids, a private school bus service or even a private driver. One can also point out the tendency of lower birth rates in high schooling families, who have access to more information on family planning

Table 3.3. Motivation of Trips by Level of Education.

		Motivation of Trips by Level of Education					
		Work			Care		
		Men	Women	Difference (%)	Men	Women	Difference (%)
Level of Education	Pre-school ed.	37.32	16.67	−123.88	25.17	39.4	36.12
	Incomplete basic ed.	55.68	30.92	−80.08	18.17	35.89	17.72
	Complete basic ed.	60.97	36.01	−69.31	17.48	33.3	15.82
	Incomplete secondary ed.	59.6	35.47	−68.03	16.55	32.16	15.61
	Complete secondary ed.	60.96	40.85	−49.23	17.5	29.97	12.47
	Incomplete university ed.	48.69	34.3	−41.95	13.21	16.91	3.70
	Complete university ed.	56.43	47.47	−18.88	16.64	24.48	7.84
	Postgraduate	59.44	47.87	−24.17	13.4	20.48	7.08

Source: Own elaboration.

and often postpone pregnancy (Saboia, Cobo, & Matos, 2012). This scenario can be related to an adoption of more traditional gender role division and a consequent more traditional sharing of the house chores between men and women in families with lower educational levels (Amâncio & Wall, 2004; IBGE, 2018).

Finally, we cross-referred the data on the level of education and age of the cohabiting children with respect specifically to the mobility of care. The findings can be analysed through the following chart. In the shades of red, we can see how mobility of care patterns alters throughout the realities of women who cohabit with children of different ages. The darker the colour, the lower the age. In blue, we see how that functions for men (Fig. 3.6).

Although values vary between ages and levels of education, one can find some patterns regarding the differences between men and women in different contexts. It is possible to see the confirmation of trends found in the previous data: the high participation of men with fewer schooling years in the tasks of care and the reduction of the differences between men and women with the increase in schooling. One curious fact that appears in this graph, however, is the great difference in the mobility of care among men and women with the highest level of education. Regarding the age of children, significant patterns associated with schooling were not found.

4.2.2. Mode of Transport

As to the mode of transport, specific differences in terms of gender, schooling and the presence of children at home were found. For a better understanding of the results, we grouped the data under non-motorised mode, collective and individual motorised[11] for this analysis. For the general population divided between men and women, the findings show the following (Figs. 3.7 and 3.8).

In agreement with other research already carried out on the use of gender and transport modes (Tanzarn, 2008), we find that women are the majority in non-motorised and collective modes, while men are the majority when referring to

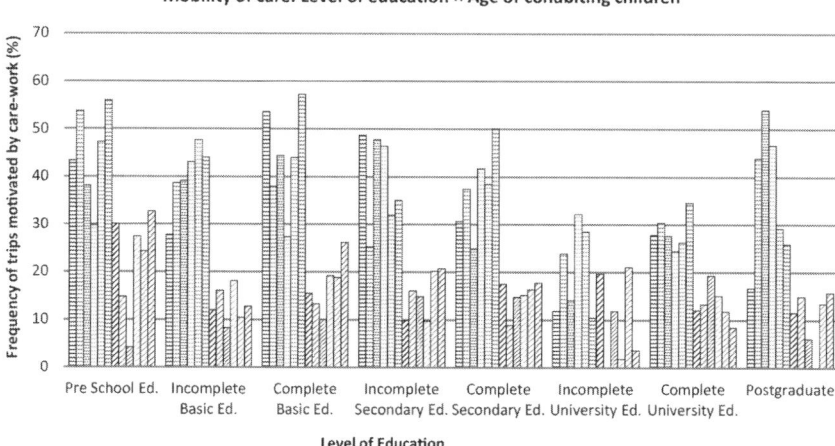

Fig. 3.6. Influence of the Educational Level and Age of Cohabiting Children in the Mobility of Care. *Source*: Own elaboration.

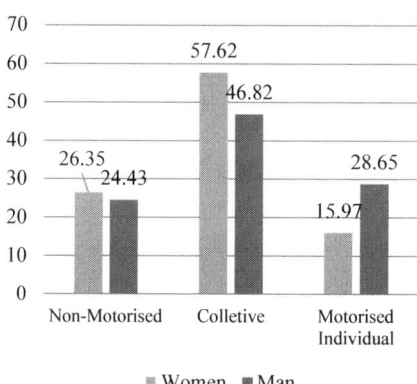

Fig. 3.7. Modes – General Population. *Source*: Own elaboration.

motorised individual mode. When comparing this data with the one of the heads of households, we noticed that there is a small decrease in non-motorised use by men and women (more significant in the case of men), maintenance of collective use and a significant increase in the use of motorised individual mode for both men and women – although the difference between genders remains unchanged in all modes. Some hypotheses can be raised regarding these changes, imagining a higher income of those in charge of the household, their greater responsibility and tasks to be performed and, according to Scheiner and Holz-Rau (2012), the priority of car use by the 'head of the family' man.

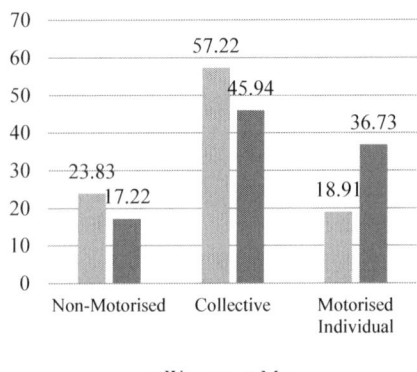

Fig. 3.8. Modes – Household Heads. *Source*: Own elaboration.

As to the presence of children at home and their influence on modes of transportation, the following data were found (Figs. 3.9–3.11).

In addition to the endorsement of differences between genders found in the general analysis of the population and persons responsible for the household, one can point out from the data some changes associated with the age of the cohabiting children. As for the non-motorised mode, it is referred mainly to walking trips since the percentage of bicycle trips in the city of Belo Horizonte is close to 2%. It was noticed that in the case of women, there is a decrease in their frequency in the first 2 years of life, and, after this age, the values remain above the average of the general stratum of women responsible for the household – being most evident when children are between 6 and 14 years of age, which may be associated with children's school age and their greater autonomy after the age of 14. In the case of men, there is also a decrease in the frequency of active trips, and only when children reach the ages of seven and eight, the values are higher than what it was seen in the general data of heads of household.

Regarding the collective mode, it is seen that the difference between men and women is the lowest when compared to the other modes. However, in most cases, women continue to be the majority in the frequency of trips. When coexisting with children younger than 12 years old, the values of use of collective transportation in the case of women were below than what was seen in the general average of heads of the household. The values for men vary by up to 3% from the difference of the reference value found, with no explicit relation with the age of the cohabiting children, except when there is the presence of 1-year-old children at home: 44%.

The main inequalities are noticed in the motorised individual mode. If the average value for men responsible for the household was of 36.73% performed by car or motorcycle, it is observed until their child's age of six, the male values are significantly higher – except for when they have children in the age of four. The highest value for the use of the motorised individual mode is when there are 1-year-old children at home, for both men (47.82%) and women (28.8%). For those cohabiting with children who are 14 years old and older, it is possible to notice that the frequency of use of this mode is below the average for both genders of those

Children and Urban Mobility 75

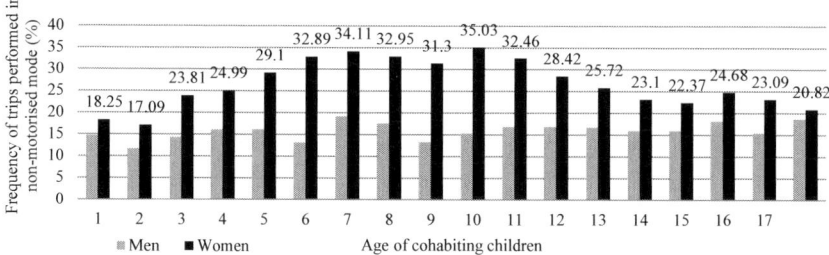

Fig. 3.9. Influence of Cohabiting Children in Non-motorised Mode.
Source: Own elaboration.

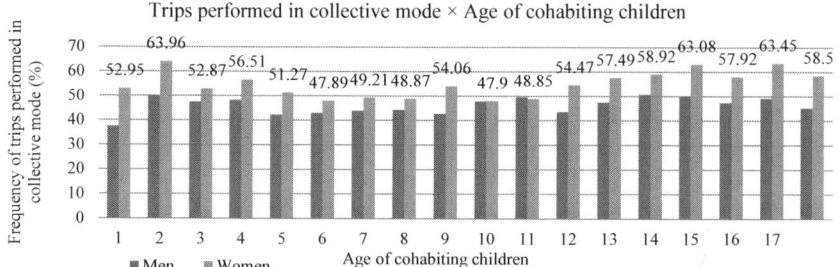

Fig. 3.10. Influence of Cohabiting Children in Collective Mode.
Source: Own elaboration.

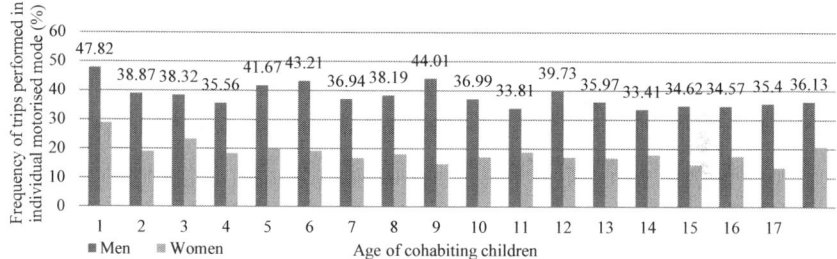

Fig. 3.11. Influence of Cohabiting Children in Motorised Individual Mode.
Source: Own elaboration.

responsible for the household. In the case of women, despite a higher oscillation of frequencies, there are also the highest values between the ages of one and six.

Concerning the age of the cohabiting children and the mode of transport used, it is possible to see that there is a clear preference for motorised individual mode until at least the sixth year of the children. We also see that there is a decrease in collective and non-motorised use by those responsible for the household when there are very young children at home. Also, it was noticed an increase in women's active mode when cohabiting with children of 6 years of age. That extends until the 14th year of age of children. Regarding the collective transportation, male mobility does not change significantly according to the age group of the children at home.

It is necessary to analyse the use of modes of transportation from a class perspective, in this study the educational level, once in our context the possession of a car is not a reality for the entire population. Thus, Fig. 3.12 shows how the possibility of access to a car is associated with certain social strata and is configured as a privilege, associated with both gender and educational level. As discussed by Jirón (2007), those who have the possibility to choose financially between using a motorised individual mode and a collective or active one very often choose the first, leaving those who cannot choose to the fate of a precarious public service or their own body. Also, the following lines point out once more the permanent inequalities between men and women in terms of access to the car and frequencies of trips carried out collectively or non-motorised. The smallest differences found between men and women are at the extremes of educational levels: in contexts of high vulnerability in households where those in charge of the household have only elementary education or in those with a postgraduate degree. In Fig. 3.12, we can see how this functions in our context.[12]

When the data are crossed to evaluate the influence of the age of coexisting children in the use of transport modes by men and women from different educational and social contexts, the following results were found (Figs. 3.13–3.15).

Crossing the data leads us to realise that the patterns and the most significant changes regarding the access difficulties of people with low educational level are more associated with this issue and with the gender matters than with the age of cohabiting children. It is clearly perceived the greater tendency to use the motorised individual mode with the increase in schooling, and the higher frequencies of the use of collective and active modes in people with lower educational

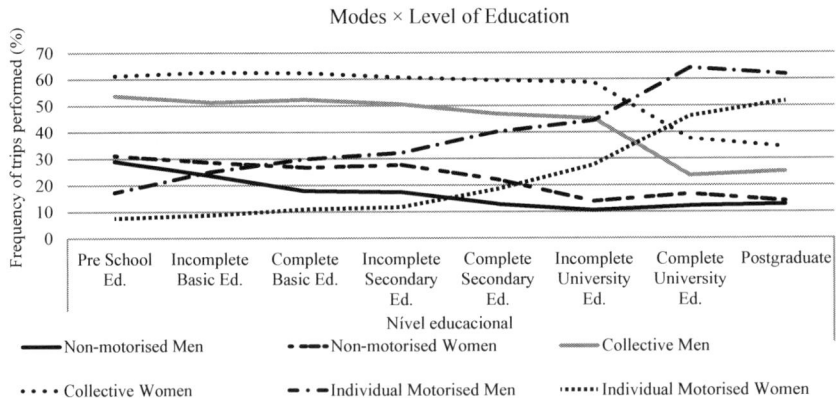

Fig. 3.12. Influence of the Level of Education in Transport Mode.
Source: Own elaboration.

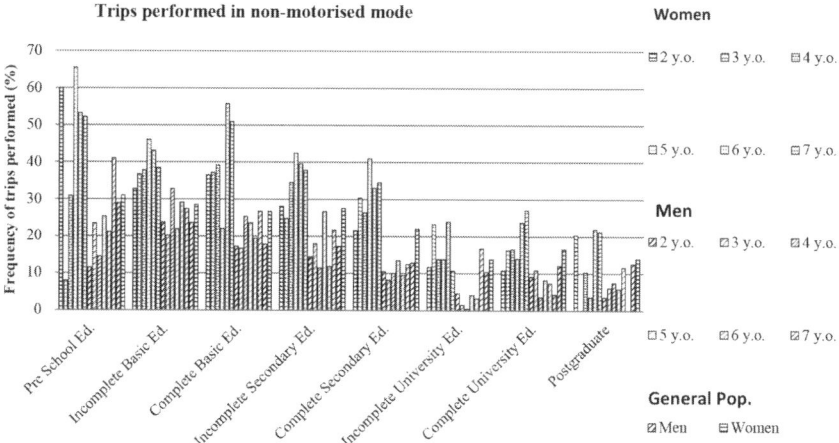

Fig. 3.13. Influence of the Age of Cohabiting Children and Level of Education in Non-motorised Use. *Source*: Own elaboration.

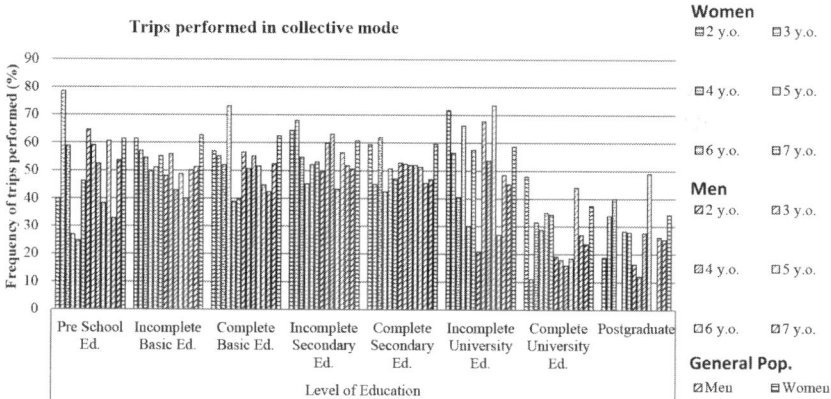

Fig. 3.14. Influence of the the Age of Cohabiting Children and Level of Education in Collective Use. *Source*: Own elaboration.

level. Moreover, the particularities with regard to the needs of young children (up to 2 years old in a very explicit way, and from 2 to 6 years old in a more lenient way), in addition to the needs of children from 7 to 14 years-old, mainly regarding the active mode, had already been perceived in the general data of the heads of household and were only confirmed in the previous charts, without significant changes in relation to schooling.

4.2.3. Ratio of Trips per Journey

It was decided to calculate the trips per journey due to the existing bibliography about multitasking trips that were already discussed. Once the format of the O–D

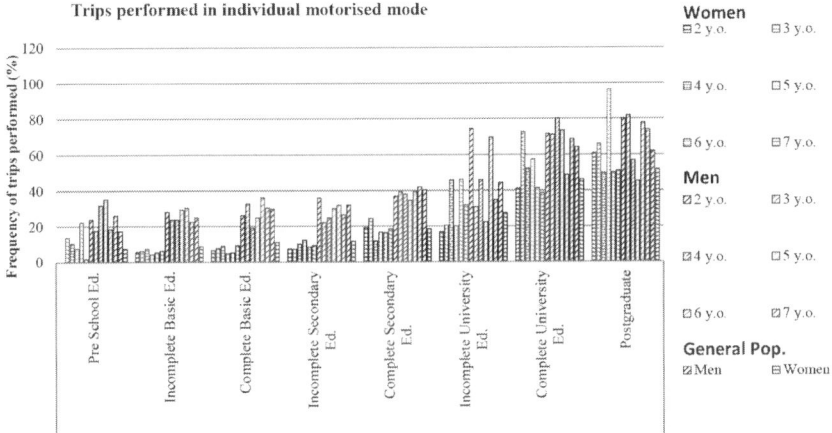

Fig. 3.15. Influence of the Age of Cohabiting Children and Level of Education in Motorised Individual Use. *Source*: Own elaboration.

Table 3.4. Ratio of Trips per Journey.

	Ratio of Trips per Journey	Men	Women
Strata	General value	1.39	1.53
	Responsible for household	1.33	1.43
	Cohabiting with children until 7 y.o.	1.45	1.49
	Low ed. level	1.49	1.67
	Medium ed. level	1.44	1.66
	High ed. level	1.26	1.38
	Low ed. + child until 7 y.o.	1.48	1.54
	Medium ed. + child until 7 y.o.	1.48	1.53
	High ed. + child until 7 y.o.	1.30	1.33

Source: Own elaboration.

Survey allows one to differentiate the trips of the journeys made by each person interviewed, it has been brought the ratio of trips by journey of the population strata that have been worked on. In order to compress data, educational levels were narrowed down to three bands: low, medium and high schooling – low for those who declared having up to elementary education, medium for those who declared to have complete or incomplete high school, and high for those who had performed at least part of higher education or up. The ratio of trips per journey indicates how many trips that population stratum performs on average for each journey, that is, if there is a ratio of 1.5 trips per journey, it means that an individual travels one and a half times each journey, or that every two trips they make a stop on the way. The results can be checked in Table 3.4.

One can see from Table 3.4 that women from selected strata always outnumber men in number of trips per journey. However, people with high schooling are those who carry out the least multitasking trips from this indicator and are also the stratum that presents the least difference between men and women. The presence of children at home did not appear to be a factor that significantly increased the number of trips among women, but it appeared to have an impact on the quantity realised by men in general.

5. CONCLUSION

Based on the data analysed, it was possible to see that the age range of the cohabiting children affects the mobility of those responsible for the household in specific ways according to their gender and educational level. We see that there is an increase in the mobility related to care work for men and women when there is the presence of children in the home, but there is a constant inequality between the number of trips they carry out for this purpose: women, in all levels of education and in all age groups of the children, perform more care trips than men. We also see that men have a higher percentage than women when we analyse the work-related trips. The motivation that presents the greatest decrease with the presence of children at home is that of the study.

Different ages of cohabiting children show different patterns of mobility of the people responsible for the household, in which in the first years, there is an increase in the male participation in the mobilities motivated by the care – never overcoming women's – and from the third year of age of the child, such participation decays. From 4 to 7 years of age, the number of trips carried out by women in charge of the household for this purpose rises to their maximum, corresponding to almost 45% of the trips carried out by them.

When analysing the differences found between men and women with different educational levels, no significant changes were observed in the mobility and use of transportation in relation to the age of the children, but the tendencies of public and active transportation evasion are explicitly seen as there is an increase in schooling and, probably, in the income of those responsible for the household. It seems that opportunities (or lack thereof) due to access to education are a greater burden on the mobility of heads of households than the presence of children in their homes. The mobility identified by Jirón (2000, 2007) as a factor not only of maintaining inequalities but of generating them is related to this reality: inequalities of income and distribution of mobility equipment by the city, for example, tend to drive those who have greater resources to use alternative, private mobility modes, while constraining those who do not have such resources to use only the available forms, generating disparities in the use of time and access to places of work, study, leisure and consumption (Jirón, 2007).

The high level of immobility of people living with small children at home and the increase in the number of motorised individual modes (cars or motorcycles) in the initial years of children also point to the inefficiency or the inadequacy of the collective transportation system and infrastructure for active mobility that addresses the demands of children and their caregivers. Micklow, Kancilia, and Warner (2015) show that in the US context, the needs of women or people with children are not identified by urban planners as a work theme, and this is a reason to be concerned about. Qualitative research has shown in more details the specific needs of those responsible for small children in the use of public transportation, such as the convenience of spaces to allocate large and medium volumes (e.g. school backpacks or grocery bags), the presence of ramps so that small children do not face difficulties to hop in and also a higher frequency of buses so that they do not come so full and offer some kind of risk for the younger ones (Jirón, 2007).

The gender perspective adopted in this study allowed us to compare the mobility of care of men and women relationally, discussing at all moments *gendered mobilities* – not just feminine mobilities. It is in contexts of higher vulnerability and higher schooling that the smaller differences between the mobilities of men and women are seen, and we also perceive the increase of the masculine mobility of care when they cohabit with children of 1 or 2 years old. It is important to emphasise that the mobility of care should not be associated with or attached to women's mobility, a connection that can once again contribute to a narrative that places care tasks on women's hands.

Despite these nuances, in all the scenarios analysed, the difference in the frequency of care work performed in the mobility between men and women always appears. To a greater or lesser degree, women performed more care-related trips regardless of schooling or the age of cohabiting children. Although the distances oscillate between men and women, the inequality remains. The gender division of labour is reflected in mobility as analysed, but the effort of this research, as directed by Hirata and Kergoat (2007), was to analyse in what conditions this distance increases or decreases.

Thinking about the concept of access as the spatial dimension of exclusion or social inclusion opens many doors for researchers and policymakers place gender inequalities in the city. Considering access in this sense is not only about the places where people arrive more or less easily – as in the concept of accessibility proposed by Neutens (2010, with Schwanen et al., 2015) – although this is already a key issue. From this point, one can stress that gender equality policies need to be debated also in the areas of urban planning and transport. Besides that, when adding to the mobility spectrum the imaginative or discursive ones, but, in addition, to add to the mobilities discussion also those that can be imaginative or discursive, Sheller and Urry (2016) suggest the task of tracking narratives and practices of mobility that may be the cause of movement or static. It seems to us that the discourses about the type of work to be done by men and women in the domestic sphere are relevant and are reflected on serious obstacles to equal access to the city. *How* have the people responsible for young children reached destinations and, perhaps more importantly, *where* have they gone and *where have they ceased to go* for this reason must also be questions raised when discussing this spatial dimension of exclusion. Considering the number of trips carried out by women based on the responsibility of care, one can affirm that there is here, as in the studies of Siqueira (2015), Elvir (2016), Kwan (2000), and Valentine (1989), a narrowing of cities for these women. No less narrow seems to be the way of men to and from work. To which extent are they capable of moving through social and geographical space?

This study shows a few more mobile borders to which we must be attentive as scientists and policymakers as well. Hjorthol (2008) has already warned about the large number of trips women perform for other family members when they have access to a car. Movement through space or hypermobility will not necessarily be related to the enlargement of one's city but may be associated with confinement to certain spaces, tasks or experiences in the geographic and social space.

The insertion of the social sciences in mobility studies has contributed to the formulation of interdisciplinary projects in the area of urban planning and transportation. By proposing a systemic view of the city and its individuals, integrated policy planning for transportation, housing and health, but also for gender and care should and can occupy the same discussion arenas.

NOTES

1. Information from the Development Agency of the Metropolitan Region of Belo Horizonte (RMBH).
2. Data available for consultation on the platform of the Brazilian Institute of Geography and Statistics https://cidades.ibge.gov.br/brasil/mg/belo-horizonte/panorama.
3. Data collected in 2012 and available on the website of the Bhtrans Mobility Observatory http://www.bhtrans.pbh.gov.br/portal/page/portal/portalpublico/Temas/ObservatorioMobilidade/Indicadores.
4. Information from the Human Development Atlas, available for consultation in http://atlasbrasil.org.br.
5. Human Development Atlas, <http://atlasbrasil.org.br>
6. Data available for consultation on the platform of the Brazilian Institute of Geography and Statistics <https://cidades.ibge.gov.br/brasil/mg/belo-horizonte/panorama>. For the most recent data, refer to the year of 2017.
7. Data available for consultation at the Belo Horizonte City Hall website: https://prefeitura.pbh.gov.br/bhtrans/informacoes/dados/mapa-de-declividades.
8. We considered as 'responsible' the person who declared to be the 'head' of the household and their partner.
9. The Child and Adolescent Statute (Brazilian Law No. 8,069, of 13 July 13 1990) considers children those who have up to 12 incomplete years of age.
10. The minimum age registered in the O-D Survey is of 1 year old.
11. The trips classified as 'Others' never reached a sum greater than 1% of the data and were therefore deleted from the charts for better visualisation. They were related to trips performed in airplanes, trucks or other modes per se, such as buggies or skates.
12. For an easier visualisation, all the lighter colours refer to women's patterns.

REFERENCES

Amâncio, L., & Wall, K. (2004). Família e Papéis de Gênero: Alguns dados recentes do Family and Gender Survey (ISSP). *A Questão Social no Novo Milênio*. Coimbra: CES/FEUC.

Best, H., & Lanzendorf, M. (2005). Division of labour and gender differences in metropolitan car use: An empirical study in Cologne, Germany. *Journal of Transport Geography*, *13*, 109–121.

Bhtrans. (2012). Relatório Completo Pesquisa Origem Destino 2011–2012. Retrieved from http://www.agenciarmbh.mg.gov.br/wp-content/uploads/2016/06/Relatorio-Completo-Pesquisa-OD-2012-1.pdf

BHTRANS. (2016a). Balanço da mobilidade Urbana de Belo Horizonte.

Bhtrans. (2016b). Manual das Pesquisas Origem Destino 2002–2012.

Brevis, H. R. (2016). Movilidad cotidiana: entre la producción y reproducción social. Una exploración a las prácticas de desplazamiento de dos mujeres en Temuco. *Revista Pilquen*, *19*(4), 14–31.

Cass, N., Shove, E., & Urry, J. (2005). Social exclusion, mobility and access. *The Sociological Review*, *53*(3), 539–555.
Castillo, R. A. (2017). Mobilidade geográfica e acessibilidade: uma proposição teórica. *Geousp – Espaço e Tempo*, *21*(3), 644–649.
De Lima, J. H., Monteiro, I. M., & Maia, M. L. A. (2017). Vagão Rosa: Segregação ou segurança? Presented at the XXXI Congresso Nacional de Pesquisa em Transporte ANPET, Recife, Brasil.
Elvir, A. M. (2016). Mulher e Mobilidade Urbana: Processos metodológicos e desafios de pesquisa na interpretação do discurso das mulheres do Coque. *Diversidade De Gênero E Sexual: Produção De Conhecimento, Aparatos Culturais E Possibilidades De Constituição De Si E Dos Outros* (Vol. 18, pp. 4072–4085). São Cristóvão: Universidade Federal de Sergipe.
Geurs, K., & Van Wee, B. (2004). Accessibility evaluation of land-use and transport strategies: Review and research directions. *Journal of Transport Geography*, *12*, 127–140.
Hirata, H. (2002). *Nova Divisão Sexual do Trabalho? Um olhar voltado para a empresa e a sociedade*. São Paulo: Boitempo
Hirata, H., & Danièle, K. (2007). Novas Configurações da Divisão Sexual do Trabalho. *Cadernos de Pesquisa*, *37*(132), 595–609.
Hirata, H., & Kergoat, D. (2007). Novas Configurações da Divisão Sexual do Trabalho. *Cadernos de Pesquisa*, *37*(132), 595–609.
Hjorthol, R. (2008). Daily mobility of men and women: A barometer of gender equality? In T. P. Uteng & T. Cresswell (Eds.), *Gendered mobilities* (pp. 193–210). Farnham: Ashgate.
IBGE - Agência de Notícias. Rubinstein, Lícia. Retrieved August 6, 2018, from https://agenciadenoticias.ibge.gov.br/agencia-noticias/2012-agencia-de-noticias/noticias/19061-retratos-as-novas-caras-das-familias.html
Jirón, P. (2007). Implicancias de género en las experiencias de movilidad cotidiana urbana en Santiago de Chile. *Revista Venezoelana de Estudios de La Mujer*, *12*(29), 173–197.
Jirón, P., & Fadda, G. (2000). Gender in the discussion of quality of life vs. Quality of place. *Open House International*, *25*(4).
Kaufmann, V., Bergman, M. M., & Joye, D. (2004). Motility: Mobility as capital. *International Journal of Urban and Regional Research*, *28*(4), 745–756.
Kwan, M.-P. (2000). Gender differences in space–time constraints. *Area*, *32*(2), 145–156.
Lyra, L. (2016). *Por onde caminham as mulheres? Um estudo sobre os percursos cotidianos de mulheres diaristas em Belo Horizonte* (Mestrado). Universidade Federal de Minas Gerais, Belo Horizonte. Retrieved from http://www.mom.arq.ufmg.br/mom/biblioteca_novo_2/arquivos/lunalyra_dissertacao.pdf
Madariaga, I. (2013). Mobility of care: Introducing new concepts in urban transport. In I. Sánchez de Madariaga & M. Roberts (Eds.), *Fair shared cities: The impact of gender planning in Europe*. (pp. 49–69) Farnham: Ashgate.
Manderscheid, K. (2014). Criticising the solitary mobile subject: Researching relational mobilities and reflecting on mobile methods. *Mobilities*, *9*(2), 188–219.
Mauttone, A., & Hernandez, D. (2017). Encuesta de movilidad del área metropolitana de Montevideo. *Principales resultados e indicadores* (p. 73). Montevideo: CAF, Intendencia de Montevideo, Intendencia de Canelones, Intendencia de San José, Ministerio de Transporte y Obras Públicas, Universidad dela República, PNUD Uruguay.
Micklow, A., Kancilia, E., & Warner, M. (2015). The need to plan for women. *Planning with a gender lens: Issue brief*. New York, NY: Cornell University.
Molinier, P. (2012). Ética e trabalho do care. *Cuidado e Cuidadoras. As várias faces do trabalho do care*. São Paulo: Atlas.
Neutens, T., Schwanen, T., Witlox, F., & De Maeyer, P., (2010). Equity of urban service delivery: a comparison of different accessibility measures. *Environ. Plann. A42*(7), 1613–1635.
Pereira, R. H. M. (n.d.). Ex-ante evaluation of the accessibility impacts of transport policy scenarios: Equity and sensitivity to travel time thresholds for Bus Rapid Transit expansion in Rio de Janeiro.
Pereira, R. H. M. (2018, March 23). Ex-ante evaluation of the accessibility impacts of transport policy scenarios: Equity and sensitivity to travel time thresholds for bus rapid transit expansion in Rio

De Janeiro. Retrieved from https://ssrn.com/abstract=3147748 or http://dx.doi.org/10.2139/ssrn.3147748

Prefeitura de São Paulo. (2016). A mobilidade das mulheres na cidade de São Paulo. *Informes Urbanos, 25*, 1–7.

Rosa, R. A. (2018). As mulheres e os territórios do cotidiano: uso do tempo e mobilidade feminina nas cidades de Belo Horizonte e Recife. 2018. 231 f. PUC-Minas, Belo Horizonte.

Saboia, A. L., Cobo, B., & Matos, G. G. (2012). Desafios e possibilidades da investigação sobre os novos arranjos familiares e a metodologia para identificação de família no Censo 2010. IBGE.

Scheiner, J., & Holz-Rau, C. (2012). Gender structures in car availability in car deficient households. *Research in Transportation Economics, 34*, 16–26.

Schwanen, T. (2007). Gender differences in chauffeuring children among dual-earner families. *The Professional Geographer, 59*(4), 447–462.

Schwanen, T., Lucas, K., Akyelken, N., Solsona, D. C., Carrasco, J.-A., & Neutens, T. (2015). Rethinking the links between social exclusion and transport disadvantage through the lens of social capital. *Transport Research Part A: Policy and Practice, 74*, 123–135.

Sheller, M., & Urry, J. (2006). The new mobilities paradigm. *Environment and Planning, 38*, 207–226.

Siqueira, L. (2015). *Por onde andam as mulheres? Percursos e medo que limitam a experiência de mulheres no centro do Recife*. Master's dissertation. Universidade Federal do Pernambuco, Recife, Brasil.

Svab, H. (2016). *Evolução dos padrões de deslocamento na Região Metropolitana de São Paulo: a necessidade de uma análise de gênero*. São Paulo: Universidade de São Paulo.

Tanzarn, N. (2008). Gendered mobilities in developing countries: The case of (urban) Uganda. In T. P. Uteng & T. Cresswell (Eds.), *Gendered mobilities* (pp. 159–171). Hampshire: Ashgate.

Toledo, J. (2019). *Análise multidimensional as barreiras que restringem a mobilidade urbana*. Master's dissertation. Universidade Federal do Rio de Janeiro, Rio de Janeiro, Brasil.

Valentine, G. (1989). The geography of women's fear. *Area, 21*(4), 385–390.

CHAPTER 4

'LIKE SARDINES IN A CAN'. GENDER, STRATIFICATION AND MOBILITY IN THE LIVES OF FEMALE HOUSEHOLD EMPLOYEES IN BOGOTÁ, COLOMBIA

Friederike Fleischer and Ivette S. Sepúlveda Sanabria

ABSTRACT

According to the Colombian Labour Ministry, in 2015, 750,000 persons officially worked as household employees. Ninety-eight per cent of these employees are women who tend to live in Bogotá's (southern) urban fringe and travel to the city's wealthier north on a daily basis. Yet public transportation in the Colombian capital is subject to stratification. Besides overcrowding and delays, petty crime and sexual harassment, fringe areas remain underserved. Based on ethnographic data, in this chapter, the authors discuss findings from a 3-year research project on female household employees' subjective experience of space. Specifically, the authors explore their capacity (motility) to be mobile. This perspective breaks with the limits of bounded categories such as 'urban', 'neighbourhood' or 'class', to highlight their situational and spatial mutability. Moreover, an investigation of motility includes people's potential to move as well as their subjective experiences of mobility. The research shows how gender intersects with local labour regimes and infrastructure to negatively affect women's mobility. Urban stratification is not only a question of locale of residence and access to services, but importantly (re)produced in the household employees' subjective experience of their daily commute, which they describe as suffering. In their limited spare time, female household employees abstain from travelling, effectively curbing their active appropriation of urban space. The research thus illuminates how spatial, social and economic dimensions mutually interact to impact on the women's lives and possibilities.

Keywords: Household employees (empleadas domésticas); gender; labour; stratification; motility; public transportation

1. INTRODUCTION

Bogotá, as other Latin American cities, is socio-economically and spatially highly stratified, as proven by indices showing income inequality, land prices and the location of informal settlements (Inostroza, Baur, & Csaplovics, 2013). As well as a centre – periphery distribution of inequality dating back to colonial times, Bogotá is divided between north and south, with a disproportioned accumulation of wealth in the city's north (Garcia & Gascón, 2016).[1] This stratification is spatially expressed in Bogotanos' mobility patterns. Whereas few wealthy residents make the journey to the city's southern parts, residents from these areas, and the urban fringe in general, frequently travel to the north, some on a daily basis (Alcaldía Mayor de Bogotá – Secretaría Distrital de Movilidad, 2015. For further detail see Appendix 'Bogotá'). Prime among these are female household employees (*empleadas domésticas*) who cross the divide between marginalised neighbourhoods and wealthy areas of the city twice daily, five to six times a week.

According to the Labour Ministry, in 2015, 750,000 persons worked as household employees in Colombia, 98% of who were women.[2] The household employee as an institution is fundamentally tied to socio-economic differentiations as women from lower classes work for higher income households. Moreover, many domestic workers migrated or were displaced from the countryside and came to the capital in search of better living conditions and safety. Thus, their mobility extends not only across local residential segregation but also across the rural–urban divide. While household employees share characteristics with other informal labourers, what sets the women apart are persisting gender ideologies that attribute them greater household and child-rearing responsibilities. Household employees' places of work are almost exclusively located in the privileged areas of the city. Yet, time constraints and locally held prejudices against lower class persons limit the benefits domestic employees could potentially derive from access to these exclusive spaces (Miralles-Guasch, 1998). The mobility and spatial experiences of empleadas domésticas are thus vital to understanding larger processes of urban mobility and social equity in Colombia and the region.

Based on ethnographic data, including participant observation and interviews with 27 women, as well as georeferencing of their daily movements, in this chapter, we discuss findings from our 2015–2018 research project on female households employees' subjective experience of space.[3] How do domestic workers use, perceive and experience urban space? How does the organisation of urban space impact their daily lives? What strategies do empleadas domésticas use to overcome urban spatial and conceptual barriers? And how do the women's practices reconfigure the city? Through these questions, we explore the issue of 'motility', that is, the women's 'capacity... to be mobile in social and geographic space' (Kaufmann, Bergman, & Joye, 2004, p. 750). This perspective breaks with the limits of bounded categories such as 'urban', 'neighbourhood' or 'class', to highlight their situational and spatial mutability. Moreover, whereas studies of spatial and socio-economic mobility focus solely on actual processes, an investigation of motility includes people's *potential* to move as well as their subjective experiences of mobility. The research shows how gender intersects with local labour regimes and infrastructure to negatively affect women's mobility. Urban stratification is not only a question of locale of residence and access to services, but importantly (re)produced in the household employee's subjective experience of their daily commute as suffering. In their limited spare time, female household employees abstain from travelling, effectively curbing their active appropriation of urban space. The research thus illuminates how spatial, social and economic dimensions mutually interact to negatively affect the living experience and life possibilities of one of the most mobile and excluded group of urban residents.

2. HOUSEHOLD LABOUR, SPACE AND MOBILITY

2.1 Empleadas Domésticas in Colombia

Since the publication of Chaney and Garcia's (1989) breakthrough study of household employees in Latin America, researchers have explored the legal and political situation of household employees in different countries in the region (Blofield, 2009; de Dios Herrero, 2006; Saldaña-Tejeda, 2012); household labour as women's work (Lautier 2003; Rico de Alonso 2001); and the relationship between employers and household employees (Casanova, 2013; Santos Alarcón, 2012). These investigations coincide in that the position of household employees is implicated with social, racial and economic hierarchies (Colen, 1990; Ehrenreich & Russell Hochschild, 2003). Economic necessity, family pressure, gender roles and class position have been identified as factors that contribute to women working in this sector despite its depreciatory and taxing nature (Gill, 1994).

Domestic labour has always been connected with migration. In recent years, as part of the paradigm of globalisation, international labour migration has been of prime interest. Studies have examined Colombian women working as household employees in different international contexts (Parreñas, 2001, 2005; Salzinger, 1991). Yet, as Harzig (2006) points out, historically, it has been rural-to-urban migration in combination with economic restructuring, economic inequalities and changes in the international division of labour, which has nourished the domestic labour sector.

A number of characteristics distinguish the sector in Latin America. Here migration to urban areas is disproportionately female, which has affected the labour force and family structures more generally (León, 2013; Rollins, 1990). In Colombia, according to García López (2012), a combination of factors has historically contributed to high numbers of women working as household employees. Beginning in the 1930s, the increasing size of families and economic pressure incited the young to look for work at an early age to help the household economy. The result was growing migration to the cities. Yet, until the mid-twentieth century, few women worked in the public sphere with the exception of waitresses, saleswomen and sex workers. Working as a household employee, in contrast, was considered appropriate for young women, especially because they usually lived with the families they worked for.[4] This labour arrangement was reflected in the urban architecture, whereby until recently, middle- and upper-class homes in Colombia included a separate room and bathroom close to the kitchen for the live-in domestic worker.

Today, according to the 'Informe Final Trabajadoras del Hogar en Colombia' (Centro de Cultura Popular José Antonio Galán, 2013), working conditions in the sector are precarious due to the high number of internally displaced in urban areas. With few options to generate income, women think their employers 'do them a favour' and give up even minimal labour rights. While the sector has been regulated by labour laws, and now offers social benefits and medical insurance, according to the Labour Ministry, only 8% of household employees have formal contracts in Colombia today.

2.2 Space and Mobility

In addition to their uncertain and unstable legal situation, household employees are excluded due to their social, economic, educational and often racial condition. This is further aggravated and indeed substantiated by their geographic marginalisation in the physical fringes and precarious areas especially in the capital's south. Female domestic workers' lives are marked by insecurity, long working hours and high levels of daily mobility.

Kaufmann et al. (2004, p. 750) employ the concept of 'motility' to describe

> the capacity of entities (e.g. goods, information or persons) to be mobile in social and geographic space, or as the way in which entities access and appropriate the capacity for socio-spatial mobility according to their circumstances.

That is, spatial possibilities do not only depend on the availability of financial means and transport, but importantly also on the appropriation of space. By using and moving through space, we make it our own and claim it for ourselves. De Certeau (1984) similarly suggests that walking realises the possibilities of space organised by the spatial order. The process 'affirms, suspects, tries out, transgresses, respects etc., the trajectories it "speaks"' (De Certeau, 1984, p. 99). Walking is thus framed as an elementary and embodied form of experiencing urban space – a productive, yet relatively unconscious, speaking/writing of the city (Collie, 2013, p. 3).

Importantly, however, the production of space is differential; not everybody has the same power in this process of appropriation: 'The actual or potential capacity for spatio-social mobility may be realised differently or have different consequences across varying socio-cultural contexts' (Kaufmann et al., 2004, p. 752). One important differential is gender. Feminist critique of discussions of space has helped to reveal the complexity of spatial agency in this respect. Authors such as Massey (1994) highlight how certain spaces are exclusionary in that they are envisioned as 'male'. Gendered space, in turn, reproduces exclusion and exclusiveness. Thus, the fear of sexual violence in public spaces and harassment in transport systems further marginalises women (Korn, 2018), making gender a determining element in accessibility and urban mobility. In the codification of space, the idea of the feminine and masculine is reproduced (Jirón, 2007; Soto, 2017).

In the same line, Uteng and Cresswell (2016) suggest that mobility *itself* constitutes gender (and race, we would add) and is constituted by it. From the common (though not universal) conception of masculinity as mobile and femininity as static to different kinds of mobility associated with gender (the male tourist, the female household employee), as well as gendered experiences of danger and safety, the interrelation between gender and mobility is vital to understanding social inequalities in contemporary cities. Yet, we argue, what is specific to the empleadas domésticas' motility is the intersection of gender, labour regimes and local conceptions of space and class.

Indeed, household employees in Bogotá are marked as 'other' in multiple ways. During her shift, the empleada wears a uniform that signals her status when running errands outside the employer's house. Yet beyond this, in Colombia, class is conceived as a corporeal quality: someone is lower class because of (supposed) habitus and looks. Skin colour, stature, sense of fashion, language and behaviour are all constructed as indicators of class. While there are no physical barriers, the multiple layers of stratification contribute to the association of parts of the city with certain socio-economic groups. The result of this socio-geographical stratification is the production of exclusionary and exclusive urban spaces. Those who do not belong to these groups are marked as outsiders, or worse, invaders. Moving in areas conceived of as upper- or middle-class spaces, empleadas domésticas are thus inherently 'out of place'.

Kaufmann et al.'s (2004) notion of motility helps us analyse the interdependent elements of mobility in that it encompasses *access* 'to different forms and degrees of mobility, *competence* to recognize and make use of access, and *appropriation* of a particular choice, including the option of non-action' (p. 750, emphasis theirs). As we will detail in the following, it is this non-action that is vital to understanding Bogotá's female household employees' gendered mobility.

3. BOGOTÁ'S PUBLIC TRANSPORTATION SYSTEM

Urban geography has focussed on experiences and social processes related to mobility and ease of access to homes, workplaces and recreational and leisure areas. From such a perspective, Ares (2010) and Urry (2011) examine the potential for mobility (motility); habitual territorial mobility (routes based on routine and repetition); obligatory mobility (occupational displacement); non-obligatory mobility (displacement for leisure purposes); and trajectories between personal spaces of activity and of residence. The research shows that transportation is extremely important in affecting people's well-being for better of worse: a well-designed and functioning public transportation system can substantially contribute to integrating the city and ameliorating the negative effects of a segregated morphology.

In the past, Bogotá's transportation system – private motorised transport and competing bus companies – was highly inefficient and congested. Licensed transit routes had multiple, individually owned or managed buses running on them. Bus drivers earned money based on the number of passengers, leading to the 'war of the centavo' – racing to pick up customers ahead of the competition. Reckless driving, disregard for bus stops or other traffic participants, poor bus maintenance and oversupply of vehicles further burdened the city (Gilbert, 2008, p. 444).

In 2000, Transmilenio, a bus rapid transit (BRT) system, was introduced to address the capital's public transportation system's shortcomings. Transmilenio was constructed in different stages and planned to eventually cover 80% of Bogotá's public transportation necessities (Ardila-Gómez, 2004). At the core are red articulated buses that run on two-lane exclusive corridors, with green feeder buses connecting more distant locations to the system's trunk routes. Buses belong to private companies contracted by the city and have to be replaced regularly; drivers are salaried employees; fares are independent of length of journey and collected by a separate, private company; and use of feeder buses is free. Transmilenio S.A., a city agency that operates on a commission basis, monitors and controls the system, using satellite tracking and wireless communication technology. Transmilenio S.A. does not receive subsidies, though public infrastructure construction and maintenance effectively means a substantial passive subsidy (Gilbert, 2008, pp. 442–443).[5]

As Cervero (2005) explains, then-mayor Enrique Peñalosa introduced Transmilenio as part of a wider urban development project that included (re)designed public spaces, pedestrianised zones and cycle paths. The aim was to improve the living experience and socially equilibrate the capital by providing low-income groups, who were unable to afford private motorised vehicles, with better transportation and free leisure facilities. Yet, critics of the project suggested early on that the new public spaces were exclusionary and bike paths would not serve residents of impoverished communities living with unpaved road and open sewage canals (Cervero, 2005).

Meanwhile, the public transportation system continues to expand. Today, Transmilenio has 138 stations and 9 terminals, distributed along the main avenues; new lines are added and complementary buses introduced to integrate the city through a wider network of services. Yet, despite significantly improving transportation, especially by ending the war of the centavo, the system suffers from a number of problems including the deterioration of stations, overcrowding and delays, security concerns and lack of competence of Transmilenio S.A. (Gilbert, 2008, pp. 447–448). Wealthier residents avoid the public transportation system altogether or alternate its use with taxis or private cars. Low-income Bogotanos, in turn, depend on public transportation and suffer the brunt of Transmilenio's shortcomings.

In fact, as we will discuss in detail in the next section, for many women at the centre of this study, Transmilenio – SITP's implementation and operation has brought greater difficulties and obstacles in terms of mobility and spatial integration. While the system has been extended through the Integrated Public Transport System (SITP) and feeder buses, routes still do not offer the necessary coverage to include informal and low-income peripheral areas of the capital. In addition, although Transmilenio has exclusive lanes, waiting time for transfers is usually between 30 and 45 minutes, leading interlocutors to consider the system inefficient and expensive. Regular buses continue to be a viable option for people who live far from Transmilenio lines or lack the economic capacity to access this system.

4. HOUSEHOLD EMPLOYEES, TRANSPORTATION AND SOCIO-SPATIAL STRATIFICATION IN BOGOTÁ

Wage labour and mobility are closely interrelated. Working as household employees structures women's daily life, from the private realm to their demands and needs related to public transportation. Importantly, however, women's mobility is circumscribed – defined – by the labour conditions of their job. Despite working in the informal sector, domestic workers have to commute during peak hours as employers expect them to arrive at a specific time. Confronted with these challenges, women employ different strategies, carefully pondering the advantages and disadvantages of different transportation means and routes. 'Effectiveness' (speed and reliability) is the prime consideration; cost is another: the more different means of transport, the more expensive the journey. As other members of the working class, household employees earn the minimum wage, a large part of which goes towards daily transportation.[6] The precariousness of their labour situation is reflected in and affects women's choice of modes of transportation (Fig. 4.1).

4.1 Work Schedules and Transportation

An important theme traversing interlocutors' narratives is their perceived shortage of time and how this is made worse by Bogotá's public transportation system.

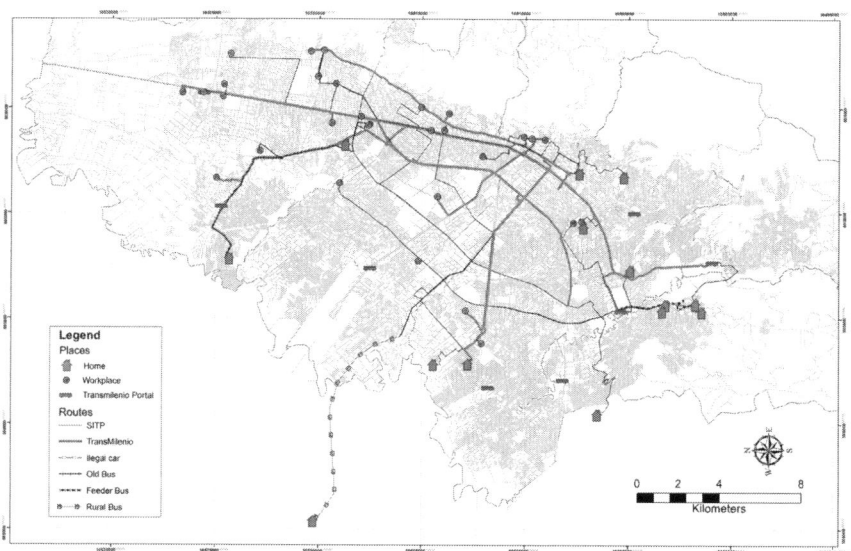

Fig. 4.1. Interlocutors' Residence-Work Journeys and Modes of Transportation.
Source: Authors.

Long, strenuous working hours are prolonged by daily journeys that expose them to insecurity and constant risks.

On average, women commute 3 hours to work and back. Peripheral residences combined with Bogotá's notorious traffic congestion add tremendous strain on interlocutors' lives. Added to this, gender ideologies define women as the prime caretakers of the family, and after interlocutors spend the day attending to employers' children and homes, they cut personal downtime or sleep to care for their own families. This double burden is even more challenging for the many female household heads. One strategy to deal with daily challenges is an extremely early start into the day. Many women get up before 4 a.m. to organise the house and cook for their dependents before leaving as early as possible to avoid the crowds on the public transportation system.

Interlocutors' early start is also due to employers' demands or needs. That is, in the chain of care management, employers depend on domestic workers in order to deal with their own tasks and demands. That is, beyond the strenuous labour conditions of domestic workers, the Colombian labour regime poses time-management challenges that affect the entire working population. Martha explains,

> Thursdays [...] I leave here at 5 a.m. because the exit from here [...] is terrible. And I have to get there early ... because Alejandro's aunt, she has a dental praxis. I have to be there super early to clean [before patients arrive].

Some employers recognise empleadas' public transportation challenges and are more flexible regarding their arrival time. This does not, however, reduce women's workload as they are still expected to complete their tasks. Thus, they leave later and face the evening rush hour.

> Thank God I don't have to stamp a card at work because I would go crazy; I almost always arrive late, even if I get up really early. I say, 'No, boss, if I leave earlier, there are even less buses, I am so tired of it'. But they are patient, and they always say, 'We know that you live very far away and that it is very difficult to get transportation'. So they let me be and I know that I have to stay later because I have to do my job. I don't see a problem with that. Well, yes, I do have a problem with it because I would like to get home earlier, but I can't because of the bus, because it is always very full when it gets here and you can hardly breathe on it. (Claudia)

Labour conditions further complicate interlocutors' lives. The majority work in a different home every day and thus have to get everything done in one day, which often means extra hours without additional pay.

> It's two additional hours. Sometimes he [the employer] says, 'Ah, but you haven't done this or that.' ... I can't work miracles. I can't. I do more or less what I am supposed to do and try to do it well ....' (Olga)

Interlocutors who work in the same home several times a week, in contrast, can spread their tasks over several days. This is more favourable in terms of the work–pay ratio. Yet, it happens mainly with people who have big houses, which overall implies more work. Leidy, a unionised domestic worker, summarises the problem: household employees' remuneration does not compensate for their effort in reaching the workplace.

> The [time and money] I spend going from here [work] to my house, I could go to Panama {laughs}. Many of these women live in Soacha and must get up at between 3 and 4 a.m. They leave wearing lots of layers, enduring the cold to get to work - on the other side of the city – on time. For 500,000 pesos, I would be crazy to go out at that time.[7] Can you imagine how long they spend sitting on those wrecks [old buses]? You could earn more making empanadas and you risk less.

Although the daily commute is such an important feature of women's everyday lives, it does not influence their job decision. Interlocutors were unanimous in that their socio-economic situation and lack of opportunities forced them to accept a position regardless of accessibility, commuting time and public transport-related difficulties. In effect, labour regimes define women's motility. Yet, given the informal nature of their work, it appears as if women could decide. Our research shows, however, that interlocutors' agency in this regard is importantly circumscribed by (1) the power relations between them and their employers (who can be more or less flexible); (2) their socio-economic situation (which defines locale of residence and the capacity to negotiate labour conditions); and (3) the type and availability of public transportation.

4.2 Means of Transportation

Interlocutors use different means of transportation to travel to and from work: Transmilenio, integrated buses (SITP), old buses (non-integrated), cars (informal taxis and ride-sharing), bicycles and walking. Prime among these is Transmilenio because women thought that it was more likely to get them to work on time.

> Even if you are squeezed in, I prefer to come on a crammed Transmilenio than on the bus that takes the Boyacá before going to Bavaria, and goes all round the houses before reaching the Americas ....All that stretch is stressful, [there is always a] traffic jam'. (Ilsa)

Yet, as outlined above, Transmilenio has various structural problems, many of which affect especially low-income, peripheral residents who rely on public transportation almost exclusively. Interlocutors' principal complaint was the lack of buses and routes, which leads to overcrowding and longer waiting times.

> They take ages to come is what I think. There are very few buses and when they finally arrive, they all come in a row; three in 10 minutes and then none for the next hour. I don't know how they do it; who sends them? And it's the same everywhere; when they come, they all come at once. (Angela)

Another relevant aspect, as described by Beuf (2012), is that decisions about Transmilenio lines – along which city roads and where they run to – are influenced by vested interests of real estate developers. Thus, suburban locations in Bogotá's north-west have been connected and subsequently experienced new urban growth. Meanwhile, southern parts of the city, home to the majority of Transmilenio customers, remain underserved.

Indeed, one major challenge is reaching the Transmilenio stations. One option is by feeder buses that connect distant localities to Transmilenio trunk routes. These small buses, however, have their own problems: interlocutors emphasise the long waiting time and large crowds of people at the bus stops, in addition to insecurity.

> It's four or five blocks from my house to the feeder [...]. Last week was really difficult as there were no buses. I live on the road to Villavicencio, which is always full of trucks carrying produce, cattle, etc. It gets very congested, and [...] sometimes traffic accidents stop the flow and no feeders go up to the neighbourhood. So you have to wait, but if not bus comes, you have to walk. (Lorena)

Walking is in fact is an important 'mode of mobility', a strategy household employees fall back on to circumvent bottlenecks, access urban transportation or reach their places of work. Olga highlights walking as a way to deal with unreliable buses: 'Its takes me, what? One hour. Sometimes the little bus I take just doesn't come, and so I have to walk and its like this' {signals a deep incline with her hands}.

SITP buses offer an option to reach the stations or to get from them to employers' homes. Yet their service is limited and walking remains important to overcome this shortcoming, as Claudia explains:

> I take the SITP here and it leaves me at the terminal and from there I take the Transmilenio and I get off and from there I walk 5 or 6 blocks up because its on the other side of the mountain.

Yet, the SITP has other inconveniences such as low frequency and delays caused by traffic jams. Nancy:

> The SITP buses are always late and they often don't even stop..., sometimes you wait for it and it doesn't stop, sometimes it's empty but the driver doesn't feel like stopping, then I have to see [what to do], I have such a hard time with transportation.

Drivers' negligence, as signalled here, is part of customer complaints that public transportation does not comply with what they consider its duty, and such experiences negatively affect interlocutors' trust in the system. Nevertheless, SITP and old buses are attractive for the return trip when interlocutors are not as pressed for time as in the morning: chances to get a seat are higher, and the service is cheaper, even though using the old buses contributes to the continued contamination and congestion of the city. This highlights the heavy physical price household employees pay in return for very little financial gain, while subjected to a work schedule that is the same as or determined by the demands of formal employment.

Curiously, some women trust the old buses (not linked to the SITP) more than the new, integrated public transportation system. Not because they offer good service, but because interlocutors are familiar with their routes and dynamics, allowing them to better organise their commute. Yaneth:

> I know how to take the bus and where it leaves me .... But I can't take those Transmilenios, I get lost and have to ask which route to take.

Maria also says,

> Yes, the buses are always late, but you know more or less when it is due and so go down on time. The first leaves at 4:30 a.m., the second at 4:45 a.m., the other at 5 a.m., the other at 5:15 a.m., and so on. So you leave just in time and don't have to hang around on the street.

Yet, as insinuated here, conventional public transport also poses dangers: extremely old vehicles and theft were the women's main concern.

> One day I was on the bus and opening my bag [...] when a woman [signalled] that I was about to get robbed. I turned to look and there was this man beside me. My bag was full, and, well, you carry your bag on the side so that you don't bother other people, and of course, that miserable thief had opened my bag, and I had my wallet and cell phone there. (Claudia)

4.3 Spatial Segregation

Interlocutors' homes are not only physically far from their places of employment but also morphologically distinct. Indeed, the localities between which women's lives are organised appear worlds apart. At the same time, they are inherently connected, among other things, through household employees' daily travels and social imaginaries about urban space and class.

Household employees live principally in peripheral areas of the city, subject to higher levels of insecurity and crime.[8] Since bus stops are often far away, women employ protective strategies to get there. Some ask family members or neighbours to accompany them to the feeder bus in the early morning hours to avoid being mugged. Others choose alternative bus routes they consider safer.

> I get up at 3:30 a.m., I shower and then call my daughter; we are a team. We always try to leave together. It's frightening at that time because we have to cross a desolate park with no surveillance, and lately there have been many muggings. (Andrea)

Interlocutors' safety is further complicated by the unreliability of connecting public transportation services, as described previously. Empleadas' socio-economic condition puts them at higher risk, and their experiences make them feel unsafe in their living environments.

Location of employers' homes further affects interlocutors' motility, not only in terms of distance but also because of the spatial context. More centrally located residences have more access roads and are served by more modes of transportation. Yet, traffic jams and customer volume are more frequent/higher and prolong women's commute. Workplaces further north and/or in higher strata neighbourhoods, in turn, are often within closed compounds. Usually, there is no direct public transportation access; hence, more transfers and/or different modes of transportation are required, which increases commuting time and costs. The women often have to walk to reach their places of work.

> To get transport from here to there, I have to take the Carrera 68, get off at Gratamira and walk because there is no bus that takes me there. When I leave at noon, I have the same problem. Sometimes I wait an hour for the SITP and it doesn't come, so I have to go back to Gratamira and take the bus from there because there is no other option. Transport is very bad, apart from the fact that the SITP is always late, it can take up to an hour and a half, if you miss it, you have wait another half hour. So the truth is, I prefer to walk. (Martha)

Employers' homes within the municipal area of Bogotá obviously pose the greatest challenge in terms of travelling time and costs, as told by Lorena:

> For a time, I worked for some people that lived in Sindamanoi, behind Chía. So I had to get to Calle 170, the end-station, and from there take an inter-municipal bus that left me at the entrance gate [to the compound]. They are like country houses, so there is a bus that picks people up at the gate, but if not, you have to call the employer to come and pick you up. When they are not there you have to walk for almost an hour [from the gate to their house].

While interlocutors recognise the difficulties in accessing the privileged spaces where they work, they also identify these areas as safe. They emphasise that they feel safer when they run errands than they do in their own neighbourhoods. '[It's] very safe, because there are many offices and so a lot of surveillance and all that' (Nubia).

Security and personal safety – or lack thereof – is in fact one of the dominant narratives connecting the segregated city with public transportation in its effect on interlocutors' lives.

4.4 Perceptions and Experiences of Safety

Interlocutors' accounts of insecurity emphasised two issues: violence and aggression related to overcrowding and criminal acts such as theft and mugging. Claudia:

> One day they scratched my finger, the other day they stepped on me terribly, on Thursday I took Transmilenio and two men were getting into a fight .... I don't know what happened [...] but people had to separate them because they were going to hit each other. No, it's terrible what you see every day, and the same on the SITP, you get on, and there are people who are very slow, and others start to treat them badly and they fight.

Complementing this association of overcrowding and conflicts with specific means of transportation are the many accounts of theft and mugging inside all types of buses, at bus stops, inside the stations and on the way to and from the public transportation system. Interlocutors shared a permanent sense of insecurity, fear and mistrust, which affects their motility and interaction with others. Again, Claudia:

> [The bus] is super late and if you are lucky, you can catch it just as it goes down [to the stop], but sometimes you don't make it, and in Molinos, there are these cars that pick people up. I don't know where they go. They ask me, 'Where are you going, *negra*, can I take you?' And they ask you [...] because they see you standing there [at the stop] for an hour. I try to wait here at the traffic light because [...] the cars cannot stop here, [...] so I take the bus from the traffic lights, and there are small restaurants here, so wait here because they say it's dangerous over there. And, yes, one day I was waiting, and some young guys on bicycles passed and they were going to rob me, but [...] I went in among a crowd, and they left.

Many of the testimonies reveal a lack of intervention by the police, which only heightens their sense of insecurity and mistrust of the system as a whole.

Interlocutors also reported incidents of theft in the neighbourhoods where they work. Yet, interestingly, in these cases, they mostly played down the significance of the experiences, reflecting and reproducing the differential valuing of urban space. Lorena explained:

> Well, there is insecurity in the North too, but not like the South. Let's say, in the South people are really intolerant. If you go out here in the North you go by taxi. But in the South, you just need to look at somebody the wrong way and that's enough, its dangerous, there are fights between groups. People are more heated than in the North, I guess.

Ilsa, in turn, had her motorcycle stolen in the residential compound where she worked but assured, 'Well ... the truth is that I never heard of anything being stolen in these apartments, or of a cell phone being stolen in [this compound] ... nothing like that.' Here we can see the power of the urban imaginary: interlocutors reproduce and reinforce popular dichotomous imaginaries that exist about the capital's north and south, considering one as safe while associating the other with heightened insecurity. Evidently, these perceptions influence women's general experience of space and impinge on their motility.

5. CONCLUSION

As we have shown in this chapter, gender intersects with local labour regimes and infrastructure to negatively affect female household employees' mobility in Bogotá. The women organise their lives around the functioning – or malfunctioning – of the public transportation system. Transmilenio – SITP was introduced as a system that would connect different means of transportation – trunk road buses, feeders and complementary buses – and equalise the stratified city. Yet interlocutors often preferred the old buses with wider circulation routes that stop everywhere and pass more frequently, highlighting empleadas domésticas' two main daily challenges: time demands and the strenuousness of their work.

Examining urban mobility and social equity through the lens of motility, the research shows that urban stratification is (re)produced in household employee's subjective experience of mobility and space, which they describe as 'suffering': suffering long waits, being squashed and abused and not having a voice. The women are also subject to insecurity in their neighbourhoods, which effectively have the highest crime rates in the capital, and from discrimination in the areas where they work. Marked by appearance and race as 'others', here they are treated with suspicion and contempt. In combination with their overall time constraints, it is not surprising that the women do not 'appropriate' the privileged spaces where they work.

Besides representing themselves as hardworking and honest, household employees' principal form of agency is to refrain from travelling in their spare time, thus limiting their active appropriation of urban space. Inspired by Auyero's (2012) notion of waiting as a form of domination through which citizens are formed, we argue that the urban poor's socially and spatially marginalised position in the urban landscape, in combination with feeling 'treated like cattle' on their journeys to earn a living, reinforce their sense of being considered second-class citizens. Yet it is above all domestic workers' gender that affects their motility: care work is considered women's work, both by their employers as in their own homes. At the same time, as women they feel more vulnerable and exposed. The research thus illuminates how spatial, social and economic dimensions mutually interact to (negatively) impact the female household employees' lives and possibilities.

NOTES

1. The 1948 'Bogotazo' violent protests in reaction to the killing of the popular left-wing leader Jorge Eliécer Gaítan caused businesses and upper class residents to move to the north of the city.
2. These are official numbers, yet informality runs high in the sector.
3. This research project is situated in the field of urban anthropology and uses qualitative data to analyse the realities and subjective experiences of domestic workers in relation to socio-economic inequality, spatial segregation and mobility. Besides participant

observation and unstructured interviews, we accompanied several women on their daily trajectories through the city to observe and analyse the ways in which they interact with urban space. Interlocutors were contacted via snowballing and were of different age, ethnic and socio-economic groups. To protect interlocutors' privacy, all names are pseudonyms.

4. In an interesting cross-cultural parallel, this has also been the reason for the rapid growth of female migrants working as household employees in reform-period China.

5. This includes bus lanes and stations, garages, bridges and other related infrastructure.

6. Even though household employees should receive the legally guaranteed transportation subsidy, the majority of women in this study did not benefit from that provision.

7. The official monthly minimum wage in 2017 was COP $737,717.

8. According to the 'Informe Calidad de Vida de Bogotá' (2017), localities with the highest levels of micro-trafficking, robbery, extortion and sexual violence are Ciudad Bolívar, Bosa, Kennedy, Los Mártires and Santa Fe. In terms of homicide rates, the localities of Santafé (64.2), Los Mártires (54.2) and Ciudad Bolívar (35) have the highest rates.

9. The metropolitan area of Bogotá had over 10 million residents in 2015.

10. Women use motorcycles less than men as a means of transport. In contrast, women rely more on individual public transport (taxi) than men.

11. According to *moovit insights*, public transit average commuting in Bogotá is 97 minutes on a weekday, and 32% of public transit customers ride for more than 2 hours every day. On average, people wait for 20 minutes at a stop or station, and 40% of users wait for over 20 minutes every day. The average distance travelled in a single trip is 8 km, while 16% travel for over 12 km in a single direction (see https://moovitapp.com/insights/en/Moovit_Insights_Public_Transit_Index_Colombia_Bogota-762).

REFERENCES

Alcaldía Mayor de Bogotá – Secretaría Distrital de Movilidad. (2015). Encuesta de Movilidad. Retrieved from http://movilidadBogota.gov.co/web/node/1990

Ardila-Gómez, A. (2004). *Transit planning in Curitiba and Bogotá*: Roles in Interaction, Risk, and Change. Cambridge, MA: Massachusetts Institute of Technology.

Ares, S. (2010). Espacio de vida y movilidad territorial habitual en Chapadmalal, Buenos Aires, Argentina. *Revista Colombiana de Geografía, 19*, 27–40.

Auyero, J. (2012). *Patients of the state: The politics of waiting*. Durham, NC: Duke University Press.

Beuf, A. (2012). De las luchas urbanas a las grandes inversiones. La nueva urbanidad periférica en Bogotá. *Bulletin de l'Institut Français d'Études Andines, 41*(3), 473–501.

Blofield, M. (2009). Feudal enclaves and political reforms: Domestic workers in Latin America. *Latin American Research Review, 44*(1), 158–190.

Casanova, E. (2013). Embodied inequality. The experience of domestic work in urban Ecuador. *Gender & Society, 27*(4), 561–585.

Centro de Cultura Popular José Antonio Galán. (2013). Informe Final Trabajadoras del Hogar en Colombia. Retrieved from http://www.slideshare.net/Sintraimagra/informe-final-trabajadoras-del-hogar-en-colombia-1

Cervero, R. (2005). Progressive transport and the poor: Bogotá's bold steps forward. *Access, 27*, 24–30.

Chaney, E. M., & Garcia Castro, M. (Eds.). (1989). *Muchachas no more: Household workers in Latin America and the Caribbean*. Philadelphia, PA: Temple University Press.

Colen, S. (1990). 'Housekeeping' for the green card: West Indian household workers, the state, and stratified reproduction in New York, NY. In R. Sanjek & S. Colen (Eds.), *At work in homes: Household workers in world perspective*. American Ethnological Society Monograph Series 3 (pp. 89–118). Washington, DC: American Ethnological Society.

Collie, N. (2013). Walking in the city: Urban space, stories, and gender. *Gender Forum. An Internet Journal for Gender Studies, 42*, 3–14. Retrieved from http://www.genderforum.org/issues/gender-and-urban-space/walking-in-the-city-urban-space-stories-and-gender/

De Certeau, M. (1984). *The practice of everyday life*. Berkeley, CA: University of California Press.
de Dios Herrero, M. (2006). El trabajo de las empleadas domésticas: entre lo doméstico (privado) y lo asalariado (público). *La Aljaba*, *10*, 157–174.
Ehrenreich, B., & Russell Hochschild, A. (Eds.). (2003). *Global woman: Nannies, maids, and sex workers in the new economy*. New York, NY: Holt, Metropolitan Books.
García López, A. C. (2012). Trabajo a cambio de pertenencia, empleadas domésticas en Bogotá, 1950–1980. *Revista Grafia*, *9*, 159–174.
Garcia, L. A., & Gascón, D. L. (2016). Anexo 02. Portafolio de Mapas. Secretaría Distrital de Planeación. Retrieved from http://www.sdp.gov.co/sites/default/files/POT/2-DOCUMENTO_DE_SEGUIMIENTO_Y_EVALUACION_14-06-19/Anexo02_Portafolio_de_Mapas_S%26E.pdf
Gilbert, A. (2008). Bus rapid transit: Is Transmilenio a miracle cure? *Transport Reviews*, *28*(4), 439–467.
Gill, L. (1994). *Precarious dependencies: Gender, class, and domestic service in Bolivia*. New York, NY: Columbia University Press.
Harzig, C. (2006). Domestics of the world (unite?): Labour migration systems and personal trajectories of household workers in historical and global perspective. *Journal of American Ethnic History*, *25*(2/3), 48–73.
Informe Calidad de Vida de Bogotá. (2017). Bogotá Cómo Vamos. Retrieved from https://bit.ly/2RywCRn
Inostroza, L., Baur, R., & Csaplovics, E. (2013). Urban sprawl and fragmentation in Latin America: A dynamic quantification and characterisation of spatial patterns. *Journal of Environmental Management*, *115*, 87–97.
Jirón, P. (2007). Implicancias de género en las experiencias de movilidad cotidiana urbana en Santiago de Chile. *Revista Venezolana de Estudios de la Mujer*, *12*(28), 173–197. Retrieved from https://bit.ly/2QCuuXr
Kaufmann, V., Bergman, M., & Joye, D. (2004). Motility: Mobility as capital. *International Journal of Urban and Regional Research*, *28*(4), 745–756.
Korn, J. (2018). *Riding scared: Sexual violence and women's mobility on public transportation in Santiago, Chile*. Urban Studies Senior Seminar Papers, 24. Retrieved from https://repository.upenn.edu/senior_seminar/24
Lautier, B. (2003). Las empleadas domésticas latinoamericanas y la sociología del trabajo: algunas observaciones acerca del caso brasileño. *Revista Mexicana de Sociología*, *65*(4), 789–814.
León, M. (2013). Proyecto de Investigación-acción: trabajo doméstico y servicio doméstico en Colombia. *Revista de Estudios Sociales*, *45*, 198–211.
Massey, D. (1994). *Space, place, and gender*. Minneapolis, MN: University of Minnesota Press.
Miralles-Guasch, C. (1998). La movilidad de las mujeres en la ciudad: Un análisis desde la ecología urbana. *Ecología Política*, *15*, 123–130.
Parreñas Slazar, R. (2001). *Servants of globalization: Women, migration, and domestic work*. Stanford, CA: Stanford University Press.
Parreñas Slazar, R. (2005). *Children of global migration: Transnational migration and gendered woes*. Stanford, CA: Stanford University Press.
Rico de Alonso, A. (2001). Familia, Genero, Pobreza Urbana en Colombia: Supervivencia y Futuro. *Papel Político*, *13*, 115–135.
Rodriguez, D. A., & Targa, F. (2004). Value of accessibility to Bogotá's bus rapid transit system. *Transport Reviews*, *24*(5), 587–610.
Rollins, J. (1990). Ideology and servitude. In R. Sanjek & S. Colen (Eds.), *At work in homes: Household workers in world perspective*. American Ethnological Society Monograph Series 3 (pp. 74–88). Washington, DC: American Ethnological Society.
Saldaña-Tejeda, A. (2012). Why should I not take an apple or a fruit if I wash their underwear? Food, social classification and paid domestic work in Mexico. *Journal of Intercultural Studies*, *33*(2), 121–137.
Salzinger, L. (1991). A maid by any other name: The transformation of 'dirty work' by central American immigrants. In M. Buraway (Ed.), *Ethnography unbound: Power and resistance in the modern metropolis* (pp. 139–160). Berkeley, CA: University of California Press.

Santos Alarcón, D. S. (2012). Aproximación a un Mundo Oculto: La experiencia del trabajo doméstico en refugiadas Colombianas. Tesis de Maestría en Sociología, Facultad Latinoamericana de Ciencias Sociales, Sede Ecuador.

Soto, P. (2017). Diferencias de género en la movilidad urbana. Las experiencias de viaje de las mujeres en el Metro de la Ciudad de México. *Revista Transporte y Territorio, 16*, 127–146. Retrieved from https://bit.ly/2IJSDZu.

Urry, J. (2011). *Mobilities*. Cambridge: Polity Press.

Uteng, T. P., & Cresswell, T. (Eds.). (2016). *Gendered mobilities*. Milton Park, CA: Routledge.

APPENDIX
Bogotá

Bogotá is Latin America's third-largest and densest city (3,900 persons per km^2). In 2014, Colombia's capital had about 7.9 million inhabitants, a number which is suggested to rise to 8,264,029 by 2019,[9] though informal urban settlements make these numbers imprecise. The city area extends 1,587 km^2 and has an elevation of 2,640 m.

Bogotá is characterised by its particular segregation pattern: working-class neighbourhoods and informal settlements are located in the south and the peripheries, while the northern part of the city has a significantly higher standard of living. The city's socio-spatial segregation is reflected in its administrative division into a six-tiered classification system of urban neighbourhoods with over 50% of the urban population living in the lowest two strata areas. The classification is based on the quality of structures and amenities of urban neighbourhoods (including land use, topography and public services) and assigned to buildings, and is the basis for public service costs. In the scheme, only strata 3 and 4 pay the actual costs of water, electricity, garbage collection, etc., while the higher strata subsidise the costs of the lowest two that do not pay anything. Importantly, conceived as an equalising mechanism, in public discourse, the classification has become a descriptor of persons.

Public Transportation System

Bogotá is highly mono-functional with separate administrative, industrial, residential and recreational areas, which causes disarticulation between places of residence and the location of jobs. Thus, (public) transportation is extremely important.

During the final decades of the twentieth century, the city's physical infrastructure was increasingly unable to keep up with a growing population. Thus, in 1997, mayoral candidate Enrique Peñalosa proposed Transmilenio as part of a general transportation reform plan for Bogotá 'to address mobility challenges, reclaim public spaces for pedestrians, and increase city residents' access to green space' (Rodriguez & Targa, 2004, p. 593).

Transmilenio is an integrated BRT system with exclusive bus lanes, stations and terminals adapted for large-capacity buses and integrated fare that connects with smaller feeder buses in residential areas on the outskirts of the city. In 2015, the system had nine operating lines with about 113 km of exclusive bus lanes. Nine bus terminals (*portales*) connect with feeder routes and the complementary SITP, which was 83% implemented. The system is planned to cover the entire city in 2030. It is more expensive than other public transportation.

General Mobility Statistics and Patterns

According to the 2015 urban mobility study, households in peripheral, lower strata locations such as Usme, Bosa and Ciudad Bolívar had on average one vehicle for every four homes, while in central, high strata locales such as Chapinero, there is one vehicle per household. Indeed, Bogotá's lower strata residents principally rely on public transportation and walking to move around the city, whereas the three upper strata principally use cars and taxi.

In 2015, the total number of public transportation journeys was 15,275,312. Analysis of the modes of transport for the total number of journeys according to stratum shows that about 92% of public transportation users belong to the lowest three strata, while private car use is concentrated in strata 3 and 4 (62%). Yet the main choice of public transportation for the lower strata is not Transmilenio but small public buses (*colectivos*) and SITP buses (covering half of all journeys). Between 2011 and 2015, strata 1 and 2 residents increasingly relied on illegal or informal transportation modes as well as on feeder buses.

The survey showed no evident correlation between type of journey (leisure, work, etc.) and medium of transportation. The collective public transport also presents similar travel rates for men and women, with a higher degree of use by people between 15 and 24 years of age.[10]

The daily distribution of journeys in the city shows the typical urban pattern with three peak periods: between 6 and 7 a.m.; 11.45 a.m. and 12.45 p.m.; and 5.30 and 6.30 p.m. The highest number of journeys per household is in stratum 1, which has the highest number of persons per household. Usme, in Bogotá's south, has the highest number of journeys per household, followed by Antonio Nariño.

According to the survey, the mean travel time in the city is 56.09 minutes. The journeys from Soacha and Bosa are the longest with an average of 70.38 minutes, while, in other localities and in the Candelaria, trip duration is 45 minutes on average. The longest travel times are connected to those means of transport that involve walking and change of vehicle or transfer between routes, whereas the shortest times are those that do not involve motorised modes.[11]

Interlocutors

Most of our interlocutors migrated as children from rural areas in Santander, Cundinamarca, Boyacá or Caldas, in search of work. They mainly live in peripheral, low strata localities such as Usme, Soacha, Altos de Cazuca, Ciudad Bolívar and Tintal. On average, the women interviewed spent between one and a half to two hours each way (home–work, work–home); that is, 3–4 hours a day on public transport. According to the women, transportation in the city does not cover users' needs, as there is no constant flow of vehicles or sufficient routes. They also complain about the costs of the Transmilenio system.

SOURCES

Moovit insights, facts and usage statistics about public transit in Bogotá, Colombia. Retrieved from https://moovitapp.com/insights/en/Moovit_Insights_Public_Transit_Index_Colombia_Bogota-762

Departamento Administrativo Nacional de Estadística (DANE), Proyecciones e Población. Retrieved from https://www.dane.gov.co/index.php/estadisticas-por-tema/demografia-y-poblacion/proyecciones-de-poblacion

Alcaldía Mayor de Bogotá – Secretaría Distrital de Movilidad, Encuesta de Movilidad 2015. Retrieved from http://movilidadBogota.gov.co/web/node/1990

CHAPTER 5

SUSTAINABLE TRANSPORT AND GENDER EQUITY: INSIGHTS FROM SANTIAGO, CHILE

Lake Sagaris and Ignacio Tiznado-Aitken

ABSTRACT

Sustainable transport is often defined according to energy efficiency and environmental impacts. With global approval during Habitat III, however, a set of Sustainable Development Goals have become the focus for human development until 2030, underlining the relevance of health, equity and other social issues.

These goals raise the challenge of achieving significant progress towards 'transport justice' in diverse societies and contexts. While exclusion occurs for different reasons, discrimination, based on cultural roles, combines with sexual harassment and other mobility barriers to limit women's mobility. This makes gender an area of particular interest and potential insight for considering equity within sustainability and its social components.

Using data from Metropolitan Santiago to ground a conceptual exploration, this chapter examines the equity implications of women's travel patterns and sustainable transport. Key findings underline the importance of considering non-work trip purposes and achieving better land-use combinations to accommodate care-oriented trips. Moreover, barriers linked to unsafe public transport environments limit women's mobility and, therefore, their participation. Women account for a disproportionately high number of walking trips, a situation that can be interpreted as 'greater sustainability' in terms of energy use and emissions, but suggests significant inequalities in access. Environmental and economic sustainability gains may be achieved at a high social cost, unless specific measures are taken.

Keywords: Walking; gender equity; social sustainability; transport justice; Santiago de Chile; planning

1. INTRODUCTION: GENDER AND EQUITY IN SUSTAINABLE TRANSPORT

Sustainable transport is often defined according to energy efficiency and environmental impacts, but during Habitat III (UN, 2016), countries worldwide launched new commitments to a set of Sustainable Development Goals, as the focus for human development until 2030, underlining the relevance of health, equity and other social issues.

These goals raise the challenge of achieving significant progress towards 'transport justice' (Lucas, 2004; Manzi & Lucas, 2010; Martens, 2017) in diverse societies and contexts. While exclusion occurs for different reasons, discrimination based on cultural roles and mobility barriers, such as risk of sexual and other forms of harassment in public spaces, seem almost universal for women (Loukaitou-Sideris, 2014; Loukaitou-Sideris, Bornstein, Fink, Samuels, & Gerami, 2009; Porter, 2011), limiting their social, political and economic participation in society. This makes gender an area of particular interest and potential insight for considering equity within sustainability and its social dimension.

Using data from Metropolitan Santiago to ground a conceptual analysis, this chapter explores the equity implications of women and sustainable transport. As discussed in depth in this chapter, our research indicates that women account for a disproportionately high number of walking trips, which can be interpreted as 'greater sustainability' in terms of energy use and emissions but may reflect significant inequalities in access to urban opportunities. This reality overlaps and interacts with general security and gender-related security concerns in ways that underline potential conflicts between the three spheres of sustainability, when social sustainability is more precisely defined. By treating transport as gender-neutral, which involves treating men and women as if their experience were the same when they engage with transport systems, we find many barriers that affect women differently or more than men. This analysis points to substantial equity considerations, some contemplated in current formulations of transport 'justice', while others require a more complex formulation of 'equity' and 'justice' driven by gender analysis methods, as they can be applied to specific contexts.

This chapter explores these issues using an interdisciplinary analysis that combines quantitative methods (origin–destination survey data and an intercept survey) and qualitative methods (analysis, participatory workshops and focus groups). This chapter contributes to the emerging literature on these trends and considers the intersections and tensions emerging from sustainability, equity, gender and active transport debates. The next section provides a summary of key concepts and methods, followed by main results. The chapter concludes with a discussion of implications for planning 'sustainable' transportation.

2. KEY CONCEPTS AND METHODS: GENDER AND TRANSPORT 'JUSTICE'

While 'sex' refers to the biological differences between women and men, the term 'gender' encompasses cultural norms, values and other complex components that constitute differences between the roles, abilities, expectations or other aspects of being female or male. Recognising that these vary in different contexts, Hanson's definition and caveats provide a solid working definition. She notes that two contradictory notions of gender co-exist: one as biologically determined and the other as a social construct. These two visions are essential when we look at gender and mobility, since even the terms 'men' and 'women' involve some clear, but other messy and heterogeneous meanings (Hanson, 2010, p. 8).

These 'messy' categories interact in contradictory ways with unsustainable transport, defined as 'automobility', a concept developed by Beckmann (2001), Urry (2004) and Sheller and Urry (2000). These authors trace how publicity and planning have placed cars at the centre of social imaginaries, modern societies, economies and cities, turning them into virtually mythical embodiments of human desire and technological progress. A car-oriented urban planning paradigm emerged in Chile during the last years of military rule (1973–1990). Pro-car publicity flooded the airwaves from the mid-1980s onward, fostering a social imaginary that treated walking and cycling as obsolete travel modes (Sagaris, 2014a, 2014b), while urban highway concessions with heavy subsidies sped the adoption of car-oriented urban planning from the 1990s onward (Silva, 2004, 2011).

In Chile as elsewhere in developing countries, low average incomes, which make cars out of reach for the majority of households, accentuate the injustice of a car-oriented mobility paradigm. Given this context, issues of 'transport justice' emerge even more sharply, particularly given a socio-political context deeply shaped by the human rights violations and neoliberal reforms of the military regime. These have limited and distorted the exercise of fundamental civil rights, which are relevant to citizens' involvement in improving transport systems and equity. This is further complicated by an institutional environment strongly marked by the authoritarian principles inherited from the regime, particularly the disempowerment of local and regional governments that, elsewhere in the world, play a crucial role in urban planning. Transport in Chile is primarily planned by the national ministry of transport: even Santiago's public transport system is run by the national ministry rather than a local or metropolitan transport agency that responds to democratically elected authorities. There is virtually no transparency or accountability for public transport decisions, at least as understood in developed cities such as Toronto, New York or London, or elsewhere in Latin America, such as Bogotá and Buenos Aires, where strong city governments have made significant innovations in public transit, cycling and walking.

To date, we have focussed on 'transport justice' as an open-ended concept, in the context of previous work on 'social sustainability' (Sagaris & Arora, 2016; Sagaris, 2014a; Sagaris, Tiznado-Aitken, & Steiniger, 2017). We consider human agency and the right to participate fully in the political decisions of a given place and time as central to our discussion of transport 'justice'. This builds from work developing Lefevre's thinking about the 'right to the city' (Harvey, 2008) and the 'just city' (Fainstein, 2010), as a necessary object of social and urban planning. Similarly, Manzi and Lucas (2010) examine the social sustainability of cities in a context of institutional, economic and environmental 'imperatives' to guarantee justice, democracy and eco-efficiency, by improving burden-sharing, care and access. Other authors, particularly Banister (2007), Newman and Jennings (2008) and Low and Gleeson (2003), identify the importance of forging new social values and building greater participation from citizens into the social side of sustainability, as does de Vasconcellos (1997, 2001, 2015), who has pioneered much significant research on equity and inclusion in Latin America.

The complexity and richness of 'social sustainability' as a concept require more attention to nuances, as many civil society organisations in particular have pointed out (Fig. 5.1). Issues of equality, equity and freedom to live life to the full (Sen, 1999) underline the challenge of achieving significant progress towards transport justice amidst societies that may or may not have made significant progress towards greater social equity and more democratic governance systems.

Although there is considerable discussion of what justice means in practice in the field of transport (Pereira et al., 2017), Martens (2016) has contributed a substantial summary of the theoretical approaches and practical issues inherent in 'transport justice', noting its role as both substantive (pertaining to the interdisciplinary content of planning) and prescriptive (pertaining to what *should be*). His arguments explore social justice theories and their potential applications to public transport. He builds on *accessibility to destinations*, rather than mobility per se, as the central good to be provided by transportation for all users and under most circumstances (Martens, 2016).

This definition, however, is narrowly focussed on transportation in its primordial function of moving people. Today, research on transport and health underlines the vital need for transportation to reduce emissions, address its own impacts on road safety, particularly premature mortality and disability and incorporate priority objectives that reflect current knowledge about the powerful role of active transport, mainly walking and cycling, in improving health through physical activity and stress reduction (Frumkin, Frank, & Jackson, 2004; Mindell, Watkins, & Cohen 2011; Nieuwenhuijsen & Khreis, 2019; Rydin et al., 2012).

From both a health and an economic perspective, walking and cycling should be major components of 'transport justice'. A city where children cannot walk or cycle to school, for example, does enormous damage to their mental, physical and social development, whereas the opposite has been shown to be highly beneficial (Chillón et al., 2012; David & Weinstein, 1987; Deka & Von Hagen 2015; Frank, Engelke, & Schmid, 2003; Frumkin et al., 2004; Hillman, 1999; Hillman, Adams, & Whitelegg, 1990; Lorenc, Brunton, Oliver, Oliver, & Oakley, 2008; Rudner 2012; Timperio, Crawford, Telford, & Salmon, 2004).

Fig. 5.1. Three Different Views of 'Equality' and 'Equity' Illustrate the Wicked Problem Behind Terms Many People Take for Granted. In Transportation, Walking and Walkability are Often Neglected in Both Planning and Research, Despite Their Crucial Interactions with Gender, Equity, Health, Road Safety and Urban Security Issues. *Sources*: (top) open use Infographic Robert Wood Johnson Foundation (RWJF 2017), https://www.rwjf.org/en/library/infographics/visualizing-health-equity.html; (middle) equity versus equality, open source graphic created by Interaction Institute for Social Change (IISC 2016) | Artist: Angus Maguire, https://interactioninstitute.org/illustrating-equality-vs-equity (IISC 2016); and (bottom) Free toolbox, Story Based Strategy (Douglas 2016). Retrieved from https://www.storybasedstrategy.org/the4thbox, all three graphics most recently accessed (1 April 2020).

Similarly, cities, where a large number of young people are killed or permanently disabled by traffic crashes, also perpetuate socially unjust conditions, particularly where a disproportionate number are low-income, pedestrians or cyclists (WHO, 2013, 2015). Making walking and cycling safe is a crucial aspect of transport justice, particularly in developing countries where these are significant and, in the case of walking, often majority modes. With such high numbers of women walking, as this research reveals, gender concerns should reinforce concerns for road safety, which impacts their mental and physical health and their participation in work and other aspects of city life.

Similarly, cities where women's mobility is restricted, limiting their access to better education, employment, cultural, networking and other opportunities, generate multiple forms of injustice. As per the definition above, while the source of gender differences may be the object of many different views, where discrimination (deliberate or through lack of concern) affects a specific social group, equity concerns require better understanding or democracy itself can suffer (Tilly, 2007).

This perspective goes beyond merely considering the justice inherent in a particular transport system or mode. Emerging research suggests that elements such as automobility, access to affordable public transport, road safety, social safety, human health externalities and community severance, that is barriers that isolate specific places and/or social groups, should be considered (Feitelson, 2002; Isalou, Litman, & Shahmoradi, 2014; Jenny Mindell & Karlsen, 2012) when evaluating how socially sustainable and how 'just' a particular transport system is.

This chapter uses a gender perspective to explore the social aspects of sustainability and relevant aspects of transport justice in two ways: (i) using origin–destination data (SECTRA-UAHurtado, 2015) to better understand how transport systems reinforce and/or could potentially offset social and other forms of inequality and (ii) data from a specific intercept survey on women, harassment and public transport and complementary results from three focus groups in Metropolitan Santiago. This data comes from *Ella se mueve segura*/She moves safely (Allen, Pereyra, Sagaris, & Cárdenas, 2019), a three-city study using a global methodology.

Using this approach, combining the origin–destination survey, an interception survey and focus groups, we were able to perform a more comprehensive and in-depth analysis of the role of gender within the social sustainability of cities, to better understand travel patterns and experiences, and their relationship with social sustainability within transport 'justice'.

This research forms part of an ongoing collaboration among researchers in Chile, India, Ecuador, Argentina, the United States and Europe, which has used scenario analysis and other methods to explore 'sustainable' transport, understood as contextually sensitive combinations of walk–bike–bus arrangements. We see these interactions among city streetscapes, transport modes and people as generating an 'ecology of modes', each with its own particular 'niche', defined mainly by distance, in conjunction with trip purpose, traveller's ability/needs and other factors. Thus, in a more sustainable city, the majority of short trips (0–2 km) should be walking; intermediate trips (1–8 km depending) by personal cycle, bike-share, cycle-taxi or other cycle-assisted methods; longer trips (over 5 km) in medium to high-density areas, by bus or public transport (collective taxis, Metro, among others).

Longer trips in rural or suburban areas may be best served by special bus services or private vehicles, depending on context (Sagaris & Arora, 2015, 2018; Sagaris et al., 2017).

From this perspective, the use of cars to cover distances shorter than 5 km reveals an 'excessive' dependency, which is unsustainable. Planners can analyse travel patterns from this perspective and establish targets for modal shifts, which can then guide the investment and spatial decisions necessary to implement them (Karner & Sagaris, 2016; Sagaris et al., 2017), based on goals for shifting short (under 2–5 km) car trips primarily to walking and cycling, campaigns to change behaviour and values, complete street designs and investment priorities.

Based on this understanding of an ecology of modes, our conceptual framework recognises an equivalent 'ecology of actors and advocacy', as is apparent in the case of driving and cycling, but less evident for walking and public transit. It is beyond the purview of this chapter to explore advocacy and human agency as they relate to each mode. This concept is of interest, however, to the final discussion of equity, women and walking. For more details on specific methods applied, please see Appendix 2 (qualitative methods and general research framework) and Appendix 3 (quantitative methods and sources).

3. WHAT ORIGIN–DESTINATION DATA REVEAL ABOUT WOMEN'S TRAVEL IN SANTIAGO

To get a sense of the variety of travel patterns and experiences in Metropolitan Santiago, data for 45 of the 52 *comunas* or administrative districts that compose the city were examined (Fig. 5.2). Key characteristics of this city, Chile's largest metropolitan region, including gender-related information (ComunidadMujer, 2016) are summarised in the Appendix.

We started by analysing the modal share and investment in each transport mode, examining the main trends observed. We then developed a contextual perspective by looking at poverty, which is very concentrated in this highly segregated city; overall travel patterns by mode (walk, cycle, bus-Metro, car and other) and how women's travel is reflected in these modes and places. After that, we looked at women's trip purposes, identifying specific concerns for transport planning.

3.1 Modal Share Evolution and Investment by Transport Mode

An analysis of official data on investment for the years 2010–2016 from the government's *Balance de Gestión Integral* (GobiernoChile, 2016), Santiago's regional strategy and 2025 transportation master plan (GORE, 2014; MTT, 2013) and the modal share between 2001 and 2012 reveals several significant trends (Tables 5.1 and 5.2). These include very high investment in train/Metro and cars, with relatively low investment in bus corridors serving a large percentage of trips (25%), and very low investment in cycling (4–6%) and walking (34%). Notwithstanding, a combination of advocacy and strategic investment of a minimal sum, just US$48 million, doubled cycling's modal share (2006–2012). Walking, which received less than 3% of total investment, retains a major modal share, although it has declined slightly.

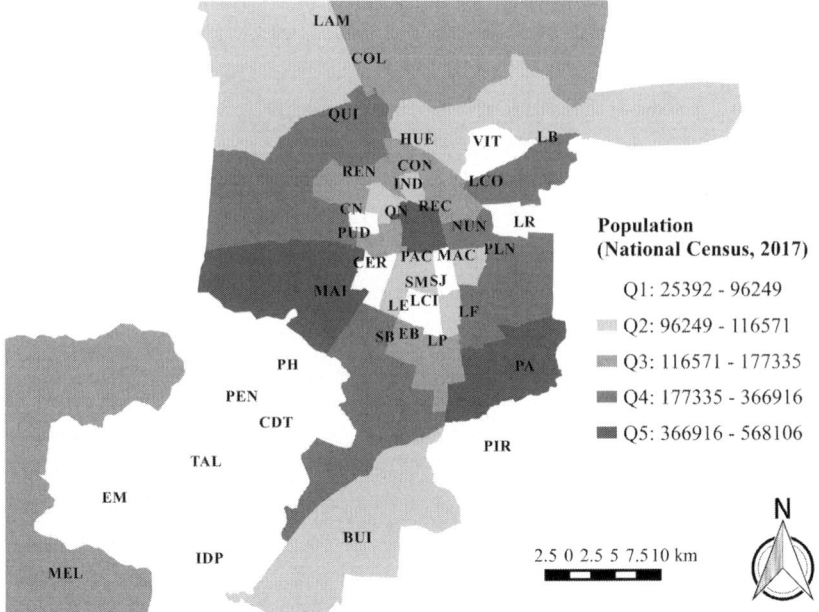

Fig. 5.2. Spatial Distribution and Population of the Comunas, with the Poorest Spread Through Most of the City, with the Jurisdictions in the Centre (SAN = Santiago Centre; PRO = Providencia) Having More Mixed Incomes, and Four Towards the City's Eastern Edge (LB = Lo Barnechea, VI = Vitacura, LCO = Las Condes and LR = LaReina) Posting Very High Incomes. *Source*: Own elaboration, based on National Census (INE 2018).

Table 5.1. Modal Share in Santiago: Soaring Automobility in Recent Decades.

	2001	% Modal Share 2001	2012	% Modal Share 2012	Trends
Walking	5,969,296	38.3%	6,039,050	34.6%	Going down
Car	3,272,982	21.0%	4,555,468	26,1%	Rising
Public Transport	4,691,275	30.1%	4,136,575	23.7%	Plunging
Public Transport combined with others public/private	187,028	1.2%	383,986	2.2%	Rising
Bicycle	327,298	2.1%	680,702	3.9%	Doubling
Basic and Collective Taxis	576,668	3.7%	733,064	4.2%	Increasing
Others	561,083	3.6%	925,057	5.3%	
Total	**15,585,630**		**17,453,901**		

Source: Own elaboration using origin–destination data from 2001 and 2012 (SECTRA, 2004; 2015).
Notes: (1) Comparison between 2001 and 2012 was made only for 38 comunas to analyse an equivalent study area. (2) The 2012 origin–destination survey combines Metro–bus trips into a single modal category making it difficult to identify the exact modal share for buses, bus–Metro and Metro only trips, although the Informe Difusión reports that of the almost 26% of BIP trips for 45 comunas, 52% are bus only, 22% Metro only, and 26% involve bus–Metro combinations (p. 26 on Main Report from SECTRA (2015)).

Table 5.2. Public Investment* in Transportation in Recent Years, Millions USD.

Projects	2010–2016		Chile's 2025 Master Plan		Modal Share	
	MM US Dollars. 1 Dollar = 650 Chilean Pesos	Share of Budget (%)	MM US Dollars. 1 Dollar = 650 Chilean Pesos	Share of Budget (%)	Mode	Percentage
Transport plans: Metro and trains	1,730	47.0	10,920	48.0	Metro	12.30
Concessions (major highways)	1,035	28.1	8,190	36.0	Cars	26.10
Roads (trunk and highways, 5%, plus local, 4%)	343	9.3	1,820	8.0		
Bus corridors*	454	12.3	1,365	6.0	Buses	20.20
Cycleways	15	0.4	455	2.0	Bikes	3.90
Walking	102	2.8			Walking	34.60
Total	US$3,680	100.00	US$22,750	100.00%		

Source: Own elaboration, based on Ministry of Transport and Telecommunications, Chile, Plan Maestro Transporte 2025, 2013; BGI (2016); Murray et al. (2017).
*It is not possible to assign all the trips to only one public transport mode. Since Transantiago is an integrated system between Metro and buses, some of the trips have two or more trip stages, and some combine bus and Metro. So the percentage showed is all public transport trips that have at least one trip stage in that mode. *Source:* Own elaboration using origin–destination data from 2012 (SECTRA, 2015).

The focus on investment in highways and facilities for cars has correlated with soaring car use throughout the capital, reflecting the imposition of a car-oriented urban planning model. Because walking and public transport remain majority transport modes, this trend has serious equity implications. Indeed, just 40% of households have cars in Santiago, but some have two or more (SECTRA, 2015), revealing that middle- to high-income families, which concentrate income, also concentrate car ownership. This scenario is barely challenged by billions of dollars of investment in Metro (MTT, 2013), the underground train system, and fails to consider the importance of the walk–bike–bus trio to greater equity and sustainability, that is, the 'ecology of modes', introduced in the methods section.

3.2 Poverty and Modal Share

Because of extreme segregation (Sabatini, Wormald, Sierralta, & Peters, 2009), *comunas* are a good proxy for poverty, which is concentrated mainly in the periphery but exists in virtually every comuna. Table 5.3 ranks *comunas* for poverty in two ways: by the absolute number of people living below the official poverty line (columns 1–3, on the left) and by the percentage of the total population living in poverty (columns 4–6, on the right). The absolute number is important, because it reflects the overall magnitude of poverty, affecting 10% (more than 600,000 people) of the population. The percentage is also significant, however, as it indicates how poverty has become concentrated in specific *comunas,* often in marginal parts of the city or in satellite suburban locations. This impacts profoundly on

Table 5.3. Poverty in Santiago Comunas (Ranked by No. of Persons and Percentage of Population).

Ranked by Number of People Living in Poverty			Ranked by Percentage of Total Population Living in Poverty		
Comuna	U(rban) or R(ural)	Number of People	Comuna	U(rban) or R(ural)	Percentage of Total Population
Puente Alto	U	85,128	La Granja	U	20.0
San Bernardo	U	50,998	Melipilla	R	19.5
La Pintana	U	35,108	San Bernardo	U	17.9
La Granja	U	27,903	La Pintana	U	17.0
La Florida	U	26,235	Isla de Maipo	R	15.4
El Bosque	U	24,933	Cerro Navia	U	15.4
Cerro Navia	U	23,801	Puente Alto	U	14.6
Peñalolén	U	22,124	Independencia	U	14.2
Melipilla	R	21,708	Calera de Tango	R	13.4
Pudahuel	U	20,858	El Bosque	U	13.2
Providencia	U	4,311	San Miguel	U	4.6
Lo Barnechea	U	4,115	Lo Barnechea	U	4.2
Las Condes	U	3,641	Maipú	U	3.9
El Monte	R	3,223	Providencia	U	3.0
Calera de Tango	R	3,105	Pirque	R	2.7
La Reina	U	1,277	Las Condes	U	1.3
Ñuñoa	U	1,153	La Reina	U	1.3
Pirque	R	568	Ñuñoa	U	0.6
Vitacura	U	246	Vitacura	U	0.3

Source: Own elaboration using origin–destination data from 2012 (SECTRA, 2015).
Notes: For readability, this table highlights *comunas* (administrative jurisdictions) with the highest (light grey) and lowest (dark grey) poverty levels, looking at poverty measured as an absolute number and as a per cent of total population.

the resources available to elected municipal councils and staff that manage each *comuna*. Metropolitan Santiago overall has no elected government, although reforms are currently underway in that direction.

Thus, gender issues play out in a city that is already segregated along income lines, a factor that complicates access to work, education and other crucial social benefits and activities.

The highest number of trips by car is associated with the four high-income *comunas*, Vitacura (64.4% of trips), Lo Barnechea (62.3%), Las Condes (57.4%) and La Reina (52.2%). High walking levels are apparent in low-income *comunas*, with walking accounting for over half of daily trips in seven *comunas*: Lampa (58.5%), Pedro Aguirre Cerda (57.6%), Pudahuel (57.2%), Conchalí (54.3%), El Bosque (52.3%), Cerro Navia (51.3%) and Lo Espejo (50.6%). Walking, then, is associated with poverty to a substantial degree, possibly because of the high costs of owning and using a car, as well as the costs of the public transport fare (Iglesias et al., 2019). Moreover, women account for 56% or more of those walking in all but one of these *comunas* (Conchalí, Fig. 5.3).

The overall sustainability of current travel patterns is remarkable, given that improving traffic conditions and infrastructure for cars has been the focus of the vast

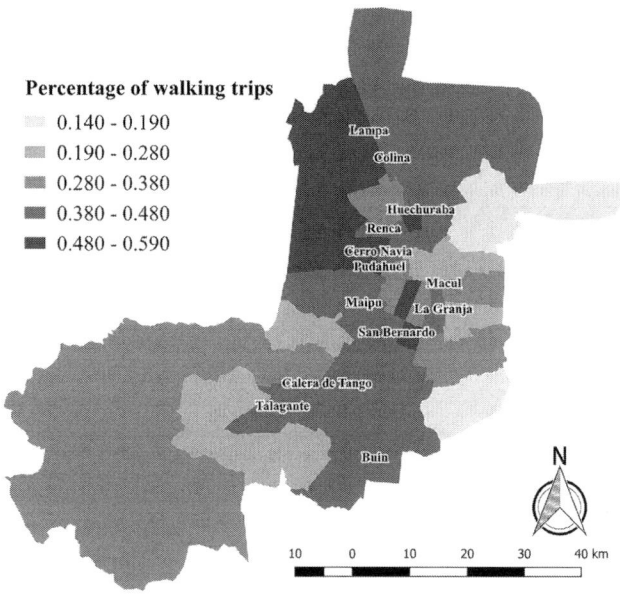

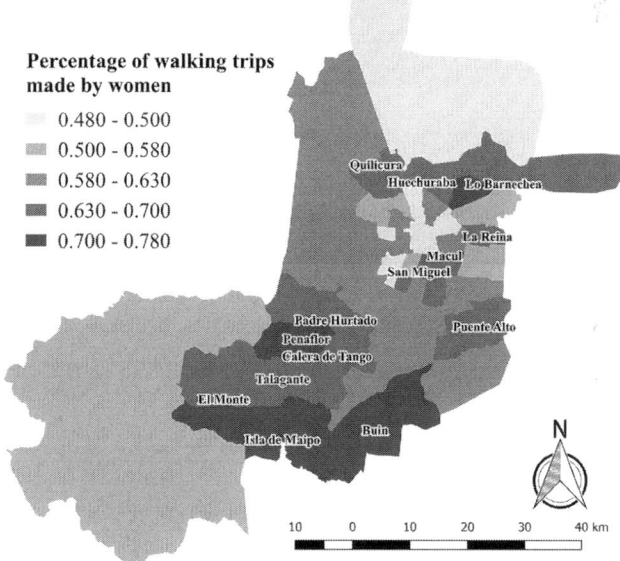

Fig. 5.3. Distribution of Walking Trips in General (Above) and Walking Trips Made Mainly by Women (Below), Revealing the High Dependence on Walking as a Major Transport Mode in Low-Income Comunas. Moreover, Women Account for a Disproportionately High Percentage of Those Trips. *Source*: Own elaboration using data from SECTRA (2015).

Table 5.4. Overall Sustainability (%).

Comuna	Total Trips	Car (%)	PT (%)	Walk (%)	Cycle (%)	Collective Taxi (%)	Metro Combinations (%)	Sustainable Transport Modes (%)
Cerro Navia	11,12,233	16.8	20.6	51.3	6.3	1.8	0.2	80.3
Conchalí	11,81,460	17.4	22.9	54.3	1.0	0.9	0.0	79.1
Pudahuel	25,12,603	16.0	18.9	57.2	1.7	0.1	0.5	78.3
San Ramón	7,17,635	17.4	24.5	47.3	4.2	1.5	0.6	78.1
P. A. Cerda	13,50,540	17.9	14.1	57.6	3.5	1.6	0.2	77.1
Providencia	33,15,625	36.2	26.1	24.9	5.0	0.4	1.5	57.7
Calera de Tango	1,50,093	21.2	0.0	44.9	8.6	3.8	0.1	57.4
Colina	11,67,011	17.5	0.1	48.3	3.8	4.4	0.0	56.6
Cerrillos	9,44,953	36.5	18.9	32.9	1.4	2.8	0.0	56.0
Ñuñoa	26,13,827	40.5	21.4	27.1	5.9	0.5	0.4	55.4
Las Condes	38,62,497.716	57.4	21.2	13.7	3.3	0.1	1.0	39.3
Lo Barnechea	9,18,876.115	62.3	11.1	18.6	3.1	0.6	0.3	33.7
Vitacura	12,27,400.397	64.4	11.4	16.4	3.0	0.2	0.4	31.4
Pirque	1,43,143.4871	45.9	0.2	14.4	4.7	0.0	0.1	19.5

Source: Own elaboration using origin–destination data from 2012 (SECTRA, 2015).
Notes: Again, for brevity and readability, this table has been shortened by selecting the five most, five middling and four least sustainable districts. For the city overall, an impressive total of 24 districts (rows) post 66% or more combined modal share for public transport, walking, cycling, collective taxi and Metro, considered 'sustainable' (dark grey), while another 14 are 'partly sustainable', a combined modal share over 50% but under 66%. Just seven districts classify as 'unsustainable' (light grey), with under half of daily transport via sustainable modes. Three are rural areas with limited access to public transport and economic activities requiring trucks and other forms of motorised transport. Among the modes (columns), walking, cycling and public transport are considered sustainable modes (dark grey), collective and individual taxis partially sustainable (yellow), and cars unsustainable (light grey).

majority of transport-related investment in the past 20 years. On average, motorised travel by car (26%) and public transport (25%) account for over half of trips, reflecting large distances covered by workers and others who cross the city to reach opportunities in the wealthier *comunas* of Santiago, Providencia, Las Condes and Vitacura. Walking (34.4%) and cycling (4%), however, are very important, with some *comunas* posting levels well above average for the three sustainable modes combined (Table 5.4).

As discussed under methods, travel modes can be associated with trip distance, either real or optimum: the vast majority of walking trips in Santiago range from 0 to 2 km. Walking trips, then, may be sustainable in the sense of energy and emissions, but suggest a lack of social sustainability, as they reveal a limited range of destinations for those *comunas* where this is the main mode. For those travellers, mainly women, who account for most of those walking, this would not be a problem if the amenities available within each *comuna* were of equivalent high number and quality. However, in recent decades, the city's most important opportunities (jobs, education, health centres, museums, stores, cultural centres, libraries, government offices, among others) have become ever more concentrated along a narrow strip of *comunas* (municipal jurisdictions) running from the central business district (Santiago centre) through Providencia, Las Condes, Vitacura and, increasingly, Lo Barnechea (Suazo, 2017).

If we look more closely at the percentage of women travelling by mode and *comuna* (Table 5.5), we can see that in just five *comunas* they account for over half

Sustainable Transport and Gender Equity

Table 5.5. Where Do Women Travel Most, by Each Mode?

Where Do More Women Travel by Car?			Where Do More Women Walk?			Where Do More Women Cycle?			Where Do More Women Take Public Transport?		
Comuna	% Trips	%W	Comuna	% Trips	%W	Comuna	% Trips	%W	Comuna	% Trips	%W
Lo Prado	25.2	58.4	Isla De Maipo	26.9	77.8	Quinta Normal	6.1	50.4	Colina	0.1	72.6
La Reina	52.2	58.1	Buin	47.9	75.4	Ñuñoa	5.9	42.5	Renca	24.9	59.6
Vitacura	64.4	53.0	Vitacura	16.4	75.2	Providencia	5.0	42.5	La Reina	18.8	58.6
Las Condes	57.4	52.7	Peñaflor	37.0	71.9	Quilicura	5.4	36.5	Padre Hurtado	0.5	58.5
Colina	17.5	50.6	San Joaquín	42.2	69.5	Pudahuel	1.7	33.3	Ñuñoa	21.4	58.4
Padre Hurtado	23.3	50.0	Calera De Tango	44.9	69.1	La Reina	4.5	32.2	Peñalolén	18.0	57.7
Ñuñoa	40.5	49.1	Huechuraba	45.8	68.1	Vitacura	3.0	31.4	Conchalí	22.9	57.6
Macul	29.1	48.7	Quilicura	33.0	67.0	Peñalolén	4.5	31.1	Quilicura	26.2	56.2
La Florida	37.2	46.4	Padre Hurtado	27.6	66.6	Isla De Maipo	24.0	30.9	Lo Prado	22.3	55.9
La Pintana	18.5	46.3	San Ramón	47.3	66.6	Cerro Navia	6.3	30.5	Vitacura	11.4	55.4
Calera De Tango	21.2	46.2	Talagante	42.2	66.0	Monte	7.7	28.2	Lo Barnechea	11.1	55.3
Providencia	36.2	46.1	La Reina	21.0	66.0	Macul	4.1	27.7	Independencia	23.3	55.2
In just five comunas, women account for more than half of those using cars			*Women account for a disproportionately high percentage of those walking in these 12 comunas. Over half of walking trips in 40 of the 45 comunas analysed*			*Women account for the half of cyclists in one comuna only, and more than 30% in 10 comunas*			*Women account for over half of public transport users in these 12 comunas, and in 26 of the total 45 comunas*		

Source: Own elaboration using origin–destination data from 2012 (SECTRA, 2015).

of car users, perhaps reflecting trip chaining by middle- and high-income women, who take children to school, realise extensive care-related activities and often work. Car ownership reveals levels of concentration similar to those for income, with high-income families having as many as five . Women, however, account for the majority, sometimes a vast majority, of those walking.

Collective taxis, which follow fixed routes and pick up as many as four passengers at a time, are particularly relevant to women, who account for over half of users in 34 of the 45 *comunas* and 100% of users in the wealthy *comuna* of Las Condes. The role of taxis and paratransit systems such as collective taxis is under-represented and not well understood in discussions of sustainable transport, although an emerging literature has explored their importance. Conditions in Chilean cities suggest these may be particularly important to women, as they often accompany young children, older adults or people with health or other disabilities (Domarchi et al., 2019).

Cycling, meanwhile, is enjoying powerful growth, with modal share doubling to 4% between 2006 and 2012 and the number of cyclists on main routes climbing by rates of 20–25% (UyT & CiudadViva, 2012). This reflects powerful advocacy and a Dutch-assisted development programme that led to a fourfold expansion in cycling infrastructure between 2006 and 2012 (Sagaris, 2015). Cycling rates have continued to rise quickly in recent years. The development of amenities, however, has followed the same pattern as other urban amenities and basic services, focussing mainly on three mid- to high-income areas: Santiago and Providencia and Ñuñoa.

Indeed, low-income *comunas* with particularly high cycling modal shares have seen little or no investment in appropriate infrastructure. In these *comunas*, where walking rates are high, especially among women, the rates of women cycling are particularly low. This probably reflects the fact that women are more risk adverse than men and, therefore, more sensitive to safety, preferring, for example, greater segregation from motorised traffic (Caulfield, Brick, & McCarthy, 2012). Widths of the few existing cycle tracks and the residual spaces on often busy roads do not offer safe travel conditions for women using cargo bikes. Currently, cargo bikes are mainly used by recyclers who make their livings plying city neighbourhoods to collect metal, cardboard and other scraps. There is no firm data on this sector, but observations reveal that a significant minority of cargo bike users are women.

Women are often considered a key 'indicator' for quality cycling facilities, with rates equalling or slightly surpassing those of men in cycle-inclusive countries, particularly the Netherlands and the city of Copenhagen (Garrard, Rose, & Lo, 2008; Pucher & Buehler, 2008). Cycling could potentially offer a low-cost and healthy alternative to walking trips, which could substantially expand women's access to specific urban amenities or to the Metro underground train system, which is widely perceived as safer than public transport in buses, and which serves the high-amenity city centres well. This potential would be particularly relevant in a more intermodal and sustainable transport planning paradigm, but to date it remains unrealised, since transport users are considered gender-neutral and transport systems are planned primarily for working trips.

3.3. Trip Purpose

Women's trips are known for 'trip chaining' (Primerano, Taylor, Pitaksringkarn, & Tisato, 2008), that is, going from one destination to another, then another, as women fulfil responsibilities in the family and the work spheres, a pattern evident in Santiago too. This study, however, examined trip purpose in itself as potentially relevant to gender, equity and sustainable transport. This analysis started by examining trips by mode, age and gender (Table 5.6), which revealed clear gender-related travel patterns.

Women of different ages account for just over half of commuting trips (13% of women's vs 25% of men's trips), reflecting their lower participation in the workforce, while they accounted for two or three times the share of shopping, health, formalities and care visits, with similar results if the analysis is done on weekdays

Table 5.6. Gender, Age and Trip Purpose (%).

Trip Purpose	Percentage of Trips	Sex	On Week Days						Total (%)
			Age 16–20 (%)	Age 21–29 (%)	Age 30–59 (%)	Age 60–64 (%)	Age 65–75 (%)	Age 76 or more (%)	
Work	37.70	Men	0.10	3.50	17.2	1.80	1.80	0.20	24.60
		Women	0.10	2.10	9.40	0.80	0.70	0.10	13.10
Shopping	17.30	Men	0.10	0.50	2.50	0.30	0.80	0.80	4.90
		Women	0.20	1.20	6.10	1.10	2.30	1.50	12.40
Others (health, various)	16.50	Men	0.10	0.80	3.10	0.50	1.00	1.00	6.60
		Women	0.20	0.80	5.10	0.80	1.80	1.20	9.90
Visit, pick up or drop off	12.80	Men	0.30	0.70	2.60	0.20	0.50	0.30	4.50
		Women	0.20	1.20	5.60	0.40	0.70	0.20	8.30
Education	10.20	Men	2.40	2.30	0.50	0.00	0.00	0.00	5.30
		Women	2.40	2.10	0.40	0.00	0.00	0.00	4.90
Recreation, eat or drink something	5.60	Men	0.30	0.60	1.60	0.20	0.20	0.20	3.00
		Women	0.20	0.50	1.30	0.10	0.30	0.30	2.50

On weekends Trip purpose	Percentage of trips	Sex	Age 16–20 (%)	Age 21–29 (%)	Age 30–59 (%)	Age 60–64 (%)	Age 65–75 (%)	Age 76 or more (%)	Total, purpose (%)
Shopping	35.40	Men	0.90	1.70	7.40	0.70	1.50	0.90	13.10
		Women	1.40	2.10	13.7	1.20	2.40	1.40	22.30
Work	19.60	Men	0.10	2.10	8.50	1.00	1.00	0.20	12.90
		Women	0.00	1.30	4.70	0.30	0.30	0.10	6.70
Visit, pick up or drop off	16.00	Men	0.80	1.90	4.00	0.20	0.90	0.30	8.20
		Women	0.50	1.30	4.40	0.30	1.00	0.40	7.80
Recreation, eat or drink something	14.60	Men	1.30	1.60	4.00	0.20	0.50	0.20	7.90
		Women	0.90	1.00	3.60	0.40	0.50	0.40	6.70
Others (health, various)	12.80	Men	0.20	1.20	2.90	0.30	0.80	0.60	6.00
		Women	0.40	0.40	3.80	0.40	1.00	0.80	6.90
Education	1.50	Men	0.30	0.40	0.10	0.00	0.10	0.00	0.90
		Women	0.20	0.30	0.10	0.00	0.00	0.00	0.60

Source: Own elaboration using origin–destination data from 2012 (SECTRA, 2015). Original table based on Grieco et al. (1989).
Note: Rows with women's care-related trips are shaded to aid reading. The categories with darker outlines are those combined into the 'care' category used in Table 5.5.

Table 5.7. Trip Purpose Ranked Using 'Care' Criteria (Women are Majority Realising These Trips).

Trip Purpose	Weekday	Weekend
	Percentage of Trips	Percentage of Trips
Care	47	64
Work	38	20
Studies	10	15
Recreation (self-care)	6	1

Source: Own elaboration using origin–destination data from 2012 (SECTRA, 2015).
Notes: Care trips (shopping, health, access to services, visiting, picking up or dropping someone off) account for more than any other category of trips, especially on the weekends. Women account for a disproportionate number of travellers for care during the week, but men participate more on weekends.

or weekends. This phenomenon has led some researchers to recommend considering all care-motivated trips as a single category (Sánchez de Madariaga & Zucchini, 2019). Grouping travel purpose categories in this way revealed that for both working days and weekends, the care-related trips where women travellers predominate account for the majority (47%) of all travel on both workdays and weekends (Table 5.7).

This analysis raises some interesting questions about the challenges to 'sustainable' transport posed by gender and, presumably, other social differences, and the opportunities inherent in rising to meet these challenges in appropriate ways. We discuss this further in the next sections.

4. SAFETY PERCEPTION AND SEXUAL HARASSMENT IN SANTIAGO'S PUBLIC TRANSPORT SYSTEM

Women's travel patterns presented above provide insight into travel purposes and modes used by women in Santiago. The Santiago component of the study *Safe and Sound, Ella se mueve segura* ('She moves safely', ESMS) offers additional insight into how gender violence affects women's use of public transport, limiting their travel behaviour. This section is based mainly on that study.

This ESMS study involved both a survey and four focus groups, one in El Bosque (low-income *comuna*), one in Santiago (low- and middle-income *comuna*) and one in Ñuñoa (middle and high-income *comuna*). The survey, which was designed to be representative for men and women using public transport in Santiago, found that 9 of 10 women had experienced some form of verbal or physical harassment, and 1 of every 100 had experienced all forms of harassment, including sexual assault. Harassment by word or gesture accounted for half of the reported cases, while physical harassment (masturbation, being chased) accounted for 24%, physical assault (being grabbed or handled) accounted for 19% of experiences and 6.5% involved being photographed or filmed.

The walk to or from public transport was identified as the place where most harassment took place (Fig. 5.4), followed by buses, and the Metro underground

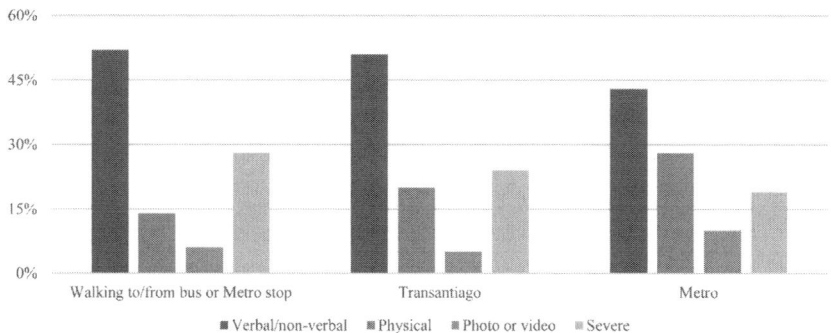

Fig. 5.4. Sexual Harassment Reported by Women Is Remarkably Consistent Across Modes, Including Walking Trips (Access/Egress) Related to Public Transit. Metro is the Only Part of the Travel Chain Covered by a Security System. *Source*: Own elaboration based on data from the Ella se mueve segura survey (based on Allen et al., 2018).

train system, which is the only component of the transport system with its own security guards and other measures. Both women and men experienced harassment, with 83% of those responsible for these experiences being men. The number of women affected by the most severe forms of harassment more than doubled the men affected. These results suggest that a closer look at offenders could be very revealing since there are some indications that a very small number of men may be responsible for most of these situations.

While most men (70%) reported few changes in their travel behaviour, one of every two women responded to these risks by changing the time of day travelled, two of five their transport mode and two of five decided not to travel. Travelling after dark, lengthy waits, overcrowded buses, walks to and from bus stops were considered most risky by women, with similar but lesser levels of concern expressed by men.

Strategies used by men to reduce risk included remaining mostly in their own neighbourhood or taking personal defence classes. Among women, remaining mostly in their own neighbourhood, avoiding specific sectors, changing routes and travelling only when someone else was available to accompany them were the main responses.

The focus groups revealed high levels of apprehension and also passivity in responding, with some debate over who was responsible for reducing risk. Participants identified specific people, for example, a man who repeatedly harassed women waiting in line for buses at the La Cisterna intermodal transfer station, or specific places en route, such as an abandoned water tower with an informal camp of homeless adolescents and young adults, as problematic. A woman's safety audit, prepared and tested as part of the research project and conducted in El Bosque, revealed that despite many good design solutions, these were not enough on their own to resolve social issues associated with poverty, drug addiction and exclusion associated with both delinquency and fear.

The focus groups also revealed that women have personal curfews, that is time constraints, beyond which they do not leave their homes, sometimes as early as 7 p.m. Closer questioning revealed that these are influenced by their habitual public transport mode, so for Metro users, their curfew began when the Metro closed, between 10.30 and 11.30 p.m. Cyclists had the most flexibility for getting around the city, with personal curfews often beyond midnight. Only one incident, witnessed or reported by an acquaintance, was typically enough to change a woman's travel behaviour for a very long time, if not permanently. Moreover, women repeatedly expressed that they teach their evasion strategies and defence methods (particularly the use of sharp pins) to their daughters.

Low-income women from El Bosque reported they avoid public transport as much as possible, reducing their trips or combining them into a single trip by taxi to avoid the bus. This behaviour was confirmed by the survey, which found that personal safety, comfort and convenience were strong motivators for women to wish to change from public transport to their own private car, although this last option is often not possible, given the high costs and low incomes involved.

5. DISCUSSION: CHALLENGES AND OPPORTUNITIES FOR SUSTAINABLE TRANSPORT

This study has placed equity at the centre of social sustainability. It recognises that there are many overlaps among the three spheres of sustainability, as occurs when jobs, mainly associated with the economic sphere, have important implications in the social sphere. At the same time, equity is primarily a social value, although it has enormous implications for both the economic and the environmental aspects of sustainability. Health, including physical activity as part of active transport and road safety, could be considered the intimate human reflection of environmental sustainability, translated to the social sphere. Clearly, there are also serious implications for economic sustainability, where non-communicable diseases are becoming the major cause of death and disability in a growing number of countries, and health care systems and family budgets are heavily burdened by related conditions, such as obesity, diabetes II, cardiovascular, cancer and other ailments.

These results reflect an exploration of how a gender analysis of origin–destination data and a mixed methods approach to perceptions of gender violence and safety in public transport systems contributed to a better understanding of the equity aspects of social sustainability. They reveal that even in a city, such as Metropolitan Santiago, which has transitioned towards a car-oriented planning paradigm, walking remains important, particularly for women. They indicate that there are important equity challenges associated with this pattern, which is positive from an environmental and economic sustainability perspective but could inhibit social participation of women in society and accessing key urban opportunities in cities. For girls and women around the world, walking as a standalone trip, walking to and from, and travelling in public transport are fraught with road safety, sexual harassment and social security issues that limit their participation in the benefits of city living (Allen, 2016). Local research confirmed these are significant challenges in Santiago.

These implications can be grouped according to their:

- *Impacts on women themselves*, and their full integration into the social and civic life of their communities (equity from a rights perspective): women in low-income *comunas* (the majority) have reduced access to major urban amenities and, given the spatial concentration of wealth and, increasingly jobs (Suazo, 2017; Tiznado-Aitken et al., 2018), in high-income *comunas*, reduced opportunities for income and development for themselves and their families. This hurts women, but it also hurts societies that limit their options. CAF (2017a, 2017b), the Latin American Development Bank, attributes the 5% growth rates achieved by Latin American countries (2002–2008) to the fact that 70 million women joined the workforce and estimates that if women could participate equally with men in their country's economies, by 2025, they would contribute an additional US$25 billion.
- *Impacts on public transport systems*, struggling to retain users amidst multiple pressures from automobility and real estate interests to switch to cars or costly Metro lines. These currently fail to consider walking (and cycling) access as an integral part of planning, designing and operating (Koglin & Rye, 2014). Nor, in most cases, do they address comfort and security issues from a gender perspective. This would involve explicit consideration of mobility involving baby carriages, carts, walkers, wheelchairs and other equipment, introducing safety elements for children and people with disabilities. Additional security elements such as panic buttons, drop-off on request (especially at night) and bikes-on-transit policies (external racks, internal spaces on trains and buses) would allow night shift workers to move more quickly and safely to public transport trunk routes and reduce wait times at lonely bus stops on feeder lines. In the health care sector, where women are the majority of nurses and a growing share of physicians, night shifts are important to participating in the labour market. For women doing internships in different professions, limitations on their ability to travel at night can seriously hamper their personal and professional development.
- *Implications for cycling, cycle taxis, bike-share and folding bikes*, as these could both expand the radius of access well beyond walking distances (by a circumference of 2–8 km) and alleviate the burden of carrying purchases, small children and adults, depending on the type of vehicles and infrastructure available. In conditions such as those revealed by this study, cycling emerges as highly strategic, to expand the range and comfort of all users and trips, but particularly women and care-related travel. This could complement walking, as it offers similar health and could improve access to critical urban amenities. Cycling with appropriate accessories for carrying children and cargo could improve walking conditions and make it easier for women — and men as values evolve towards greater equity in gender roles — to fulfil their tasks while still preserving the health, environmental and safety benefits of active transport. Cycle taxis such as the cycle rickshaw systems common throughout India could complement personal ownership with collective services suited diverse conditions and needs, creating jobs without increasing costs to the prohibitive (for many) levels of motorised transport.

- *Potential for retaining or enhancing positive health and access benefits*, through spatial and other planning approaches such as complete streets, traffic-calming, car-free precincts and other mechanisms. A more integrated 'ecology of modes' approach to transport could significantly improve security, safety and environmental conditions for walking by significantly reducing motorised trips in areas of the city with high densities of residences, commercial or other trip-attracting activities. Similarly, educational policies that locate primary and secondary schools within walking and cycling distances would enhance both travel and environmental quality. They could also improve children's autonomy, liberating parents from taxi duties, and providing them with more freedom for other activities. Health trips could reverse direction, with primary health care workers visiting neighbourhoods on foot and by bicycle, thereby improving understanding of the urban context shaping people's food, physical activity and other habits. Linking walking and cycling more directly and easily to public transport, with intermodal policies and applications, would also help to retain health benefits while improving overall access to the city.
- *Implications for transportation planning and institutions*, which with few exceptions suffer from extreme fragmentation, and a lack of deliberative participatory approaches that could contribute to shifting behaviour and values towards more active transport-centred planning. Planning for more than one mode is a major challenge in cities like Santiago, where national ministries rather than local governments are responsible for different aspects of transport planning and often compete rather than collaborate on policy arrangements and investment. Geels (2014), Bulkeley, Broto, Hodson, and Marvin (2011), Newman and Jennings (2008), Low and Gleeson (2003) and Banister (2007) have all explored these issues, mostly from a positionality located in developed countries, where driving is the majority transport mode. More research is required to explore how to preserve high walking shares and increase cycling while still improving equity and inclusion in developing countries, where travel patterns may be radically different, despite recent transitions towards greater automobility.

Addressing safety concerns, whether related to traffic or delinquency and sexual harassment, remains an additional and major challenge in many urban environments in both developed and developing cities, as the Santiago research indicates.

What is encouraging, however, is that this perspective indicates the importance of active transport, mainly walking, as the potential basis for a more sustainable transport system, from a social as well as economic and environmental perspectives. The predominance of non-work trips, moreover, has important implications for combining transport and land use planning, given that local governments typically have more influence over where local schools, health facilities and shops are located. From a service perspective, it suggests that public transport planning that does not consider access and egress trips from the system cannot be considered 'sustainable' from a social perspective. Moreover, it strongly suggests that safety, health and (dis)ability considerations should play a central role in planning for sustainable transport in the twenty-first century.

In the past 20 years, cycling has enjoyed a powerful renaissance around the world (Buehler & Pucher, 2017; Pucher & Buehler 2017; Pucher, Buehler, & Seinen, 2011). Advocacy by local, national and international cycling organisations (particularly the Dutch, Danish and European Cycling federations and the World Cycling Alliance) has played a key role in pushing this progress, as have visionary planners, designers (CROW et al., 2007; Godefrooij, Pardo, & Sagaris, 2009; Mokhtarian & Handy 2008) and engineers (Forester, 2012; Parkin, 2012; Tiwari, Arora, Jain, & Godefrooij, 2008). Walking and walkability have recently attracted significant advocacy, through gatherings such as the Walk 21 conference, but public transit remains primarily the domain of transport engineers and related professionals.

As mentioned earlier, then, 'ecologies of modes' potentially have equivalent 'ecologies of actors', the human faces necessary to push innovative policies onto public agendas and keep them there long enough for significant change. In this sense, women's lives are multipurpose, and their trips reflect their dependency on more sustainable transport modes to serve a more diverse gamut of needs and activities. This generates trip chaining, which in itself can contribute to more efficient use of transport time, infrastructure and other resources. Women's participation in sustainable transport debates can help push more interdisciplinary approaches that in turn could help build stronger advocacy for a 'sustainability trio', in which an intermodal focus improves walk–bike–bus interactions, to reinforce gender-related aspects and social sustainability in general (Sagaris, Steiniger, & Tiznado-Aitken, 2017).

Security issues threaten to undermine this potential, however, as women faced with hostile walking and public transport conditions increasingly consider cars a safer, more comfortable and convenient transport mode. Collective taxis can help to offset these concerns, but to date their role in supplementing public transport, particularly to address women's and children's needs, has been under-researched and, if care is not taken, these may be displaced by 'modernisation', whether in favour of cars, public transit in general or bus rapid systems with their often exclusive corridors.

Another area for further research would be a closer look at potential correlations between poverty, safety, gender and transport choices, throughout the life cycle and across time. Knowing more about how positive behaviours such as the high levels of walking identified in this study reflect personal or collective values, cultures and other factors could help to identify key levers when policymakers seek to retain the high modal shares of walking and public transit while improving social equity issues associated with each. These issues are particularly crucial in developing countries, where many have very high modal shares for walking (e.g. Nairobi) or cycling (Delhi and other Indian and Asian cities). There the challenge is as much convincing people to continue with active transport, as it is persuading them not to leap into cars or at least not to use cars for short trips.

Placing a high priority on walking and cycling networks as the foundational components of a sustainable transport grid could significantly improve gender equality and social justice aspects of 'sustainable' transport, including public transport, which requires walking or cycling trips as part of accessing the public transport system. This possibility is not receiving enough attention amidst debates about Uberisation, mobility as a service, 'smart' cities, self-driving cars and other phenomena, much of it driven by commercial rather than sustainability interests.

ACKNOWLEDGEMENTS

This research was supported by the Center for Excellence in BRT+ and Center for Excellence and the Centro de Desarrollo Urbano Sustentable (CEDEUS) at the Pontificia Universidad Católica de Chile, with funding from Conicyt, FONDAP No. 15110020. The *Ella se mueve segura* study received funding from CAF, the Latin American Development Bank and the FIA Foundation.

REFERENCES

Allen, H. (2016). *Safe and sound* (p. 57). London: FIA Foundation.

Allen, H., Pereyra, L., Sagaris, L., & Cárdenas, G. (2019). *Ella se mueve segura, Un estudio sobre la seguridad personal de las mujeres y el transporte público en tres ciudades de América Latina*. Buenos Aires: CAF y FIA Foundation.

Allen, H., Sagaris, L., Pereyra, L., & Cárdenas, G. (2018). *Ella se mueve segura – Women Safety and Public Transport in Three Latin American Cities*. London: Brussels. Retrieved from https://scioteca.caf.com/bitstream/handle/123456789/1407/Ella%20se%20mueve%20segura%20-%20A%20study%20on%20womens%20personal%20safety.pdf?sequence=5&isAllowed=y

Asociación de Investigaciones de Mercado (AIM) Chile. (2016). *Nuevos Grupos Socioeconómicos* 2018. Retrieved from http://www.aimchile.cl/wp-content/uploads/Nuevos-Grupos-Socioeconomicos-AIM-febrero-2018-FINAL-2.pdf

Banister, D. (2007). Sustainable transport: Challenges and opportunities. *Transportmetrica*, *3*(2), 91–106.

Beckmann, J. (2001). Automobility—a social problem and theoretical concept. Environment and Planning D: Society and Space, *19*(5), 593–607.

Buehler, R., & Pucher, J. (2017). Trends in walking and cycling safety: Recent evidence from high-income countries, with a focus on the United States and Germany. *American Journal of Public Health*, *107*(2), 281–287.

Bulkeley, H., Broto, V. C., Hodson, M., & Marvin, S. (2011). *Cities and low carbon transitions*. London: Routledge.

CAF. (2017a). El determinante papel de las mujeres en el desarrollo económico de América Latina. Retrieved from https://www.caf.com/es/actualidad/noticias/2017/03/el-determinante-papel-de-las-mujeres-en-el-desarrollo-economico-de-america-latina/

CAF. (2017b). Mujeres y desarrollo económico. Retrieved from https://www.caf.com/es/actualidad/noticias/2017/03/mujeres-y-desarrollo-economico/

Caulfield, B., Brick, E., & McCarthy, O. T., (2012). Determining bicycle infrastructure preferences – A case study of Dublin. *Transportation Research Part D: Transportation and Environment*, *17*(5), 413–417.

Chillón, P., Ortega, F., Ruiz, J. R., Evenson, K. R., Labayen, I., Martínez-Vizcaino, … Sjöström, M. (2012). Bicycling to school is associated with improvements in physical fitness over a 6-year follow-up period in Swedish children. *Preventive Medicine*, *55*, 108–112.

ComunidadMujer. (2016). Género, educación y trabajo: La Brecha Persistente. Primer estudio sobre la desigualdad de género en el ciclo de vida. Una revisión de los últimos 25 años. ComunidadMujer. Santiago, Chile, Comunidad Mujer, Banco Interamericano de Desarrollo: 48. Retrieved from https://www.comunidadmujer.cl/get/httpwww-informeget-cl/

CROW, Talens, H., Ploeger, J., Kroeze, P. A., Diteweg, R., Dijkstra, A., … Zeegers, Th. (2007). *Design manual for bicycle traffic*. Utrecht: CROW.

David, T. G., & Weinstein, C. S. (1987). *Spaces for children: The built environment and child development*. New York, NY: Plenum Press.

De Vasconcellos, E. A. (1997). The demand for cars in developing countries. *Transportation Research A Policy and Practice*, *31*(3), 245–258.

De Vasconcellos, E. A. (2001). *Urban transport, environment, and equity: The case for developing countries*. London: Earthscan Publications.

De Vasconcellos, E. A. (2015). Transporte urbano y movilidad: reflexiones y propuestas para países en desarrollo. Buenos Aires: UNSAMedita.

Deka, D., & Von Hagen, L. A. (2015). The evolution of school siting and its implications for active transportation in New Jersey. *International Journal of Sustainable Transportation*, 9(8), 602–611.

Domarchi, C., Coeymans, J. E., & de Dios Ortúzar, J. (2019). Shared taxis: modelling the choice of a paratransit mode in Santiago de Chile. *Transportation*, 46(6), 2243-2268.

Douglas, L. (2016). The elusive pursuit of equity. Retrieved from https://secondlineblog.org/2016/11/the-elusive-pursuit-of-equity/

Fainstein, S. S. (2010). *The just city*. Ithaca, NY: Cornell University Press.

Feitelson, E. (2002). Introducing environmental equity dimensions into the sustainable transport discourse: Issues and pitfalls. *Transportation Research Part D: Transport and Environment*, 7(2), 99–118.

Forester, J. (2012). *Effective cycling*. Cambridge, MA: MIT Press.

Frank, L. D., Engelke, P. O., & Schmid, T. (2003). *Health and community design: The impact of the built environment on physical activity*. Washington, DC: Island Press.

Frumkin, H., Frank, L. D., & Jackson, R. (2004). *Urban sprawl and public health: Designing, planning, and building for healthy communities*. Washington, DC: Island Press.

Garrard, J., Rose, G., & Lo, S. K. (2008). Promoting transportation cycling for women: The role of bicycle infrastructure. *Preventive Medicine*, 46, 55–59.

Geels, F. W. (2014). Regime resistance against low-carbon transitions: Introducing politics and power into the multi-level perspective. *Theory, Culture & Society*, 31(5), 21–40.

GobiernoChile. (2016). Balance de Gestión integral (BGI). Retrieved from http://www.dipres.gob.cl/598/w3-propertyvalue-15229.html

Godefrooij, T., Pardo, C., & Sagaris, L. (2009). *Cycling-inclusive policy development: A handbook*. Utrecht: Interface for Cycling Expertise, GTZ, Federal Ministry for Economic Cooperation and Development.

GORE. (2014). *Estrategia Regional de Desarrollo Capital Ciudadana 2012–2021*. Santiago: Gobierno Regional (GORE).

Grieco, M., Pickup, L., & Whipp, R. (1989). *Gender, transport, and employment : the impact of travel constraints*. Aldershot, Hants; Brookfield, WI: Gower.

Hanson, S. (2010). Gender and mobility: new approaches for informing sustainability. Gender, Place & Culture, 17(1), 5–23. doi:10.1080/09663690903498225

Harvey, D. (2008). The right to the city. *New Left Review*, 53(Sept.–Oct.), 23–40.

Hillman, M. (1999). The impact of transport policy on children's development. Paper presented at the Canterbury Safe Routes to School Seminar, C. C. C. U. College, Christ Church University College, Canterbury, UK.

Hillman, M., Adams, J., & Whitelegg, J. (1990). *One false move: A study of children's independent mobility*. London, Policy Studies Institute.

Iglesias, V., Giraldez, F., Tiznado-Aitken, I., & Muñoz, J. C. (2019). How Uneven is the Urban Mobility Playing Field? Inequalities among Socioeconomic Groups in Santiago De Chile. *Transportation Research Record*. DOI: https://doi.org/10.1177/0361198119849588

IISC. (2016). Equality vs. equity. Collaboration between Interaction Institute for Social Change and the Artist Angus Maguire. Retrieved from http://madewithangus.com/portfolio/equality-vs-equity/

INE. (2018). Censo Nacional de Chile/National census. Retrieved from http://www.censo2017.cl

Isalou, A. A., Litman, T., & Shahmoradi, B. (2014). Testing the housing and transportation affordability index in a developing world context: A sustainability comparison of central and suburban districts in Qom, Iran. *Transport Policy*, 33, 33–39.

Karner, A., & Sagaris, L. (2016). *Testing a new approach to planning sustainable transport using data from Metropolitan Santiago de Chile and the San Francisco Bay Area*. Washington, DC: Transportation Research Board.

Koglin, T., & Rye, T. (2014). The marginalisation of bicycling in modernist urban transport planning. *Journal of Transport Health*, 1(4), 214–222.

Lorenc, T., Brunton, G., Oliver, S., Oliver, K., & Oakley, A. (2008). Attitudes to walking and cycling among children, young people and parents: A systematic review. *Journal of Epidemiology and Community Health*, 62(10), 852–857.

Loukaitou-Sideris, A. (2014). Fear and safety in transit environments from the women's perspective. *Security Journal*, 27(2), 242–256.

Loukaitou-Sideris, A., Bornstein, A., Fink, C., Samuels, L., & Gerami, S. (2009, October). *How to ease women's fear of transportation environments: Case Studies and Best Practices*, Mineta Transportation Institute, San Jose State University, CA, USA (p. 82).

Low, N., & Gleeson, B. (2003). *Making urban transport sustainable*. Houndmills: Palgrave Macmillan.

Lucas, K. (2004). *Running on empty: Transport, social exclusion and environmental justice*. Bristol: Policy Press.

Manzi, T., & Lucas, K. (2010). *Social sustainability in urban areas*. New York, NY: Earthscan.

Martens, K. (2016). *Transport justice*. New York, NY: Routledge.

Martens, K. (2017). *Transport justice*. New York, NY: Routledge.

Mindell, J., & Karlsen, S. (2012). Community severance and health: What do we actually know? *Journal of Urban Health*, 89(2), 232–246.

Mindell, J., Watkins, S., & Cohen, J. (2011). *Health on the move 2. Policies for health promoting transport*. Stockport: Transport and Health Study Group.

Mokhtarian, P., & Handy, S. (2008). *Neighborhood design and the accessibility of the elderly: An empirical analysis in Northern California*. Transportation Research Board 87th Annual Meeting, Washington, DC.

MTT. (2013). Plan Maestro de Transporte de Santiago 2025. Santiago, Chile, Ministerio de Transporte y Telecomunicaciones.

Murray, C., Monetti, E., & Ween, C. (2017). *Real Estate and Urban Development in South America: Understanding Local Regulations and Investment Methods in a Highly Urbanised Continent*. New York: Routledge.

National Census (2017). National Institute of Statistics (INE). Government of Chile. Retrieved from https://www.censo2017.cl/

Newman, P., & Jennings, I. (2008). *Cities as sustainable ecosystems: Principles and practices*. Washington, DC: Island Press.

Nieuwenhuijsen, M., & Khreis, H. (2019). Urban and transport planning, environment and health. In M. Nieuwenhuijsen & H. Khreis (Eds.), *Integrating human health into urban and transport planning* (pp. 3–16). Basel: Springer.

Parkin, J. (2012). *Cycling and sustainability*. Bingley: Emerald Publishing Limited.

Pereira, R. H. M., Schwanen, T., & Banister, D. (2017). Distributive justice and equity in transportation. *Transport Reviews*, 37(2), 170–191. https://doi.org/10.1080/01441647.2016.1257660

Porter, G. (2011). 'I think a woman who travels a lot is befriending other men and that's why she travels': Mobility constraints and their implications for rural women and girls in sub-Saharan Africa. *Gender, Place and Culture*, 18(1), 65–81.

Primerano, F., Taylor, M. A. P., Pitaksringkarn, L., & Tisato, P. (2008). Defining and understanding trip chaining behaviour. *Transportation*, 35, 55–72.

Pucher, J., & Buehler, R. (2008). Making Cycling Irresistible: Lessons from The Netherlands, Denmark and Germany. *Transport Reviews*, 28(4), 495–528.

Pucher, J., & Buehler, R. (2017). Cycling towards a more sustainable transport future. *Transport Reviews*, 37(6), 689–694.

Pucher, J., Buehler, R., & Seinen, M. (2011). Bicycling renaissance in North America? An update and re-appraisal of cycling trends and policies. *Transportation Research Part A*, 45, 451–475.

Rudner, J. (2012). Public knowing of risk and children's independent mobility. *Progress in Planning*, 78(1), 1–50.

RWJF. (2017). Visualizing health equity: One size does not fit all infographic. Retrieved from https://www.rwjf.org/en/library/infographics/visualizing-health-equity.html

Rydin, Y., Bleahu, A., Davies, M., Dávila, J. D., Friel, S., De Grandis, G., … Wilson, J. (2012). Shaping cities for health: Complexity and the planning of urban environments in the 21st century. *The Lancet*, 379(June 2), 2079–2108.

Sabatini, F., Wormald, G., Sierralta, C., & Peters, P. A. (2009). Residential segregation in santiago: Scale-related effects and trends, 1992–2002. In B. R. Roberts & R. H. Wilson (Eds.), *Urban segregation and governance in the Americas* (p. 244). New York, NY: Palgrave Macmillan.

Sagaris, L. (2014a). Citizen participation for sustainable transport: The case of living city in Santiago, Chile (1997–2012). *Journal of Transport Geography*, 41(December), 74–83.

Sagaris, L. (2014b). Citizens' anti-highway revolt in post-pinochet Chile: Catalyzing innovation in transport planning. *Planning Practice & Research*, *29*(3), 268–280.

Sagaris, L. (2015). Lessons from 40 years of planning for cycle-inclusion: Reflections from Santiago, Chile. *Natural Resources Forum*, *39*(1), 64–81.

Sagaris, L., & Arora, A. (2015). Rethinking sustainable transportation as bike-bus intermodal integration. In D. Henscher & J. C. Muñoz (Eds.), Thredbo International Series. Santiago: Chile.

Sagaris, L., & Arora, A. (2016). Evaluating how cycle-bus integration could contribute to sustainable transport. *Research in Transportation Economics*, *59*(November), 218–227.

Sagaris, L., & Arora, A. (2018). Cycling for social justice in democratizing contexts: Rethinking sustainable mobilities. In T. Priya & K. Lucas (Eds.), *Urban mobilities in the Global South* (p. 248). London: Routledge.

Sagaris, L., Tiznado-Aitken, I., & Steiniger, S. (2017). Exploring the social and spatial potential of an intermodal approach to transport planning. *International Journal of Sustainable Transportation*, *11*(10), 721–736.

Sánchez de Madariaga, I., & Zucchini, E. (2019). Measuring *mobilities of care*, a challenge for transport agendas. In C. Lindkvist Scholten & T. Joelsson (Eds.), *Integrating gender into transport planning, from one to many tracks* (pp. 145–174). Cham: Palgrave Macmillan.

Secretaria de Planificación de Transporte (SECTRA). (2004). O-D Survey from 2001. Planning and Development Coordination, Transport and Telecommunications Ministry, Government of Chile. Available at: http://www.sectra.gob.cl/biblioteca/detalle1.asp?mfn=818

Secretaria de Planificación de Transporte (SECTRA). (2015). O-D Survey from 2012. Planning and Development Coordination, Transport and Telecommunications Ministry, Government of Chile. Available at: http://www.sectra.gob.cl/encuestas_movilidad/encuestas_movilidad.htm

SECTRA-UAHurtado. (2015). Estudio de Origen – Destino Santiago RM. *Origin–destination surveys*. Santiago: SECTRA, Ministry of Transport, Government of Chile.

Sen, A. (1999). *Development as freedom*. Oxford: Oxford University Press, Alfred Knopf.

Sheller, M., & Urry, J. (2000). The City and The Car. *International Journal of Urban and Regional Research*, *24*(4).

Silva, E. (2004). *The model highway: Chilean neoliberalism, capital city planning and the making of Santiago's Costanera Norte*. 2004 Bridges Summer Research Report 24-VI-2011. Center for Latin American Studies. Retrieved from http://www.clas.berkeley.edu/Research/graduate/summer2004/bridges/silva/index.html

Silva, E. (2011). Deliberate improvisation: Planning highway franchises in Santiago, Chile. *Planning Theory*, *10*(1), 35–52.

Suazo, G. (2017). *Characterization of activity displacement in Santiago de Chile in 1990–2015: Impact on travel times in the city and its camps*. Master of Science thesis, Pontificia Universidad Católica de Chile, Chile.

Tilly, C. (2007). *Democracy*. Cambridge: Cambridge University Press.

Timperio, A., Crawford, D., Telford, A., & Salmon, J. (2004). Perceptions about the local neighborhood and walking and cycling among children. *Preventive Medicine*, *38*, 39–47.

Tiwari, G., Arora, A., Jain, H., & Godefrooij, T. (2008). *Bicycling in Asia*. Utrecht: Interface for Cycling Expertise.

Tiznado-Aitken, I., Muñoz, J. C., & Hurtubia, R. (2018). The role of accessibility to public transport and quality of walking environment on urban equity: the case of Santiago de Chile. *Transportation research record*, *2672*(35), 129–138.

UN. (2016). Sustainable Development Goals. Retrieved from http://www.undp.org/content/undp/es/home/sustainable-development-goals.html. Accessed on September 1, 2019,

Urry, J. (2004). The System of Automobility. *Theory, Culture & Society*, *21*(4–5), 25–39. Retrieved from http://journals2.scholarsportal.info.myaccess.library.utoronto.ca/tmp/10531457860267822187.pdf

UyT, C., & CiudadViva. (2012). *Plan Nosotros Contamos Informe Técnico No. 1.*, Santiago, Chile. Retrieved from https://www.uyt.cl/estudios-y-proyectos. Accessed on January 25, 2019.

WHO. (2013). *Pedestrian safety: A road safety manual for decision-makers and practitioners* (p. 111). Geneva: World Health Organization,.

WHO. (2015). *Global status report on road safety*. Geneva: World Health Organization.

APPENDIX 1

Table A1. Gender and Transport in Santiago: An Overview.

Variables	Santiago
Key City Characteristics	Large metropolitan region, with extensive links to ports on the Pacific coast (100 km westward), mineral producing areas in the north, fruit and forestry production areas in the south
Socio-Spatial Pattern	Highly segregated by socio-economic level. 21.8% of the total population live in seven municipalities, located from the historical city centre towards the northeast area, and concentrate the High Class (AB) and High-Medium Class (C1a) population, which earn almost 28 and 13 times more than the Poor Class, respectively (AIM, 2016). Moreover, they concentrate 53.5% of the new construction space for commercial activities and services between 2009 and 2015 (Suazo, 2017)
Population	6,940,209 (45 comunas analysed, according to National Census, 2017)
Older Adults (Over 60)	1,069,103 (45 comunas analysed, according to National Census, 2017)
Rural/Urban	96.3% urban, 3.7% rural (45 comunas analysed, according to National Census, 2017)
Poverty	Income poverty: 6.6% and multidimensional poverty: 19.6% (MDS, 2015). Wealth is heavily concentrated in the city's eastern neighbourhoods
Women Household Heads	43% (the whole metropolitan region, 52 comunas) (National Census, 2017)
Women's Employment	Women are heavily concentrated in jobs reflecting traditional roles related to caring and service, particularly household help, teaching, social services and health, retail and tourism. Their participation in the work force has risen from 40% (1990) to 66% (2014) but remains among the lowest for both OECD and LAC countries. Moreover, in Santiago, their participation in the work force stands at 48%, compared to 72.7% for men
Care-Related Tasks	Women generally dedicate three times as many hours to care-related duties as do their male counterparts (see additional analysis in this study), with 63% reporting this is the main reason their participation in the labour force is so low
Gender Gap	Chile's gender gap, that is the difference between women's state and men's, shows relative equality among children up to about 15 years old (measured mainly by education), but from 30 on (measured mainly by women's employment income over men's) rises steadily to reach 30% (40–49 years old) and 53.3% as women turn 60 and retire
Life Satisfaction (Measured Using UNDP Methodology)	While 90% of high-income individuals report high levels of satisfaction with their lives (7 or more on a scale of 10), as income falls satisfaction also drops, to 68% among middle income and 58% among low-income respondents
GDP	44.4% of Chile's GDP
Area	15,403 km^2 (the whole metropolitan region, 52 comunas)
Density	462 people per km^2 (the whole metropolitan region, 52 comunas)
Governance	Highly centralised: the national transport ministry runs Transantiago, the city's bus system, with limited participation, transparency accountability
Administrative Areas	Fifty-two comunas with elected mayor and city council; appointed regional Intendente, with very limited planning powers, and elected regional council (recent innovation)

Variables	Santiago
Key Transport Characteristics	Sustainable transport (walk–bike–bus) 67.6% of daily trips (34 comunas of the Greater Santiago)
Automobility	Share of car trips under 5 km (more suited to active transport modes): 53% (34 comunas of the Greater Santiago)
Data	Relatively reliable and complete origin–destination surveys (mostly 2012, 2001 used for comparison); National Census (2017)

Source: Own elaboration using regional data from Estrategia Regional de Desarrollo 2012–2025 (GORE, 2014; SECTRA, 2015) and gender data from a recent report on the status of women in Chile (Informe Comunidad de la Mujer, GET, BID, 2016), unless otherwise noted.

APPENDIX 2: GENERAL METHODOLOGY AND QUALITATIVE METHODS APPLIED

Van den Broeck (2015) underlines the need for research projects, particularly where they involve qualitative research methods, to be explicit about their epistemology and theories, to establish a general research *strategy,* and within this framework select and apply specific *methods.* We consider these distinctions central to our work, particularly as they deeply influence how our qualitative data is analyzed, on its own and in dialogue with our quantitative work.

In terms of epistemology, we consider cities open, adaptive and highly complex human, "natural" and technological ecologies/systems, in which different forms of communication and knowledge must be mobilized if planning is to maximize benefits and minimize costs. By benefits we are referring to the achievement of values and specific goals associated with "sustainability", as defined by the global **Sustainable Development Goals** (UN Habitat, Quito 2016), **with equity.**

To consider equity in a systematic way, we apply a **gender focus**, based on the observation that while motives and forms of discrimination vary widely across cities, countries and cultures, women and girls — the majority in virtually all human societies — face specific kinds of constraints and limitations due to their biologically assigned gender. This makes contrasts of interest for exploratory and more advanced research, although we underline that this perspective and results **do not apply across all categories** forming the basis for discrimination and exclusion.

We consider the city an open, adaptive, complex system (Byrne, 2003; Byrne, 2005), with an essentially *social* ecology of actors (Evans, 2002) who shape and are shaped by particular niches, composed of neighborhoods, cities and regions. Consistent with this view, we employ a variety of methods to identify key issues and evaluate their depth and validity. These are applied within an overall framework, or strategy, of participatory action research (PAR), to permanently mobilize diverse perspectives, positionalities, and sources of both academic and experiential knowledge. We believe both are necessary to a scientific approach to city-based research, with "scientific" used in Byrne's sense, of a systematic form of knowledge.

PAR is particularly apt for applied research that seeks to apply existing theories and draw lessons from practice that can refresh, challenge or replace prior theoretical assumptions.

Given our focus on sustainability with equity, social events are contextualized within historical, macro- and meso-level institutional and other forces (Freire, 1998). Dialogue and partnership in empowering environments help to shift from a subject (researcher) - object (those researched) to a collaborative, subject-subject relationship.

Specific qualitative methods applied follow a similar pattern, with applies Booher and Innes' principales of DIAD (Diversity, Interdependence and Authentic Dialogue, which we understand as similar to deliberation, as studied by Gastil xx or Forester xx) involving:

- A **participatory group**, usually framed as an "advisory council", involving skilled and representative individuals from diverse instances within local/regional/national government and citizen organizations, individuals of interest and/or with interest in the subject, other actors from the private sector, professionals, and academics, particularly researchers. We strive for an even balance of the sexes (difficult in transport-related subjects) and low, middle and high-income individuals, again a challenge given patterns of exclusion from higher education, and the tendency for more educated people to participate more.
- Participatory **workshops to develop initial questions and methods**, then contribute during both qualitative and quantitative data processing, confirmation of observations, evaluation and decisions about conclusions and, where relevant, recommendations. On this last, we tend to seek specific recommendations that can be taken into other fora — government policy and program meetings and events, citizen organizations, among others — as we consider the theory-action, researcher-practitioner nexus highly dynamic and important to cultivate.
- Ongoing **circles of participation**, where the specific partners and/or their roles may vary over time and according to the specific project. At the heart of these circles is the core group, composed of citizen, professional and academic urban planners, each embedded in their own circles of contexts (networks or, in our terms, trees and forests of relationships and interactions). Around the core group, and at different distances, which can be measured according to the type, quality and frequency of communication, are other organizations and instances, all coming mainly from our three sectors of focus: citizen organizations, local/regional/national government, private and academic actors.
- To illustrate with an example, for the **focus groups or participatory workshops** conducted as part of the research for *Ella se mueve segura*, we built on an existing relationship with community and government actors associated with our Kool Routes to Skools project, reinforcing our relationship with other departments in the municipal government (especially those focusing on women, disabled and elderly groups), and partnered with the local Women's Centre to recruit, holding the group in a local school. Participants are offered the option of **confidentiality**, but most prefer **attribution,** a situation that is consistent throughout our research. We find community members and leaders are tired of "experts" taking their knowledge and using it for other purposes. They want their knowledge to be recognized and respected. The focus groups followed a script, however, very similar to that recommended for this purpose (see for example, pp. 152-153, Silverman 2015).
- Similarly, most participatory group activities seek to build **ongoing relationships with participants**, so we work hard to provide feedback, report on what we (think we) have found, offer specific opportunities to validate and revalidate our findings.
- We employ diverse forms of **ethnography** extensively in other research projects, reversing the usual approach of "participant observers", ie researchers who also participate, to work as **"observing participants", that is participants who**

also do research. This reflects our community base, as a **community-university collaboration** between Living City (Ciudad Viva), a national citizens group that does citizen-led urban planning, and the Centre for Sustainable Urban Development, based in Transport Engineering, at the Pontificia Universidad Católica de Chile, with strong links to its BRT+ Centre of Excellence in Bus Rapid Transit.

- Data processing involves categorization and analysis, which typically starts from our qualitative results, then passes through a survey or quantitative phase, then involves triangulation between both methodological approaches, to identify consistencies and surprises, which require further analysis or additional research.

APPENDIX 3: QUANTITATIVE METHODS FOR PRIMARY AND SECONDARY DATA

We see an ongoing dialogue between quantitative and qualitative methods as central to doing research on cities that is useful to communities and active citizens, to academics both in Chile and abroad, and to practitioners. We strongly believe that progress toward sustainability with equity requires strong participation from all three.

3.1 THE *ELLA SE MUEVE SEGURA SURVEY* IN THREE SANTIAGO DISTRICTS

An intercept-survey to public transport users was conducted. The aim of this survey was studying the security perception when people using the system. The questions explored the access to public transport and the travel experience by bus or subway, exploring the effects of safety perception on the travel behavior: when, how and for what.

The survey was conducted in bus stops and metro stations in 3 districts of the city: Ñuñoa (high income district), Santiago (middle income district) and El Bosque (low income district). The stops were categorized based on the amenity of the urban environment surrounding each public transport stop and bus or Metro frequency at every stop. Public transport users were surveyed in 4 different periods: 2 in peak hours and 2 in off-peak hours.

790 surveys were obtained: Ñuñoa (241), Santiago (359) and El Bosque (204). The survey was statistically representative of men (404 surveys) and women (386 surveys) of 18 years using Public Transportation in Santiago, Ñuñoa and El Bosque at 95% with sampling error of 10%.

3.2 SANTIAGO'S ORIGIN-DESTINATION SURVEY FROM 2012 AND ADDITIONAL DATA

The Ministry of Social Development (MDS) advised by the Executive Secretariat of the Transportation Infrastructure Planning Commission (SECTRA), mandate the application of origin-destination surveys called "Mobility Surveys".

The Mobility Surveys are the main source of information used in any transport planning process. These surveys provide key background on the mobility patterns of a city and provide the data required for the calibration of transport models. Since 2010, 12 mobility surveys have been carried out in Chile.

The last origin-destination survey of Santiago was conducted in 2012 and it was the main source of data of our work. This survey gathered georeferenced information on the travel patterns in cities, the socioeconomic characteristics of travelers, detailed information on non-motorized trips and measurements of vehicle flows, occupation and the levels of service in public and private transport.

The 2012 survey version included the traditional urban areas of the Santiago Province plus urban areas of the peripheral districts of the Region. Thus, 45 districts are part of this survey and not the usual 34 that comprise the urban nucleus, called Greater Santiago.

Thus, 18,000 household surveys were conducted in 45 municipalities in the metropolitan region, with a minimum of 160 surveys in each one and a confidence interval of less than 8% in each one. The expansion factors used in the study allows to take the results of the sample to the total number of households included in the 45 municipalities under study.

For addition information we consulted the CASEN survey on poverty by municipal jurisdiction (*comuna*) within the Chilean population (MDS, 2013) and the national association of marketing for information on emerging socioeconomic groups (AIMChile, 2016).

CHAPTER 6

GENDERED EXPLORATION OF EMOTIVE AND INSTRUMENTAL WELL-BEING FOR CYCLIST WOMAN IN LATIN AMERICA

Beatriz Mella Lira

ABSTRACT

The research and practices associated to expand the use of active travel have shown extensive benefits on the overall assessment of well-being. However, cycling is still unequal considering age and gender. Therefore, further research is needed for contributing to the wider and more inclusive use of the bicycle for women.

The chapter aims to explore and differentiate the emotive and instrumental subjective well-being (SWB) factors that make cycling especially favourable for women, contributing to their general well-being. The chapter also inquiries about the factors that expand women's opportunities as consequence of cycling.

The research is focussed in the context of Latin American cities, building on the experience of experts in Santiago, Bogotá, Buenos Aires and Mexico City. These cities have had a substantial increase in urban cycling, and yet low rates of cycling women when compared to men.

The nature of the research is qualitative as it considers semi-structured interviews with 21 women experts from non-governmental organisations, academia, government and cycling organisations. The questions have been framed under the concepts of the SWB, considering emotive and instrumental factors.

The findings show that self-esteem, freedom, empowerment and happiness are some of the emotive factors that have emerged from the analysis of interviews.

On the side of instrumental factors, cycling emerges as relevant for women's care role, entrance to the labour market and for strengthening social relationships leading to the promotion of social capital. Social factors have also emerged, mostly related to the advantages of socialisation, democracy and cycling as a political symbol.

Keywords: Cycling; women; Latin America; well-being; social equity; gender; subjective well-being

1. INTRODUCTION

Transport planners have the challenge of expanding the factors that determine the benefits of transportation projects. Nowadays, transport projects are mainly based on the measurement of the cost-benefit, and consequently, the factors associated with the benefits are mostly utilitarian. A more holistic response that can recognise other relevant aspects while travelling can mean a fundamental change in the understanding of transport problems and solutions. Users' travel satisfaction (Bergstad et al., 2011) helps directing this challenge towards daily travel, resulting in the understanding of the satisfaction using private, public and active transport users. Active travel tends to have the highest levels of satisfaction (Páez & Whalen, 2010; Smith, 2017; St-Louis, Manaugh, van Lierop, & El-Geneidy, 2014; Whalen, Páez, & Carrasco, 2013), while public transport users tend to assess their experience more negatively (Abenoza, Cats, & Susilo, 2017; De Vos, Mokhtarian, Schwanen, Van Acker, & Witlox, 2016; Ettema, Friman, Gärling, Olsson, & Fujii, 2012).

Existing literature suggests that women use the bicycle at considerably lower rates than men, despite the expanding bicycle infrastructure that is being provided in cities and despite the well-being benefits. Therefore, this chapter aims to explore which well-being factors make cycling especially favourable for women, considering both instrumental and emotive factors that can impact their general well-being. Considering this purpose, the research was developed through a qualitative approach, using semi-structured interviews with 21 women experts on cycling. They were selected under the base of being related to cycling schemes, being part of the public sector or participate as private advisors, or for being members of non-governmental organisations (NGOs) promoting cycling activism. The discussions were framed considering to what extent certain emotive and instrumental factors could impact in cyclist women's well-being.

The findings reflect the factors that impact women's well-being in the practice of cycling. Security aspects related to street sexual harassment and *bicimachismos* negatively affect their experience. However, cycling can produce relevant positive impacts for women's well-being, through enhancing the self-esteem and empowerment, facilitating freedom and autonomy, and utterly improving the feelings of happiness. On the instrumental side, cycling has been shown as relevant for women's care role, entrance to the labour market and strengthening social relationships that could lead to the promotion of social capital.

The chapter highlights the relevance of fostering cycling for women in the context of Latin America. In the following section, the chapter provides evidence of the links between cycling and well-being, previously explored in the literature. After the literature review, the methodology and the analysis of the interviews are developed. Finally, the chapter suggests some key policymaking aspects that should be considered for fostering the participation of women in Latin America.

2. WHY THE STUDY IS CENTRED IN WOMAN CYCLISTS IN LATIN AMERICA

Trip characteristics, cultural norms and infrastructure preferences are some of the reasons why women cycle less than men (Aldred, Woodcock, & Goodman, 2016). The daily trips for women tend to be more complex compared to men, and aspects of care are still relevant either with children or other family members. Contrarily, there are still cultural stigmas and barriers related to the use of bicycle impacting negatively on women's cycling - such as the risk of tolerance, perception of security and cultural stereotypes. Although cycling infrastructure tends to be relevant for both genders, for example, with respect to the existence of segregated infrastructure (Aldred et al., 2016), in the case of women it tends to be more relevant since they prefer streets with less traffic and away from structuring streets (Beecham & Wood, 2014). Moreover, certain infrastructure tends to reinforce the male dominance paradigm of cycling policy (Lam, 2018).

The existing literature in Europe (United Kingdom, Germany, Denmark or Holland) is not necessarily a reflection of Latin American cities. However, this literature helps to understand the context and trends, and what their main challenges have been. London, for example, has a lower bicycle travel rate than other countries in the region, and historically, the cycling profile has corresponded mainly to men, whites, in a good physical condition, as well as young people. Aldred et al. (2016) have analysed if in the current context, women are better represented, and if there is more diversity in cycling, or women have adapted to existing users.

In the Latin American context, and in recent years, Mexico City has sustained a consistent increase in the use of the bicycle as primary transport mode – currently only a 2.2%. Of that number, only 24% are women, which equates to approximately 33,000 women cyclists in Mexico City, by the end of 2016. However, the numbers are expected to exponentially growth after the implementation of the Gender and Mobility Strategic Plan, an initiative of the local government which aims to contribute to safety, comfort, accessibility and shorter travel times. They recognise the need for incorporating new patterns of mobility, solving the harassment and violence issues, as well as increasing the participation of women in the transport initiatives.

The methodology of *Perfil Ciclista* (cyclist profile) for Mexican cities (Secretaria de Desarrollo Agrario, Territorial y Urbano, & Institute for Transportation and Development Policy (ITDP), 2018) allows analysing information about the uses, practices, motivations and attitudes of cyclists. The report has published fundamental aspects to understand the cycling profile of women in five Mexican cities. The percentage of women's bicycle trips in Mexican cities fluctuates between 0.18% and 1.3% (Morelia) compared to the percentage of men's bicycle trips that fluctuates between 1.63% and 9.26% (León). The main barriers to the use of bicycles as reported by women in most cities are lack of public safety, in their dimension of violence and sexual harassment. Regarding incentives, the study has revealed that more and better cycling infrastructure is the most critical factor for women. The study has facilitated the methodology that could be applied in other Mexican and Latin American cities, for different agents in the civic society, government or academia.

In the case of Santiago, Chile, cycling modal share, in the case of women, has increased from 10% to about 30% in recent years (Sagaris & Tiznado-Aiken, 2017). The spatial distribution of trips in Santiago and the profile of cyclists have also changed. The southern area of the city (associated with a lower socio-economic profile and longer trips) is not the largest producer of trips by bicycle. Furthermore, in the commune of Santiago (centre), women represent 67% of the trips destined for other communes (Waintrub, Peña, Niehaus, Vega, & Galilea, 2016). However, it seems a central issue to review the quantity, quality and type of cycling infrastructure that meets the requirements of women since they tend to better recognise the safety conditions of the streets (Waintrub et al., 2016). Today in the city there is an increase in the number of cyclists, although women are only a quarter of that total. The reasons coincide with the international experiences that refer to women's trips having to fulfil more diversified roles and several activities during the journeys (Primerano et al., 2008), as well as based-care activities involving another family member (Sagaris & Tiznado-Aiken, 2017).

It is interesting to highlight in the case of Buenos Aires, Argentina, the efforts and interest from the *Subsecretaria de Movilidad Sustentable y Segura*, developing a qualitative study that reflects the barriers and limitations experienced by women when using the bicycle as the primary mode. The study has also been developed in the context of promoting inclusive policies of mobility in Latin America. Similar to Mexican cities, the *Encuesta de Movilidad Domiciliaria* (Residence Mobility Survey) shows that only 3% of all the trips in the Metropolitan Region of Buenos Aires are made by bicycle. The gender imbalance is also related, as less than 20% of the total of trips by bicycle are made by women (Diaz & Rojas, 2017).

In Bogotá, Colombia, there are currently more than 620,000 daily trips by bicycle. According to the Mobility Survey (2011–2015), 4.9% of daily trips are made by bicycle, and of these trips, women's cycling participation corresponds to 23%. The personal safety and prevention of traffic risks are the most significant triggers of the comparatively lower participation of women (Osorio Diaz & Pinillos Ramirez, 2017). Similar to the previous cases, the man uses the bicycle three times more than the woman for study and work purposes. Again, the development and management of the road network, together with the generation of segregated bike path infrastructure, is one of the main challenges for overcoming barriers. By 2017, Bogotá had a network of 476 km of CicloRutas connecting cyclists to major BRT routes, parks and community centres (C40 Cities Finance Facility, 2018). Road safety and personal safety are determining factors in the mobility of women cyclists in Bogotá's scenario.

3. WHY CYCLING SHOULD BE LINKED TO WELL-BEING?

The concept of subjective well-being (SWB) has gained recent attention (Nordbakke & Schwanen, 2014), as an interdisciplinary conceptualisation interpreted through the lens of an individual's perceptions and experiences (Singleton, 2018). SWB can be defined as the degree to which an individual positively evaluates the overall quality of their lives (Ettema, Gärling, Olsson, & Friman, 2010). The 'subjectivity' relates to individual perceptions and experiences that establish individual evaluation (Nordbakke & Schwanen, 2014). The temporality of the benefits is a difference between satisfaction and SWB, as the latest relates to a more extended period of time, as well as the effects produced in people's lives (for differences between eudaimonic and hedonic well-being) (Mokhtarian, 2019; Nordbakke & Schwanen, 2014).

Delbosc (2012) has shown, in regards of the definition of well-being, that accessibility is one of the factors that influence the most people's well-being, listing a series of factors that directly influence psychological well-being, such as poverty, employment, interpersonal relations and health. The evidence shows that transport disadvantages have a high impact on well-being (Currie et al., 2010; Delbosc & Currie, 2011), and, in turn, that well-being also has a connection with transport equity (Reardon, Mahoney, & Guo,, 2019). The effect that the activities at the destination affect how people perceive the entire trip has also been documented (Bergstad et al., 2011).

Bergstad et al. (2011) have already suggested that travel satisfaction is related to SWB, and that there is a difference between emotive (also called symbolic-affective) and instrumental reasons. For the purposes of this study, the instrumental factors are those that tend to be defined based on the utility, such as modal choice and destination requirements, which serve as a means to achieve the purpose of the trip. Emotive factors offer an alternative to utilitarian evaluation of travel, since they respond to self-reports of specific emotions that arise from and are related to travel. This differentiation is key in this study, since the instrumental reasons do not cover the complexity of the problem, and emotional factors complement how travel decisions are made, in this case, by female cyclists.

This type of differentiation has already been considered when defining the reasons for car use (Gatersleben, 2007; Steg, Vlek, & Slotegraaf, 2001). Regarding the use of the bicycle, there is evidence about the links for users of bike-sharing systems and well-being (Ma, Zhang, Ding, & Wang, 2018). In terms of the impacts in the commute, Olsson et al. (2013) and Kahneman, Krueger, Schkade, Schwarz, and Stone (2004) have established a relationship between SWB factors with emotional perceptions while commuting. Understanding the emotive and instrumental reasons for selecting a particular transport mode can help with the recognition of the overall assessment of the activities performed (Bergstad et al., 2011). Although the concept of SWB has been already analysed in the context of vulnerable and elderly groups (De Vos, Schwanen, Acker, & Witlox, 2013; Mokhtarian, 2019; Nordbakke & Schwanen, 2014), it has not been directly addressed concerning gender differences. Moreover, understanding how SWB is impacted by cycling could promote an increasing amount of cycling women in the region.

4. METHODOLOGY

The chapter aims to explore the emotive and instrumental SWB factors that make cycling especially favourable for women, contributing to their general well-being. The research considers a qualitative approach through semi-structured interviews with 21 women experts on cycling schemes, consultants, public sector, activists and NGO leaders. All interviewees are part of an institution related to encouraging cycling, either from NGOs, academia or secretaries of transport in the government. Although the background of the interviewees is diverse (architects, activists, educators, environmentalists, publicists and geographers, among others), the common factor was approaching women that have endeavoured to solve the challenges of making the bicycle a transformative tool for women in different areas of their lives.

The questions of the semi-structured interviews were framed under the concepts of the SWB, considering emotive and instrumental factors. The questions of the interviews have considered four topics: differences between male and woman in the use of the bicycle; factors that favour the use of the bicycle for women; how using the bicycle can help or affect the access to job opportunities; and what are the opportunities that increase, particularly for women, with the use of the bicycle.

The analysis has been conducted using thematic analysis, helping to report the main themes that have shaped the differences and similarities between the interviewees. This analysis has helped framing a qualitative and exploratory approach, coding and comparing the interviews, and diving into the main concepts that interviewees have suggested during the conversations.

5. ANALYSIS

The thematic analysis made it possible to emerge the themes presented in the following text.

5.1. Instrumental Factors

5.1.1. Security and Sexual Harassment

As it has been explored in the existing literature, several interviewees mentioned security – one of the interviewees reporting that 'there are many women who do not pedal out of fear.' This relates to both the physical safety and street security of being harassed when riding a bicycle. The general opinion is that women are more exposed to street harassment: more unprotected, which makes the trip different to men. The issue of security is relevant and related to women's appropriation of the public space within the society. In the case of Santiago, street harassment has recently been included as part of a political bill and incorporated as a municipal ordinance in a couple of municipalities. While there is not yet a legal figure at the national level, the harassed person can report the aggressor, who receives an economic fine paid to the local police court.

According to some interviewees, the situation of street harassment tends, however, to be more bearable when riding a bicycle – compared to the situation when walking. Several interviewees have commented on the advantages of the speed when using the bicycle. The bicycle becomes a better alternative than walking along paths that are not well lighted or even when compared to highly crowded public transportation. The understanding and recognition of the built environment are fundamental in the case of Latin American cities since the urban form is a well-known determinant of cycling activity, which directly affects women when determining their route.

5.1.2. Care Role and Labour Market

Time savings for women has nuances. It cannot be measured simply by considering the minutes a regular trip takes – generally considering a linear origin–destination trip. Women tend to make more trips, which usually have to do with other members of the family, as children or another family member. In this sense, the bicycle is a particularly valuable tool, since it allows managing more trips, of a variety of distances, without monetary expenses associated with those trips. Literature and practice show that the care role continues to be fulfilled to a greater extent by women – although there are increasing cases in which man shares more responsibility. Just as there are imbalances concerning household roles, there are also imbalances regarding trip purposes, trip chains and daytime distribution of needs (Priya Uteng, 2016). In some cases, women could spend up to 60% of their income in mobilisation to their jobs, which means that the relative margin of economic gains might be undermined (Mella Lira, 2020). This comparison gets more exacerbated when transport costs are high since she will spend more money on transportation, compared to the benefits of having a job. The solution in most cases means staying at home, taking care of the children and saving that expense. Furthermore, women who are in a more vulnerable situation do not usually have a job but have more than one, which is added to be in charge of family activities – what in turn increases transport costs.

The cost of travel is a powerful element of the decision within the household, and the reason why many women end up choosing to stay at home. Currently, women do not have equal remuneration as men, so the scale of salaries and positions is lower in the case of women. By having access to lower paid or precarious jobs, it is even less economically convenient to go to work. However, in societies where success is measured according to material standards, there is still much prejudice in the use of the bicycle. One of the interviewees, for example, comments that people's mentality is what affects the image of the cyclist the most, but it does not necessarily affect women more than men.

5.1.3. Technical Skills

The analysis of the interviews shows a deep recognition of the bicycle as a vehicle for social mobility, which allows women to enter the labour market. However, having a bicycle as a mode of transport means having to acquire one – especially in contexts where there is no public bicycle system. The 'freedom' of riding a bicycle should be supported through financial incentives to buy a bicycle. In the same way, the 'maintenance' of the bicycle should cease to be an activity unusual to women. In the case of Santiago and Mexico, there are already groups that not only promote and teach women to ride a bicycle but also educate them in terms of maintaining them. Some interviewees have mentioned how the use of tools must be part of the cycling culture, independent of gender, but it is especially relevant in the case of women. Women who tend to have more technical skills for repairing a bicycle also feel more empowered to overcome the different situations in which they are involved. The skills acquired, backed by technical knowledge of the use of bicycle repair tools, are essential for a more significant intrusion of urban cycling for women.

5.2. Emotive Factors

5.2.1. Self-Esteem and Empowerment

Self-esteem and personal improvement are strong and positive concepts emerging from the interviews, not being documented in the existing literature and different from the use of other transport modes. One of the interviewees, for example, considers that the bicycle has done more for the emancipation of women than anything else. At least in terms of mobility, the bicycle allows women to feel freedom. Several interviewees mention the inconveniences of using public transport and the benefits of cycling in comparison. Self-esteem and the feeling of happiness are also mentioned by most of the interviewees. Being able to control the routes, speed and times produces physical and mental well-being that does not compare with the use of other transport modes.

Feelings of empowerment add to the improvements in the self-esteem. For many interviewees, empowerment is recurrent, since they feel they own the personal space in which they physically move with the bicycle being a small extension of the human body. Women, in particular, can generate a non-direct benefit because it contributes to this empowerment of the street, of urban space. Empowerment also relates feelings of gender equality – the bicycle as a symbol of equality. The bicycle favours the process of feminism understood as equal rights for men and women.

5.2.2. Freedom and Autonomy

The interviewees have mentioned in different ways that the bicycle facilitates freedom and autonomy – both strongly related to the previous point on self-esteem and empowerment. Most of the interviewees agreed on the idea of men historically having a greater right for using the streets and public spaces, so the bicycle represents for women an instrument of empowerment that allows them to move freely from one place to another. There is a symbolic but also a practical autonomy of using the bicycle. It allows moving anywhere, for free and by own means.

5.2.3. Happiness

Most of the interviewees agree that the sum of the physical and mental benefits of using the bicycle produces a greater sense of happiness. Both the immediate experience of using the bicycle and the long-term experience are incentives for prolonged use of this transport mode. Contrarily, considering the disadvantages of using motorised public transport modes, the bicycle is positioned much better than others. Car use remains primarily masculine in Latin American cities – derived from a patriarchal culture. In this context, the bicycle is a way to break with the limitations of conventional transport modes.

5.3. Social Factors

From the analysis of the interviews, it was possible to account for a third group of factors of SWB, associated with the interaction with other members of society. Among these are concepts such as *bicimachismos* (which also connect to the emotive dimension), socialisation with others and bicycle as a political symbol of democracy.

5.3.1. Bicimachismos

Bicimachismos are probably the best evidence of gender differences between men and women when using the bicycle as the primary transport mode. Although there is an agreement among the interviewees that the differences do not lie in the transport mode itself, they reveal certain aspects that arise in the case of women. Gender biases, or as they have also been called *micromachismos*, are expressed and evidenced on the bicycle.

Another interesting factor is that how men and women move by bicycle is a manifestation of what happens in public space. Several of the interviewees consider that in both walking and cycling, women are located in the space of physical vulnerability compared to men. The vulnerability does not depend on physical capability, but in the way in which men tend to use the space. The use of the streets by men in this context resembles the 'manspreading', evidenced in the use of seats in public transport when men sit with their legs open occupying more than one seat. In the same way, the interviewees suggest that women tend to feel more vulnerable in the use of public space, and therefore in the street when riding a bicycle.

5.3.2. Socialisation with Others

The interviewees have also mentioned that the visual encounter between people is within the advantages of using the bicycle. They recognise that seeing another woman on bicycle fuels the feeling of empathy – which does not necessarily happen with the man. Women tend to be more empathetic among themselves, recognising themselves in the same space, avoiding the same type of difficulties when riding a bicycle. They also relate this idea with participation in producing public space within the city. The bicycle implies slowing down compared to motorised vehicles, which positively affects the construction of the urban space.

Some interviewees have mentioned that women create networks and meet people when cycling. Cycling for women can also be an instance to meet other people, open spaces for women of community participation. Cycling promotes socialisation with other people in the street and allows for communication, at least visual, that does not occur in other modes.

5.3.3. Symbol of Democracy
One of the interviewees has been emphatic about the role of the bicycle for women, being a political symbol of democracy, values and ethics. This thought, in other words, has been shared in terms of women having the same rights as men in the streets, even though there is a perception of having the means for using the public space differently. Another expert explains that cycling with dress and heel is a regular practice – at least in Mexico. Others have made the connection of cycling in the public space, where women acquire knowledge of their legal rights – speed, closeness to cars, preferences of cyclists and hierarchies, among others. Cycling has also been recognised by some interviewees as a political symbol. Being a cyclist woman contributes to the value and ethical revolution. It is in the line of generating changes in feminism, in education; it contributes to making the environment more conducive.

6. CONCLUSIONS

The study explores the factors that make bicycle use especially favourable for women. The thematic analysis has allowed the themes to emerge from the interviews, which has resulted in three categories of the SWB: instrumental, emotive and social considerations. Even though the study starts defining the instrumental and emotive factors, previously considered in the literature, the analysis has evidenced the need of complementing these factors with social considerations – shaped by the sociocultural context and understood through the lens of social interactions. Although these three categories have allowed organising the spectrum of responses of the interviewees, the resulted factors are interconnected in the context of the narratives. For example, talking about the inclusion of women in the labour market can be directly related to the existence of *micromachisms* in other areas beyond the election of a transport mode. Correspondingly, decisions based on the household economy may affect the personal empowerment and the possibilities of individual entrepreneurship for women. Undoubtedly, an even more exhaustive exploration is relevant for each one of these areas and factors in particular. In this sense, the contribution of this chapter is an overview of some of the relevant issues to be considered in studies that account for still existent gender gaps.

The findings of this study allow reflecting on the factors that impact women's well-being in the practice of cycling. The results show that security aspects related to street sexual harassment and *bicimachismos* negatively affect the women's experience and well-being. However, when cycling, women report relevant positive impacts on their well-being. Some of the key concepts arising from the interviews highlight how the self-esteem and empowerment are enhanced when cycling. Freedom and autonomy are rare concepts to be found in the transport literature, and yet, they utterly improve the feelings of happiness. Regarding the instrumental factors, the interviewees have referred to cycling as a relevant tool for accomplishing care roles, for facilitating the entrance to the labour market and for strengthening social relationships that could lead to the promotion of social capital.

From the analysis of the interviews, some keys can be suggested for strengthening the participation of women in the universe of new cyclists in the streets of Latin America. These are, among others:

- Mechanical knowledge to solve bicycle problems, more education and improvement of the personal skills for solving mechanical issues with the bicycle.
- Promotion of the bicycle as a vehicle for empowering women in the use of public space. Building a stronger narrative about the use of public space, rights and citizen participation will gather more people to use the streets. Having more people in the streets favours the virtuous circle of promoting more women going out on the street.
- The infrastructure needs to be considered beyond the construction of more cycle lanes. Promoting more (and better) facilities , such as parking spaces, in offices and companies. Encourage the use of ramps and covered parking. Improve climate protection and security.
- Incentives from public health. Consider the use of bicycle as a way of 'saving health' and not only economic resources. Promoting more empirical research and public policy connecting the use of bicycle with the improvement of health conditions can help. The bicycle helps to improve fitness but most importantly, it can be relevant in fighting diseases.

ACKNOWLEDGEMENTS

Sincere thanks to the women cyclists, activists, mothers, academics and professionals, who agreed to give some of their time for interviewing them. We had exciting and engaging conversations, and all of them were fundamental for the development of this research, which will be a kick-off to a more extensive mixed-methods research in the future.

REFERENCES

Abenoza, R. F., Cats, O., & Susilo, Y. O. (2017). Travel satisfaction with public transport: Determinants, user classes, regional disparities and their evolution. *Transportation Research Part A: Policy and Practice*, 95, 64–84. https://doi.org/10.1016/j.tra.2016.11.011

Aldred, R., Woodcock, J., & Goodman, A. (2016). Does more cycling mean more diversity in cycling? *Transport Reviews*, 36(1), 28–44. https://doi.org/10.1080/01441647.2015.1014451

Beecham, R., & Wood, J. (2014). Exploring gendered cycling behaviours within a large-scale behavioural data-set. *Transportation Planning and Technology*, 37(1), 83–97. https://doi.org/10.1080/03081060.2013.844903

Bergstad, C. J., Gamble, A., Gärling, T., Hagman, O., Polk, M., Ettema, D., … Olsson, L. E. (2011). Subjective well-being related to satisfaction with daily travel. *Transportation*, 38(1), 1–15. https://doi.org/10.1007/s11116-010-9283-z

C40 Cities Finance Facility (2018). Cycling Infrastructure in Cities: Bogotá's Quinto Centenario Cycle Avenue - Creating the Enabling Environment.

Currie, G., Richardson, T., Smyth, P., Vella-Brodrick, D., Hine, J., Lucas, K., … Stanley, J. (2010). Investigating links between transport disadvantage, social exclusion and well-being in

Melbourne – Updated results. *Research in Transportation Economics*, *29*(1), 287–295. https://doi.org/10.1016/j.tranpol.2009.02.002
De Vos, J., Mokhtarian, P. L., Schwanen, T., Van Acker, V., & Witlox, F. (2016). Travel mode choice and travel satisfaction: Bridging the gap between decision utility and experienced utility. *Transportation*, *43*(5), 771–796. http://dx.doi.org/10.1007/s11116-015-9619-9
De Vos, J., Schwanen, T., Acker, V. V., & Witlox, F. (2013). Travel and subjective well-being: A focus on findings, methods and future research needs. *Transport Reviews*, *33*(4), 421–442. https://doi.org/10.1080/01441647.2013.815665
Delbosc, A. (2012). The role of well-being in transport policy. *Transport Policy*, *23*, 25–33. https://doi.org/10.1016/j.tranpol.2012.06.005
Delbosc, A., & Currie, G. (2011). Exploring the relative influences of transport disadvantage and social exclusion on well-being. *Transport Policy*, *18*(4), 555–562. https://doi.org/10.1016/j.tranpol.2011.01.011
Diaz, R., & Rojas, F. (2017). Mujeres y ciclismo urbano: Promoviendo políticas inclusivas de movilidad en América Latina. Retrieved from https://publications.iadb.org/es/mujeres-y-ciclismo-urbano-promoviendo-politicas-inclusivas-de-movilidad-en-america-latina
Ettema, D., Friman, M., Gärling, T., Olsson, L. E., & Fujii, S. (2012). How in-vehicle activities affect work commuters' satisfaction with public transport. *Journal of Transport Geography*, *24*(C), 215–222.
Ettema, D., Gärling, T., Olsson, L. E., & Friman, M. (2010). Out-of-home activities, daily travel, and subjective well-being. *Transportation Research Part A: Policy and Practice*, *44*(9), 723–732.
Gatersleben, B. (2007). Affective and symbolic aspects of car use. In T. Gärling & L. Steg (Eds.), *Threats from car traffic to the quality of urban life* (pp. 219–233). Bingley: Emerald Publishing Limited. https://doi.org/10.1108/9780080481449-012
Kahneman, D., Krueger, A. B., Schkade, D. A., Schwarz, N., & Stone, A. A. (2004). A survey method for characterizing daily life experience: The day reconstruction method. *Science (New York, N.Y.)*, *306*(5702), 1776–1780. https://doi.org/10.1126/science.1103572
Lam, T. F. (2018). Hackney: A cycling borough for whom? *Applied Mobilities*, *3*(2), 115–132. https://doi.org/10.1080/23800127.2017.1305151
Ma, L., Zhang, X., Ding, X., & Wang, G. (2018). Bike sharing and users' subjective well-being: An empirical study in China. *Transportation Research Part A: Policy and Practice*, *118*(C), 14–24.
Mella Lira, B. (2020). *Urban and social equity impacts from transport. Evidence and approaches from Santiago de Chile*. London: University College London.
Mokhtarian, P. L. (2019). Subjective well-being and travel: Retrospect and prospect. *Transportation*, *46*(2), 493–513.
Nordbakke, S., & Schwanen, T. (2014). *Well-being and mobility: A theoretical framework and literature review focusing on older people*. *Mobilities*, *9*(1), 104–129. https://www.tandfonline.com/doi/abs/10.1080/17450101.2013.784542
Olsson, L. E., Gärling, T., Ettema, D., Friman, M., & Fujii, S. (2013). Happiness and satisfaction with work commute. *Social Indicators Research*, *111*(1), 255–263. https://doi.org/10.1007/s11205-012-0003-2
Osorio Diaz, P., & Pinillos Ramirez, M. (2017). *La mujer usuaria de la bicicleta como modo de transporte en BogotÃ¡: Retos y oportunidades*. 212.
Páez, A., & Whalen, K. (2010). Enjoyment of commute: A comparison of different transportation modes. *Transportation Research Part A: Policy and Practice*, *44*(7), 537–549. Retrieved from https://www.worldtransitresearch.info/research/3523
Priya Uteng, T. (2016). *Gendered Mobilities* (1st ed.). Routledge. https://doi.org/10.4324/9781315584201
Primerano, F., Taylor, M. A. P., Pitaksringkarn, L., & Tisato, P. (2008). Defining and understanding trip chaining behaviour. *Transportation*, *35*(1), 55–72. https://doi.org/10.1007/s11116-007-9134-8
Reardon, L., Mahoney, L., & Guo, W. (2019). Applying a subjective well-being lens to transport equity. In *Measuring transport equity*. Amsterdam: Elsevier.
Sagaris, L., & Tiznado-Aiken, I. (2017). *Equidad e inclusión en la movilidad de América Latina: Un análisis de género*. [Conference Presentation]. Retrieved from https://conicyt.cl/gendersummit12/wp-content/uploads/2017/12/2-Lake-Sagaris-CEPAL.pdf

Secretaria de Desarrollo Agrario, Territorial y Urbano, & Institute for Transportation and Development Policy (ITDP). (2018). Ciudades mexicanas. Pedaleando por un desarrollo bajo en carbono. Resultados del Perfil Ciclista en cinco ciudades. gob.mx. Retrieved from http://www.gob.mx/sedatu/documentos/resultados-del-perfil-ciclista-en-cinco-ciudades

Singleton, P. (2018). Walking (and cycling) to well-being: Modal and other determinants of subjective well-being during the commute. *Travel Behaviour and Society*, *16*, 1–30. https://doi.org/10.1016/j.tbs.2018.02.005

Smith, O. (2017). Commute well-being differences by mode: Evidence from Portland, Oregon. *Journal of Transport & Health*, *4*, 246–254. Retrieved from https://pdxscholar.library.pdx.edu/usp_fac/183/

Steg, L., Vlek, C., & Slotegraaf, G. (2001). Instrumental-reasoned and symbolic-affective motives for using a motor car. *Transportation Research Part F: Traffic Psychology and Behaviour*, *4*(3), 151–169.

St-Louis, E., Manaugh, K., van Lierop, D., & El-Geneidy, A. (2014). The happy commuter: A comparison of commuter satisfaction across modes. *Transportation Research Part F: Traffic Psychology and Behaviour*, *26*, 160–170. https://doi.org/10.1016/j.trf.2014.07.004

Waintrub, N., Peña, C., Niehaus, M., Vega, R., & Galilea, P. (2016). Understanding cyclist traffic behaviour: Contrasting cycle path designs in Santiago de Chile. *Research in Transportation Economics*, *59*(C), 228–235.

Whalen, K. E., Páez, A., & Carrasco, J. A. (2013). Mode choice of university students commuting to school and the role of active travel. *Journal of Transport Geography*, *31*(C), 132–142.

CHAPTER 7

ACTIVE COMMUTE TO SCHOOL, PHYSICAL ACTIVITY AND HEALTH OF HISPANIC HIGH SCHOOL STUDENTS IN THE UNITED STATES

Ivis García and Keuntae Kim

ABSTRACT

Increasing physical activity can reduce obesity risk among adolescents. This study analyses how behaviours, ethnicity and various sociocultural characteristics may influence the likelihood of engaging in active commute and other healthy activities. The authors analyse data from the 2010 National Youth Physical Activity and Nutrition Survey. The sample included US Hispanic high school students from 9th to 12th grade. Quasi-Poisson regression was used to understand the association between 24 possible variables and the number of days physically active at least 60 minutes per day. This study will present findings by race and ethnicity: non-Hispanic whites and blacks, as well as Hispanics. The research findings uncover that walking is the most predominant physical activity among Hispanics, especially from school to home, which indicates engagement in active transportation. This study shows the need for tailoring physical activity and health programmes by race and ethnicity. Interventions that encourage active commute can be effective for adolescents to achieve physical activity guidelines – at least 60 minutes per day.

Keywords: NYPANS data; adolescents; complex survey data analysis; walking; biking; exercise

1. INTRODUCTION

Urbanisation and population growth have created mobility challenges among Hispanic communities living across the Americas. In both Latin American and US cities, as the population grows, people might drive more while bike and walk less – which could lead to sedentary and unhealthy lifestyles. With both urban mobility and health equity in mind, Latin American cities such as Bogotá (Colombia), Mexico City (Mexico), Rio de Janeiro, São Paulo and Curitiba (Brazil) have improved biking infrastructure substantially. Meanwhile, US urban areas like Boulder (Colorado), Portland (Oregon) and Chicago (Illinois) have also invested in biking projects that promote active transportation and wellness. Similarly, most urban areas in the Americas are also the most walkable (Angotti & Irazábal, 2017). The current chapter seeks to explore physical activity, especially among Hispanic high school students, an important issue related to urban mobility.

Investments to improve biking and walking will be necessary for all cities of the Americas as they move into the future as well as they promote general well-being. The trend of increasing greenhouse emissions is likely to continue in the Americas. Therefore, it is crucial to invest in walking and biking infrastructure to counteract the effects of climate change. Furthermore, the promotion of active travel among youth is essential to achieve the long-term development goals of the United Nations (UN) Sustainable Development Goals: (1) ensuring healthy lives and promoting the well-being for all ages, (2) bike and walk to keep clear air and (3) educate young people on climate change to put them on an environmentally sustainable path early on (UN, 2019).

According to Dellinger and Staunton (2002), five decades ago, children in the United States lived an active life. Mobility to school by walking was a part of children's daily routine physical activity in urban areas, but the number of children who walk to school has substantially decreased. Researchers found that about 50% of elementary and middle school students walked or cycled to their schools in the 1960s (Dellinger & Staunton, 2002). However, the percentage of kids and young people walking to school declined to about 15% since the 2000s. Although these statistics do not exist for Hispanic youth, a Research Brief by the Robert Wood Johnson Foundation indicates parallel declines in Hispanic youth physical activity; these rates decline further with increasing age (Nyberg, Ramirez, & Gallion, 2011).

Active commuting can increase the recommended levels of physical activity – that is, 60 minutes per day, which is the recommended amount by the US Physical Activity Guidelines for Americans (Mendoza et al., 2011). Hispanic adolescents in Colombia that walked or biked to and from school were less likely to be overweight than those that drove or took public transit (Arango et al., 2011). About one-third of Colombian children between 6 and 17 years old were physically active for at least 60 daily minutes, and 71.7% reported walking or biking as their primary mode of transport to or from school in the previous week (González et al., 2018).

Similarly, a study by Banerjee, Uhm, and Bahl (2014) observing the associated benefits of walking to school in Los Angeles Hispanic-majority schools demonstrated that walking not only provides a child with a regular dose of physical activity but also instils lifelong health behaviours. Researchers emphasise the role of teaching parents the importance of active commute as we as teaching children walking habits early on and suggest that commuting to and from school by walking is the best way to achieve these habits (McDonald, Deakin, & Aalborg, 2010).

Walking is a household decision within ecological factors described previously, such as the age of the student, neighbourhood conditions, and so on (Banerjee et al., 2014; McDonald et al., 2010). Parents' employment status and household automobile ownership contribute to commuting choices at the household level. If parents have a positive attitude towards walking and engage in regular physical activity, then they are more likely to encourage their children to walk (Banerjee et al., 2014). Parents who are physically active also teach their children the value of walking by modelling. Besides, parents' perception of traffic around the school also plays a role in the decision-making process for commuting to and from school (McDonald et al., 2010). If parents feel that the streets around the schools have heavy traffic, then they are less inclined to allow their children to walk or cycle to school. An escalation in road traffic – as more vehicles are needed for transporting adolescents to and from schools – has, therefore, resulted in a downfall of physical activity.

Neighbourhood perception (safe or unsafe) also influences parents' commuting decisions for their children; usually, urban areas (e.g. Los Angeles or Chicago) and thus urban mobility are perceived as less safe (Banerjee et al., 2014; Timperio, Crawford, Telford, & Salmon, 2004). Most parents do not allow their kids to walk or cycle to school even though the distance is commutable because of safety concerns over the potential harm from traffic accidents and unknown strangers (Banerjee et al., 2014; McDonald et al., 2010). Risk elements such as gangs, drugs, prostitution and crime also influence the perception of risks and deter people from engaging in active transportation (García & Ara, 2018). To further compound safety concerns, parents often do not have adequate time to invest in supervised walking with their children (Faulkner, Richichi, Buliung, Fusco, & Moola, 2010). Thus, they choose the most convenient mobility alternative by deciding to drive or use public transportation (i.e. carpool, school bus, public transit or van). This allows the parent to go to their next activity, usually work, on time.

The literature indicates that walking and cycling is more likely to occur when schools within 1 mile from home (Ewing, Schoeer, & Greene, 2004). It takes about 20 minutes to walk 1 mile. This is also true for most walking outside of school, including parks (Cohen et al., 2007). However, even for children who live close, the primary mobility modes to school for most students are by automobile or bus (Ewing et al., 2004). Convenience (ease of dropping their kids to school on the way to work) was the single primary factor for youth commuting to school by car (Faulkner et al., 2010). The study by Faulkner et al. (2010) showed that most parents did not want to get up 20 minutes earlier to have their children walk to school. Other factors included the weight of the backpack, distance from school, lack of complete sidewalks, as well as weather, traffic and walkability conditions (Schlossberg, Greene, Phillips, Johnson, & Parker, 2006). There is also a strong relationship between adolescents walking and parental safety concerns related to both being hit by a car or being a victim of a crime while walking to school (Oluyomi et al., 2014).

Studies demonstrate that positive or negative attitudes, intentions and social norms from themselves, parents and others can influence active commute to school among children and adolescents (Ball, Jeffery, Abbott, McNaughton, & Crawford, 2010; McDonald et al., 2010; Oluyomi et al., 2014). Despite the aforementioned empirical evidence, research gaps exist regarding the understanding of the contribution of active commute to the achievement of physical activity guidelines (60 minutes per day), particularly among Hispanic adolescents. Therefore, this study aims to assess the relationship between active commute to and from schools among Hispanic adolescents in the United States.

Although the book's overall focus is on exploring issues related to urban mobility and social equity in Latin American urban areas, this chapter seeks to explore these issues among Hispanic high school students living in the United States. More specifically, the chapter examined cross-sectional associations between active commute to school and physical activity among non-Hispanic white, Hispanic and black youth living in the United States. The associations between other factors (such as neighbourhood environment, home environment and lifestyle factors) and physical activity are also explored.

The next section explains why Hispanics are the chosen study population. The following section is a literature review that concentrates on the associations between physical activity, active commute and their impact on health. The literature review is followed by a methods section – a discussion of the 2010 National Youth Physical Activity and Nutrition Study (NYPANS) as well as the usage of the quasi-Poisson regression. The methods section is then followed by the results, discussion and policy recommendations.

2. HISPANICS IN THE UNITED STATES

We concentrated on the Hispanic population because it has grown dramatically in the United States in the last five decades and is expected to continue growing. Between 1970 and 2010, according to the US Census, the Hispanic population increased from 9.1 to 50.5 million, accounting for a 455% change (Ennis, Ríos-Vargas, & Albert, 2011). While the proportion of non-Hispanic white children in the United States has declined from 60% to 51% from 2000 to 2016, the Hispanic population has grown from 17% to 25% in the same period (Child Trends, 2018). Census Bureau's population projections indicate that by 2050, the Hispanic population at least will double, making up 30% of the US population (Ennis et al., 2011).

According to the US Census, the Hispanic ethnicity category includes a group of people from different races, who trace the origin of their ancestors to Spanish-speaking countries in the Caribbean, Spanish-speaking Central and South America, Mexico and Spain. The 2010 Census estimated 50.5 million Hispanics in the United States, comprising 16% of the total US population of 308.7 million (Ennis et al., 2011). The highest concentration of Hispanics is in traditional areas where Hispanics have immigrated (California, Texas, Florida, etc.) and some dispersal across the United States (García, 2014). In 2010, more than a total of 6.7 million Hispanics (13%) lived in five cities: New York, Los Angeles, Houston, San

Antonio and Chicago (García, 2014). To give some context, according to the 2010 US Census Bureau, 81% of the US population lived in urban areas (Garfinkel-Castro, Kim, Hamidi, & Ewing, 2017).

The health status of Hispanics in the United States is largely shaped by genetics, cultural and language barriers, as well as healthcare access, insurance coverage and its utilisation. The Center for Disease Control and Prevention (CDC) reported in 2010 the following leading causes of death among Hispanics at the national level: cancer, heart disease, accidents, stroke and diabetes (Heron, 2010). Obesity, which may influence the risk of stroke, heart disease and diabetes, was slightly higher among Hispanics than for non-Hispanics whites (66% vs 65%, respectively) – while, blacks had the highest rates of all (The Office of Minority Health, 2014).

Health disparities are also related to income and wealth. For example, lower income families are more likely to not live close to a full supermarket with fresh fruits and vegetables (Hendrickson, Smith, & Eikenberry, 2006). The median income for white households in 2017 was $63,704, compared to $60,734 for Native Hawaiians and Pacific Islanders, $49,793 for Hispanics, $41,882 for American Indians and Alaskan Natives, and $40,232 for African Americans (US Census Bureau, 2017).

As discussed in the previous sections, physical activity, walking and biking can lower the risk of becoming obese. The 2010 NYPANS provides data on behaviours related to physical activity for different ethnic and racial groups. Still, until now, researchers have not concentrated on Hispanics as a subgroup of primary interest. This study is particularly interested in Hispanics that attend high school, which is 12–19 year olds in the United States, a population that has been growing and will continue to grow in the next decades. With these changing demographics, an understanding of this population and their physical activity, health habits and active commute patterns are needed to create public health programmes that target this growing population shaping the US landscape for decades to come.

3. PHYSICAL ACTIVITY AND HEALTH: RACIAL AND ETHNIC DIFFERENCES

This study observes associations between 24 possible variables and the number of days physically active at least 60 minutes per day (see Table 7.2). US Physical Activity Guidelines for Americans recommend that youth spend 60 minutes or more of physical activity daily (CDC, 2018; Hallal, Victora, Azevedo, & Wells, 2006; Song, Carroll, Lee, & Fulton, 2015). The following section concentrates on physical activity, active comment and other kinds of activities related to fitness behaviours and the impact on health. We will also discuss why it is vital for planners to increase their knowledge of Hispanics to be better able to further health equity among this group.

There is a large body of research on active travel and physical activity in the Latin American region that has discussed, for example, how biking and walking routes can serve as a larger programme that contributes to promoting health equity between low-middle and high-income individuals (Sarmiento & Beard, 2013; Sarmiento et al., 2017). By creating neighbourhoods that are more walkable and bikeable, Latin American political leaders like Bogotá's Mayor Enrique Peñalosa created cities that are not only more equitable but also more liveable. Bike lanes (ciclovías) in Bogotá are reducing traffic, improving air quality and contributing to street safety (Angotti & Irazábal, 2017).

The prevalence of childhood obesity has increased markedly in the last three decades (Ogden, Carroll, Kit, & Flegal, 2014; Wang & Lim, 2012) and is a public health issue in the Americas (Wang & Beydoun, 2007). In the United States, about one-third of youth ages, 2–19 years are either overweight or obese (Ogden et al., 2014) and nearly a quarter of high school students are either overweight or obese (CDC, 2018). Playing video games and watching TV for more than 2 hours/day is associated with being overweight (Lowry, 2009). Similarly, there are associations between being obese and not eating fruits and vegetables (Lowry, 2009). Until now, studies have not discussed the relationship between engaging in at least 60 minutes of physical activity – most times achieved by walking among high school students (Song et al., 2015) – and eating healthy, watching TV and playing video games.

Youth who are obese are predisposed to experience a decline in life expectancy along with health-related conditions and psychological issues (Jonides, Buschbacher, & Barlow, 2002; Perrin, Bloom, & Gortmaker, 2007; Rønningen, Wammer, Grabner, & Valderhaug, 2019; Schwimmer, Burwinkle, & Varni, 2003; Swallen, Reither, Haas, & Meier, 2005). While the evidence on the association between physical activity and obesity has been somewhat ambiguous, physical activity engagement has shown beneficial effects on adolescent's risk of becoming obese, general health, and well-being status (Gordon-Larsen, McMurray, & Popkin, 2000; Hallal et al., 2006; Trost, Kerr, Ward, & Pate, 2001). Given that most high school students achieve their recommended amount of physical activity (60 minutes per day) by walking (Song et al., 2015), we can then assume that walking might reduce obesity, increase overall health and result in fewer illnesses down the line.

Unquestionably, disparities in childhood obesity exist among racially, ethnically and diverse sociocultural groups (Caprio et al., 2008; Freedman, Khan, Serdula, Ogden, & Dietz, 2006; Taveras, Gillman, Kleinman, Rich-Edwards, & Rifas-Shiman, 2010). Hispanic adolescents have not been the exception, and obesity rates are of concern (Crawford et al., 2013; Isasi, Rastogi, & Molina, 2016; Liu, Probst, Harun, Bennett, & Torres, 2009). The prevalence of obesity among Hispanic adolescents is higher compared to their white peers (CDC, 2018). Obesity increases the risk of developing comorbidities, including cardiovascular diseases and diabetes, which are two diseases noted among the top five causes of death for Hispanics living in the United States (Dominguez et al., 2015). Walking and biking are thus an excellent way of promoting health equity.

In addition to the well-documented health benefits for adolescents to participate in physical activity (Hallal et al., 2012; Reichert, Menezes, Wells, Dumith, & Hallal, 2009), adolescents may be more likely to walk to and from school, as well as walk to other destination such as parks (Cohen et al., 2007; Ewing et al., 2004). Adolescents also spend more time engaging in sports, particularly team sports, rather than individual sports (Dinç, 2011). However, the engagement in walking, biking or participating in sports does not necessarily translate to the frequency or a more significant amount of time of moderate to vigorous physical activity (Smpokos, Linardakis, Papadaki, Lionis, & Kafatos, 2012).

Ignoring intensity, simply exercising by engaging in walking might not be correlated to not being obese, because diet also plays an important role (Epstein, Wing, Penner, & Kress, 1985). Furthermore, studies suggest that Hispanics change their eating patterns to US patterns, which might contribute to obesity (Liu et al., 2009; Wojcicki, Schwartz, Jiménez-Cruz, Bacardi-Gascon, & Heyman, 2012). However, in general, more vigorous exercise is correlated with a healthy diet; in other words, the more people were conscious of their health like reducing sugar, fats, sodium and eat fewer calories, the more they exercise (Sallis, Pinski, Grossman, Patterson, & Nader, 1988). In the same manner that people might develop a culture of healthy habits that include both diet and exercise, individuals, families and communities based on class, age, ethnicity, race and many other multiple, and intersecting identities might develop a lifestyle corresponding to the culture of the group they belong to that support or rejects physical activity, including walking to and from school (Gill, 2017; Pérez-Escamilla and & Putnik, 2007).

Other than culture, poverty and being low-income is associated with having access to healthy foods, being able to play sports, buy a bike or comfortable running shoes as well as living close to school, a park, to a protected biking trail or afford a gym membership. Hispanics are usually in the middle between blacks and whites in the United States in terms of their socioeconomic characteristics. Hispanics do better in terms of income and homeownership than blacks, but they lagged behind blacks in terms of their educational attainment and poverty rates. This is particularly true for first-generation individuals (García, 2014). Hispanics lagged in all socioeconomic measures when compared to whites. These race and ethnic disparities are also reflected in diet and physical activity patents as well as obesity rates and health outcomes (Gordon-Larsen & Popkin, 2011). Age, being too old or too young, having a disability and not having access to a car also limit one's mobility (Titheridge, Achuthan, Mackett, & Solomon, 2009; Titheridge, Wixey, Jones, & Chritodolou, 2007).

We recognise that there is a complex interaction between individual and structural aspects such as race, ethnicity, age, socioeconomic status and culture, which might limit or enhanced physical activity. Hispanic youth simply exhibit different physical activity patterns. For example, Song et al. (2015) found that Hispanic adolescents engage in active video games, running/jogging and dance regularly as non-competitive sports or individual physical activities. This means that Hispanics might benefit significantly from having an active park near their homes with football fields, basketball and volleyball courts. Research has uncovered that walking is the most predominant physical activity among Hispanic adolescents in urban areas such as Miami, the Bronx, Chicago and San Diego, which may indicate some opportunities for engagement in active transportation (Arredondo et al., 2016; Song et al., 2015).

Psychosocial factors also influence engagement in physical activity and active commute. Researchers have found that self-efficacy partially mediates the relationship between social influence and physical activity (Duncan, Strycker, & Chaumeton, 2015). Youth may have high intentions to commute to and from school actively.

Still, other environmental factors, such as the lack of sidewalks or high crime in a neighbourhood, may limit their engagement in this type of physical activity (Villa-González, Ruiz, Mendoza, & Chillón, 2017). The built environment, if people live in urban or suburban areas, also relates to physical activity and obesity (Garfinkel-Castro et al., 2017; Garfinkel-Castro, Kim, Shima, & Ewing, 2014). Mobility is affected by where one lives; if there is access to walking and biking, infrastructure matters greatly (Manderscheid, 2016). That being said, planners and decision makers should learn about physical activity, active commute and other health/fitness patterns of Hispanics, compared to other groups, so that they can advocate for their needs and wants more effectively both at the individual and neighbourhood level.

4. METHOD

4.1. Statistical Analysis

This study aims to address a question about how much active commute to school by students can contribute to an increase in the degree of being physically active and physical activity participation. Our dependent variables are all count variables, but the number of days of being physically active represents an underdispersed frequency distribution – that is, the mean value is greater than the variance. On the other hand, the other dependent variable – the number of days exercising during the past 7 days – has an overdispersed count frequency distribution, which we generally handle in research.

Using quasi-Poisson regression in R, we calculated the odds of all independent and control variables on physical activity levels measured by the number of days. Statistical significance is determined at the $p < 0.05$. To analyse gender and race/ethnicity differences in the relationships between active commute and physical activity levels, subset data were drawn from the total sample data, and the quasi-Poisson regression was conducted by using the same variables for comparison across the multiple quasi-Poisson regression models. To reflect the survey design effects and sampling strategies in the NYPANS data, all analyses were performed using the survey package in R, and all estimates were weighted to provide coefficients of national estimates (Lumley, 2010).

4.2. Data Source

This study uses data from the 2010 NYPANS. Conducted by the Center for Disease Control and Prevention (CDC), NYPANS includes a 120-item questionnaire about physical activities, nutritional behaviours, measured obesity, weight and height to calculate the body mass indices and basic demographic characteristics such as race, ethnicity, age, sex and school grades. Details for the CDC's protocols for collecting these data, including weight and height, could be found in the NYPANS data user's manual. As an anonymous and self-administered survey taken with premeditated parental permissions, the 120-item questionnaire was delivered to 9th to 12th grade high school students and implemented during a regular class period in the spring of 2010.

4.3. Participants

Using the three-stage cluster design, 12,907 students in 168 schools were initially sampled in all 50 states, including the District of Columbia, and 11,458 students in 138 sampled schools participated in the survey. The school and student response rates were 82% and 88%, respectively, and the overall response rate was 73%. To get national estimates and avoid oversampling of black and Hispanic students, analysis weights were applied to all estimates in the data based on student sex, race, ethnicity and grade level. Among survey data of physical activity and behaviours of youth students, NYPANS is the nationwide survey data and the only data that also includes relevant behavioural pattern like active commuting to school and built environment information such as neighbourhood safety and the degree of proximity of amenities in students' neighbourhoods.

4.4. Study Measures

In this study, we have 24 variables of interest and we observe how they relate to the number of days physically active at least 60 minutes per day (see Table 7.2). In the survey questionnaire, active commute data were collected by asking students the number of days they walk or bike to school during the past 7 days, the number of days they were physically active at least 60 minutes per day during the past 7 days. Therefore, among 11,458 response data, we excluded response data in these variables that have missing responses. In the demographic characteristic variables, sex, race/ethnicity and grades variables are also important, and we also excluded data with missing responses to these questions. The depended variable is the number of days physically active at least 60 minutes a day. The BMI is the only continuous variable in this study. Missing responses found in these control variables were removed to get survey data with complete responses. After removing all missing responses in the variables, 7,992 (70%) US high school students between 9th and 12th grades are finally selected.

NYPANS collected response data of high school students' physical activity and relevant information by designing 12-month, 7-day and 24-hour recall questions. For an analytic purpose, 12-month recall questions do not represent accurate information due to the limited capacity of students' memory, and 24-hour recall questions do not reflect students' normal physical activity and behaviours.

5. RESULTS

5.1. Descriptive Statistics of the Survey Responses

National estimates in this study are based on a sample of 7,398 high school students (grade 9th to 12th). Table 7.1 shows the demographic and physical activity characteristic of the sampled respondents used in this study. The average BMI is about 23, and the BMI values range from about 13 to 53. No significant difference

Table 7.1. Demographic Characteristics and Physical Activity Behaviours in NYPANS Survey Data Sample ($n = 7,398$).

	Total	White, Non-Hispanic	Black, Non-Hispanic	Hispanic	Other Races
Total number of respondents in the sample	7,398	3,191	1,475	2,177	555
Percentage	100.0	43.2	19.9	29.4	7.5
Male[a]	49.5	22.0	9.4	14.2	3.9
Female[a]	50.5	21.1	10.5	15.2	3.7
Total	100.0	43.1	19.9	29.4	7.6
9th grade[a]	24.6	10.5	4.7	7.7	1.7
10th grade[a]	25.2	11.1	5.0	7.3	1.8
11th grade[a]	24.8	10.6	5.4	7.1	1.7
12th grade[a]	25.4	11.0	4.9	7.4	2.1
Total	100.0	43.2	20.0	29.5	7.3
Median BMI	23.2	22.9	23.7	23.4	22.8
Engaged in physical activity for at least 60 minutes[b]	61.6	63.3	57.8	62.5	58.9
Walked or rode bike to school[b]	18.5	10.9	21.4	27.1	21.1
Walked or rode bike from school[b]	25.3	17.3	15.8	35.5	29.6
Physical activity: walking[b]	80.2	81.4	75.1	81.6	82.0
Physical activity: biking[b]	26.5	28.8	18.7	28.8	25.6

[a]All percentage values represent the proportion of respondents to the entire survey data sample ($n = 7,398$).
[b]The percentages represent the proportion of students engaging in physical activities for at least 60 minutes during the week within each race group.

in BMI is identified across racial groups, but black high school students have the largest average BMI, whereas white high school students have the lowest BMI, except for the other race students. The proportion of students by gender and grades is almost equally sampled. However, the proportions of students in the sample are not equal across race and ethnicity. Approximately 43% of the students in the sample were white high school students, and 30% and 20% of the students were Hispanic and black high school students, respectively. This unequal sample sizes by race and ethnicity groups are adjusted by using the sampling weights that are already calculated in the NYPANS data. Grades sample almost the same number of students.

In the active commute (walking/biking) variable, 18.5% of the students walk or bike to school every week at least once, while the percentage walking and biking home from school was higher at 25.3%. Hispanics were more likely than any other group to walk or bike to school at 27.1%, compared to their black (21.4%) and white (10.9%) counterparts. These patterns are also reflected trips from school to home but at a much higher rate – for Hispanics 35.5%, for blacks 15.8% and for whites 17.3%. The most common physical activity among high school students was walking – 80.2% engaged in this activity. Hispanics participated in walking as their physical activity at school the most compared to any other group (81.6%). The rates for biking followed a similar trend.

5.2. Race/Ethnicity Differences in Effects of Active Commuting and Other Physical Activity Behaviours

Table 7.2 shows the complex survey data quasi-Poisson regression results by race and ethnicity. We specifically explore NYPANS Survey Question 9, "The number of days physically active at least 60 minutes per day" as the dependent variable. We will only discuss the categories that were significantly related to it. Hispanic and black students in the 11th grade were more likely to engage in physical activity for 60 minutes or more daily than those in the 10th grade and the 12th grade. The number of white and Hispanic students that are physically active at least 60 minutes per day and actively commute to school is significant. Meanwhile, it is not significant for blacks.

Both white and Hispanic students that engaged in physical activity at least 60 minutes per day had positive attitudes towards physical activity – they reported that when they participated in physical activities, their 'body feels good'. Blacks did not feel this way. It is more likely for whites, Hispanics and blacks, who engaged in physical activity at least 60 minutes per day to use home fitness equipment. Whites who engaged in physical activity at least 60 minutes per day were significantly affected by their perception of neighbourhood safety and parental supports, such as playing sports with them and providing transportation. For Hispanic students, on the other hand, having parks, playgrounds and gyms near their home negatively affect their physical activity status. One possible explanation for this may be related to their neighbourhood safety; neighbourhoods where Hispanic students live tend to be low-income and deteriorated neighbourhoods with parks, playgrounds and gyms of poor conditions. These amenities in Hispanic neighbourhoods tend to be places where crimes are likely to occur, and this may prevent Hispanic students from going to these places for their physical activities. As with white students, Hispanic high school students tend to be more physically active when their parents provide them with transportation to get to sports facilities. For black high school students, the quasi-Poisson regression results on neighbourhood characteristics show that their level of physical activeness is likely to increase when they have sports equipment at home. As with white and Hispanic students, black high school students also tend to be physically active when their parents provide transportation.

All groups depend on their parents, driving them to school. Whites are more likely to ride their bike to and from school. Whites, blacks and Hispanics are more likely to walk from school to home than from home to school. Whites are more likely than any other group to engage in physical activity for 60 or more minutes per day.

Regarding nutrition, there is a relationship between blacks not eating breakfast and not exercising for at least 60 minutes per day. Moreover, there is a relationship between whites (vs black and Hispanics) exercising for at least 60 minutes per day and eating vegetables at least three times a day. Hispanics and whites who ate fruits or drank 100% fruit juices at least twice a day are also more likely to exercise for the recommended amount. There are other behaviours associated with achieving less physical activity and, thus, walking, like playing video games and watching

Table 7.2. Complex Survey Data Quasi-Poisson Regression Results: Race/Ethnicity Effects.

Dependent Variable:

Question 9: The Number of Days Physically Active at Least 60 Minutes per Day

	White[a]		Hispanic[b]		Black[c]	
	Odds Ratio	(95% CI)	Odds Ratio	(95% CI)	Odds Ratio	(95% CI)
BMI	0.999	(0.995, 1.003)	1.001	(0.997, 1.005)	0.997	(0.993, 1.001)
School grades (9th grade as a reference group)						
10th grade	0.976*	(0.950, 1.003)	0.963	(0.892, 1.039)	0.931**	(0.874, 0.992)
11th grade	0.966	(0.907, 1.028)	0.942*	(0.881, 1.008)	0.937*	(0.874, 1.005)
12th grade	0.949**	(0.907, 0.993)	0.941	(0.856, 1.033)	0.944	(0.867, 1.026)
Days for active commute	1.017***	(1.006, 1.027)	1.021***	(1.008, 1.035)	1.010	(0.996, 1.024)
Attitudes towards physical activity: body feels good	1.048***	(1.030, 1.065)	1.034**	(1.007, 1.060)	1.023	(0.986, 1.063)
Sports equipment at home	1.034***	(1.011, 1.057)	1.035***	(1.011, 1.059)	1.036**	(1.003, 1.069)
Parks, playground, gyms nearby	1.003	(0.986, 1.019)	0.974***	(0.958, 0.990)	1.002	(0.975, 1.028)
Neighbourhood safety	1.023**	(1.003, 1.043)	1.006	(0.975, 1.037)	0.991	(0.959, 1.023)
Parental support: playing sport with students (not playing sports as a reference)						
One to two times/week	1.042*	(0.999, 1.085)	0.998	(0.925, 1.078)	0.944	(0.845, 1.053)
Three to four times/week	1.057**	(1.013, 1.103)	1.037	(0.956, 1.124)	1.045	(0.966, 1.131)
Five to six times/week	1.084***	(1.028, 1.142)	1.009	(0.911, 1.119)	0.960	(0.771, 1.195)
Daily	1.105***	(1.047, 1.165)	1.103	(0.958, 1.270)	1.054	(0.946, 1.176)
Parental support: providing transportation (no transportation as a reference)						
One to two times/week	1.004	(0.946, 1.065)	1.026	(0.953, 1.105)	1.033	(0.943, 1.130)
Three to four times/week	1.054	(0.989, 1.124)	1.162***	(1.080, 1.250)	1.166***	(1.061, 1.283)
Five to six times/week	1.169***	(1.102, 1.240)	1.265***	(1.185, 1.351)	1.212***	(1.067, 1.376)
Daily	1.226***	(1.171, 1.284)	1.335***	(1.254, 1.423)	1.223***	(1.104, 1.353)
Days for bike riding after school	1.019***	(1.010, 1.028)	1.010	(0.993, 1.027)	1.009	(0.992, 1.026)
Days for walking after school	1.010***	(1.005, 1.016)	1.014***	(1.006, 1.022)	1.014**	(1.003, 1.026)
Days eating breakfast	1.004	(0.999, 1.010)	1.001	(0.993, 1.009)	1.021**	(1.003, 1.039)

Eating vegetables three plus times/day: no ('yes' as a reference)	0.940**	(0.896, 0.986)	0.947	(0.882, 1.017)	1.031	(0.959, 1.111)
Eating fruits or drinking 100% fruit juices two plus times/day: no ('yes' as a reference)	0.948***	(0.918, 0.980)	0.985	(0.930, 1.044)	0.908***	(0.865, 0.955)
Hours playing computer games per day	0.984***	(0.975, 0.994)	0.985*	(0.970, 1.000)	0.971***	(0.956, 0.987)
Hours watching TV per day	0.992	(0.982, 1.003)	0.994	(0.981, 1.007)	1.012	(0.992, 1.033)
Observations	3,378		2,383		1,637	
McFadden's R^2	0.202		0.163		0.135	

*$p < 0.05$; **$p < 0.01$; and ***$p < 0.001$.
[a]Dispersion parameter: 0.624 (underdispersion).
[b]Dispersion parameter: 0.692 (underdispersion).
[c]Dispersion Parameter: 0.806 (underdispersion).

Note: Seven-day response variables are used in this study. Also, all raw responses in NYPANS are stored as numeric values. Some variables represent simple count variables – for instance, the number of days doing exercises during the past 7 days – but other variables use numeric values to represent categories. Notably, some categorical variables have orders across groups, so we need to be careful of dealing with these ordered categorical variables: for ordered categorical variables based on Likert scales, we use numeric value as it is to represent order among categories; for purely ordered variables, we treated them as nominal variables and calculated probability of falling within each category group compared with the reference group. Based on these criteria, data clean-up for defining count and categorical variables is also conducted before analysis.

TV for more than 3 hours per day. Only 13.9% of whites reported watching TV or video games for more than 3 hours in comparison to 40.1% for blacks and 26.1% for Hispanics. All of the youth who engaged in 3 hours or more playing computer games per day were less likely to achieve 60 minutes or more of physical activity.

6. DISCUSSION AND POLICY RECOMMENDATIONS

There are several limitations to our analysis. First, the data are nationwide; we could not analyse the differences that exist in smaller geographies like states or cities. Because of this, the survey does not consider differences relating to low-income or minority neighbourhoods. Second, another possible limitation is the time had been used for asking about physical activity (7 days). Third, the behaviours can have been influenced by the seasons. In the winter, the children are more likely to do not walk or active commute to go to school or home.

The following paragraphs summarise nine main findings or strengths of this study. First, this study showed that Hispanics that engaged in physical activity at least 60 minutes per day had positive attitudes towards exercise, which might have contributed to engaging in physical activity such as walking, to begin with. Second, our study demonstrated that walking is the most prevalent physical activity adolescents engage in. Third, we found that those who engage in walking are more likely to meet the physical activity requirements of 60 minutes per day, especially when combined with other kinds of physical activity such as sports. Fourth, this analysis helped us to understand that having sports equipment at home increased their opportunities to engage in physical activity.

Fifth, we also found that Hispanics, in particular, were influenced by having a park or a gym nearby – these contributed to increasing the likelihood of their physical activity. Parks and gyms provide places for Hispanics to walk and jog, as well as engage in more active sports such as basketball and football. Policymakers and planners in Latin America and the United States should try to expand opportunities to increase physical activity by investing and developing parks, particularly in low-income neighbourhoods (Cohen et al., 2007).

Six, this study notes, there might be differences between age, sex, ethnicity, race and the use of parks for exercise. More studies are needed to understand these relationships. Other studies have shown how parks are used if they are less than 1 mile or 20 minutes away (Cohen et al., 2007; Ewing et al., 2004), so that would be an important factor to consider while planning. However, parks are not always safe, and perceptions of safety may affect walking in one's neighbourhood (Cohen et al., 2007; Jacobs, 1992).

Seventh, this study showed that their perceptions of neighbourhood safety did not influence Hispanics and blacks' physical activity. Nonetheless, our study showed that whites were less physically active if they perceived their neighbourhood to be unsafe. Concerns about safety might be affected by gender, age, race, ethnicity and other factors. Safety has been cited as the main reason why parents drive their kids to school, regardless of race and ethnicity (McDonald et al., 2010). Mobility to and from school using active transportation can increase the time that students spend engaging in physical activities overall. As students get old enough to walk or bike to school, for example, after the 10th grade, they might participate more in these activities. When they start owning cars or carpool with friends, they might be less likely to walk or bike to school, for instance, in the 12th grade. As demonstrated by the survey, white and Hispanic students are more likely to commute to school walking or biking than blacks.

Eight, Hispanics who also exercise for at least 60 minutes per day were more likely than any other group to walk or bike to school. This means that Hispanics would walk even less if they did not walk to school. At least walking to school is a form of exercise. If it were not for walking to school, Hispanic youth perhaps would be more obese. Hispanics had higher obesity rates than blacks and whites.

Ninth, Hispanics were much less likely to generally ride bikes and, therefore, to commute to school in a bike, in comparison to whites. While four out of every five Hispanic youth reported walking, only one out of every three reported biking. The literature explains many reasons for this, for example, Hispanics are less likely to bike because their parents did not ride a bike or they tend to live in lower income neighbourhoods where there is poor biking infrastructure, or their bikes are likely to be stolen (Lusk, Anastasio, Shaffer, Wu, & Li, 2017).

Not all youth come back home in the same mode of travel as some students join the foot commuters while coming back home. All groups were more likely to go back home walking. The reason could be that busy parents drive their children to school on their way to their workplaces yet are unable to pick them up when school ends. Consequently, more young people are going back home on foot than young people coming to school in the morning. That being said, if resources are limited, a 'walking back home' intervention might be more effective. In addition, programmes like these need administrative support and school intervention to make it successful since parents, volunteers or school employees may find it time-consuming to monitor all the students during the walk to/from school.

Nonetheless, this type of intervention along with community education, improving crosswalks, signage, placemaking and the creation of walking trails in low-income and majority Hispanic neighbourhoods, is promising in fostering life-long health-promoting habits while addressing safety concerns and other barriers that impede walkability (García, 2017; Zambrana & Oostema, 2017). Finally, regarding school interventions, it is essential to recognise the role of teachers and administrators in teaching both parents and students about health practices (McDonald et al., 2010).

It is also important to highlight the role of parents in terms of educating young people in developing healthy habits, including healthy eating and engaging in physical activity (Banerjee et al., 2014). Parents and family members could be role models in healthy behaviours. For example, young people are more likely to walk or bike because their parents also engage in walking or biking. Indoor and outdoor activities involving the community could be helpful to change behaviours too.

In terms of policy recommendations for planners and other decision makers in Latin America as well as in the United States, not engaging schools in active transportation programmes would be a missed opportunity. Understanding the long-term benefits of walking, policymakers, parents and school administrators nationwide already have organised supervised walking (e.g. safe passage programmes) where youth from across a neighbourhood can walk to/from school under the supervision of a designated responsible adult (McDonald et al., 2010). Programmes like Safe Passage could be furthered supported and funded. Apart from increasing walking rates, research demonstrates that organised walking increased youth road safety skills.

Additionally, making changes in the built environment in Latin America and the United States could have massive effects on engaging in active commute. According to Ewing et al. (2004), "built environment of low densities, little mixing of land uses, long blocks, incomplete sidewalks, and other hallmarks of sprawl" made kids depend on automobiles to commute to school (p. 55). Moreover, on the one hand, major roads or railroads in the path of school acted as a deterrent as well as the lack of connectivity in street networks. On the other hand, straight streets, short block lengths and good street connectivity facilitate walkability in urban areas (Calthorpe, 1995). All these being established, public awareness (school administration, parents and children), organised walks as well as improvements to build environment factors that address safety concerns seem to be the solution for increasing walking rates among youth – which is the most common physical activity among adolescents.

Urban planners in cities of the Americas, both in Latin America and the United States, need to work more closely with public health specialists to be able to understand how other behaviours affect engaging in physical activity. This study showed that there is a positive relationship between physical activity and eating vegetables and fruits among white youth, while there is a negative relationship between playing video games for 3 or more hours per day among African Americans and Hispanics. School programmes, as well as community programmes that encourage healthy behaviours, should target active commute, with other activities like encouraging healthy eating and less sedentary behaviours by way of utilising neighbourhood parks or going to the gym. All of these school or after-school programmes should be available in low-income neighbourhoods. However, this research has demonstrated that more analysis with data segregation by race, ethnicity, age and gender is needed.

It is crucial to think about how planners and others that work in the built environment can promote the long-term development of the United Nations (UN), such as ensuring healthy lives and well-being for all at all ages, active travel to reduce air pollution and young education on climate change. It is also important to increase the knowledge of planners in active transport, so they can effectively create places that promote health equity and inclusive urban mobility policies.

REFERENCES

Angotti, T., & Irazábal, C. (2017). Planning Latin American cities: Dependencies and 'best practices'. *Latin American Perspectives*, 44(2), 4–17. https://doi.org/10.1177/0094582X16689556

Arango, C. M., Parra, D. C., Eyler, A., Sarmiento, O., Mantilla, S., Gomez, L. F., & Lobelo, F. (2011). Walking or bicycling to school and weight status among adolescents from Monteria, Colombia. *Journal of Physical Activity & Health*, 8(2), 171–177.

Arredondo, E. M., Sotres-Alvarez, D., Stoutenberg, M., Davis, S. M., Crespo, N. C., Carnethon, M. R., ... Evenson, K. R. (2016). Physical activity levels in U.S. Latino/Hispanic adults: Results from the Hispanic community health study/study of Latinos. *American Journal of Preventive Medicine*, 50(4), 500–508. https://doi.org/10.1016/j.amepre.2015.08.029

Ball, K., Jeffery, R. W., Abbott, G., McNaughton, S. A., & Crawford, D. (2010). Is healthy behavior contagious: Associations of social norms with physical activity and healthy eating. *The International Journal of Behavioral Nutrition and Physical Activity*, *7*(December), 86. https://doi.org/10.1186/1479-5868-7-86

Banerjee, T., Uhm, J., & Bahl, D. (2014). Walking to school: The experience of children in inner city Los Angeles and implications for policy. *Journal of Planning Education and Research*, *34*(2), 123–140. https://doi.org/10.1177/0739456X14522494

Calthorpe, P. (1995). *The next American metropolis: Ecology, community, and the American dream* (3rd ed.). New York, NY: Princeton Architectural Press.

Caprio, S., Daniels, S. R., Drewnowski, A., Kaufman, F. R., Palinkas, L. A., Rosenbloom, A. L., … Kirkman, M. S. (2008). Influence of race, ethnicity, and culture on childhood obesity: Implications for prevention and treatment. *Obesity*, *16*(12), 2566–2577. https://doi.org/10.1038/oby.2008.398

CDC. (2018). Childhood obesity facts. Retrieved from https://www.cdc.gov/obesity/data/childhood.html

Child Trends. (2018). Racial and ethnic composition of the child population. *Child Trends* (blog). Retrieved from https://www.childtrends.org/indicators/racial-and-ethnic-composition-of-the-child-population

Cohen, D. A., McKenzie, T. L., Sehgal, A., Williamson, S., Golinelli, D., & Lurie, N. (2007). Contribution of public parks to physical activity. *American Journal of Public Health*, *97*(3), 509–514. https://doi.org/10.2105/AJPH.2005.072447

Crawford, P., Schneider, C., Martin, A., Spezzano, T., Algert, S., Ganthavorn, C., … Donohue, S. (2013). Communitywide strategies key to preventing childhood obesity. *California Agriculture*, *67*(1), 13–20.

Dellinger, A. M., & Staunton, C. E. (2002). Barriers to children walking and biking to school – United States, 1999. *Morbidity and Mortality Weekly Report (MMWR)*, *51*(32), 701–704. Retrieved from https://trid.trb.org/view.aspx?id=725924

Dinç, Z. (2011). Social self-efficacy of adolescents who participate in individual and team sports. *Social Behavior and Personality: An International Journal*, *39*(10), 1417.

Dominguez, K., Penman-Aguilar, A., Chang, M.-H., Moonesinghe, R., Castellanos, T., Rodriguez-Lainz, A., & Schieber, R. (2015). Vital signs: Leading causes of death, prevalence of diseases and risk factors, and use of health services among Hispanics in the United States – 2009–2013. *MMWR. Morbidity and Mortality Weekly Report*, *64*(17), 469–478.

Duncan, S. C., Strycker, L. A., & Chaumeton, N. R. (2015). Personal, family, and peer correlates of general and sport physical activity among African American, Latino, and white girls. *Journal of Health Disparities Research and Practice*, *8*(2), 12–28.

Ennis, S., Ríos-Vargas, M., & Albert, N. (2011). The Hispanic population: 2010. Retrieved from https://www.census.gov/prod/cen2010/briefs/c2010br-04.pdf

Epstein, L. H., Wing, R. R., Penner, B. C., & Kress, M. J. (1985). Effect of diet and controlled exercise on weight loss in obese children. *The Journal of Pediatrics*, *107*(3), 358–361. https://doi.org/10.1016/S0022-3476(85)80506-0

Ewing, R. H., Schoeer, W., & Greene, W. (2004). School location and student travel: Analysis of factors affecting mode choice. *Transportation Research Record*, *1895*, 55–63.

Faulkner, G. E. J., Richichi, V., Buliung, R. N., Fusco, C., & Moola, F. (2010). What's 'quickest and easiest?': Parental decision making about school trip mode. *The International Journal of Behavioral Nutrition and Physical Activity*, *7*(August), 62. https://doi.org/10.1186/1479-5868-7-62

Freedman, D. S., Khan, L. K., Serdula, M. K., Ogden, C. L., & Dietz, W. H. (2006). Racial and ethnic differences in secular trends for childhood BMI, weight, and height. *Obesity*, *14*(2), 301–308. https://doi.org/10.1038/oby.2006.39

García, I. (2014). *Making the case for change: Report series*. Chicago, IL: Nathalie P. Voorhees Center for Neighborhood and Community Improvement, and the Illinois Latino Family Commission. Retrieved from https://www.voorheescenter.com/publications

García, I. (2017). Community engagement in an urban daylighting project: A case study of a Salt Lake City creek. *Journal of Urban Planning, Landscape & Environmental Design*, *2*(3), 53–63.

García, I., & Ara, S. (2018). Active transportation and perceptions of safety: A case study of a regional trail and a transit corridor in Salt Lake City, Utah. *Focus: The Journal of Planning Practice & Education, 14*(1), 37–43.

Garfinkel-Castro, A., Kim, K., Hamidi, S., & Ewing, R. (2017). Obesity and the built environment at different urban scales: Examining the literature. *Nutrition Reviews, 75*(Suppl. 1), 51–61. https://doi.org/10.1093/nutrit/nuw037

Garfinkel-Castro, A., Kim, K., Shima, H., & Ewing, R. (2014). The built environment and obesity. In R. S. Ahima (Ed.), *Metabolic syndrome: A comprehensive textbook* (pp. 1–14). Cham: Springer International Publishing. https://doi.org/10.1007/978-3-319-12125-3_17-1

Gill, D. L. (2017, April). Gender and cultural diversity in sport, exercise, and performance psychology. *Oxford Research Encyclopedia of Psychology.* https://doi.org/10.1093/acrefore/9780190236557.013.148

González, S. A., Triana, C. A., Abaunza, C., Aldana, L., Arias-Gómez, L. F., Bermúdez, J., … Sarmiento, O. L. (2018). Results from Colombia's 2018 report card on physical activity for children and youth. *Journal of Physical Activity and Health, 15*(s2), S335–S337. https://doi.org/10.1123/jpah.2018-0507

Gordon-Larsen, P., & Popkin, B. (2011). Understanding socioeconomic and racial/ethnic status disparities in diet, exercise and weight: Underlying contextual factors and pathways. *Journal of the American Dietetic Association, 111*(12), 1816–1819. https://doi.org/10.1016/j.jada.2011.09.017

Gordon-Larsen, P., McMurray, R. G., & Popkin, B. M. (2000). Determinants of adolescent physical activity and inactivity patterns. *Pediatrics, 105*(6), e83. https://doi.org/10.1542/peds.105.6.e83

Hallal, P. C., Reichert, F. F., Ekelund, U., Dumith, S. C., Menezes, A. M., Victora, C. G., & Wells, J. (2012). Bidirectional cross-sectional and prospective associations between physical activity and body composition in adolescence: Birth cohort study. *Journal of Sports Sciences, 30*(2), 185–192. https://doi.org/10.1080/02640414.2011.631570

Hallal, P. C., Victora, C. G., Azevedo, M. R., & Wells, J. C. K. (2006). Adolescent physical activity and health. *Sports Medicine, 36*(12), 1019–1030. https://doi.org/10.2165/00007256-200636120-00003

Hendrickson, D., Smith, C., & Eikenberry, N. (2006). Fruit and vegetable access in four low-income food deserts communities in Minnesota. *Agriculture and Human Values, 23*(3), 371–383. https://doi.org/10.1007/s10460-006-9002-8

Heron, M. (2010). Deaths: Leading causes for 2010. *National Vital Statistics Reports: From the Center for Disease Control and Prevention, National Center for Health Statistics, National Vital Statistics System, 62*(6), 1–97. Retrieved from http://www.cdc.gov/nchs/data/nvsr/nvsr62/nvsr62_06.pdf

Isasi, C. R., Rastogi, D., & Molina, K. (2016). Health issues in Hispanic/Latino youth. *Journal of Latina/o Psychology, 4*(2), 67–82. https://doi.org/10.1037/lat0000054

Jacobs, J. (1992). *The death and life of great American cities* (Reissue ed.). New York, NY: Vintage.

Jonides, L., Buschbacher, V., & Barlow, S. E. (2002). Management of child and adolescent obesity: Psychological, emotional, and behavioral assessment. *Pediatrics, 110*(Suppl. 1), 215–221.

Lee, C. A., Chrisinger, B., Greenlee, A. J., Garcia Zambrana, I., & Jackson, A. (2020). Beyond Recruitment: Comparing Experiences of Climate and Diversity between International Students and Domestic Students of Color in U.S. Urban Planning Programs. *Journal of Planning Education and Research, March*, 1–7. https://doi.org/10.1177/0739456X20902241.

Liu, J., Probst, J. C., Harun, N., Bennett, K. J., & Torres, M. E. (2009). Acculturation, physical activity, and obesity among Hispanic adolescents. *Ethnicity & Health, 14*(5), 509–525. https://doi.org/10.1080/13557850902890209

Lowry, I. S. (2009). *Migration and metropolitan growth: Two analytical models*. San Francisco, CA: Chandler Publishing Company.

Lumley, T. (2010). *Complex surveys: A guide to analysis using R* (1st ed.). Hoboken, NJ: Wiley.

Lusk, A. C., Anastasio, A., Shaffer, N., Wu, J., & Li, Y. (2017). Biking practices and preferences in a lower income, primarily minority neighborhood: Learning what residents want. *Preventive Medicine Reports, 7*(September), 232–238. https://doi.org/10.1016/j.pmedr.2017.01.006

Manderscheid, K. (2016). Unequal mobilities. In T. Onhmacht, H. Maksim, & M. Bergman (Eds.), *Mobilities and inequality*. New York, NY: Routledge. https://doi.org/10.4324/9781315595719-8

McDonald, N. C., Deakin, E., & Aalborg, A. E. (2010). Influence of the social environment on children's school travel. *Preventive Medicine, 50*(January), 65–68. https://doi.org/10.1016/j.ypmed.2009.08.016

Mendoza, J. A., Watson, K., Nguyen, N., Cerin, E., Baranowski, T., & Nicklas, T. A. (2011). Active commuting to school and association with physical activity and adiposity among US youth. *Journal of Physical Activity & Health*, *8*(4), 488–495.

Nyberg, K., Ramirez, A., & Gallion, K. (2011). *Addressing nutrition, overweight and obesity among Latino youth*. Washington, DC: Robert Wood Johnson Foundation. Retrieved from https://www.rwjf.org/content/dam/farm/reports/issue_briefs/2011/rwjf71859

Ogden, C. L., Carroll, M. D., Kit, B. K., & Flegal, K. M. (2014). Prevalence of childhood and adult obesity in the United States, 2011–2012. *Journal of the American Medical Association*, *311*(8), 806–814. https://doi.org/10.1001/jama.2014.732

Oluyomi, A. O., Lee, C., Nehme, E., Dowdy, D., Ory, M. G., & Hoelscher, D. M. (2014). Parental safety concerns and active school commute: Correlates across multiple domains in the home-to-school journey. *The International Journal of Behavioral Nutrition and Physical Activity*, *11*(March), 32. https://doi.org/10.1186/1479-5868-11-32

Pérez-Escamilla, R., & Putnik, P. (2007). The role of acculturation in nutrition, lifestyle, and incidence of type 2 diabetes among Latinos. *The Journal of Nutrition*, *137*(4), 860–870. https://doi.org/10.1093/jn/137.4.860

Perrin, J. M., Bloom, S. R., & Gortmaker, S. L. (2007). The increase of childhood chronic conditions in the United States. *Journal of the American Medical Association*, *297*(24), 2755–2759. https://doi.org/10.1001/jama.297.24.2755

Reichert, F. F., Menezes, A. M. B., Wells, J. C. K., Dumith, S. C., & Hallal, P. C. (2009). Physical activity as a predictor of adolescent body fatness: A systematic review. *Sports Medicine (Auckland, N.Z.)*, *39*(4), 279–294. https://doi.org/10.2165/00007256-200939040-00002

Rønningen, R., Wammer, A. C. P., Grabner, N. H., & Valderhaug, T. G. (2019). Associations between lifetime adversity and obesity treatment in patients with morbid obesity. *Obesity Facts*, *12*(1), 1–13. https://doi.org/10.1159/000494333

Sallis, J. F., Pinski, R. B., Grossman, R. M., Patterson, T. L., & Nader, P. R. (1988). The development of self-efficacy scales for healthrelated diet and exercise behaviors. *Health Education Research*, *3*(3), 283–292. https://doi.org/10.1093/her/3.3.283

Sarmiento, C. S., & Beard, V. A. (2013). Traversing the border: Community-based planning and transnational migrants. *Journal of Planning Education and Research*, *33*(3), 336–347. https://doi.org/10.1177/0739456X13499934

Sarmiento, O. L., Castillo, A. D. D., Triana, C. A., Acevedo, M. J., Gonzalez, S. A., & Pratt, M. (2017). Reclaiming the streets for people: Insights from Ciclovías Recreativas in Latin America. *Preventive Medicine*, *103*, S34–S40. https://doi.org/10.1016/j.ypmed.2016.07.028

Schlossberg, M., Greene, J., Phillips, P. P., Johnson, B., & Parker, B. (2006). School trips: Effects of urban form and distance on travel mode. *Journal of the American Planning Association*, *72*(3), 337–346.

Schwimmer, J. B., Burwinkle, T. M., & Varni, J. W. (2003). Health-related quality of life of severely obese children and adolescents. *Journal of the American Medical Association*, *289*(14), 1813–1819. https://doi.org/10.1001/jama.289.14.1813

Smpokos, E. A., Linardakis, M., Papadaki, A., Lionis, C., & Kafatos, A. (2012). Secular trends in fitness, moderate-to-vigorous physical activity, and TV-viewing among first grade school children of Crete, Greece between 1992/93 and 2006/07. *Journal of Science and Medicine in Sport*, *15*(2), 129–135. https://doi.org/10.1016/j.jsams.2011.08.006

Song, M., Carroll, D. D., Lee, S. M., & Fulton, J. E. (2015). Physical activities of US high school students – 2010 National Youth Physical Activity and Nutrition Survey. *Journal of Physical Activity and Health*, *12*(6 Suppl. 1), S11–S17. https://doi.org/10.1123/jpah.2014-0117

Swallen, K. C., Reither, E. N., Haas, S. A., & Meier, A. M. (2005). Overweight, obesity, and health-related quality of life among adolescents: The national longitudinal study of adolescent health. *Pediatrics*, *115*(2), 340–347. https://doi.org/10.1542/peds.2004-0678

Taveras, E. M., Gillman, M. W., Kleinman, K., Rich-Edwards, J. W., & Rifas-Shiman, S. L. (2010). Racial/ethnic differences in early-life risk factors for childhood obesity. *Pediatrics*, *125*(4), 686–695. https://doi.org/10.1542/peds.2009-2100

The Office of Minority Health. (2014). *Hispanic/Latino profile*. Retrieved from http://minorityhealth.hhs.gov/templates/browse.aspx?lvl=2&lvlID=54

Timperio, A., Crawford, D., Telford, A., & Salmon, J. (2004). Perceptions about the local neighborhood and walking and cycling among children. *Preventive Medicine*, *38*(1), 39–47. https://doi.org/10.1016/j.ypmed.2003.09.026

Titheridge, H., Achuthan, K., Mackett, R., & Solomon, J. (2009). Assessing the extent of transport social exclusion among the elderly. *Journal of Transport and Land Use*, *2*(2), 31–48.

Titheridge, H., Wixey, S., Jones, P., & Chritodolou, G. (2007, August). Measuring accessibility as experienced by young people. Paper Presented at Access to Destinations, Minneapolis. Retrieved from http://discovery.ucl.ac.uk/151577/

Trost, S. G., Kerr, L. M., Ward, D. S., & Pate, R. R. (2001). Physical activity and determinants of physical activity in obese and non-obese children. *International Journal of Obesity*, *25*(6), 822–829. https://doi.org/10.1038/sj.ijo.0801621

Villa-González, E., Ruiz, J. R., Mendoza, J. A., & Chillón, P. (2017). Effects of a school-based intervention on active commuting to school and health-related fitness. *BMC Public Health*, *17*(January), 20. https://doi.org/10.1186/s12889-016-3934-8

Wang, Y., & Beydoun, M. A. (2007). The obesity epidemic in the United States – Gender, age, socioeconomic, racial/ethnic, and geographic characteristics: A systematic review and meta-regression analysis. *Epidemiologic Reviews*, *29*, 6–28. https://doi.org/10.1093/epirev/mxm007

Wang, Y., & Lim, H. (2012). The global childhood obesity epidemic and the association between socio-economic status and childhood obesity. *International Review of Psychiatry (Abingdon, England)*, *24*(3), 176–188. https://doi.org/10.3109/09540261.2012.688195

Wojcicki, J. M., Schwartz, N., Jiménez-Cruz, A., Bacardi-Gascon, M., & Heyman, M. B. (2012). Acculturation, dietary practices and risk for childhood obesity in an ethnically heterogeneous population of Latino school children in the San Francisco Bay Area. *Journal of Immigrant and Minority Health*, *14*(4), 533–539. https://doi.org/10.1007/s10903-011-9553-7

Zambrana, I., & Oostema, C. (2017, October). Active and public transportation connectivity between North Temple TOD and Jordan Park River Trail. TREC Final Reports NITC-RR-990. Portland, OR: Transportation Research and Education Center. https://doi.org/10.15760/trec.

CHAPTER 8

CHILDREN'S MOBILITY AND PLAYABILITY IN THE NEIGHBOURHOOD OF RÍO PIEDRAS: PERSPECTIVES FROM CHILDREN AND ADULTS

Norma I. Peña-Rivera and Enery López-Navarrete

ABSTRACT

Transportation planning has conventionally examined mobility from the standpoint of the efficiency of transportation systems, based on trips as units of analysis, overlooking the social needs of excluded groups, such as children. Understanding children's geographies provides insight into one of the basic social needs of children, intrinsically related to mobility: play. Disadvantages in mobility, along with other social conditions further limit children's autonomy in their neighbourhood. This chapter proposes the term playability as a concept that intertwines both needs. A case study of neighbourhood analyses the playability needs of children from their perspective and that of the community. Findings suggest that, in a walkable, built environment, issues from criminal activity directly influence children's playability, even more than automobile presence. Furthermore, community perspective on playability, as mostly limited to structured play in designated spaces and time, separates mobility from play and thus limits opportunities for social inclusion. A change in both, acknowledging children's need for play and mobility, and their reciprocity, and incorporating measures to improve it, may provide a different framework for transportation and urban planning at the local level, one that seeks greater social inclusion of children.

Keywords: Children; mobility; play; playability; transportation; social inclusion

1. INTRODUCTION

Since the 1950s, city and transportation planning in the United States (USA) have emphasised the need for a transportation system oriented towards time and efficiency (Meyer & Miller, 2001; Vuchic, 2000). The focus has been on making people, goods and services more mobile; moving them as quickly as possible. Mobility requires having an efficient transportation system. Thus, the core of conventional transportation planning is to reduce congestion, where greater mobility is the key metric (Texas A&M Transportation Institute, 2019). Such orientation is the result of a historical planning and policy practice which privileges road transportation and private transport over public transit while also limiting the development of alternative modes of transportation and separating land-use and transportation planning (Preston & Raje, 2007). This perspective remains prevalent but it falls short of recognising human development and social needs. 'Mobility' transcends just the action of moving (i.e. infrastructure development and accessibility) and should include the forms in which people travel according to physical, social and urban scales (Ansell, 2009; Cresswell, 2010; Danenberg, Doumpa, & Karssenberg, 2018).

Alternative definitions of mobility emphasise the need to understand the physical, spatial and socioeconomic attributes of an individual and their capacity to move, to promote access to destinations and ensure social inclusion (Fransen et al., 2015; Sheller & Urry, 2006; Urry, 2007). This socialised definition alludes to the importance of taking a more in-depth look at the conditions of vulnerable social groups, defined as groups or individuals with characteristics that may result in experiences which socially exclude them.

Children, particularly those of non-driving age, are considered as a vulnerable group given the cognitive capacities that are associated with their development stage and level of autonomy. When talking about children, understanding their geographies (e.g. place and time) in which their childhood is constructed provides insight into their mobility (Holloway & Valentine, 2000; Murray & Cortés-Morales, 2019). Children's capacity to move primarily depends on their access to safe walking spaces, yet this mode of transportation is not at the core of transportation planning. Thus, the transportation system and the city as a whole exclude children, as they do not belong to the 'average' population (i.e. an adult that can drive a private vehicle) (Legendre, Ripaud, Brisset, & Munchenbach, 2013; McCahill & Ebeling, 2015).

In Western countries, such as the USA, equity concerns regarding vulnerable groups and transportation have mainly focussed on providing adults with access to public transit (McCahill & Ebeling, 2015). Individuals vulnerable because of their age, gender, disability or social identities, living in poor conditions with low-incomes, are prone to social exclusion. By overlooking the scales and needs of vulnerable groups, transportation planning and policy has limited their mobilities causing major disadvantages.

The combination of mobility disadvantages and other persistent social disadvantages of people generates 'mobility poverty', which Lucas (2012) has examined. Conditions such as low-income, poor housing, lack of information, poor transit and high fares limit people's capability to have access to goods, services, social networks and capital. Such inaccessibility exacerbates pre-existing economic and political exclusion, as well as decision-making (Lucas, 2012). This chapter focusses on children's mobility poverty and how it socially excludes them from participating in city dynamics, particularly examining their access to free, active play.

1.1 Children's Mobility

Children's mobility varies according to their developmental state and living context. Play has an interdependent relationship with mobility that is similar to when a child learns to crawl and walk: it occurs given an intrinsic and ambiguous urge to experiment and discover (Gleave & Cole-Hamilton, 2012; Lester & Russell, 2008; Sutton-Smith, 1997). Play is also children's medium for mobility and vice versa. Thus, the more a child can move in his or her environment, such as their local neighbourhood, the higher the opportunity to improve his or her development (Marzi & Reimers, 2018; Schoeppe, Duncan, Badland, Oliver, & Browne, 2014). Child mobility is about not only transporting him or herself from point 'A' to point 'B': it is a building block of child development. This requires considering play as an integral activity of children in the city and one which requires mobility:

> [...] Children's mobilities are not only about transport, but relate to mobilities at all scales from micro-mobilities of the body to the movements, and imagined movements of ideas, objects, communications and policies. (Murray & Cortés-Morales, 2019; Location 951–956)

We call children's capability to play by moving freely and actively around their neighbourhoods 'playability'. Playability includes children's license to move around a space, supported and trusted by their households. This definition of playability considers the scales that influence child-neighbourhood relationships as well as immediate and larger contextual conditions (Bronfrenbrenner, 1979; KaBOOM!, 2016; Leventhal & Brooks-Gunn, 2000; Murray & Cortés-Morales, 2019). Children's playability is the means by which children actively participate in their cities. Thus, it is important to integrate playful forms of children's mobility, as play and mobility go together when exploring and negotiating effectively for the development and use of urban spaces. Play is essential to children's mobility (Lester & Russell, 2010; Sutton-Smith, 1997). Thus, as mobility and social conditions affect children's access to free, active play in cities and neighbourhoods, or their playability, it becomes necessary to study their relationship to better understand how to integrate children's needs in local and regional transportation planning.

1.2 Mobility Disadvantages of Children

The mobility poverty in which some children develop results in social exclusion by making, among other things, free play inaccessible in the neighbourhood. Childhood mobility disadvantages include lack of or poor sidewalks in their neighbourhoods, streets dominated by cars, adult concern about going outside, lack of information about modes of transport and poor or non-existent public transit in their neighbourhood. Mobility poverty interacts with other disadvantages such as socioeconomic status, health and literacy to affect their children's access to numerous opportunities such as education, social networks, access to food and other services. In order to simplify this relationship, it is useful to say

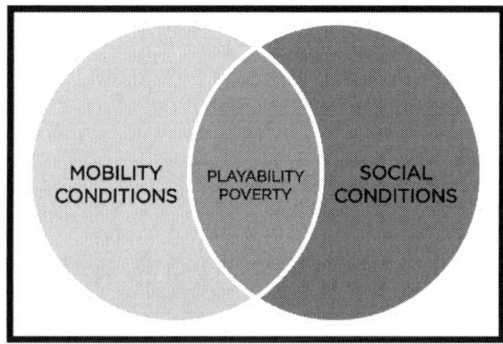

Fig. 8.1. Conditions That Create Playability Poverty.

that limited mobility and social disadvantages that affect children together produce 'playability poverty' given that children's ability to play is directly related to their mobility, as Fig. 8.1 shows.

1.3 The Importance of Playability of Children

Playability deserves special attention because it is a social activity that brings about children's autonomy – an important goal of children's development and one of their rights (James, Jenks, & Prout, 1998; Kraftl, 2013).

Research has identified children's need for outdoor free play, both for health and for developmental reasons (Ansari, Pettit, & Gershoff, 2015; Gill, 2014; Marzi & Reimers, 2018). One noticeable impact is on children's obesity (Herrington & Brussoni, 2015), and children's contact with nature and the outside environment has a direct impact on their executive functions and behaviours (Christensen & O'Brien, 2003; Hughes & Graham, 2002; Leventhal & Brooks-Gunn, 2000). For decades, studies have advocated for spaces to be designed and planned for and with children to meet their needs and build life competencies (Chawla, 2002; Christensen & O'Brien, 2003; Hart, 1979; Karsten & van Vliet, 2006; Shackell, Butler, Doyle, & Ball, 2008; Tranter, 2015). This matter is at the heart of children's development.

Furthermore, children have a right to play in the city (Cushing & van Vliet, 2017; Harvey, 2003; Mitchell, 2003; UNCRC, 1989). They must be included in society as citizens at all times, not just once they become adults (Murray & Cortés-Morales, 2019). As established by Article 31 of the United Nations Convention on the Rights of the Child (UNCRC, 1989) children's need to play is a basic human right. This article recognises:

> [...]the right of the child to rest and leisure, to engage in play and recreational activities appropriate to the age of the child and to participate freely in cultural life and the arts. (UNCRC, 1989)

In practice, children's interdependency with caregivers or other authority figures means that they have heteronomy rather than autonomy. But this does not mean that they always have to submit and give up their needs for empowerment and agency (Bustelo, 2007). Children's social rights imply that society, as a whole, is responsible for children's legitimate citizenship (Bustelo, 2007). The Child Friendly City movement recognises that a sustainable transportation system is important as it gives children access to urban opportunities and initiatives for freedom and risk all necessary to support children's playability (UNICEF, 2018).

The more a child can move in his or her environment, the higher the opportunity to improve his or her development (Ginsburg, 2007; Yogman, Garner, Hutchinson, Hirsh-Pasek, & Golinkoff, 2018). This requires considering play as an integral childhood activity in the city which requires mobility. Thus, it becomes important to integrate 'playful forms' of children's mobility, as play and mobility go together when exploring and negotiating effectively in urban spaces. KaBOOM! (n.d.) provides examples of cities and communities weaving, reimagining and visibilising play in non-traditional playscapes.

A study presented in this chapter explores the relationship between mobility and child social disadvantage and the importance of access to free, active play in the neighbourhood (playability) by asking: how mobility and social disadvantages of children affect their playability in the neighbourhood from the perspective of children and adults?

The following sections of this chapter first review research and discuss practices that facilitate children's mobility in cities and neighbourhoods, through the lens of how they promote children's playability. Subsequent sections present methods and findings from the study that observed children while playing in a neighbourhood and interviewed adults about their perspectives on playability in the same neighbourhood. Findings identify interactions between mobility and social conditions affecting playability, such as crime, the street and dedicated, urban spaces.

2 LITERATURE REVIEW

2.1 Definitions of Play and Its Relationship to Children's Mobility in the Neighbourhood

Play is the way children discover themselves, their surroundings and how to interact with others and their surroundings (Brown & Vaughan, 2009). Play is intrinsically motivated by children's needs. It evolves as their ability to move increases, providing autonomy to an individual. Tonucci (2007) exposes the importance of play for children comparing it to the needs of humans:

> Children's ability to play freely and spontaneously is similar to adults' most elevated and extraordinary experiences such as scientific research, exploration, art, and mysticism; precisely the experiences in which humans find themselves in front of complexity, where he or she finds again the possibility of letting himself or herself be guided by the great motor of pleasure. (p. 43)

Perceiving play as a means to an end could hamper children's biological intrinsic nature (Gleave & Cole-Hamilton, 2012). The activity of playing is not only purposive, like school trips but is both a means and an end in and of itself.

An important distinction becomes necessary between play types particularly between structured and unstructured. Adult-led and directed, structured play implies a pre-determined set of rules, time and place and tends to follow agendas. This form of play falls into supervised organised games or programmes that address a specific issue (generally sports, arts or skill based). On the other hand, unstructured or free play is freely chosen and self-directed by the child. The child is able to determine the space and moment in which he or she independently engages in its process as an end (8 80 Cities, 2017; Gibson, Cornell & Gill, 2017; Gray, 2011). Intrinsically motivated and led by imagination, themes and symbols, free play is mainly fluid, flexible and is an open-ended way in which a child or individual can express themselves (8 80 Cities, 2017). Given its ambiguity and spontaneity, free play may not be understood according to adult norms. Thus, unstructured play appears as a waste of time based on outcomes versus process.

However, research shows how contemporary lifestyles limit children's playability. Gray (2011) has exposed how outdoor play has declined even more than indoor play. This has led to rises in forms of psychopathology among children, such as anxiety, depression and narcissism. Social and cultural expectations have overscheduled children's free time by allocating them into spaces with minimum risk exposure and extracurricular activities that can make children marketable when growing up (Gill, 2007; Lanza, 2012; Tantia, Welch & Lin, 2015). Although skills are important, children need opportunities to develop, at their own pace. Gray (2011) argues how 'play is, first and foremost, done for its own sake' (p. 454). Children need more opportunities to be and play freely to gain independent mobility.

2.2 Opportunities to Play in the City: Place, Access and Mobility

Opportunities for free, active play in the city depend, in part, on the built environment. Diversity of the built and natural environmental resources and access to play and exploration are key determinants for a child friendly, play-oriented place (Freeman & Tranter, 2011; Marketta, 2004). The two main urban design-models in the Global North, which the Global South has adopted in some cities, are, in very general terms, the traditional city and, its counterpart, the suburb ('sub'). Of course, as cities have grown and developed they have become more varied than this two-type model suggests (Brenner, 2014). Yet generalisations are useful to guide particular examinations of related issues. These two models have been objects of great discussion among urban transportation planners, discussing the benefits and potential drawbacks, such as social exclusion and the degradation of the land and air (Transportation Research Board, 1998).

The Congress for the New Urbanism ('CNU', n.d.) promoted principles for the so-called neo-traditional cities and neighbourhoods, with the purpose of addressing city and subproblems (Duany, Plater-Zyberk, & Speck, 2000). In the beginning, CNU proposed three basic principles for urban settlements and new developments: design, density and diversity. Urban planning should consider human scale, with moderate to higher densities and a mix of residential and commercial uses, designed to promote more sustainable cities.

In the USA, the federal and local governments adopted the sustainable cities concept, integrating CNU ideas and others. The term 'livable cities' evolved, arguing for compact developments and the transformation of cities in favour of improving the human experience and protecting the environment (Fairchild & Revord, 2017). Movements such as the Project for Public Spaces ('PPS'), which was founded in 1975, expanded on the idea of providing better places to live, mainly in the city, but including other urban or suburban areas (Project for Public Spaces, 2019). PPS emphasises the need for public space of good quality that 'maximises shared value'. The movement has spread to more than 50 countries, and the US Congress supports its approach for transforming public spaces for all.

Each one of the two urban models offers different play affordances as well as support for autonomous or independent mobility of children. For example, the traditional city has a rather human scale, meaning it is walkable given its protective and interesting design, as well as with connected blocks in some cases, promoting short distance walking (Duany, Plater-Zyberk, & COMPANY, 2014). The traditional city is also diverse in its social and economic composition. Thus, it has a mix of land-uses for commercial and residential activities that are accessible in terms of transit, in addition to active modes of transportation. Recognising that children play everywhere and anywhere, this urban design is amenable to free, active play since it provides for access to places to play given the scale and support for active transportation, not to mention the security that a diverse population with 'eyes on the street' and mix of land-uses can support (Danenberg et al., 2018; Jacobs, 1961; KaBOOM!, 2016).

Subs have the opposite characteristics: large scale, single use for residential purposes, as well as disconnected networks of streets and roads with multiple dead-ends. Such design is oriented for the exclusive use of private vehicles. Zoning ordinances (inspired by Euclidean ideas for separating spaces and developing a classification system of land-uses) have been a quintessential urban planning tool to implement the separation of space, but result in the separation of everyday life as well (Lefebvre, 1992). Zoning, while it can help to protect natural areas and separate industrial areas from the population, also promotes socially exclusionary gated communities and unsustainable private vehicle-orientated transportation systems, resulting in the privatisation of everyday activities, either in the private vehicle or in the private house.

Single-use residential subs directly socially exclude children since they are non-drivers. Many sub developments have sidewalks, and streets that tend to be low-speed, which support access to free, active play. Nonetheless, the fact that subs are for single, residential use reduces the opportunities for free, active play since there are no constant 'eyes on the street' given the lack of need for residents to be outside to be undertaking diverse activities such as grocery shopping, banking or anything else. Thus, children's access to active play on the street or sidewalk becomes more of a structured type of activity that depends on the agendas of parents and neighbours (Tantia et al., 2015). This limitation also applies to parks. Designated space exclusive for play, parks detach play from everyday activities as children and parents need to make the time and move there for a single purpose.

Research has explored and questioned children's independent or interdependent mobility in different countries and physical environments (Hillman, Adams, & Whitelegg, 1990; Kyttä, Hirvonen, Rudner, Pirjola, & Laatikainen, 2015; Legendre et al., 2013; Mikkelsen & Christensen, 2009; Nansen et al., 2015; Shaw et al., 2012), while other studies have delved into how home zones impact children's play (Forman, 2017; Gill, 2016, 2014; Karsten & van Vliet, 2006; Play England, 2016;

Tranter & Doyle, 1996). Other authors propose unregulated play experiences in open spaces, such as parks, in which children can experience more freedom (Leichter-Saxby & Law, 2015; Mohd Latfi & Abdul Karim, 2012). Planning for spontaneous play in a variety of public spaces maximises the usage of an area, widens children's opportunities to increase their playability forms, appropriate to their developmental level, by not circumscribing them to traditional playground equipment targeted to specific age groups.

Some benefits include diversifying playscapes, which broadens accessibility and social interactions with different peers (Gill, 2014). Gill (2016) has also documented how these play spaces can encourage opportunities for children's physical activity and increase their time spent outdoors, empowering community members to activate their neighbourhood. Play England (2016) considers restricting speed limits in order to calm traffic and increase play. Although these alternative playscapes make children visible in public spaces, Sutton (2008) draws attention to certain disadvantages perceived by adult stakeholders that limit the inclusion of play in these spaces. Examples include its depreciation given lack of understanding and parental permits, menace of risky and tormenting behaviours and prioritisation given to development. But a clear turn towards diversifying playscapes, counting with the street as a major asset, is apparent.

2.3 Social Disadvantages of Children's Capability to Play Outside in the Neighbourhood

Social disadvantages, such as poverty, have a direct impact on the capability of children to play outside in the neighbourhood, directly because of family conditions and indirectly given characteristics of the living area. The family of the child moderates the effects of poverty on children since it decides where to put their scarce resources, like investing in their education or not. Families also become mediators of the effects of poverty when caretakers suffer, mentally or physically, given economic stressors (Engle & Black, 2008). Thus, the socioeconomic conditions of families, their resources, attitudes and aspirations can determine, for example, the time and place for playing outside. Based on studies in the United States, lower-income households tend to have lower leisure-time physical activity (Kakinami et al., 2018). Furthermore, playing outside in the neighbourhood is less of an option for lower-income households (Johnston & Gao, 2009). Also, everyday life stressors related to their economic situation tend to reduce the time, resources and opportunities for children to play outside or at home (Milteer, Ginsburg, Council on Communications and Media Committee on Psychosocial Aspects of Child and Family Health, & Mulligan, 2012).

The characteristics of low-income neighbourhoods affect children's capability to play outside since these living areas tend to have criminal activity and few opportunities for socialisation (Engle & Black, 2008). Furthermore, neighbourhoods of concentrated poverty have fewer play areas, which tend to be unsafe because of drug-dealing violence and vandalism. Given safety and other needs (such as getting nutritious food) structured, after-school programmes in areas of concentrated poverty, mainly populated by African-Americans and Latinos, serve to fulfil what parents consider fundamental necessities (Afterschool Alliance, 2016). After-school programmes provide for services that otherwise poor families could not have access. Support for children to stay in school and succeed, through after-school programmes, becomes key to improving material conditions of low-income families. However, even if after-school programmes are helpful in promoting academic interests and keeping children safe, disconnecting education to playability misses excellent opportunities.

3. CHILDREN'S PLAYABILITY EXAMINED: METHOD

The study is based on a mixed-methods approach to explore children's playability. The questions that guided the study were: what are the perceptions of adults about children's mobility and social disadvantages that affect their playability? What are their definitions of play, the roles of the children in the community and their relationships? The objective of the study with children was to identify how children can play as they move and interact in their neighbourhood, bearing in mind contextual mobility and social disadvantages of the neighbourhood. The study area was Río Piedras, a neighbourhood in the municipality of San Juan, in Puerto Rico.

The study employed different techniques for adults and for children. Children-oriented techniques were those commonly used when identifying local geographical locations and interactions with them. The purpose was to provide information for qualitative and spatial analysis. Techniques included formal and informal observations of children, children taken photographs, walking child-led tour, children and other participants' annotation of memories and activities on community mappings (Driskell, 2002; Lucas, 2012; O'Brien, 2003; Ragan, 2009; Tonucci, 2007; Wridt, 2005). Adult-oriented techniques included individualised, semi-structured interviews and small group discussions. Adult participants included parents and community leaders from Río Piedras – a neighbourhood located in San Juan, Puerto Rico.

The study involved 20 children, between the ages of 4 and 13. Children were recruited through a community summer camp during June 2016. Twelve children out of twenty (seven girls and five boys) assented to participate in the study. The rest were not interested. Activities such as the photo shooting tour and mapping worked as warm-ups introducing the issue of playability in the community and developing related vocabulary (see Figs. 8.2 and 8.3).

Summer camp facilitators that assisted in the process suggested places for the photo shooting tour. This intervention consisted of more structured instructions that children, for the most part, followed. In Fig. 8.3, children map out locations in which society expects them to play, where they actually play or desire to play. The third activity was drawing on the sidewalk, which ended up on the street as well (see Fig. 8.4).

The subsequent part of the study focussed on adults living in the same neighbourhood. Their selection was based on their participation in community activities and organised groups. Fifteen participants provided in-depth information on their perspectives about children, play and mobility in the neighbourhood, in the context of social disadvantages.

Fig. 8.2. Photo Shooting Tour. Capetillo, San Juan, Puerto Rico, 2016.

Fig. 8.3. Children Drawing on Map of Their Community and Final Map. Capetillo, San Juan, Puerto Rico, 2016.

3.1 Study Area

The study area is a neighbourhood named Río Piedras. Río Piedras is an ethnically diverse community of approximately 10,000 people, which is part of the Municipality of San Juan – capital of the archipelago of Puerto Rico. Puerto Rico is an island territory of the USA located in the Caribbean, having a population of approximately 3.5 million people, based on estimates from the US Census Bureau (2016). Ten per cent of the population of Puerto Rico lives in San Juan, 380,149 inhabitants. Puerto Rico has transportation trends strongly oriented to the use of the private vehicle. The Puerto Rico State Highway System is composed of 4,814 miles, within a territorial extension of 3,515 square miles, which results in great ubiquity of roads and streets. More than 40% of the households have two or more private vehicles, and only, 4% have no private vehicles. Average travel time to work is 28 minutes; comparable to continental US patterns, where average travel time is actually lower: 26 minutes (US Census Bureau, 2017).

Fig. 8.4. Drawing with Chalks on the Sidewalk and Street, Capetillo, San Juan, Puerto Rico, 2016.

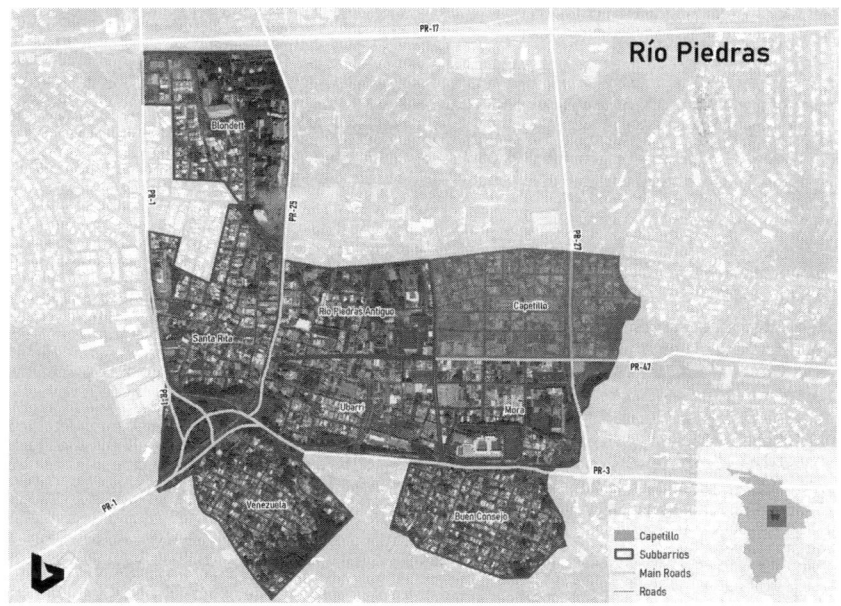

Fig. 8.5. Río Piedras Neighbourhood and its Eight Sub-Barrios, San Juan, Puerto Rico 2015 [Map]. 1:7,500. *Sources*: QGIS Development Team (2018); Áreas de Tecnología de Información, OGP (n.d.); Junta de Planificación (n.d.).

Río Piedras is composed of eight neighbourhoods or sub-barrios, where approximately 10,000 people live (see Fig. 8.5). It has a historical main square plaza that is located next to a church. Various commercial as well as government buildings surround it. Streets are one-way for the most part and slow-speed.

Half a dozen schools are located in the neighbourhood, and there are two train stations, as well two bus terminals at walking distance.

Río Piedras has a higher building density than urbanisations in Puerto Rico. It has single-family housing units, coexisting with two-story to five-story condos, with commercial uses on the first floor, for the most part. An urbanisation in Puerto Rico is similar to a US suburb in terms of single-family housing, land-use segregation. However, urbanisations are of higher density where plots are 300–600 m² on average, instead of one or half of an acre.

The construction of mega malls, urbanisations and new roads since the 1980s have negatively impacted Río Piedras during the last decades. Reduced population and related economic activity have resulted in urban blight. Furthermore, economic depression in Puerto Rico, starting around 2006, mixed with related migration to the USA, and recent category-five hurricane impacts (Hurricanes Irma and María, 2017), has left most segments of Río Piedras without population. Its historic core centre has around 200 people living (Río Piedras Antiguo), with most buildings empty. Some pockets have more population and commercial activity, mainly where immigrants from other Caribbean islands live.

Capetillo is one of the eight neighbourhoods or sub-barrios that compose the core urban centre of Río Piedras. According to the US Census Bureau (2015), Capetillo had 1,936 inhabitants. It has two bus terminals. However, the distance to the nearest train station is longer than 800 m – an average walking distance. Capetillo is further divided into Capetillo Arriba (above) and Capetillo Abajo (below) by the

Fig. 8.6. Map of Capetillo Sub-Barrio and Critical Sites for Play in Capetillo from the Perspective of Children. San Juan, Puerto Rico, 2015. *Sources*: QGIS Development Team (2018); Áreas de Tecnología de Información, OGP (n.d.); Junta de Planificación (n.d.).

José Celso Barbosa Avenue (PR-27), a six-lane roadway of 3.04 km in length (see Fig. 8.6). Road PR-27 is a major artery that connects Río Piedras with the region of San Juan. During 2009, the annual average of daily traffic (AADT) at PR-27 was 54,936, which shows an increase from 40,400 in 2000 (DTOP, 2010). The area where the study took place was on Capetillo Abajo, located on the east side of the artery Road PR-27. This area has approximately 10 blocks, and it is enclosed by a channelised creek on its east side.

4. FINDINGS

Our study shows that children's mobility and social disadvantages seem to affect their playability, based on their perspectives and that of the adults, at least in three meaningful ways. First, adults' perception of crime in the neighbourhood appears more influential on children's playability than their perception of the lack of safety on the street related to the presence of cars. This diminishes children's playability. Second, while adults prefer to keep children out of the street, children find their way to improve their playability opportunities. Finally, the community provides for time-structured, place-determined activities precisely for children, deemed as 'play', and defends separated places for them.

4.1 Perception of Crime in a Poor Neighbourhood: Worse Than Presence of Cars for Supporting Children's Playability

Crime and adults' perception of it seem very detrimental to children's playability in the neighbourhood. Other good social and physical conditions of the build environment do not matter in the face of criminal activity or the perception of it. Children simply cannot go out to play freely when a drug-dealing point is nearby, or when a homeless person is around. Drug-dealing activity was the main limitation on children being allowed to play around the neighbourhood. The epicentre of this activity is located between the community garden and a small public playground. Children reported that often parents would not allow children to go to either one of such places, unless it is with another adult. Children were very aware of the danger drug dealing represents to their lives. Older children were the ones most vocal and aware of criminal activity in the community. They expressed a sense of great injustice referring to the presence of the drug-dealing point, especially since it limits their access to another area in which they used to play: a green lot hidden with trees next to a channelised creek, situated next to a dead-end street and the drug-dealing point. One child said: 'They took the forest away from us.'

In terms of homelessness, children mentioned that guardians limit their access to the basketball court and the main square plaza – some of the children's play area – as a safety measure. Dozens of homeless people live on the green spaces around the court and get weekly services. While the court is a place where many of its activities for children are structured – such as tournaments – children consider it a place that provides missed opportunities for play; plus, it is one of the few places with 'beautiful trees with flowers' as one of the children mentioned during a visit to the court. Regardless, children's perspective is different from their counterparts. From their point of view, homeless people belong to the community, and hence, they can benefit from the same, shared, space, where homeless people can live and children can play at the same time. Actual criminal activity and adults' perception of it, as well as children's awareness of it, was very significant in affecting children's playability even when desirable places to play were accessible in terms of the distance, sidewalk availability and low-speed streets surrounding them.

4.2 The Street Saves the Day: Children Subvert Time and Space Structure in Favour of Greater Playability

The street emerged as the quintessential play space in the low-income neighbourhood, from the perspective of children. While adults instructed children, young and older, to stay off the street, children seemed to consider it an extension of the summer camp premises. During the sidewalk-drawing with chalks section of the study – a structured, adult-directed activity – they slowly 'took over' the street to play more freely and with greater mobility. First, they drew pictures of their homes, animals, flowers and other figures on the sidewalk, then on the street. Within minutes, they added interactive games, like drawing a baseball quadrant and hopscotch and played with them on the street. As they started to take on more space on the street, and more children engaged, they ended up partially closing the segment of the street in front of where the community garden is located. It seemed a natural chain of events and facilitators let their spontaneity flow. They observed, and provided loose parts, like used boxes and containers, to support children when they were forming a barrier for private vehicles (see Fig. 8.7).

Actually, older children seemed to have a sense of entitlement over the street. One of the older ones, 11 years old, even controlled the cars by stopping them and asking where they were going, and if they could instead take a different route, since they were playing on the street. He knew some of the drivers, probably family or neighbours. This action seemed fun to him; a part of playing. Older children served as role models to young ones in taking initiative in playing on the street and collaborating in drawing maps of the neighbourhood, as well.

This taking over of the street was probably the highlight of the study, where play was semi-structured, and adult direction was loose enough to provide for children's

Fig. 8.7. Children Forming Barriers for Traffic Calming on the North and South Sides Corners of the Street. Capetillo, San Juan, Puerto Rico 2016.

opportunity to improve their playability. Nonetheless, during the interviews with adults, it was evident that other opportunities to improve playability occur in the neighbourhood in terms of using the street. Various community leaders reported commonly seeing children riding their bicycles on the street, in particular during evenings and even during night-time. At least one community leader is aware of the street as 'their place to play' but mainly because there is no better option. This notion is tied to the idea that better options include the public plaza in the core area of the neighbourhood, the court or a park, as some adults reported. Yet, all of them considered streets more prohibitive than not given the dominant presence of private vehicles.

Although not as significant as crime and its perception, children complained about the number and speed at which private vehicles take over the road 'as if it was only theirs'. Nonetheless, children were eager to reclaim the street as a place to play and did it during the study, as this section explains. Access to the street was very important to improving children's playability.

4.3 Time-Structured and Place-Determined 'Play' in the Neighbourhood

Playability of children in the neighbourhood, from the perspective of adults, is rather contingent on the availability of dedicated spaces and the coordination of pre-determined activities. Community initiatives include after-school tutoring at the community garden, a yearly children festival, sports tournaments, a yearly summer camp, also at the garden, and church activities for children on weekends. These are for the most part occasional activities that community organisers coordinate during the year rather than integrated to everyday life. Tutoring sessions are more frequent though and offer an opportunity for children to meet other children, sometimes eat a snack and engage with books and teenage volunteers from the neighbourhood or from the university, who provide the service. Generally, they considered children's health and shelter more critical than free play, which are not necessarily related in their minds. While participants did not identify free time to play, it does not mean it does not occur or that they do not support it. But no conscious recognition was evident from the interviews, which might have to do with the perspective of play as 'entertainment', as a participant called it.

These children-oriented alternatives, that presumably would keep them off the streets, rest on community organisations proactively recruiting children and youth, in order to assure their participation. Even when activities are generally walking distance, some guardians are not available to take the children themselves. In many cases, leaders would go and pick up children from their homes and take them to the activity venues, in a van or walking.

These activities have a limited impact on supporting children's mobility since they are not every day and rely on private vehicles, in some instances, to access them. The positive side is that more frequent activities, such as tutoring and annual events, take place in open spaces, and one of them – the festival – on the street. Even when children can play anytime and anywhere, community offered opportunities to engage with other children through pre-determined children activities can limit the flexibility and spontaneity needed for children's playability.

Based on participants' perspectives, the need to determine places "for" children is intertwined with time-structured activities. Adults were very aware of the need for children's play opportunities and included the issue in their agendas. It was very noticeable at a recount of a participatory budgeting process that took place in the community a couple of years before. More than half a dozen of the projects that participants identified were related to open space and parks, primarily to address children's needs, and the community in general. This is partly because the area has very little green and open space. Actually, a major win in the budgeting process was adding outdoor workout equipment as well as ping pong tables and a children's play area in the main square plaza. Priorities for child-dedicated spaces also include building a library where they can do school work, since currently there is none, and children end up using the nearest Burger King, where Wi-Fi is free, for such purposes.

4. DISCUSSION

Traditional neighbourhoods, like Río Piedras, combine moderate density, land-use diversity and human-scale design to promote desirable built environments for liveable, vibrant and sustainable communities, where children can play. However, economic and social conditions in Río Piedras have increased social disadvantages for the population. Criminal activity in particular, related to the desolation of the neighbourhood and poverty, overwhelms its built-environment advantages for playability. In this case, the social disadvantages of the neighbourhood and its population – including children and their families – seem much more significant than mobility disadvantages and their impact on children's playability.

By all means, protecting children, and anyone for that matter, from crime and violence in the neighbourhood is of vital importance. While literature is filled with strategies to use the built environment to deter criminal activity, communities have a say in curbing crime when it is viewed as part of a web of social dynamics that include playability as defined in this chapter (Gómez, Johnson, Selva, & Sallis, 2004; Irving, 2015). On the one hand, perceptions of high crime affect and even can promote it. On the other hand, from the urban standpoint, Jacobs (1961) made very clear that the more people are outside on public, urban spaces, such as the sidewalk and the street, the more 'eyes on the street' help monitor and create safer places. Thus, children playing out on sidewalks and streets can itself promote greater liveability, as such organic, socialised and friendly vigilance may compete with criminal activity. Of course, the idea is not to put children in the middle of warfare, as neither is letting them play in any street at the mercy of private vehicles. The idea is to actively promote better playability for children in the neighbourhood, which also suggests the need for socialising children's playability. That is, based on the premise that children have social rights, society is responsible for children's well-being including their playability, not only their legal guardians. This suggests that a community can include in their agendas improving children's playability in the neighbourhood, out on the street, given it is one of the most preferred and accessible public areas for multiple purposes and audiences.

The importance of streets for uses other than private vehicles has become widely recognised in urban transportation and planning (McCann & Rynne, 2010). What started as a 'complete streets' movement has turned into 'complete communities' (Ohland & Brooks, 2012). The complete streets concept promotes revisiting the street as a desirable public space for social interaction, requiring revamping its design in favour of sharing its uses and adding facilities for multiple modes of transportation, mainly active ones or micro-transportation – walking, scooters, skateboards, bicycles and other means. Such changes improve children's mobility, as well as that of the population as a whole, and playability. Recognising the ubiquity of streets in the USA, and presence and access to them in most cities and neighbourhoods, revamping streets became a central part of promoting greater liveability of communities. Children can play out more and with greater autonomy in communities where the street is safer from private vehicles, has more 'eyes on the street' and presumably, less crime around.

Improving children's playability on streets and sidewalks, instead of or in addition to, the creation of parks or playgrounds as part of community agendas and urban transportation planning makes sense from an economic standpoint. When children's play becomes a service, it ends up providing them with education, housing, health services and developmental opportunities in a safe, holistic environment. Such service has to be programmed and should occur in a dedicated space – parks, courts or plazas, in isolation. This poses a challenge for playability since identifying specific lots and buildings as play places limits the possibilities, opportunities and quality of playability. Play as another function of the city requires compliance with zoning and permits and land lots. This leaves play to compete and depend on the willingness and feasibility of local governments to fund it. A different view of play as playability, where children's mobility is central, and part of everyday life on the street, reduces the need for investing funds in dedicated spaces. Strategies to incorporate playability in the neighbourhoods as part of everyday life supposes flexibility of space, time and funds to support it. Parks, playgrounds and courts may be necessary in many neighbourhoods. However, in those plagued with crime and violence, and in the context of economic scarcity, fostering playability on the street seems like an option to bring about transformation and well-being, with reduced economic investment and greater community action.

5. CONCLUSION

Streets show plenty of opportunities for free play, especially when other public spaces are limited or unsafe. In contexts where funds are highly compromised with other issues, appropriating the street for play is of particular importance for the improvement of children's mobility and related development. Streets present a desirable alternative that may help overcome common social exclusion based on playability. This is of vital importance where criminality is continuously present in child specialised designated spaces and seems like it cannot be removed.

There is a need to have parents, caregivers, neighbours, leaders and volunteers identify such alternative spaces so that children can gain autonomy and play out. Neighbourhoods with greater playability require adults' recognition of children's social rights, which include play. Children can greatly benefit from the support of advocates that move an agenda for social inclusion in transportation and urban planning.

Community efforts that prioritise general education to improve children's capabilities to integrate into society can also incorporate opportunities for improving playability. Playability needs to be added to community urban planning agendas, processes and goals to increase and transform child-friendly neighbourhoods that foster playability.

Neighbourhoods can address their playability to become more just. Children need not only dedicated parks, playgrounds and courts but also access to unintended sidewalks and shared streets – common public spaces. Sidewalks and streets should be revitalised as safe public spaces to play.

REFERENCES

8 80 Cities. (2017). *Building better cities with young children and families.* Retrieved from https://www.880cities.org/wp-content/uploads/2017/11/BvLF-8-80-Cities-Report-Final.pdf

Afterschool Alliance. (2016). *America after 3pm: Special report: After school in communities of concentrated poverty.* Retrieved from http://www.afterschoolalliance.org/aa3pm/concentrated_poverty.pdf

Ansari, A., Pettit, K., & Gershoff, E. (2015). Combating obesity in head start: Outdoor play and change in children's BMI. *Journal of Developmental & Behavioral Pediatrics, 36*(8), 605–612.

Ansell, N. (2009). Childhood and the politics of scale: Descaling children's geographies? *Progress in Human Geography, 33*(2), 190–209.

Áreas de Tecnología de Información, OGP. (n.d.). *Geodatos CRIM, ACT.* Retrieved from http://www.gis.pr.gov/Pages/default.aspx

Brenner, N. (2014). *Implosions/explosions: Towards a study of planetary urbanization.* Berlin: Jovis.

Bronfrenbrenner, U. (1979). *La ecología del desarrollo humano.* Barcelona: Ediciones Paidós.

Brown, S., & Vaughan, C. (2009). *Play: How it shapes the brain, opens the imagination, and invigorates the soul.* Kindle DX Version. Retrieved from Amazon.com

Bustelo, E. (2007). *El Recreo de la Infancia: argumentos para otro comienzo.* Buenos Aires, Argentina: Siglo Veintiuno.

Chawla, L. (2002). *Growing up in an urbanizing world.* Paris: UNESCO Publishing.

Christensen, P., & O'Brien, M. (Eds.). (2003). *Children in the city: Home, neighbourhood and the city.* Routledge, USA and Canada: The Falmer Press.

Congress for the New Urbanism. (n.d.). *What is new urbanism?* Retrieved from https://www.cnu.org/resources/what-new-urbanism

Cresswell, T. (2010). Mobilities I: Catching up. *Progress in Human Geography, 35*(4), 550–558.

Cushing, D. F., & van Vliet, W. (2017). Children's right to the city: The emergence of youth councils in the United States. *Children's Geographies, 15*(3), 319–333.

Danenberg, R., Doumpa, V., & Karssenber, H. (2018). *The city at eye level for kids.* Rotterdam: STIPO Publishing.

Driskell, D. (2002). *Creating better cities with children and youth.* Paris: UNESCO Publishing.

DTOP. (2010). *Traffic data report 2000–2009.* Retrieved from https://data.pr.gov/Transportaci-n/Annual-Average-Daily-Traffic-AADT-Transito-Promedi/7kaq-zyym

Duany, A., & Plater-Zyberk, E., & COMPANY. (2014). *The lexicon of new urbanism.* Retrieved from https://www.dpz.com/uploads/Books/Lexicon-2014.pdf

Duany, A., Plater-Zyberk, E., & Speck, J. (2000). *Suburban nation: The rise of sprawl and the decline of the American dream.* New York, NY: North Point Press.

Engle, P. L., & Black, M. M. (2008). The effect of poverty on child development. *Annals of the New York Academy of Sciences, 1136*, 243–256.

Fairchild, D. G., & Revord, P. J. (2017). Planning livable communities: Findings from HUD's regional planning and community challenge grant programs. *Cityscape, 19*(3), 3–8.

Forman, H. (2017). Residential street design and play: A literature review of policy and research on residential street design and its influence on children's independent outdoor activity. Playing Out, Bristol, United Kingdom. Retrieved from https://playingout.net/wp-content/uploads/2017/02/Helen-Forman-Street-design-and-play.pdf

Fransen, K., Neutens, T., Farber, S., De Maeyer, P., Deruyter, G., & Witlox, F. (2015). Identifying public transport gaps using time-dependent accessibility levels. *Journal Transport Geography, 48*, 176–187.

Freeman, C., & Tranter, P. (2011). *Children and their urban environment: Changing worlds*. Kindle DX Version. Retrieved from Amazon.com

Gibson, J. L., Cornell, M., & Gill, T. (2017). A systematic review of research into the impact of loose parts play on children's cognitive, social and emotional development. *School Mental Health, 4*, 295–309. Retrieved from https://link.springer.com/content/pdf/10.1007%2Fs12310-017-9220-9.pdf

Gill, T. (2007). *No Fear: Growing up in a risk averse society*. UK: Calouste Gulbenkian Foundation.

Gill, T. (2014). The benefits of children's engagement with nature: A systematic literature review. *Children, Youth and Environments, 24*(2), 10–34.

Gill, T. (2016). *Street play initiatives in disadvantaged areas: Experiences and emerging issues*. Play England. Retrieved from http://www.playengland.org.uk/wp-content/uploads/2017/07/StreetPlayReport2web.pdf

Ginsburg, K. R. (2007). The importance of play in promoting healthy child development and maintaining strong parent–child bonds. *Pediatrics, 119*(1), 182–191. Retrieved from https://pediatrics.aappublications.org/content/119/1/182

Gleave, J., & Cole-Hamilton, I. (2012). A world without play: A literature review on the effects of a lack of play on children's lives. Play England, UK. Retrieved from https://www.playengland.org.uk/media/371031/a-world-without-play-literature-review-2012.pdf.

Gómez, J. E., Johnson, B. A., Selva, M., & Sallis, J. F. (2004). Violent crime and outdoor physical activity among inner-city youth. *Preventative Medicine, 39*(5), 876–881.

Gray, P. (2011). The decline of play and the rise of psychopathology in children and adolescents. *American Journal of Play, 3*(4), 443–463. Retrieved from https://www.psychologytoday.com/files/attachments/1195/ajp-decline-play-published.pdf

Hart, R. A. (1979). *Children's experience of place: A developmental study*. New York, NY: Irvington Press.

Harvey, D. (2003). The right to the city. *International Journal of Urban and Regional Research, 27*, 939–941.

Herrington, S., & Brussoni, M. (2015). Beyond physical activity: The importance of play and nature-based play spaces for children's health and development. *Current Obesity Reports, 4*, 477–483. Retrieved from https://www.researchgate.net/publication/282153607_Beyond_Physical_Activity_The_Importance_of_Play_and_Nature-Based_Play_Spaces_for_Children's_Health_and_Development

Hillman, M., Adams, J., & Whitelegg, J. (1990). *One false move…A study of children's independent mobility*. London: Policy Studies Institute.

Holloway, S., & Valentine, G. (2000). Children's geographies and the new social studies of childhood. In S. Holloway & G. Valentine (Eds.), *Children's geographies: Playing, living, and learning* (pp. 1–28). London: Routledge.

Hughes, C., & Graham, A. (2002). Measuring executive functions in childhood: Problems and solutions? *Child and Adolescent Mental Health, 7*(3), 131–142.

Irving, C. (2015). Crime prevention through environmental design: Application to Christchurch City planning practices. *Lincoln Planning Review, 7*(1–2), 44–47.

Jacobs, J. (1961). *The death and life of great American cities*. New York, NY: Vintage.

James, A., Jenks, C., & Prout, A. (1998). *Theorising childhood*. Oxford: Polity Press.

Johnston, R. A., & Gao, S. (2009). Public versus private mobility for the poor: Transit improvements versus increased car ownership in the Sacramento Region. Retrieved from https://transweb.sjsu.

edu/sites/default/files/2403-public-private-mobility-poor-transit-improvements-car-ownership-sacramento.pdf
Junta de Planificación, Gobierno de Puerto Rico. (n.d.). Geodatos. Retrieved from https://jp.pr.gov
KaBOOM!. (2016). Play everywhere playbook. Retrieved from https://kaboom.org/resources/play_research/publications
KaBOOM!. (n.d.). Playability – KaBOOM! news. Retrieved from https://kaboom.org/about_kaboom/kaboom_news?tag=playability
Kakinami, L., Wissa, R., Khan, R., Paradis, G., Barnett, T. A., & Gauvin, L. (2018). The association between income and leisure-time physical activity is moderated by utilitarian lifestyles: A nationally representative US population (NHANES 1999–2014). *Preventive Medicine*, *113*, 147–152.
Karsten, L., & van Vliet, W. (2006). Children in the city: Reclaiming the street. *Children, Youth, and Environments*, *16*(1), 151–167.
Kraftl, P. (2013). Towards geographies of "alternative" education: A case study of UK home schooling families. *Transactions*, *38*(3), 436–450.
Kyttä, M., Hirvonen, J., Rudner, J., Pirjola, I., & Laatikainen, T. (2015). The last free-range children? Children's independent mobility in Finland in the 1990s and 2010s. *Journal of Transport Geography*, *47*, 1–12. Retrieved from https://www.sciencedirect.com/science/article/pii/S0966692315001271
Lanza, M. (2012). *Playborhood: Turn your neighborhood into a place for play*. California, CA: Free Play Press.
Lefebvre, H. (1992). *The production of space* (D. Nicholson-Smith Trans.). Cambridge, MA: Blackwell.
Legendre, A., Ripaud, E., Brisset, E., & Munchenbach, D. (2013). Different types of children's independent mobility in French Brittany. Université de Rennes 2. Retrieved from https://halshs.archives-ouvertes.fr/halshs-00857237/document
Leichter-Saxby, M., & Law, S. (2015). *The new adventure playground movement*. Notebook Publishing.
Lester, S., & Russell, W. (2008). *Play for a change: Play, policy and practice: A review of contemporary perspectives*. Play England, United Kingdom.
Lester, S., & Russell, W. (2010). *Children's Right to Play: An Examination of the Importance of Play in the Lives of Children Worldwide*. The Netherlands: Bernard van Leer Foundation.
Leventhal, T., & Brooks-Gunn, J. (2000). The neighborhoods they live in: The effects of neighborhood residence on child and adolescent outcomes. *Psychological Bulletin*, *126*(2), 309–337.
Lucas, K. (2012). Transport and social exclusion: Where are we now? *Transport Policy*, *20*, 105–113.
Marketta, K. (2004). The extent of children's independent mobility and the number of actualized affordances as criteria for child-friendly environments. *Journal of Environmental Psychology*, *24*(2), 179–198.
Marzi, I., & Reimers, A. K. (2018). Children's independent mobility: Current knowledge, future directions, and public health implications. *International Journal of Environmental Research and Public Health*, *15*(11), 2441. Retrieved from https://www.ncbi.nlm.nih.gov/pmc/articles/PMC6267483/
McCahill, C., & Ebeling, M. (2015). Tools for measuring accessibility in an equity framework. Paper presented at *Congress for new urbanism 23rd annual meeting*, Congress for New Urbanism, Dallas.
McCann, B., & Rynne, S. (2010). Complete streets: Best policy and implementation practices. Planning Advisory Service Report 559. American Planning Association.
Meyer, M. D., & Miller, E. J. (2001). *Urban transportation planning: A decision-oriented approach*. New York, NY: McGraw-Hill.
Mikkelsen, M. R., & Christensen, P. (2009). Is children's independent mobility really independent? A study of children's mobility combining ethnography and GPS/mobile phone technologies. *Mobilities*, *4*, 37–58.
Milteer, R. M., Ginsburg, K. R., Council on Communications and Media Committee on Psychosocial Aspects of Child and Family Health, & Mulligan, D. A. (2012). The importance of play in promoting healthy child development and maintaining strong parent–child bond: Focus on children in poverty. *Pediatrics*, *129*, e204. Retrieved from https://pediatrics.aappublications.org/content/129/1/e204: American Academy of Pediatrics
Mitchell, D. (2003). *The right to the city: Social justice and the fight for public space*. New York, NY: The Guilford Press.

Mohd Lafti, M. F., & Abdul Karim, H. (2012). Suitability of planning guidelines for children playing spaces. *Procedia – Social and Behavioral Sciences*, *32*, 304–314. Retrieved from https://www.sciencedirect.com/science/article/pii/S1877042812008312

Murray, L., & Cortés-Morales, S. (2019). *Children's mobilities: Interdependent, imagined, relational.* Kindle version. Retrieved from Amazon.com

Nansen, B., Gibbs, L., MacDougal, C., Vetere, F., Ross, N. J., & McKendrick, J. (2015). Children's independent mobility: Compositions, collaborations and compromises. *Children's Geographies*, *13*, 467–481.

O'Brien, M. (2003). Regenerating children's neighborhoods: What do children want? In P. Christensen & M. O'Brien (Eds.), *Children in the city: Home, Neighbourhood and Community.* (pp. 141–161). New York, NY: Routledge.

Ohland, G., & Brooks, A. (2012). *Are we there yet? Creating complete communities for 21st century America.* Reconnecting America, USA. Retrieved from http://reconnectingamerica.org/assets/PDFs/20121001AreWeThereYet-web.pdf

Play England. (2016). *Why temporary street closures for play make sense for public health.* Play England, United Kingdom. Retrieved from http://www.playengland.org.uk/wp-content/uploads/2017/07/StreetPlayReport1web-4.pdf

Preston, J., & Raje, F. (2007). Accesibility, mobility and transport-related social exclusion. *Journal of Transport Geography*, *15*(3), 151–160.

Project for Public Spaces. (2019, August). PPS. Retrieved from https://www.pps.org

QGIS Development Team. (2018). QGIS 3.2 geographic information system. Open Source Geospatial Foundation Project. Retrieved from http://qgis.osgeo.org

Ragan, D. (2009). Community youth mapping annotated bibliography. Retrieved from http://youthrex.com/wp-content/uploads/2015/10/Youth-Asset-Mapping-Annotated-Bibliography.pdf

Schoeppe, S., Duncan, M. J., Badland, H. M., Oliver, M., & Browne, M. (2014). Associations between children's independent mobility and physical activity. *BMC Public Health*, *14*(1), 91. Retrieved from https://www.ncbi.nlm.nih.gov/pmc/articles/PMC3932047/pdf/1471-2458-14-91.pdf

Shackell, A., Butler, N., Doyle, P., & Ball, D. (2008). *Design for play: A guide to creating successful play spaces.* Play England, United Kingdom. Retrieved from http://www.playengland.org.uk/media/70684/design-for-play.pdf

Shaw, B., Watson, B., Frauendienst, B., Redecker, A., Jones, T., & Hillman, M. (2012). *Children's independent mobility: A comparative study in England and Germany (1971–2010).* London : Policy Studies Institute.

Sheller, M., & Urry, J. (2006). The new mobilities paradigm. *Environment and Planning A*, *38*, 207–226.

Sutton, L. (2008). The state of play: Disadvantage, play and children's well-being. *Social Policy and Society*, *7*(4), 537–549.

Sutton-Smith, B. (1997). *The ambiguity of play.* Cambridge, MA: Harvard University Press.

Tantia, P., Welch, S., & Lin, S. (2015). Using behavioral economics to create playable cities. KaBOOM! & Ideas 42. Retrieved from https://kaboom.org/resources/play_research/publications

Texas A&M Transportation Institute. (2019, September). *Urban mobility report.* College Station, TX: Texas A&M Transportation Institute. Retrieved from https://mobility.tamu.edu/umr/

Tonucci, F. (2007). *La ciudad de los niños: Un modo nuevo de pensar la ciudad* – 1ª ed. (M. Merlino, Trans.). Buenos Aires: Editorial Losada.

Transportation Research Board. (1998). *The costs of sprawl – Revisited.* TCRP Report 39. Washington, DC: National Academy Press.

Tranter, P. (2015). Children's play in their local neighborhoods: Rediscovering the value of residential streets. In B. Evans, & J. Horton (Eds.), *Play, recreation, health and well being, geographies of children and young people* (Vol. 9). Singapore: Springer. http://dx.doi.org/10.1007/978-981-4585-96-5_37-1

Tranter, P., & Doyle, J. (1996). Reclaiming the residential street as play space. *International Play Journal*, *4*, 81–97.

UNCRC. (1989). United Nations convention on the rights of the child. Retrieved from https://www.unicef.org.uk/what-we-do/un-convention-child-rights/

UNICEF. (2018). *Shaping urbanization for children: A handbook on child-responsive urban planning.* UNICEF. Retrieved from https://s25924.pcdn.co/wp-content/uploads/2018/10/2018 08-26-Handbook-Child-responsive-Urban-Planning-on-line.pdf

Urry, J. (2007). *Mobilities*. Oxford: Polity Press.
US Census Bureau. (2015). American community survey. Retrieved from https://www.census.gov/acs/www/data/data-tables-and-tools/subject-tables/
US Census Bureau. (2016). American Community Survey - Population Estimates.
US Census Bureau. (2017). 2016 American community survey content test: Journey to work. Retrieved from https://www.census.gov/library/working-papers/2017/acs/2017_McKenzie_01.html
Vuchic, V. R. (2000). *Transportation for livable cities* (2nd ed.). New Brunswick, NJ: Center for Urban Policy Research, Rutgers University.
Wridt, P. (2005). The neighborhood atlas project: An example of participatory action research in geography education. *Research in Geographic Education*, 5, 25–47.
Yogman, M., Garner, A., Hutchinson, J., Hirsh-Pasek, K., & Golinkoff, R. M. (2018). The power of play: A pediatric role in enhancing development in young children. *Pediatrics*, *142*(3), 1–17. Retrieved from https://pediatrics.aappublications.org/content/142/3/e20182058

CHAPTER 9

MOBILITY AND EQUITY: THE PROBLEM OF ACCESS TO CITY SPACES BY INDIVIDUALS SUBMITTED TO PSYCHIATRIC HOSPITALISATION

Luiza Morena Alves Lopes

ABSTRACT

Since the late 1980s, the Brazilian Psychiatric Reform, alongside the anti-asylum movement, has promoted a change in the way of treating people with mental suffering in the country. This process produced transformations in the flows and forms in which individuals with mental illnesses use the city, intending to make the city itself less unequal.

Taking into account that accessibility measures must consider individual, temporal, transportation and land-use elements as relevant, this study will focus on the relation between mobility and access, looking at subjects who were submitted to prolonged psychiatric hospitalisation and got discharged to live in the Residential Therapeutic Services – RTS, in Belo Horizonte, Brazil. In order to do that, the study used focus groups, observation, shadowing and in-depth interviews as methodologies strategies.

The results of the study demonstrate that: (a) there are a variety of ways of accessing the city; (b) displacements outside the facilities are characterised by the proximity of the destinations and by being made, mostly, on foot; (c) there is a restriction regarding the use of public transport system; and (d) access to money is a determinant factor for the accomplishment of mobility practices in *city spaces. However, it is also observed that the mobility and access to the city can exert an effect of autonomy by allowing governance of the subjects' own time and destination.*

Keywords: Anti-asylum movement; Residential Therapeutic Services; mobility; occupational therapy; city; mental health

1. INTRODUCTION

The discussions that transformed the way we observe and understand mobility in social sciences raise an important question: who is able to move? Just as interesting as that question, from an analytical point of view, is its negative form: who is not able to move? Or who is prevented from moving?

In the Brazilian mental health field, we may think that similar questions were posed by the anti-asylum movement to question the Model of Mental Health Care offered to people with mental illnesses, which prevented them from moving through the city. Some of those questions were: why restrict their freedom? What are the consequences of preventing this population from accessing public places? These questions had led the country to a period of Psychiatric Reform, marked by significant changes in the realm of public access, as researchers have already pointed out (Amarante, 1995; Lobosque, 1997).

From the point of view of public administration, we have witnessed discussions emerge about the democratisation of access to public spaces, considering the singularities of the population. Public policies in the fields of urban mobility and health have, in this sense, considered the problem of access for their elaboration. However, there still seems to be a gap between the policy itself and its implementation, resulting in continuous problems to various groups of the population, such as people with disabilities, women or the elderly.

Since the lack of mobility generated by psychiatric hospitalisation restricts this population's access to urban spaces, this research aims to contribute to the discussion, describing and analysing urban access by people submitted to long-term psychiatric hospitalisation, considering the aforementioned process of transformation in the changed for Model of Mental Health Care.

In order to accomplish that, this chapter begins with a brief discussion on some theoretical questions about mobility, access and mental health policy. The methodological section details the procedures for choosing samples, collecting and analysing data. Results are presented alongside the discussion of the theme, in which the findings are placed in relation to each other and to the theory used. Some final considerations conclude the chapter.

2. THEORETICAL DISCUSSION

The relation between freedom and mobility is addressed by Mimi Sheller (2008) through the investigation of different forms of these two elements: whether or not one is able to move through space is a measure of freedom. In this sense, Sheller (2008) realises that among the different forms of freedom of mobility, constraints of physical, spatial, temporal and social nature are present. This idea is connected to central elements of the accessibility measures, listed by Wachs and Kumagai (1973).

We can also find studies in the literature concerning impacts of environmental design on people's adequate access and outdoor mobility. Clarke, Ailshire, and Lantz (2009) showed that there is a direct relationship between the conditions of sidewalks and the increase or decrease of the disablement process. Sze and Christensen (2017) point out that good practices of accessible design should be addressed to everyone's needs, including those of people with disabilities.

In this context, the perspective of social equity seems relevant, since it can be understood as the recognition of singularities in the application of norms (Campos, 2006). Differing from the concept of equality, equity proposes that solutions should be found according to the needs of each situation, considering 'in each person a subject with relative degree of freedom and autonomy' (Campos, 2006, p. 25).

These reflections are also perceived in the construction of public policies to ensure accessibility for all in Brazil, such as Law n. 10.098, from December 2000, which establishes basic criteria and general rules for promoting accessibility for people with disabilities or reduced mobility (Brasil, 2000a). Although there is a movement to guarantee their rights through legislation, we still perceive a great distance between what is on paper and what is planned and executed in this area in the country.

In terms of accessibility, mobility and disability, there are still issues to be addressed concerning people in mental distress. Since the late 1980s, regardless of the discussion about mental illnesses being a disability or not, the care policies concerning this parcel of the population have undergone changes that directly affect accessibility and mobility. As highlighted by Foucault (1978) and Basaglia (2001), the first treatment spaces for this population, called asylums, played an important role in regulating the relations between freedom and patient mobility. This regulation was marked by the impediment of mobility in spaces outside the asylums.

Similar to the problem of accessibility, mental health policies now have a legislative framework and civil society organisations to ensure that treatment spaces play a different role in the relations between freedom and mobility, now stimulating people in mental distress to access different spaces throughout the cities (Arruda, 2016; Vieceli, 2014).

The distance between what is stated in the law and what the Psychiatric Reform Policy has ensured as real guarantees is a subject worthy of investigation. Until 2015, 8,613 psychiatric beds have been closed throughout Brazil; 2,209 psychosocial care centres and 289 therapeutic residential services were opened (Brasil, 2010, 2015). These and other facilities were created to replace the asylums, all of which were articulated inside a network called the psychosocial attention network (RAPS, the initials in Portuguese).

Different forms of care were built after this policy change, among which urban spaces are considered privileged spaces of intervention (Costa & Brasil, 2014). Contrarily, this form of distribution of institutions in a network has also been criticised. Negative effects have been observed, such as the fragmentation of care and new forms of chronification (Pande & Amarante, 2011).

Sidewalks, problems with traffic speed, crossing streets and getting on the bus are difficulties encountered by people with mental distress, people with hearing, visual and motor disabilities or advanced age (Imrie & Kumar, 2010). This suggests that structural improvements would equally benefit people with needs arising from different types of disabilities and other city pedestrians, as pointed out by Sze and Christensen (2017).

It is worth asking: looking at the city equitably, is there any kind of structural necessity that is specifically required by the conditions of mental suffering?

Weyler (2006) indicates that a special difficulty in navigating the city is something to be considered for this population, especially taking into account situations of prolonged hospitalisation. Other studies show that prolonged hospitalisation periods, as well as times of crisis, cause significant disruptions in relationships and support systems (Dalmolin & da Penha Vasconcellos, 2007).

One of the contributions brought by the field of mental healthcare is challenging the idea that mental illness alone should be considered as an incapacity to social living or make it impracticable. This questioning led to the observation that acute moments may generate some incapacity, usually temporary, as well as moments when symptoms are milder. It is also observed that the development of the condition itself may bring significant losses, long-term ones, especially if associated with the prolonged use of medications, lack of social support and prolonged hospitalisations (Dalmolin & da Penha Vasconcellos, 2007; Pande & Amarante, 2011).

Thus, both the accessibility policy and the mental health policy seem committed to the same goal: democratise urban spaces so that people, in their uniqueness, can participate in the construction of the city.

3. RESEARCH PROBLEM

Due to the transformation in mental healthcare practices, the city of Belo Horizonte (see Appendix) went through a unique situation while organising the closure of the last psychiatric hospital at the city's healthcare system (SUS), the Serra Verde Clinic (SVC). While organising the closure, the Municipal Health Department had to open an intermediary facility that would house patients coming from SVC and, then, organise their discharge. This location became known as Transitory Hospital, where I worked for two and a half years.

The Transitory Hospital was opened in 2012 and received 149 patients for their last years in this type of institution, after an average of 25 consecutive years of hospitalisation. The closure occurred three and a half years after the opening and all the patients were discharged. Belo Horizonte ended up hosting many of these patients in its Residential Therapeutic Services – RTS. Some other individuals went back to their families and some went to RTSs in other cities.

RTS are

> community inserted dwellings, designed to accommodate long-term inpatients (two years or more uninterrupted), from psychiatric hospitals and custody hospitals, among others (...) that do not have family and social bonds. (Brasil, 2000b)

Described as home-based health services, these facilities staff include supervisors, caregivers and interns. To promote healthcare for residents, this team must be in constant articulation with other health and mental health institutions; it must also maintain a constant dialogue with the neighbourhood, in order to facilitate and sometimes mediate the relationship between residents of the RTS and their neighbours.

Considering mobility as a measure of freedom and observing different mobility constraints (Sheller, 2008), we can think that SVC, Transitory Hospital and RAPS facilities play different roles in mediating the relationship between patients and urban spaces: SVC, as a total institution, did not allow patients to access urban or exterior spaces; Transitory Hospital allowed external access in some specific conditions; RAPS facilities encourage such access.

Many studies have made important contributions by investigating the construction of hospital discharge (Franco, 2012), revealing that patients consider their mobility within the city as a parameter for their quality of life outside the hospital (Santos Junior, Silveira, Gualda, & Salim, 2011) and the loss of memories of the city as a hindrance to their return to life in their spaces (Weyler, 2006).

With that said, I ask: how was the process of accessing the city initiated in the Transitory Hospital and continued in the therapeutic residential services? Based on the mobility practices of the participants, this study aims to describe and discuss the urban access of the inpatients, through movements performed in the external spaces of the two facilities. The following indicators will be adopted as research guidelines: motivators and access impediments, autonomy and transportation used.

4. METHODOLOGY

This chapter was produced based on a research for a Master's programme, conducted between 2016 and 2018. As in the research, this chapter drew on qualitative methodology and quantitative resources to describe and analyse urban access and mobility (Table 9.1).

The first investigation was conducted in the Transitory Hospital context. Since this hospital had already closed when the research was carried out, it was not possible to observe patients in their daily lives. Instead, one focus group and eight interviews were conducted with employees from all different professional categories that composed the hospital staff.

The focus group was composed by professionals with higher education degrees. Interviews were held with employees without higher education, following the same script used in the focus group. I have also made some consultation of medical records and, since I was part of the Transitory Hospital team, I have also considered my memories.

Focus groups and interviews explored how patients moved around the hospital and how they performed mobility around the city. In this process, individual mobility and characteristics of patients were addressed and attention was drawn, by focal group participants, to the relations between motor and communication skills, on the one hand, and mobility and access, on the other hand.

Table 9.1. Methodological Strategies to Data Collection and Analysis.

Facilities	Goals	Method	Outcomes
1 Transitory Hospital	Describe patients' mobility and urban access	Focus group Memories Semi-structured interview Medical records	Mobility framework
1 Transitory Hospital	Choose the sample for research's second part	Mobility framework analysis RTS description	Indicators for sample selection
2 RTSs	Describe patients' mobility and urban access	Semi-structured interview	Mobility and urban access description of each resident
		Daily life observation	Description of interactions between residents, workers and visitors of each RTS Contributions to mobility and urban access description of each resident
		Shadowing	Mobility and urban access description of one resident

Source: Own elaboration.

In this chapter, I will focus on the information gathered about the movement around the city.

Crossing data from these sources allowed the description of the mobility of 134 of the 149 patients admitted to the Transitory Hospital. This description has been systematised in the 'Mobility Framework'. The 15 missing cases are those which participants did not clearly remember, so they were not considered. The final work on these data consisted of grouping mobilities into two categories and four subcategories. Once assembled, this framework was evaluated and approved by three Transitory Hospital employees.

The criteria for choosing patients to participate in the second stage of the research took into account those four subcategories and the characteristics of the ten RTSs. These facilities have been opened to house most of the patients from the Transitory Hospital. In order to select the RTSs, the following aspects were considered: (a) duration of hospitalisation at the SVC; (b) types of mobility presented during hospitalisation; and (c) age. In relation to those criteria, I searched for diversity among the RTSs. The presence of wheelchair users was used as a criterion to ensure that this particularity could be observed in contrast to the lack of it. Finally, gender was used as an inclusion criterion. Three different RTSs were chosen.

The second stage of data collection was conducted using new strategies: 86 hours of observation were performed in the three RTSs, according to the goals exposed in Table 9.1; also, 41 interviews with 14 employees of the three facilities were conducted, as well as the shadowing of one resident.

All three strategies sought to gather the following information: mobilities motives, forms, subjects and places. Interviews were made nominally. Each employee was asked to answer the same questionnaire more than once, having a different resident as their reference for each time.

Shadowing was used to approximate the understanding of mobility practices because, according to Jirón (2001), shadowing as a methodology implies participating in activities of their daily life through constant dialogue and interaction. Given the configuration of the RTS and the peculiarities of the residents, it was possible to apply this technique with only one of them.

In order to record information at this stage, a field notebook was used, as well as photos and video recordings. This material was analysed through a categorisation process, using the Atlas.ti software as a tool. The categories were organised into four large groups: subjects, places, motives and forms of mobility. The research was submitted and approved by the ethics committee.

5. RESULTS AND DISCUSSION

5.1. Mobility and Access at the Transitory Hospital

The 149 patients who arrived at the Transitional Hospital were mostly men. Although they had been hospitalised for a long time, most people arrived without any personal belongings. They wore simple, loose clothes, and almost all of them had deep cracks on the soles of their feet. Many had sunburned skin. It was hard to presume their ages by their appearance, since they all had physical features of elderly people. A small number of patients needed a wheelchair because of medical necessities and someone to guide the chair. Many of them did not establish verbal communication, refusing any form of interaction or using other contact strategies.

Ages varied from about 40 to 80 years old. Diagnoses were not used as guidelines by participants to describe their patients, since most of them arrived there with the same diagnosis (F29 – unspecified nonorganic psychosis). In addition to that, some issues noted by the participants concerned social exclusion, instead of situations of psychiatric crisis (focus group).

Regarding family support, many patients were considered abandoned, some received sporadic visitors who paid them part of their legal benefits, and a small part of the patients received visitors and part of their benefits regularly. This financial benefit, also called BPC, was not granted to all patients, but only to those who had requested it through a legal representative and undergone the medical examination demanded by the social services.

There was a small monthly sum managed by the staff to cover some expenses, preferably used on patients with no income, such as meals, bus fares, taxis and some personal items such as slippers or underwear.

The Transitory Hospital was located in an old neighbourhood in Belo Horizonte, surrounded by a variety of businesses, a small square and a church. We can say that its location was privileged from the point of view of access. However, considering that proximity is not sufficient for the promotion of access (Wachs & Kumagai, 1973), another feature had to be observed.

During the focal group, the employees concluded that there was a differentiation between an internal world, inside the hospital and an outside world, even though impressions of these worlds differed among participants. These worlds seemed to differ both in relation to the physical structure and its 'inhabitants' and

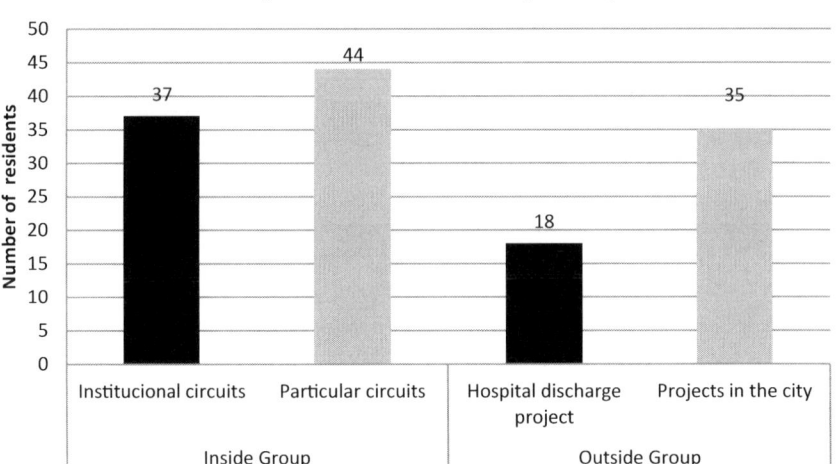

Fig. 9.1. Mobility at the Transitory Hospital. *Source*: Own elaboration.

in relation to living together and social norms, in a dialogue with Goffman (1974). The direction of the hospital did not allow patients to leave without the accompaniment of an employee, a norm that I will consider as a bureaucratic impediment.

The description and categorisation (Fig. 9.1) of mobility also revealed this differentiation between the internal and external spaces of the hospital, locating, among the patients, those who wanted and demanded to access the external world and those who developed circuits that only articulated spaces inside the hospital.

Patients categorised as belonging to the 'Inside Group' presented clear boundaries with respect to the spaces where movements occurred, so that the institutional world massively overshadowed the outside world. Here, we have patients who were somehow afraid of leaving the hospital or disregarded this possibility for themselves, either because of physical issues or mental issues. Mental issues were found due to a high degree of subjective devastation or the increase of psychiatric symptoms.

The subcategories of this group were constructed in accordance with these different issues, so that psychic issues are represented in the subgroup called 'Particular Circuits – 1' and the physical problems and the issues of high degree of subjective devastation are contained in the subgroup called 'Institutional Circuits – 2'. In this group, we have represented patients who are both dependent and independent concerning locomotion.

The 'Outside Group' was characterised by a high degree of 'demands', so that patients of this group took an active position in the relationship with workers, articulating their access to external spaces through different means of communication. Here, we have, for example, the patients who refused the coffee offered inside the hospital because the coffee at the nearby bakery was better for their taste.

Mobility and Equity

It is important to note that, as we observed with the Inside Group, this group has patients who move around independently and patients who are dependent on others, but all of them show some level of communication skills: those who do not use verbal language communicate well by gestures or sounds, being persistent in their demands. What seems to make an important difference between the wheelchair users of both groups is the willingness to access urban spaces and the ability to communicate this desire to the interlocutor, which in this case was the staff.

It was possible to note a difference between those who considered their access to external spaces as a way to build or reinforce their urgent demand for hospital discharge and those who seemed to not worry about being discharged, although they could continue to access the street. The first group was named 'Discharge Project – 3' and the second, 'Projects in the City – 4'.

The predominance of the 'Inside Group' among the described mobilities, however, is not a big surprise, as these people spent many years restricted to the internal spaces of the institutions. A reason given to this predominance, beyond those already mentioned, was the lack of belonging, as one employee said: *If I do not feel that I belong to a place, I have difficulty to move in order to access it* (employee interview). Some symptoms also seemed to work as refusals: moments of intensification of delusional constructions and hallucinations, dullness, depressed mood.

The number of patients represented in the 'Outside Group', especially in the subcategory 'Projects in the City – 4' is significant, suggesting that, despite the difficulties of access, being in urban spaces was important for many of them. These projects often represented unpretentious desires, such as having a coffee at the bakery or simply sitting on the bench at the square. Among the destinations, most were food-related establishments, as listed in Table 9.2.

For some bedridden patients, however, access to the city was definitely different. Even with the difficulties of getting out of bed, some members of this group were able to provoke workers into bringing them objects and food that were not found inside the hospital. Faced with the impossibility or difficulty of being in external spaces, these patients used to ask for a piece of the world outside the institution, thus configuring a way to access the city. An example of such a situation was Felipe, a bedridden patient, who provoked the team into bringing him pictures of football players and the flag of his team to be hung around his bed.

When in town, wheelchair and non-wheelchair patients used different means of transportation during their routes, as detailed in Table 9.2.

The patients showed some difficulty with the ban on cigarette smoking inside public transportation vehicles, a law that has been in place in the country for over 10 years, but seemed to be completely new to them. In addition, cigarette consumption was high, configuring a close relationship between the subjects and the drug.

The 'on foot' mode of transportation was used more frequently, maybe because of the commercial variety found right next to the hospital.

The repetition of these experiences produced effects on how patients responded to adversity. In addition, this strategy also had effects on the hospital neighbours, who began to recognise the patients and to become interested in their stories. This helped produce some important changes in the patients' routine and, at the same time, it transformed the neighbours' own behaviour when interacting with these citizens.

Table 9.2. Transportation Use Difficulties.

Means of Transportation	Frequency	Difficulties	Destination
On foot	High	Sidewalks: irregularities, holes Pedestrian semaphore waiting time Speed of cars Lack of ramps on the sidewalks for wheelchair	Bakery, ice-cream shop, restaurant, church, school, fruit-shop, square
Bus	Low	Waiting time for the arrival and for boarding the vehicle Step height for boarding Vehicle speed Ratchets Ban on cigarette smoking inside public transportation vehicles Use of a wheelchair lift	School, another neighbourhood square, bakery, museum
Taxi	Low	Money Wheelchair adapted taxi availability	Another neighbourhood square, bakery, museum, health service
Ambulance	Low	City ambulance availability Fear	Another health service

Source: Own elaboration.

It is possible to conclude that over 50% of the patients did not access external spaces during hospitalisation. Among those who did, all needed a professional who would accompany them or bring them objects and food; food stores were mentioned as popular destinations, as well as the small neighbourhood square. Difficulty in using public transportation, bureaucratic impediments and individual restrictions, such as fear and lack of belonging, were listed as constraints to access. Finally, the perception of changes in the relationship between the neighbourhood and patients was pointed out as an effect of the work that was being performed by the staff.

5.2. Mobility and Access in Residential Therapeutic Services

The 16 residents who have been chosen to participate in the second stage of the research present the following profile (Table 9.3).

Considering urban access, three different mobility profiles have been found. They can be grouped according to frequency, diversity of means of transportation and facilities used, and autonomy for access (Table 9.4).

As in the hospital, the mobilities described in the RTSs were mostly observed in the internal spaces of the facilities. The advanced age of residents was pointed out as a reason, as well as their trouble in accessing their own money. Tide House supervisor explained:

> We already had the experience of using public transportation and sometimes we had problems because you get on the bus and it's a little full and nobody gives up the seat. When we have to get on buses with high steps, it's a bit difficult for them. (...) And here is a variable that I think is also important: money. Most patients actually receive the BPC, but the family retains the benefit and sometimes only gives them two hundred reais every three months. (Tide House supervisory interview).

Mobility and Equity 201

Table 9.3. Resident's Profile.

	Tide House RTS Type I	Dom Pedro House RTS Type I	Wheel House RTS Type II
Survey participants age and hospital subgroup categorisation	Luizinho – 52 y, 1	Nelson – 59 y, 3	Flávia – 58 y, 2
1: Particular circuits	Ivo – 72 y, 2	Neguinho – 48 y, 4	Bela – 51 y, 2
2: Institutional circuits	Drica – 85 y, 1	Raquel – 56 y, 4	Felipe – 45 y, 4
3: Discharge project	Sabiá – 67 y, 3	Pai Ioiô – 53 y, 1	Tereza – 87 y, 4
4: Projects in the city	Carola – 74 y, 1	Tião – 49 y, 1	
	Bárbara – 50 y, 3	Lila – 58 y, 4	
Average length of hospitalisation CSV	30 years	21 years	27 years
Physical condition for movement	Independent of external support	Independent of external support	Dependent on external support
Communication skills	Two resident with nonverbal communication – low performance	One resident with nonverbal communication – high performance	Three residents with nonverbal communication – average performance
	Four residents with verbal communication – average performance	Two residents with verbal communication – high performance	One resident with verbal communication – low performance
		Three residents with verbal communication – average performance	

Source: Own elaboration.
Notes: RTS, Residential Therapeutic Service and CSV, Serra Verde Clinic.

The area of concentration of the mobilities performed by Tide House residents, when in Transitory Hospital, was predominantly inside, as we observed in subgroups 1 and 2. Thus, we may think that what is expressed in these RTS was already somehow pointed out when we investigated the hospital.

The profile of the residents of Wheel House is also relevant: completely dependent on other people to move them, these residents also face embarrassing situations when using public transportation. In fact, this mode of transportation was not mentioned during the interviews. For the routes that exceed the distance to the square next to the house, they use taxis, financed by public money.[1] In this case, the supervisor did not mention the difficulty of access to money as being an embarrassment.

Contrarily, the state of the sidewalks was observed as something that hindered access to the square, which is very close to the house. In this regard, the neighbourhood was very welcoming, providing, on its own, structural improvements on the sidewalks, such as the construction of access ramps. This helped Felipe participate in the festivities that took place there and Tereza to drink non-alcoholic beer while sitting at the square.

Both Tereza and Felipe were already carrying out 'Projects in the City – 4' while they were hospitalised, many of which were performed through objects

Table 9.4. Residential Therapeutics Service Mobility Profile.

RTS	Output Frequency	Autonomy	Means of Transport	Places Accessed
Tide House	Low	Medium – none of the residents leaves without an escort	Taxi Ambulance On foot	Hospital Basic health unit Supermarket
Wheel House	Average	Low – all the residents need someone to transfer them from the bed to wheelchair and to drive it	Taxi Ambulance On foot	Square Hospital
Dom Pedro House	High	High – two residents have the key to the house and permission to go out alone	Taxi On foot Bus Uber Ambulance	Bar Restaurant Bakery Supermarket Basic health unit School Coexistence Centre Other SRTs Beauty saloon Psychosocial care centre

Source: Own elaboration.
Note: RTS, Residential Therapeutic Service.

brought into the hospital. In the RTS, this type of resource was not cited or observed because access occurred in the traditional format of presence of residents in external spaces.

Residents and employees of this RTS use, with significant dexterity, different means of communication, ranging from words, sounds and small body movements to the development of an accurate practice of listening, both mechanically and symbolically. Insistence and repetition are resources widely used by both speakers and listeners, so many moments were recorded when residents demanded to be taken to the streets. At Tide House, this kind of demand did not appear as often.

These communication resources were also significantly present at Dom Pedro House. In this RTS, however, the independence for mobility allowed residents to have a higher frequency of access to external spaces. And not only a higher frequency, but greater variability. Many of them used their own resources to finance spending during these outings.

This coincides with the profile of younger, more independent residents, with a less restricted access to their rightful benefits. They are those, among those surveyed, who had spent less time in the hospital, with a predominance of subgroups 3 and 4. Also, the organisation of work inside this RTS seemed to be concerned with increasing street access.

Two residents of this RTS, Nelson and Neguinho, have the house keys, so that they have greater freedom to enter and leave the residence. Continuing with his project, which started at the hospital, Nelson was attending high school while at the RTS and was also attending the Coexistence Centre, a facility that offers workshops for RAPS patients, twice a week. For these routes, he used the bus and Uber, during the day and night. In addition to these displacements, he described other minor ones, made on foot, near the house.

Shadowing Nelson walking on the street, I realised that he guides himself in a very peculiar way: trash cans and objects thrown on the ground serve as beacons for the direction and rhythm of his movement. Some objects are taken to the RTS and used as decoration, such as a picture frame in the living room. Other than that, it was also striking to realise that the reported use of the Coexistence Centre by the resident did not necessarily coincide with his actual use of this space, thus indicating a certain level of freedom (field notebook).

At the bus stop, Nelson was aware of the language of the city, explaining that he knew that the bus was coming because the other one had just stopped across the street, referring to the same bus going in the opposite direction. He also showed familiarity with the people from the neighbourhood (field notebook).

Pai Ioiô, another resident of this house, made some significant changes in his mobility forms, as well as in the areas of concentration of his movements. At the RTS, he hired, with his own resources, a therapeutic companion who helped him navigate the neighbourhood and reach greater distances. He presented a good development of these skills, as reported by the supervisor. In addition to the work of approaching his family, he moved to his brother's house in another city inside the state. If in the hospital, Pai Ioiô was known for his 'Particular Circuits – 1', in the RTS he is remembered as a resident who, relearning to walk around the city, managed to return to his family life.

Observing these differences among the residents of the three houses, we noticed a certain gradation of frequency and variety of access, so that characteristics such as advanced age and longer length of stay appear in the house where access is less frequent and less varied, whereas shorter time of hospitalisation and younger age appear in the home where access is more varied and frequent. It is curious to note that psychiatric issues such as symptom worsening were not listed in any of the houses as barriers or facilitators of access. Similarly, the use of wheelchairs and dependence for handling, albeit making it more complicated, did not seem to restrict access.

6. FINAL CONSIDERATIONS

When we asked about mobility and urban access practices developed by the subjects of this research, we intended to look at a large universe and try to capture some elements that could describe a transition process. In this way, it is important to highlight that barriers to accessibility were found in the individual sphere, such as feelings of fear, unwillingness, difficulty in accessing one's own money, difficulties in using public transportation; and in the structural sphere, such as institutional restrictions to urban access, inadequate provision of public transportation, social exclusion.

Contrarily, we also found a variety of movements that revealed diverse functions for urban access: leisure, shopping, meals, school activities, healthcare.

In order to make this access operational, elements such as communication skills, welcoming of neighbourhoods, as well as offering the necessary assistance for navigating the city are emphasised as relevant aspects.

Something that drew our attention both in the hospital context and in the context of the RTSs were the reports of proximity to the neighbourhood as a strategy to operationalise urban access for the research subjects and the practical effects of this approach. This reveals an interesting effect from the point of view of public policy seeking to ensure accessibility: this policy also has an impact on the relationships built between the target audience and other population groups (Wachs & Kumagai, 1973).

In other words, improving the access of people with mental illnesses to urban spaces promotes changes in the relationships that this population builds with other citizens in the city. This can be understood as a process of strengthening support networks, operating in the opposite direction formerly pointed by Dalmolin and da Penha Vasconcellos (2007), and thus favouring accessibility.

In this sense, we observed promotion of social equity and access to some rights that were not previously being accessed, such as transit through the city, regardless of the difficulties presented. The performance of hospital and RTS teams was significant for this observation.

It is important to highlight that mobility, used as a methodological resource for data collection and analysis, proved to be satisfactory to generate reflections on accessibility and on facilities' functions.

It was also found that access is, more than an act, a set of actions, promoted by different subjects. Thus, it is important to understand that this is a process: before stepping on city streets, the subject needs to want to step on those streets and, in the impossibility of walking with their own feet, he/she/they need(s) to communicate this to someone and build a way of achieving his goal. We also encountered those who seemed not to have this desire, and one of the suggested explanations was their prolonged hospitalisation periods, associated with advanced age.

If we ask ourselves if there is any kind of structural need required by the specific condition of mental suffering in terms of access, one answer is that public care policy should build intervention resources other than prolonged hospitalisations. This avoids the breakage and reduction of support networks (Dalmolin & da Penha Vasconcellos, 2007). It is also important that the current policy continues to establish and improve conditions, so that those who have been through long hospitalisations can build their own forms of access.

Although there are still many challenges for accessibility for this public, the research documented the closure of the last psychiatric hospital within the SUS of Belo Horizonte. This closure represents, among many other things, the political option of interrupting the cycle of prolonged hospitalisations based on the understanding that urban access and social living are more efficient resources regarding the care of this population.

Regarding a population historically discredited because of its capabilities, the work shows that coexistence is possible, even if it requires a public policy, with active agents that mediate relationships, favouring the construction of strategies for city life. There is still much to be done in this regard and, therefore, the continuity and development of free, universal and comprehensive public policies, produced from technical data and with effective social participation, is important. This seems to be a viable way to build more equitable and accessible cities.

NOTES

1. As in the hospital, there is a monthly resource for some expenses, including displacement. Similarly, it is a limited resource that needs to be managed according to observed priorities.
2. Data available for consultation on the platform of the Brazilian Institute of Geography and Statistics https://cidades.ibge.gov.br/brasil/mg/belo-horizonte/panorama.
3. Primary source: Fundação João Pinheiro. Centro de Estatística e Informações. Available for download at http://www.fjp.mg.gov.br/index.php/docman/cei/pib/pib-municipais/160-anexo-estatistico-pib-regioes-mg-1999-2010.
4. Information from the Development Agency of the Metropolitan Region of Belo Horizonte.
5. Data collected in 2012 and available on the website of the Bhtrans Mobility Observatory http://www.bhtrans.pbh.gov.br/portal/page/portal/portalpublico/Temas/ObservatorioMobilidade/Indicadores.
6. Primary source: Atlas do Desenvolvimento. Data available for consultation on http://www.atlasbrasil.org.br/2013/pt/perfil_m/belo-horizonte_mg.
7. Data provided by the Municipal Health Secretariat in May 2018.
8. Municipal Health Secretariat (May 2018).

ACKNOWLEDGEMENTS

I would like to thank my CEURB colleagues, especially Bruna Barradas, Gabriela Cicci and Ana Marcela Ardila, and also all the patients and workers who have contributed to this research.

REFERENCES

Amarante, P. (1995). Novos sujeitos, novos direitos: o debate em torno da Reforma Psiquiátrica. *Cadernos de Saúde Pública, Rio de Janeiro, 11*(3), 491–494, jul/set.
Arruda, A. E. (2016). *Experiências e territórios da loucura: narrativas de portadores de sofrimento mental assistidos em um serviço aberto na cidade de Belo Horizonte. 2016. 111 f.* Dissertação (Mestrado), Universidade Federal de Minas Gerais, Faculdade de Filosofia e Ciências Humanas.
Basaglia, F. (2001). *A instituição negada: relato de um hospital psiquiátrico* (p. 326). Rio de Janeiro: Graal.
Brasil. (2000a). *Lei n° 10.098, de 19 de dezembro de 2000*, que estabelece normas gerais e critérios básicos para a promoção da acessibilidade das pessoas portadoras de deficiência ou com mobilidade reduzida. DOU de 20/12/2000 (Seção 1, pg. 2).
Brasil. (2000b). Portaria n° 106, de 11 de Fevereiro de 2000, Institui os Serviços Residenciais Terapêuticos. DOU de 24/02/2000 (n° 39-E, Seção 1, p. 23).
Brasil. (2010). Ministério da Saúde. Saúde Mental em Dados – 7, ano V, n° 7. Informativo eletrônico. Brasília: junho de 2010 (acesso em Outubro de 2019).
Brasil. (2015). Ministério da Saúde. Saúde Mental em Dados – 12, ano 10, n° 12. Informativo eletrônico. Brasília: outubro de 2015 (acesso em Outubro de 2019).
Campos, G. W. de S. (2006). Reflexões Temáticas sobre Eqüidade e Saúde: o caso do SUS. *Saúde e Sociedade, 15*(2), 23–33.

Clarke, P., Ailshire, J. A., & Lantz, P. (2009). Urban built environments and trajectories of mobility disability: Findings from a national sample of community-dwelling American adults (1986-2001). *Social Science & Medicine*, *69*, 964-970.
Costa, L. A., & Brasil, F. D. (2014). Cidade, territorialidade e redes na política de saúde mental. *Cadernos de Terapia Ocupacional da UFSCar, São Carlos*, *22*(2), 435-442.
Dalmolin, B. M., & da Penha Vasconcellos, M. (2007). «Cartografias de sujeitos que vivenciam osofrimento psíquico numa comunidade urbana», *Ponto Urbe* [Online], 1 |posto online no dia 30 julho 2007, consultado o 06 maio 2019. Retrieved from http://journals.openedition.org/pontourbe/1236. doi:10.4000/pontourbe.1236
Foucault, M. (1978). *História da loucura na Idade Clássica*. São Paulo: Perspectiva.
Franco, R. F. (2012). Habitar a cidade: a (re)construção de espaços de habitação para ex-internos de um hospital psiquiátrico e sua importância para produção de subjetividade. Doctoral thesis, Universidade Federal de Minas Gerais, Belo Horizonte, Brasil.
Goffman, E. (1974). *Manicômios, prisões e conventos*. São Paulo: Perspectiva.
Imrie, R., & Kumar, K. (2010). Focusing on disability and access in the built environment. *Disability & Society*, *13*(3), 357-374. doi: 10.1080/09687599826687
Jirón, P. (2001). On becoming "la sombra/the shadow". In Buscher, M., Urry, J., & Witchger, K. *Mobile methods* (pp. 36-54). New York, NY: Routledge.
Lobosque, A. M. (1997). *Princípios para uma clínica antimanicomial* (p. 96). São Paulo: Hucitec.
Pande, M. N. R., & Amarante, P. (2011). Desafios para os centros de atenção psicossocial como serviços substitutivos: a nova cronicidade em questão. *Ciência & Saúde Coletiva*, *16*(4), 2067-2076.
Santos Junior, H. P. de O. S., Silveira, M. de F. de A., Gualda, D. M. R., & Salim, N. R. (2011). Loucos? Histórias de vida, significados do sofrimento psíquico e (des)institucionalização. In Silveira, M. de F. A., & H. P. de Santos Junior O. S. (Orgs) *Residências terapêuticas: pesquisa e prática nos processos de desinstitucionalização*. Campina Grande: EDUEPB. ISBN 978-85-7879-063-9. Retrieved from SciELO Books http://books.scielo.org
Sheller, M. (2008). Mobility, freedom and public space. In S. Bergmann & T. Sager (Eds.), *The ethics of mobilities: Rethinking place, exclusion, freedom and environment* (pp. 25-38). Ashgate Hampshire.
Sze, N. N., & Christensen, K. M. (2017). Access to urban transportation system for individuals with disabilities. *IATSS Research*, *41*, 66-73.
Vieceli, A. P. (2014). Lugares da loucura: o reencontro da cidade com a diferença. III Encontro da Associação Nacional de Pesquisa e Pós-graduação em Arquitetura e Urbanismo arquitetura, cidade e projeto: uma construção coletiva São Paulo, São Paulo.
Wachs, M., & Kumagai, T. G. (1973). Physical accessibility as social indicator. *Socio-Economic Planning Sciences*, *7*, 437-456.
Weyler, A. R. (2006). O hospício e a cidade: novas possibilidades de circulação do louco. *Imaginário, USP*, *12*(13), 381-395.

APPENDIX

A.1. Belo Horizonte Overview

Belo Horizonte is the capital of the state of Minas Gerais, located in the southeastern region of Brazil. It has a population of 2,523,794 inhabitants, distributed in nine health districts and a demographic density of 7,167 inhabitants per km^2.[2] The Belo Horizonte Metropolitan Region is made up of 34 municipalities, bringing together an approximate population of 4.8 million people and presenting a GDP of R$ 120 billion in 2010.[3] Belo Horizonte concentrates 45% of this value.[4]

Regarding forms of mobility around the city, Belo Horizonte is characterised by a high degree of motorisation, so that 36.6% of daily trips are carried out in motorised individual mode, 34.8% is carried out on foot and 28.1% in collective transportation mode.[5]

Concerning social indicators, the HDI is 0.839, unevenly distributed throughout the city's territory. The Gini is of 0.60, life expectancy is 76.4 years old and the fertility rate is 1.3 child per women.[6] The municipality has 600,000 households and 216 special zones of social interest.

The city has wide coverage of the Psychosocial Care Network – RAPS, featuring 255 services in Primary Care, where 647 professionals work, and 15 services in Specialised Care, where 741 professionals work. In addition, in the field of capacity building, the municipality has an Integrated Mental Health Residency programme. Among the services located in Specialised Care, the city has eight Psychosocial Care Centres; three Psychosocial Care Centres, Alcohol and Drugs; two Child and Youth Psychosocial Care Centres; one Psychiatric Emergency Service; one Adult Transitional Hosting Unit ; and one Child and Youth Transitional Hosting.[7]

Regarding primary care, Belo Horizonte has 33 Therapeutic Residential Services, 9 Coexistence Centres, 4 Street Clinic Teams, 49 Health Art Programme Centres, 9 Child and Youth Complementary Teams and 208 professionals distributed by the Basic Health Units.[8]

There are two State Psychiatric Hospitals in the city that serve patients from other municipalities in the state, so that the population of Belo Horizonte can perform all their treatment in other RAPS equipment.

CHAPTER 10

URBAN ACCESSIBILITY IN BELO HORIZONTE, BRAZIL: A CASE STUDY OF MOBILITY PRACTICES AND DEMANDS OF PEOPLE WITH DISABILITIES IN THE MOBILITY SYSTEMS

Ana Marcela Ardila Pinto, Marcos Fontoura De Oliveira, Bruna Barradas Cordeiro and Laíse Lorene Hasz Souza e Oliveira

ABSTRACT

Since the 1990s, several policy instruments have been produced in Belo Horizonte, Brazil, to improve accessibility to urban mobility systems, especially for people with disabilities. However, the city still faces important shortcomings in understanding the demands of the population with disabilities and in implementing an appropriate urban structure. The present work identifies mobility practices and demands for accessibility of this population based on a descriptive analysis of the city's origin/destination survey (2012) and results of a focus group with representatives of the population with disabilities and public authorities. The analysis demonstrates that the demands of persons with reduced mobility are characterised first by a high level of immobility, comparing to people without disabilities, which has important consequences on access to urban goods, especially jobs and health and educational services. Second, mobility has a relevant role in producing forms of discrimination and exclusion. Third, in addition to the problems faced by the general population, people with reduced mobility also face greater challenges in using transport systems. Ultimately, this analysis points out that the main needs for people with disabilities are related to the problems of articulation between public places and transportation systems, both in terms of infrastructure and in terms of attitude and behaviour of service providers and other citizens.

Keywords: Accessibility; urban mobility; people with disabilities; urban policies; mobility practices; universal design

1. INTRODUCTION

Since the 1990s, managers of the city of Belo Horizonte, capital of Minas Gerais, Brazil, have produced various regulatory instruments and urban mobility projects, which have as one of their goals ensuring accessibility to urban transport systems for all citizens, particularly the ones with reduced mobility, such as elderly people and individuals with impairments and disabilities (physical, intellectual, hearing or visual). However, far from being an inclusive city, Belo Horizonte still faces shortages in normative arrangements, especially regarding the implementation of physical structures and public policy management to, as stated in the municipal law (De Oliveira, 2014), 'provide wide and democratic access to the urban space, giving priority to public and non-motorized means of transportation' (Belo Horizonte, 2011, art. 2).

The accessibility legal framework of Belo Horizonte is based on Brazil's Federal legal framework, which consists of a set of federal law provisions and decrees, as well as accessibility standards as reported by the Brazilian National Standards Organization (ABNT, Associação Brasileira de Normas Técnicas in Portuguese). The development of the legal framework is distributed within various instruments, both territorial and legislative, regarding issues related to the population with disabilities. Thus, based on the Federal Constitution of 1988, in 1989, the Policy for the Integration of People with Disabilities was published, in 2000 – the laws promoting accessibility and priority of care, in 2001 – the City Statute, in 2003 – the Elderly Statute, in 2004 – the decree that regulates accessibility, in 2011 – the Access to Information Law and in 2012 – the National Urban Mobility Policy.

In 2015, a great consolidation and expansion of rights was the main goal of the Brazilian Law for Inclusion of People with Disabilities (LBI in Portuguese), designed to ensure and promote, on an equal basis, the exercise of fundamental rights and freedoms for persons with disabilities, aiming at their social inclusion and citizenship. Among other innovations, this law introduced universal design as a rule in the conception and implementation of transport projects. The legislation also includes the promulgation of the United Nations Convention on the Rights of Persons with Disabilities. The amendment to the Federal Constitution made in 2015 that now incorporates 'the right to the transport' as a new social right shall also be added to the accessibility legal framework, which allows us to conclude that, for the policies of inclusion of persons with reduced mobility, urban mobility is a main issue (Brasil, 2015).

In Belo Horizonte, the municipal legal framework distinguishes between sectoral and territorial instruments (De Oliveira & Souki, 2016). Local mobility and transport are regulated by the Municipal Master Plan, Law 7.165 (1996) and its new version, Law 1.749 (2019); the Urban Mobility Policy, Law 10.134 (2011) and the Mobility Master Plan, Decree 15.317 (2013). Two recent initiatives, both from 2018, illustrate the continued relevance of the theme of persons with reduced mobility in the formulation of urban policies in the capital of Minas Gerais. They consist in two normative instruments, those being the formulation of the *BHTrans Plan of Accessibility for Urban Mobility in Belo Horizonte* in 2018 (De Oliveira, 2018b) and the establishment of the *Permanent Accessibility Commission of Belo Horizonte* (Belo Horizonte, 2018), which seek to ensure, at least formally, the right of broad and democratic access to urban space for all people.

The local accessibility legal framework is a step forward towards improving access to public transportation and to the city in general. However, a few studies carried out in Belo Horizonte have shown that the issue of access has been treated with a special emphasis on technical and infrastructural aspects, without the participation of citizens. Thus, the framework does not sufficiently incorporate the demands of those with reduced mobility, does not recognise the diversity regarding disabilities (Ardila Pinto & Villamizar-Duarte, 2018; De Oliveira, 2018a) and does not ensure enough control over the compliance of the actions of the local government, oriented to incorporate the universal design in the city transport (De Oliveira, 2019).

An analysis of the available information highlights the shortage of data that identifies access barriers faced by the city's disabled population. Moreover, the data indicate that there are a significant amount of people with disabilities or reduced mobility. According to the 2012 origin/destination survey (OD, Pesquisa de Origem/Destino in Portuguese), carried out by Minas Gerais's State Government, 3.9% of the population of the Belo Horizonte municipality claimed to have some kind of disability, and 73% of this group did not report any travels outside their homes. Furthermore, the city's infrastructure proves to be quite lacking. According to the 2010 census (IBGE, 2010 – Brazilian Institute of Geography and Statistics), compared to other Brazilian cities, Belo Horizonte shows good overall infrastructure indicators, as 98% of its households can be accessed by paved roads and 94% have sidewalks. However, a detailed analysis shows that only 9.6% of the sidewalks in Belo Horizonte are equipped with pedestrian corner ramps. In contrast, the same 2010 census shows that in Brasília and Porto Alegre, 16.5% and 23.3% of the sidewalks, respectively, are equipped with pedestrian corner ramps (these are the highest indicators in Brazil).

These data illustrate the gap between the objectives and the implementation of the policy addressing the transformation of urban space to meet the needs of people with disabilities. It is clear that we do not have enough information about the mobility demands of this social group. The aim of the present study is to identify daily mobility practices and demands of individuals with reduced mobility. To accomplish this, we have employed quantitative and qualitative methods of research that allow tackling the practices, as well as the demands of the disabled population based on their own experiences. For this purpose, we have carried out a descriptive analysis of the mobility practices of people with disabilities (permanent and temporal) using data from the 2012 OD survey in the Belo Horizonte Metropolitan Region. To complement this analysis, we also carried out a focus group session with representatives of the city's organisations of people with disabilities and local and state government employees. Participants in the focus group were invited directly by the city government during the 2017 International Urban Accessibility Seminar organised by BH-TRANS and the World Resources Institute with support from the Minas Gerais Development Bank and the Centre of Urban Studies at UFMG.

Through these analyses, we found that the demands of people with reduced mobility are characterised, first, by the high level of immobility in comparison to people without disabilities, which critically impacts their access to urban goods, especially jobs and health and educational services. Second, mobility has a relevant role in producing forms of discrimination and exclusion. Third, in addition to the problems faced by the general population, people with reduced mobility also face greater challenges in using transport systems. Ultimately, this analysis points out that the main demands of people with disabilities are related to the problem of articulation between public places and transportation systems, both in terms of infrastructure and in terms of attitude and behaviour of service providers and other citizens. Identifying the disabled population's demands can contribute to the knowledge and progressive incorporation of the variables related to accessibility in public policies, in order to overcome the purely technical and sectoral nature of the urban policies. The variety of demands from these groups challenges experts and citizens to create more inclusive cities, with policies that allow us to move towards the full exercise of the citizenship rights and the guarantee of justice and equity.

In order to understand the practices and demands of the disabled population, we have divided the chapter into four sections. The second section contains a literature review on the relationship between disabilities and mobility. The third section presents the conceptual framework and the adopted research methods. The fourth section displays the results of the study, which are subdivided into two sections: first, the travelling practices and experiences in the city based on the 2012 OD survey data, and second, the mobility experiences and demands reported by the focus group. The latter specifically discusses accessibility for people with disabilities. The fourth and last section of the chapter presents the final considerations of our study.

2. LITERATURE REVIEW

Research on the relationship between disability and urban mobility is part of a gradual process consisting of the progressive incorporation of the social dimensions to the study of the movement of people, ideas and goods in cities. This has been visible mainly in research addressing accessibility of transport infrastructures from either physical and functional or economic and social perspectives. New approaches have been developing in the search to understand disability not as a limitation, but as an opportunity for all urban agents to incorporate the citizens' diversity and to promote democratic inclusion.

Since the 1950s, transport engineering and regional planning perspectives based on a functional and economic approach to movement have been dominating the transport studies. Factors such as distance, population size, urban functions, the structure of the goods and services market and the organisation of governments were considered significant and were incorporated into mechanics-inspired gravitational models for the analysis of physical places. The agents were understood as abstract and homogeneous individuals that make rational decisions and no clear distinction was made regarding their physical, social or cultural characteristics (Chorley & Haggett, 2013 [1967]). Thus, such understanding resulted in/ led to the overlooking of ended up and demands of specific population groups.

Following the 1970s, a significant group of authors questioned the functional and economic approach in the field of transport research and started taking into account the diversity regarding individuals' situations and demands. Kain (1968), Wachs and Kumagai (1973), and Seguí Pons and Petrus Bey (1991), among others, incorporated a perspective and characteristics of varied individuals into the mobility studies. Oviedo and Titheridge (2016) demonstrated that elderly people, people with disabilities, children, black people, women and poor people present the highest inequality levels in the city. In the same way, Schönfelder and Axhausen (2010), Gannon and Liu (1997), and Brand et al. (2012) illustrated the connection between these sociodemographic aspects and the travelling experiences, rhythms and representations of the urban agents

Other significant contributions were made by authors that emphasised the role of the individuals' demands in relation to the city's and the transport system's characteristics. Van Wee and Geurs (2004, 2011) suggest that the dimensions of land-use and distribution of activities, the components of transport, must be analysed based on the experiences of the individuals. They may be approached in terms of the relation between origin and destination, the time constraints and the availability of infrastructure in different spaces and times. Daniel Banister (2018, p. 44) debated on the mediating role of public transport policies in terms of conciliating the availability of opportunities and individual aspects, and social justice and social mobility. The author considers the public investment in transportation to be relevant, directly or indirectly, through allowances, to reduce social inequality. In the same way, Cervero (2011, p. 19) highlighted the relationship between transport planning and the public investment in mass transport. The investment of the public sector in transport is considered to be a moral issue, since mobility is not only a public good, but a human need. Public transport services provide connection, particularly for poor people and other vulnerable groups, most of them ignored by the market (Cervero, 2011, p. 5). These studies show that accessibility to transport contributes to reducing inequality and must be understood in terms of the individuals' opportunities and capabilities to enjoy urban, spatial and social benefits.

Specifically related to research on persons with disabilities within the transport field, we found studies that seek to identify the influence of disabilities on the accessibility of urban goods and services. One of the most renowned studies is Litman's (2017) that proposes the concept of vertical accessibility to understand how individual characteristics (skills and needs of individuals and groups) of elderly people and people with disabilities prevent them from using and accessing the city effectively. This concept is opposed to that of horizontal accessibility, which implies equal treatment for equals in socioeconomic aspects. The author further proposes strategies for increasing equity, including universal design, spatial mobility services, special parking for persons with disabilities and quality services for non-drivers. Likewise, Wasfi, Levinson, and El-Geneidy (2012) analysed the situation with elderly people and people with disabilities, demonstrating the difficulties that these groups face to access medical services, to work, to do shopping, etc., as well as the need for better public transport services and physical access to public and private spaces.

From a *mobility ontology* perspective, Gharebaghi et al. (2018); Rosenberg, Huang, Simonovich, and Belza (2013); and Fougeyrollas (2010), among others, proposed to integrate the spatial and social dimensions with the experiences and semantic networks of the groups of people with disabilities at three different scales of analysis: micro (an individual), meso (community/services) and macro (society/system). Through this analysis, the authors demonstrated how each mobility system enables the development of the capacities of people with disabilities. They created analytical models to identify how daily activities, places and characteristics of individuals in different disability situations are linked.

Another relevant approach to mobility practices is the environmental perspective. For the authors who support this approach, the physical environment and space are the ones that hamper the capacity of persons with disabilities to perform daily life activities, to have choices, freedom and to take part in the collective life. To geographers like Gleeson (1999) and Chouinard, Hall, and Wilton (2010), spatial, social and economic barriers are related to the segregation and marginalisation created by capitalism and to the ways in which the body and normality concepts are built, both spatially and socially. More specifically, the studies are trying to understand how different impairments and disabilities are associated with not only environmental, but also to other variables, such as '*physical-built environment, societal attitudes, and system/policy environment*', as stated by Altman, Lollar, and Rasch (2014, p. 36).

The role of urban environments and services is thus defined as that of to provide connectivity, ways and spaces to promote a healthier lifestyle, higher sociability and independence both for persons with disabilities and elderly people (Wahl, Iwarsson, & Oswald, 2012; Webber, Porter, & Menec, 2010; Yen, Michael, & Perdeu, 2009). The effects of the quality of healthcare and education services on the activity level of persons with disabilities and elderly people with reduced mobility are also being considered. By analysing the barriers of the built environment, this body of literature helps to identify which urban conditions of different physical environments contribute to the walkability capacity for these groups of people (Gell, Rosenberg, Carlson, Kerr, & Belza, 2015; Rosenberg et al., 2013).

This group of authors seeks to identify in more detail the factors that affect the mobility of these groups in public spaces by assessing the number of parking lots and car services, the quality of the curb ramps, lighting, crossings, signals, paved surfaces, sidewalks and other elements of infrastructure for the pedestrians, as well as their usability, especially for the people with motor and visual impairments. For them, the implementation of the universal design and the assistive technology are essential strategies for adapting the urban environment to the individual needs of different types of disabilities and evaluate the role of the assistive in the improvement of mobility (Gharebaghi et al., 2018; Kirchner, Gerber, & Smith, 2008; Rosenberg et al., 2013).

Based on a social perspective, some authors examined disability as a constraining factor in the use of the urban space and means of transportation, considering the built environment as the main element that hinders or favours the access to the city and its services. Particularly, some studies of accessibility in urban environments have demonstrated the relation between physical and attitudinal barriers and transport policies, urban land-use and city planning. For example, Bezyak, Sabella, and Gattis (2017) provide a description of the persistence of physical and attitudinal barriers in the transport system in the USA after the implementation of the Americans with Disabilities Act (ADA) in 1990. Moreover, Velho, Holloway, Symonds, and Balmer (2016) analyse the barriers faced by wheelchair users in public transport in London. Despite the improvement on the accessibility of London buses and the promulgation of The Disability Discrimination Act in 1995, the authors identify negative user experiences associated with technological, spatial and social barriers. Wheelchair users are not being seen as potential clients and face isolation and anxiety in a city with a crowded and rigid transport system. Hine and Mitchell (2001) also explore the travel experiences and elucidate how transport policies are being shaped by a notion of an universal disembodied subject, without taking into account the differences and disadvantages. In particular, the authors argue that a social agenda for transport has to put accessibility in the centre of the policy in order to create equality of access as a civil right.

More recently, authors from the *mobility turn* perspective have analysed the mobility practices of this population group (Parent, 2016). Goggin (2016) exposes how mobility practices link different citizenship forms at different scales. Sawchuk (2017) also analyses how the social construction of *impairments* can create *disabilities* in an ontogenetic process that changes with time. Different identity forms can conflict in their demands of resources and rights in the mobility space, thus generating unequal capacities, like, for example, pedestrians and wheelchair users or children, elderly and wheelchair users in transport systems. The studies based on this perspective contribute to the perception of disability as a more relatable, changeable and diverse form of identity, allowing the understanding of the demands of the groups with disabilities in terms of their rights and power struggles in society.

Together, all these authors acknowledge the importance of the social, spatial and political dimensions of movement in understanding the inequality in transport systems. The advances of these works allowed the recognition of the effects of disability on the economic, political and social participation of individuals in urban life. They also contributed to the understanding of the roles that urban structure and organisation of transport systems play in the accessibility for groups that, due to their individual characteristics, have specific needs. Nevertheless, the analysis is still bound to the idea of disability as an inherent condition of an individual, as a fixed identity, and in some cases, as a homogeneous situation of disability. On the other hand, especially in accessibility studies, more structural dimensions or more technical evaluations of the quality of the urban space are valued, assigning less importance to the individuals with disabilities' own perceptions. Recognising the diversity of situations, experiences and practices regarding the use of the urban space of this group represents a theoretical and methodological challenge that must be faced to move forward in the comprehension of this issue.

3. FRAMEWORKS AND METHODS

In this section, we present the main concepts that were used in this study to define the conceptual framework that facilitated the identification of methods used to pinpoint the demands of people with disabilities. Subsequently, we explain the techniques, instruments and sources used in the analysis of both practices and demands.

3.1. Conceptual Framework

For this study, we have adopted a concept of disability that recognises the ontological dimension of the agents, in terms of their capacities, practices and experiences, as well as in the way their bodies interconnect with the urban environment (Altman, Lollar, & Rasch, 2014). Our aim is to overcome the idea of abnormality, which treats people with disabilities as a segregated, special, fixed and homogeneous group (Da Silva Bampi, Guilhem, & Alves, 2010; Gharebaghi et al., 2018). We consider disability to be a result of the interdependency between biological, psychological and cultural aspects (Imrie & Kumar, 1998). It is an embodied experience, which implies the construction of social identities (Chouinard et al., 2010) that are diverse and result in different practices, experiences and meanings, which may be transient or permanent, physical or intellectual and may change over time (Sawchuk, 2017; Shakespeare, 2001). Thus, we analysed many forms of mobility, in terms of temporary and permanent disabilities, and different displacement scenarios, like public transport and public spaces.

People with disabilities face daily restrictions in travelling and develop movement practices and strategies that shed light on other forms of social differentiation and diversity (Boys, 2014; Imrie & Street, 2011). The creativity that persons with disabilities employ in order to use the space can help understand the differences in their bodies and socio-spatial practices. People with disabilities can be perceived not as unequal and vulnerable users with needs, but as agents that contribute to the construction of the strategies of relativisation and recognition of human diversities and different forms of urban use and to promote the production of richer and more creative spaces (Boys, 2014). Based on that perspective, we have carried out focus groups that allow us to identify the barriers to accessing city transport and goods and to ensure mobility in urban spaces. This analysis enables proposals for strategies to overcome the challenges imposed by the urban barriers in the future.

The demands of people with disabilities can be understood as more than just special needs, but also as the exercise of citizen's rights (Levy, 2009; Sheller, 2008), in which other forms of equity, power and justice are evident. Looking at these demands allows us to identify forms of social inequality, engendered by circulation barriers, and also to the wishes and the difficulties in carrying out the citizens' projects (Urry, 2007). They also provide us with an opportunity to identify the extent of the awareness about human diversity in urban policies, from the perspective of space construction and social practices of use of the urban space, and to understand the combination of different forms of inequality, since from an intersectional perspective, disability is interlaced with other forms of exclusion like gender, race, class or ethnicity (Hamraie, 2017).

Based on this framework, we have analysed the ways transport systems are used by people with disabilities, the barriers they face daily, as well as the demands regarding the urban space and the city residents. We have identified these practices in terms of their relation to the variables of sex and age (available in the references), level of education and integration with the job market (understood as indirect income indicators). These variables are relevant for grasping the diversity in disability cases and moving forward towards an intersectional perspective on the issue. The next section explains the methodological proposition created for the understanding of the object in question.

3.2. Data Collection and Systematisation

To examine the daily mobility practices and demands of the individuals with disabilities, this study used quantitative data from the 2012 OD survey and qualitative data from focus groups. We have analysed the sociodemographic profiles and travel profiles from the 2012 OD survey in Belo Horizonte's Metropolitan Region carried out by the Belo Horizonte Metropolitan Region Development Agency and the State Department of Metropolitan Management (SEGEM) of Minas Gerais. The universe of the survey consists of 34 municipalities of the Belo Horizonte Metropolitan Region (BHMR) (Minas Gerais, 2013, p. 72). 43,784 households were visited, giving a final sample of 30,786 households. The trust level of the statistical analysis in our work was set to 95%, the margin of error to 1% and the estimated variance to 1%. The spatial cutout was the city of Belo Horizonte and the data came from the Household Survey module, which collected data about the trips performed on the day before the day of the survey by all the dwellers of the selected residence. We conducted a descriptive statistical analysis based on Pearson's chi-squared test and the significance level of 0.05 was used to analyse various characteristics of the group.

In order to identify the problems that persons with disabilities face in BHMR and to create more democratic environments for the construction of public policies, we organised a focus group with the participation of leaders and representatives from the organisations of people with disabilities and from the state agencies of Belo Horizonte and BHMR. Through this focus group, we first sought out to identify people's own visions about their accessibility and daily life in the city and second, hear about the challenges that they face in order to travel around and take part in the public life of the city. Individual observations and collective discussions revolved around one main question: *which problems hinder full and democratic access to the urban space in the Belo Horizonte Metropolitan Region?* By the end of the session, the group drew up a document entitled ' Letter of

Belo Horizonte for the right to a city for all' ('Carta de Belo Horizonte pelo direito a uma cidade para todas e todos' in Portuguese), which was sent to the Belo Horizonte Mayor's Office and to the Minas Gerais State Government. The responses collected in the focus group were analysed using IBM SPSS Statistics (IBM, USA) software.

The focus group was held on the 24 August 2017 and had 50 participants. Among them, the participants of the organisations of people with disabilities that represented the following organisations: Coletivo BH Acessível (The Collective Accessible BH), Associação dos Usuários de Transporte Coletivo da Grande Belo Horizonte (Users of Public Transport of Greater Belo Horizonte Association), BH em Ciclo (BH in Cycle), Movimento Nossa BH (Our BH Movement), City Councils for the Rights of Persons with Disabilities and the Rights of Elderly (both of the city of Belo Horizonte), among others. The representatives of public authorities were the administrators of Empresa de Transportes e Trânsito de Belo Horizonte (BHTrans; Transport and Transit Company of Belo Horizonte), BHMR Development Agency, Department of Buildings and Roads of Minas Gerais (DEER/MG, Departamento de Edificações e Estradas de Rodagem de Minas Gerais in Portuguese), Municipal Authority of Transit and Transport of Contagem (TransCon), Superintendence of Urban Trains of Belo Horizonte (STU-BH), Municipal Department for Urban Planning of Belo Horizonte (Smapu, Secretaria Municipal de Planejamento Urbano in Portuguese), among others.

The participants set out 176 demands that were codified in order to classify and organise the diversity of statements. The coding process was carried out using a two-stage category reduction process (Miles & Huberman, 1984). In the first stage, 33 code clusters were identified, which attempted to preserve, in a more detailed manner, the participants' contribution. In the second stage, eight larger groups were created, based on dimensions related to the urban mobility and transport policy. This space for dialogue was of fundamental importance for perceiving both the necessity to include citizens' views in the local policy-making and the differences that exist within the population with disabilities.

4. RESULTS

As previously discussed, the efforts in the creation of regulatory instruments are important steps to improve access, to ensure the rights of people with disabilities and to adopt universal design as a criterion for urban design. Nevertheless, the analysis of citizens' practices and their experiences shows that the full exercise of freedom and the overcoming of barriers still require an incorporation of accessibility principles in the instruments of urban planning and transportation, in the management of mobility systems and in the daily practice of citizens. While the principles of the universal design are still far from being fully applied, the production and use of urban space still have a remarkably exclusionary character (Ardila Pinto & Villamizar-Duarte, 2018; Hamraie, 2017; Hine & Mitchell, 2001; Shakespeare & Watson, 2001).

The analysis of the practices and experiences in the present study shows that the enforcement of the rights of persons with disabilities in the scope of urban mobility is still insufficient. In order to grasp these aspects, we have analysed the practices of the population with disabilities based on the 2012 OD survey, and to understand the experiences and mobility demands, we have used the focus group study as a basis. Both methodologies, complementing each other, allowed identifying the different situations faced when using public mobility spaces for travelling in the city.

4.1. Daily Travelling Practices of People with Disabilities

The sources available for broad measurement of the movement practices of this population are quite limited. In our work, we have analysed the 2012 OD survey data. This survey measures the travelling patterns according to the different characteristics of each disability (Minas Gerais, 2013, p. 35). Regarding people with disabilities, first, we identified the sociodemographic characteristics of groups considered disabled. Then, we established the travelling patterns according to the motive, mode of transport and duration. These data allowed us to recognise the similarities and differences between distinct mobility situations according to the types of disability.

It is necessary to point out that the type of disability in the OD survey was assigned based on a self-declaration of the interviewed person. This self-declaration contains information if an individual 'has' any disability, if the disability is 'temporary' or 'permanent' and what is their type of disability (options are: motor, hearing, mental, visual or slow gait). The institutional classification of disability is limited to a given extent, not allowing further understanding of the diversity of this population, nor does it inform about other forms as exclusion such as race, gender or ethnicity. Yet, this is the most complete research available about mobility practices in the city. In order to compare the practices of the population with disabilities to the ones of the population that declared to have none, and to measure the relationship with other variables, we used the chi-square test. This analysis enables us to identify some characteristics of the practices of disabled group with more reliability.

The results demonstrate that there are 1.805 individuals (3.9% of Belo Horizonte population) that declared themselves as disabled and live in the city of Belo Horizonte. We have found that gender is distributed as follows: 44.8% are men, 55.2% are women; this distribution is quite similar to the distribution of the population 'without disabilities'. Yet, when it comes to age, there is a significant difference (P-value $= 0.000$ ($p < 0.05$)) between the groups: the most part of the persons with disabilities' population is in the group aged between 50 and 59 years (16.9%), a result similar to the results of other studies; this is related to the increase in the disability rate in the process of ageing (Sze & Christensen, 2017). However, we found that there is also a significant portion of people with disabilities considered young, in the age group of 20–29 years old (16.8%), belonging to the economically active population (Fig. 10.1).

The survey data for the city of Belo Horizonte show that among people in economically active ages (between 15 and 65 years according to the IBGE), only

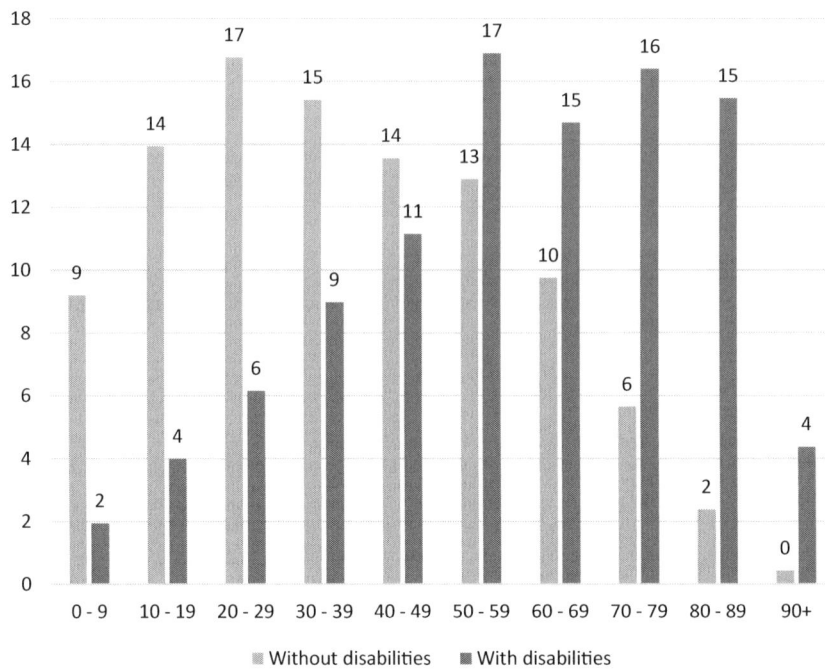

Fig. 10.1. Percentage Distribution of Persons With and Without Disabilities by Age in the City of Belo Horizonte. *Source:* Authors' calculations based on the OD survey data, taken in Belo Horizonte in 2012 (Minas Gerais, 2013).

12.5% of people with disabilities have reported employment, whereas among people who do not have disabilities this rate reached 59.6%. With respect to income, people with disabilities of Belo Horizonte show a very low level of earnings compared to the general population. These results indicate a low insertion of this population into the job market, which is associated not only with economic barriers but also with the lack of adequate access to urban mobility services (Clarke, Ailshire, Bader, Morenoff, & House, 2008; Rantakokko, Iwarsson, Portegijs, Viljanen, & Rantanen, 2015) (Fig. 10.2).

Inequalities in relation to employment may also be associated with levels of schooling in this group. The differences by level of education are evident: 37.9% of people with disabilities have incomplete primary education, and 13% are illiterate. For the group of people without disabilities, illiteracy is only at a 1.4% rate, with incomplete primary education corresponding to 27.2% of people from this group in the city of Belo Horizonte. On the other hand, only 6% of people with disabilities have completed higher education, the people without disabilities rate reaches 12.3% (P-value$= 0.000$ ($p < 0.05$)).

Low levels of education and low labour market insertions, as well as advanced age, seem to be significantly related to the structure of the trips of this population. To identify this pattern, we employed the average number of trips per individual

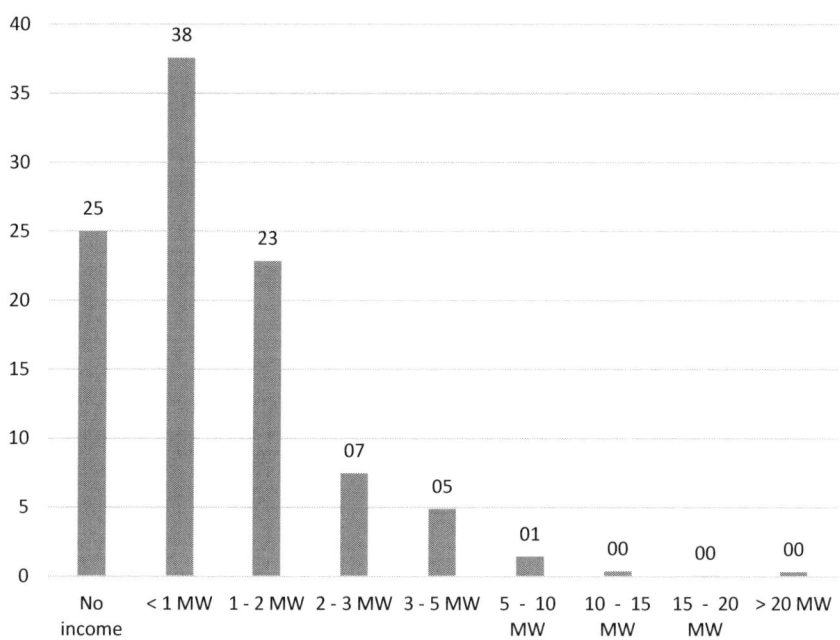

Fig. 10.2. Percentage Distribution of Per Capita Income in Minimum Wages of People with Disabilities. *Source*: Authors' calculations based on the OD survey data, taken in Belo Horizonte in 2012 (Minas Gerais, 2013).

per day. To obtain this value, the number of trips made was divided by the number of people who made those trips. For the total number of persons in the city of Belo Horizonte, the daily number of trips per person was 1.43 trips/person. In the case of people with disabilities, each individual with disabilities performed 0.62 trips per day. Another important difference can be observed when this value is compared between self-reported cases of permanent and temporary disability: the obtained values are 0.74 trips/person in case of temporary disability against 0.59 trips/person in case of permanent disability. These findings indicate that the mobility of persons with permanent disabilities is even more restricted.

Significant differences are observed when comparing diverse disability situations. The individuals that declared temporary disabilities travel more than those who declared permanent disabilities. The diversity is even more evident when we observe that while a person with temporary visual impairment makes 0.85 trips/day, a person with a permanent intellectual disability makes only 0.36 trips/day (Fig. 10.3).

Analysing the reasons for travel, besides returning home, it is important to note the significance of travels for health reasons for people with disabilities, especially in groups with motor disabilities, either temporary or permanent. It is also important to note that trips made by people with visual or hearing impairments were more diverse, with a predominance of travels to work or to go shopping (Table 10.1).

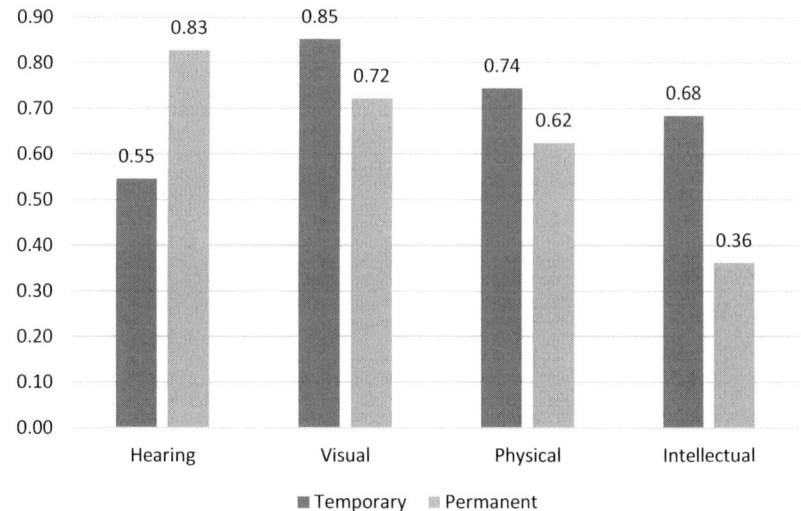

Fig. 10.3. Number of Trips per Day per Person in Belo Horizonte According to the Disability Type. *Source*: Authors' calculations based on the OD survey data, taken in Belo Horizonte in 2012 (Minas Gerais, 2013).

Table 10.1. Percentage Distribution of Reasons for Travelling in Belo Horizonte According to the Disability Type.

Type	Disability	Purpose											P-value
		A	B	C	D	E	F	G	H	I	J	K	
Physical	Without	3	13.4	0.3	3.4	3.2	2.2	2.4	1.4	46.0	2.3	22.4	0.000
Temporary	With	7	2.3	0	5.5	6.3	5.5	3.1	0	45.3	15.6	9.4	
Hearing	Without	3	13.4	0.3	3.4	3.2	2.2	2.4	1.4	46.0	2.3	22.4	0.011
Temporary	With	33.3	0	0	0	0	16.7	0	0	50.0	0	0	
Visual	Without	3	13.4	0.3	3.4	3.2	2.2	2.4	1.4	46.0	2.3	22.4	0.04
Temporary	With	4.3	4.3	0	4.3	4.3	4.3	4.3	4.3	43.5	8.9	17.5	
Intellectual	Without	3	13.4	0.3	3.4	3.2	2.2	2.4	1.4	46.0	2.3	22.4	0.000
Temporary	With	3.8	7.7	0	3.8	11.5	0	3.8	0	42.3	23.1	4	
Physical	Without	3	13.4	0.2	3.4	3.2	2.2	2.4	1.4	46.0	2.3	22.5	0.000
Permanent	With	5.4	7.3	0.6	6.7	4	4.2	4.5	1.3	47.0	12	7	
Hearing	Without	3	13.7	0.3	3.4	3.2	2.2	2.4	1.4	45.8	2.3	22.3	0.000
Permanent	With	7.3	7.3	0	6.3	2.1	3.1	3.1	1	47.9	10.4	11.5	
Visual	Without	3	13.4	0.3	3.4	3.2	2.2	2.4	1.4	46.0	2.3	22.4	0.000
Permanent	With	13.9	4.9	0	7.4	3.3	7.4	1.6	0.8	46.0	5.7	9	
Intellectual	Without	3	13.4	0.3	3.4	3.2	2.2	2.4	1.4	46.0	2.3	22.4	0.000
Permanent	With	3.7	24.8	0	3.1	0	1.9	2.5	0.6	47.9	9.9	5.6	
Slow gait	Without	3	13.5	0.2	3.4	3.2	2.1	2.4	1.4	46.0	2.4	22.4	0.000
	With	9.3	3.4	0.6	10	0.6	6.3	4	0.6	47.2	13	5	

Source: Authors' calculations based on the OD survey data in Belo Horizonte in 2012 (Minas Gerais, 2013).
Legend: A – shopping; B – studies; C – transfer; D – leisure; E – giving a ride; F – personal business; G – other; H – meal; I – home; J – health; and K – work.

Statistically, significant differences were found regarding the use of public transport, where people with disabilities tended to use public transport to a greater extent than those who did not declare disabilities; the latter employed private transport more. This difference, though small in absolute numbers, expresses an important dependence on public systems and, therefore, the need to ensure their accessibility for the group of people with disabilities. Both groups used non-motorised transport at the same rate; therefore, improvement of sidewalks and cycle lanes is of great importance to all citizens (Fig. 10.4).

The demographic profile of people with disabilities and their travel patterns demonstrate important differences from the people who declared themselves non-disabled. For the group of people with disabilities, immobility is a structuring reality of their daily life, associated with their great socioeconomic vulnerability, lower labour market insertion and low level of education. However, the diversity of disability situations is also a significant factor, and greater participation and mobility are observed among those with temporary disabilities, compared to persons with permanent disabilities.

As we described in the literature review, other studies point out that disability is not an inherent condition of individuals, but a relationship with their bodies, their socioeconomic situation and the urban environment (Altman, Lollar, & Rasch, 2014; Van Wee & Geurs, 2011). Each disability situation, in dialogue with the city, can enable or impose barriers to the participation in the dynamics of the city for groups with different corporealities (Chouinard et al., 2010; Clarke et al., 2008; Imrie & Street, 2011; Rantakokko et al., 2015; Shakespeare, 2001). Results show that inequalities are greater for those who present more permanent situations, particularly associated with intellectual disabilities. The diversity of situations

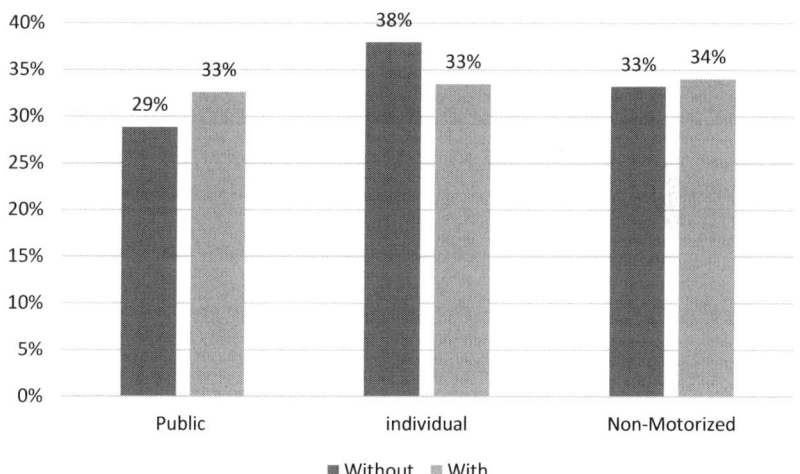

Fig. 10.4. Percentage Distribution of Modes of Transport of People with Disabilities in Belo Horizonte. *Source.* Authors' calculations based on the OD survey data, taken in Belo Horizonte in 2012 (Minas Gerais, 2013).

according to the different forms of disabilities is also relevant. The different corporealities display great variability in terms of immobility rates, labour market insertions and opportunities to access schooling. More generally speaking, the high rate of immobility and the heavy reliance on public transport for the people with disabilities of Belo Horizonte make up a challenge for public policies to ensure the right to mobility of these highly vulnerable groups.

4.2. Mobility Experiences of People with Disabilities in Belo Horizonte

The analysis of travel patterns based on the OD survey data does not provide enough information about the diversity of practices and demands of people with disabilities. From the experiences reported by the agents in the focus group, a high number of diverse issues and problems that they face daily can be noted. As Boys (2014) and Imrie and Street (2011) point out, it is necessary to understand the relational and political character of the mobility of the social group of persons with disabilities.

The results of the participatory exercise of the focus group present a complex view of the problem, which contrasts with the generalising, technical and homogenising approach seen in the legal arrangements. Together, the participants set out 176 demands on topics such as urban infrastructure, education and citizenship, relations between personnel and passengers at the boarding places and in buses, the effectiveness of public policies, modal and tariff integration, among others. In addition, the participants pointed to the lack of awareness and organisation of the civil society, the low compliance with the laws that guarantee the right to access and to the proper circulation of citizens and the strong process of privatisation of public spaces and modes of transport in the region.

The percentage distribution of responses is characterised by high dispersion, as most of the responses obtained less than 5% of mentions. Only the following items obtained a higher percentage of mentions: the holes on sidewalks (15%), the lack of education and respect from citizens (7.5%), the limited number of employees with knowledge in assisting persons with disabilities in bus systems (6.8%) and the defects in tactile paving surfaces for the visually impaired and the areas with obstacles (5.4%).

In order to arrange the problems according to their priority and to organise their connection with mobility policies, we established seven main themes. We found a higher concentration of the problems related to the physical accessibility of urban space (61%) than to the economic or social barriers to the use of the city. The category of physical accessibility includes both the devices that allow accessing public transport systems and the public spaces for collective use in general (Fig. 10.5).

Regarding physical accessibility to transport systems, the main demands are associated with the limited number of employees for the appropriate functioning of the transport services that would guarantee the operation of platforms in the traditional buses, both for people with motor disabilities and people with visual and hearing impairments (6.8%), the access to the public transport with universal design (4.8%) and the platforms and devices for deaf people (4.8%).

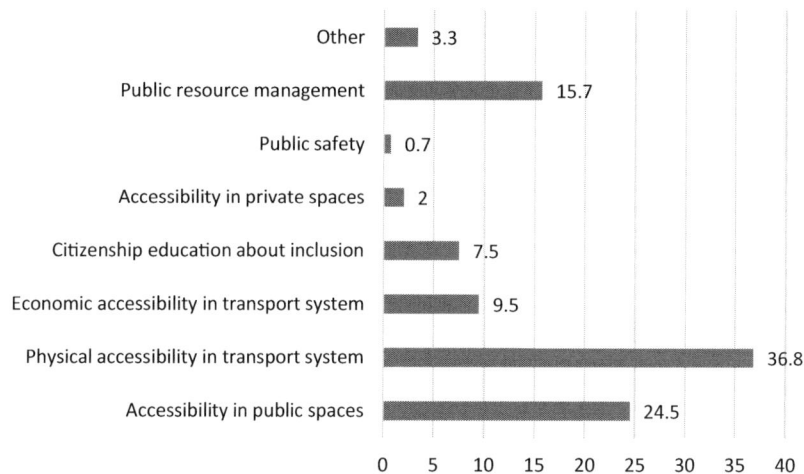

Fig. 10.5. Percentage Distribution of the Demands of the Participants of the Focus Group Regarding the Mobility for People with Disabilities in Belo Horizonte, by Thematic Axes. *Source*: Authors' calculations from the results of the accessibility workshop performed on August 24th, 2017.

Belo Horizonte was the first Brazilian city that, in 1999, introduced a high-autonomy low-floor bus with floor-level boarding as a standard model for the municipal public transport fleet. Local private operators, however, resisted the measure and slowed the annual fleet replacement rate. This led to the progressive ageing of the fleet, but the requirement was maintained by the public administrators until 2008 when it was revoked. The city that, in 2001, had 5% of its fleet consisting of these high-autonomy buses quickly removed them from circulation starting with 2008 and now have only buses that are equipped with a platform lift (De Oliveira, 2018a). It should be noted that this type of vehicle does not meet the requirements of the current Brazilian technical standards NBR 14022 (ABNT, 2006), and yet it is still being used in Belo Horizonte.

In 2014, on account of the FIFA Confederations Cup and World Cup, the BRT (bus rapid transit) system of Belo Horizonte, locally called 'Move', was implemented. Thus, the standard of vehicles with floor-level boarding was partially restored in the bus transport system, this time through the deployment of high platforms at the specialised stations of three transport corridors. By coincidence, the buses of this type represent 5% of the total operational bus fleet. Nevertheless, five years later the number of these floor-level boarding buses (that meet the accessibility requirements) remains the same, without any increase since the beginning of the operation (De Oliveira, 2018a).

The traditional bus fleet that provides services to most part of the population depends on manual operators for handling the platform lifts, which is why citizens identify the need for improvement in terms of the number of workers and the quality of care provided to persons with disabilities. In recent years, the presence of these 'agents on board' has been the subject of debates. The owners of transport companies justify dismissal of these agents from the transport systems with the reduction of travel costs. However, this dismissal has led to transport delays and new types of friction between passengers and operators.

Although the regulatory instruments and actions of public agents promote the universal design as a way of improving the quality standards of the urban mobility system, a high level of generalisation of legal provisions opens gaps for non-compliance from the part of private transport operators. The participants of the focus group pointed out that both in conventional buses and the BRT system, people with disabilities remain very dependent on operators and other citizens to solve their daily mobility demands. Thus, the limited number of workers who operate the platform lifts in conjunction with the high dependence of individuals with reduced mobility on these agents form a significant problem for the participants.

The second most important theme is related to the accessibility in public spaces (24.5%). Within this category, the high incidence of holes and the poor quality of public spaces were mentioned as the main issue (15%), followed by the defective/absent signs for visually impaired people (such as tactile paving surfaces) and the strong presence of areas with barriers (which together totalled 5.4%). The complaints regarding the public spaces can be understood as a claim for the right of appropriation and movement in these urban spaces in order to achieve a genuinely inclusive urban experience.

Imrie and Kumar (1998) point out that the configurations of the built environments have complex and daily effects on the material circumstances, identities and experiences of people with disabilities. Although the regulatory instruments prescribe the use of the universal design as a standard, and recognise the lack of physical continuity, homogeneity and adequate signalling as a shared problem, quality remains a complex and conflicting category.

Participants with visual impairment especially pointed out the difficulties for the correct implementation of tactile paving, which, if badly installed, causes more damage and hazards to walkers than its absence. Active representatives of wheelchair users specified the Portuguese pavement as a great enemy of proper circulation through the city. It was stated that this type of pavement, considered by public entities a historical heritage of the city, is always in terrible condition, especially in the central and hospital areas. It should be noted that the universal design rules set out in the plans and standards do not apply to certain areas of the city, as these areas are a subject of negotiations with cultural heritage protection laws.

On the other hand, according to local regulations, the maintenance of sidewalks in Belo Horizonte lies within the responsibility of the owners of the neighbouring properties. Thus, the sidewalks are maintained in an individual manner, yet have a collective impact on the city's walkable structure. The standardisation rules for sidewalks provided by the Belo Horizonte Mayor's Office (Belo Horizonte, 2019) seek to set up guidelines that would ensure that sidewalks are more regular, continuous, stable, slip-resistant and without abrupt changes in level or gradients that hinder pedestrian circulation. However, the city plans do not establish instruments for the renewal of urban areas, nor clear procedures and goals for expanding the range of spaces with universal design. The effective application of the guidelines for the sidewalks is dispersed and depends on the attention of various citizens to the fulfilment of the required accessibility standards. This implies a complex policy of multiple accountability and a high inconsistency and dispersion in the implementation of building standards.

The concentration of demands on the issue of the sidewalks shows strong attention of the focus group participants to the use of public spaces for the circulation of pedestrians or wheelchair users. The 2012 OD survey demonstrated that more than 33% of total travels were done on foot. Nevertheless, the organisation of the city's inner space favours the use of cars, while sidewalks remain almost invisible in mobility policies. This shows that the policies related to mobility spaces are uncoordinated, both with regard to the demands of the citizens who desire more attention to these city spaces and to the very configuration of responsibility attributions that these policies bring. At this point, it is important to emphasise that these spaces of mobility are not just places of transition, but also spaces of sociability and urban experience, which contribute to the construction of citizenship.

As stated by the perspective on disability proposed by Shakespeare and Watson (2001), all individuals, and not only the so-called 'persons with disabilities', are impaired at some level. Thus, it is important to place walking as the centrepiece of accessibility policies and to understand the relevance of the quality of pavements and other walking structures (walkways, crosswalks, etc.) to the mobility of all citizens. Greater attention to the conditions of the city's walkable structure would allow more inclusive access for everyone.

The third important demand was public resource management (15.7%). Focus group participants also shed light on the prevalence of private interests of transport system operators coupled with lack of adequate public policies (3.4%), as well as the non-compliance with laws, lack of political will and state control (giving together 2.7%) and the lack of specific accessibility policies (1.4%). All these demands demonstrate the need for greater accountability of the government and greater participation of citizens in the planning, execution and evaluation of accessibility policies. The fact that the instruments do not make any mention regarding the participation of citizens also contributes to the lack of accountability.

The fourth marked problem is related to the economic accessibility of transport (9.5%), a major issue in the development of the mobility capacity of individuals (Kaufmann, Bergman, & Joye, 2004). Though residents of RMBH over the age of 65 were entitled to free urban transport four years before this became a constitutional right, there are numerous obstacles to the exercise of this right. Each municipality of the region has its own particular procedures for issuing the gratuity card; it is an institutional barrier that hinders travelling in the region, where the activities are concentrated in the central area. There were also reported barriers related to the number of allowed trips and to the access of accompanying persons. For the people with disabilities, the care expenditures are high, and paired with their vulnerable condition, they reduce their capacity to benefit from the appropriate urban life.

Another substantial demand is related to educating citizens about inclusion (7.5%). It is directly linked to the identification of the lack of dialogue between the State and the citizens about accessibility policies (3.4%), the disrespect of the places reserved for vulnerable groups in the transport systems (2%) and the lack of organisation of the groups of people with disabilities themselves (1.4%). The participants of the focus group identified difficulties faced by the citizens in general, and particularly by the staff members, in dealing with language differences and specific demands of the population with disabilities.

The participants also pointed out the dominance of a homogenising vision, both in the policies and in the daily implementation of transport services, that understand all forms of disability within the scope of the demands of wheelchair users. Especially, deaf and blind people reported that they were always offered wheelchairs in places where they requested some assistance. This approach can be understood as a form of comprehension of this public problem, characterised by the construction of metonymic forms of language that hides or attributes the characteristics of one group to another (Ardila Pinto & Villamizar-Duarte, 2018; Kövecses, 2010).

More specific, but not less important demands for technological development in order to improve the applications that incorporate support for people with reduced mobility were also mentioned (3.4%). In 2015, PBH launched the SIU-Mobile application, which acts as a public transport access tool for its users. This application provides bus arrival forecasts, routes and schedules and has accessibility features for visually impaired persons, allowing them to express their interest in boarding by sending a message to the bus driver. This message appears on the bus control panel of the chosen line. Sheller and Urry (2006) pointed to uniting new communication technologies with urban transport systems, emphasising its influence on mobility patterns, co-presence, social exclusion and safety. The authors state that new technologies support new mobility forms and at the same time are being shaped and remodelled by them. Thus, the implementation of new technologies in urban transport proves to be a potential field to be explored in urban mobility planning.

As mentioned earlier, the analysis of focus group results presented a more complex reality than that portrayed in the policies or OD survey. People with disabilities in Belo Horizonte, like the residents of other cities around the world (Sagaris, 2014), seek to increase spaces for dialogue with public agents, service operators and citizens in general. More than just a homogeneous segregated group that needs special attention, these people fight for disability being approached as a social relationship embodied in time and space, for overcoming the reducing of individuals to the stigma of disability and for the recognition of the potential and diversity of these citizens.

5. FINAL CONSIDERATIONS

Both the academic literature and the demands of the citizens are challenging traditional views of disability. Far from being only a problem of physical accessibility to urban space or transport systems, the practices, experiences and representations of mobility of people with disabilities are part of a broader process of everyday life construction in the cities and of claiming rights to equality from the perspective of diversity. In Belo Horizonte, the technical devices and regulatory instruments have advanced significantly, but remain anchored in dichotomous, homogenising, abstract and extremely synthetic visions that pin identities and contribute to deepening the stigmas attached to these groups.

While recent regulatory instruments have introduced universal design as a guiding principle, these changes have not been enough to modify the city's mobility planning and management processes. Public spaces and transportation systems systematically contribute to increasing the exclusion of the population with disabilities, both by the quality and quantity of available physical devices and by the service of the employees. Meanwhile, the population's needs are diverse, both in terms of disability situations, as well as the spaces and agents involved in travelling practices. The urban space plays a key role in imposing barriers to travel at multiple scales.

Additionally, most people with disabilities in the city face high levels of immobility, as well as difficulties in accessing the city's goods and services, especially the services related to health, education and work. The high levels of illiteracy, unemployment and low-income contrast with the high dependence of people with disabilities on public transport and medical services. Thus, the urban space contributes to the intensification of the exclusion of these citizens, especially of the youngest and the poorest in the city. Therefore, the conditions of people with disabilities present a great accumulation of barriers and restrictions in a city that excludes and segregates its population from access to urban goods and services.

Public spaces for walking and public transport are vital to ensure the rights of both this particular group and the general population. However, the dynamics of urban management in these spaces create barriers that prevent their proper use, especially for people with disabilities. The city's transport system is deficient in ramps, turnstiles and adapted stations, as well as in enough information systems to guarantee universal, autonomous and free access for people with disabilities.

The organisational structure of the city's transport system, based on the concession system, with low enforcement capacity, does not offer technological devices nor a sufficient number of qualified employees to include people with disabilities as legitimate users of the system. From the perspective of the participants of the focus group, public policy and urban governance are based on a homogenising vision of citizens that treats them as universal, average users, without particular needs and demands. Special assistance depends on street level bureaucrats, who have high levels of administrative discretion and shape the daily experience of people with disabilities.

Furthermore, public space management is characterised by high dispersion and individualisation in the production of areas suitable for pedestrians in terms of quality and quantity. Sidewalks, ramps and other circulation areas are extremely heterogeneous and hinder a possibility of autonomous and safe use. In view of the lack of provision of adequate spaces and transport systems, the demands of the population with disabilities are varied and require structural changes in urban planning, in provision of public services and transport, as well as in the attitudes of citizens. The universal design, therefore, requires a broader and more complex application, especially in Latin American countries, with their very poor transportation systems and precarious assistance services. Political mobilisation and the creation of scenarios of participation of the citizens can contribute to the production of more diverse and democratic views on urban life.

This analysis of the practices and demands of the people with disabilities in mobility systems, based on the analysis of quantitative and qualitative methods, constitutes one of the primary efforts made in the city to acknowledge the barriers and challenges that citizens face daily to access urban transport and public spaces in the city, thus exercising their right to mobility. Some of the results show continuity of the situation in other cities. However, we have observed significant differences in regard to the forms of urban management, especially with respect to the public transport sector and to the production of public spaces.

Being a recent concern in the academic studies of the city, there is still the need to go deeper into key aspects such as the inclusion of the theme accessibility for the population with disabilities in normative instruments and in the implementation of local policies. We should particularly advance in the identification of barriers in the different transport modes, as well as in different areas of the city, with different morphological characteristics, use and activity distribution and transport availability. It is also necessary to further explore the organisation forms of this social group and the strategies employed to discuss their demands in the public sphere. Last but not least, it is also fundamental to advance in the understanding of the people's strategies, desires and expectations that challenge our notions of normality and justice with their diverse forms of appropriating and using the city.

REFERENCES

ABNT, Associação Brasileira de Normas Técnicas. (2006). *Acessibilidade em veículos de características urbanas para o transporte coletivo de passageiros.* Retrieved from http://www.cnmp.mp.br/portal/images/Comissoes/DireitosFundamentais/Acessibilidade/NBR_14022-2011_Onibus_Ed4.pdf

Altman, B. M., Lollar, D. J., & Rasch, E. K. (2014). The experience of environmental barriers among adults with disabilities: A national description. In B. M. Altman & S. N. Barnartt (Eds.), *Research in social science and disability* (Vol. 8, pp. 33–53). Bingley: Emerald Publishing Limited. https://doi.org/10.1108/S1479-354720140000008003

Ardila Pinto, A. M., & Villamizar-Duarte, N. (2018). Ciudad(anía) en movimiento: construcción social de instrumentos de políticas de movilidad en Bogotá y Belo Horizonte 1995–2015. *Universitas Humanística, 85*(85). https://doi.org/10.11144/Javeriana.uh85.cmcs

Banister, D. (2018). *Inequality in transport.* Oxfordshire: Alexandrine Press.

Belo Horizonte, PBH. (2011). Lei n.° 10.134, de 18 de março de 2011. *Institui a Política Municipal de Mobilidade Urbana.* Diário Oficial do Município – DOM, Belo Horizonte, ano XVII – Edição n.° 3788, 19 mar. (2011). Poder Executivo. Prefeitura de Belo Horizonte. Secretaria Municipal de Governo.

Belo Horizonte, PBH. (2018). Portaria do Código de Posturas: Regras para a padronização de passeios no município de Belo Horizonte. Secretaria Municipal de Política Urbana. Retrieved from https://prefeitura.pbh.gov.br/sites/default/files/estrutura-de-governo/politica-urbana/PASSEIO/padrao_de_passeios_municipal.pdf

Belo Horizonte, PBH. (2019). *Política Municipal de Mobilidade Urbana. Diário Oficial do Município.* Vol. Edição n.° 3788. Retrieved from https://leismunicipais.com.br/a/mg/b/belo-horizonte/lei-ordinaria/2011/1013/10134/lei-ordinaria-n-10134-2011-institui-a-politica-municipal-de-mobilidade-urbana

Bezyak, J. L., Sabella, S. A., & Gattis, R. H. (2017). Public transportation: An investigation of barriers for people with disabilities. *Journal of Disability Policy Studies, 28*(1), 52–60.

Boys, J. (2014). *Doing disability differently: An alternative handbook on architecture, dis/ability and designing for everyday life*. London: Routledge.

Brand, P. C., Dvila, J. D., University College London, Development Planning Unit, Universidad Nacional de Colombia (Medellín), Facultad de Arquitectura y Universidad de los Andes. (2012). *Movilidad urbana y pobreza: lecciones de Medellín y Soacha, Colombia*. London: University College London Universidad Nacional de Colombia.

Brasil. (2015). Emenda Constitucional: Dá nova redação ao art. 6º da Constituição Federal, para introduzir o transporte como direito social. Constituição Federal. Retrieved from http://www.planalto.gov.br/ccivil_03/constituicao/Emendas/Emc/emc90.htm

Cervero, R. (2011). *State roles in providing affordable mass transport services for low-income residents*. Discussion Paper No. 2011-17, Vol. 2011/17. International Transport Forum.

Chorley, R. J., & Haggett, P. (2013 [1967]). *Socio-economic models in geography*. London: Routledge.

Chouinard, V., Hall, E., & Wilton, R., (2010). *Towards enabling geographies: "Disabled" bodies and minds in society and space*. Geographies of Health Series. Farnham: Ashgate.

Clarke, P., Ailshire, J. A., Bader, M., Morenoff, J. D., & House, J. S. (2008). Mobility disability and the urban built environment. *American Journal of Epidemiology, 168*(5), 506–513. https://doi.org/10.1093/aje/kwn185

Da Silva Bampi, L. N., Guilhem, D., & Alves, E. D. (2010). Social model: A new approach of the disability theme. *Revista Latino-Americana de Enfermagem, 18*(4), 816–823. https://doi.org/10.1590/S0104-11692010000400022

De Oliveira, M. F. (2014). Ausências, avanços e contradições da atual política pública de mobilidade urbana de Belo Horizonte: uma pesquisa sobre o direito de acesso amplo e democrático ao espaço urbano. Tese (Doutorado em Ciências Sociais). Belo Horizonte: Pontifícia Universidade Católica de Minas Gerais (PUC Minas).

De Oliveira, M. F., & Souki, L. G. (2016). Avanços e obstáculos na formulação da política de mobilidade urbana em Belo Horizonte. In C.A.P. Faria, C.V. Rocha, C.A.C. Filgueiras, L.G. Souki (Eds.), *Políticas públicas na América Latina*: novas territorialidades e processos. Porto Alegre: UFRGS/CEGOV.

De Oliveira, M. F. (2018a). Nota técnica de acessibilidade n.º 1 – Conceituação e análise sobre acessibilidade em ônibus urbano do transporte público coletivo – versão C. C. Belo Horizonte: BHTrans. Retrieved from https://prefeitura.pbh.gov.br/bhtrans/informacoes/acessibilidade-para-todos/notas-tecnicas-de-acessibilidade

De Oliveira, M. F. (2018b). Nota técnica de acessibilidade n.º 5 – Proposta de Plano BHTrans de Acessibilidade na Mobilidade Urbana de Belo Horizonte (Plamu-BHTrans 2018). Belo Horizonte: BHTrans. Retrieved from https://prefeitura.pbh.gov.br/sites/default/files/estrutura-de-governo/bhtrans/2018/documentos/NotaTecnica_5_D_Plamu-BHTrans_2018-10-10_0.pdf

De Oliveira, M. F. (2019). Marco legal de acessibilidade no Brasil. Belo Horizonte: Levante-BH. Retrieved from http://levantebh.com.br/politica/marco-legal-de-acessibilidade-no-brasil

Fougeyrollas, P. (2010). *La funambule, le fil et la toile: transformations réciproques du sens du handicap*. Québec [Que.: Presses de l'Université Laval. Retrieved from http://www.deslibris.ca/ID/434736

Gannon, C., & Liu, Z. (1997). *Poverty and transport. Discussion paper*. Washington, DC: World Bank. Retrieved from http://www.rhd.gov.bd/Documents/ExternalPublications/WorldBank/TransSectPub/contents/documents/B03.pdf

Gell, N. M., Rosenberg, D. E., Carlson, J., Kerr, J., & Belza, B. (2015). Built environment attributes related to GPS measured active trips in mid-life and older adults with mobility disabilities. *Disability and Health Journal, 8*(2), 290–295. https://doi.org/10.1016/j.dhjo.2014.12.002

Geurs, K. T., & van Wee, B. (2004). Accessibility evaluation of land-use and transport strategies: Review and research directions. *Journal of Transport Geography, 12*(2), 127–140. https://doi.org/10.1016/j.jtrangeo.2003.10.005

Gharebaghi, A., Mostafavi, M.-A., Edwards, G., Fougeyrollas, P., Gamache, S., & Grenier, Y. (2018). Integration of the social environment in a mobility ontology for people with motor disabilities. *Disability and Rehabilitation: Assistive Technology, 13*(6), 540–551. https://doi.org/10.1080/17483107.2017.1344887

Gleeson, B. (1999). *Geographies of disability*. London: Routledge.
Goggin, G. (2016). Disability and mobilities: Evening up social futures. *Mobilities*, *11*(4), 533–541. https://doi.org/10.1080/17450101.2016.1211821
Hamraie, A. (2017). *Building access: Universal design and the politics of disability*. Minneapolis, MN: University of Minnesota Press.
Hine, J., & Mitchell, F. (2001). Better for Everyone? Travel experiences and transport exclusion. *Urban Studies*, *38*(2), 319–332.
IBGE. (2010). Censo Demográfico 2010: Características urbanísticas do entorno dos domicílios. Retrieved from https://ww2.ibge.gov.br/home/estatistica/populacao/censo2010/entorno/entorno_tab_municipios_zip_xls.shtm
Imrie, R., & Kumar, M. (1998). Focusing on disability and access in the built environment. *Disability & Society*, *13*(3), 357–374. https://doi.org/10.1080/09687599826687
Imrie, R., & Street, E. (2011). *Architectural design and regulation*. Chichester: Wiley-Blackwell.
Kain, J. F. (1968). Housing segregation, Negro employment, and metropolitan decentralization. *The Quarterly Journal of Economics*, *82*(2), 175. https://doi.org/10.2307/1885893
Kaufmann, V., Bergman, M. M., & Joye, D. (2004). Motility: Mobility as capital. *International Journal of Urban and Regional Research*, *28*(4), 745–756. https://doi.org/10.1111/j.0309-1317.2004.00549.x
Kirchner, C. E., Gerber, E. G., & Smith, B. C. (2008). Designed to deter. *American Journal of Preventive Medicine*, *34*(4), 349–352. https://doi.org/10.1016/j.amepre.2008.01.005
Kövecses, Z., & Benczes, R. (2010). *Metaphor: A practical introduction* (2nd ed.). New York, NY: Oxford Univ. Press.
Levy, J. (2009). Os Novos Espaços da Mobilidade. *GEOgraphia*, *3*(6), 7. https://doi.org/10.22409/GEOgraphia2001.v3i6.a13407
Litman, T. (2017). Evaluating transportation equity guidance for incorporating distributional impacts in transportation planning. Victoria Transport Policy Institute. Retrieved from http://www.vtpi.org/equity.pdf
Miles, M. B., & Huberman, A. M. (1984). *Qualitative data analysis: A sourcebook of new methods*. Beverly Hills, CA: Sage Publications.
Minas, G., SEGEM, & ADRMBH. (2013). Relatório completo pesquisa origem e destino 2011/2012. Belo Horizonte: Governo do Estado De Minas Gerais. Secretaria de Estado Extraordinária de Gestão Metropolitana (SEGEM); Agência De Desenvolvimento da Região Metropolitana de Belo Horizonte. Retrieved from http://www.agenciarmbh.mg.gov.br/wp-content/uploads/2016/06/Relatorio-Completo-Pesquisa-OD-2012-1.pdf
Oviedo, H. D., & Titheridge, H. (2016). Mobilities of the periphery: Informality, access and social exclusion in the urban fringe in Colombia. *Journal of Transport Geography*, *55*(7), 152–164. https://doi.org/10.1016/j.jtrangeo.2015.12.004
Parent, L. (2016). The wheeling interview: Mobile methods and disability. *Mobilities*, *11*(4), 521–532. https://doi.org/10.1080/17450101.2016.1211820
Rantakokko, M., Iwarsson, S., Portegijs, E., Viljanen, A., & Rantanen, T. (2015). Associations between environmental characteristics and life-space mobility in community-dwelling older people. *Journal of Aging and Health*, *27*(4), 606–621. https://doi.org/10.1177/0898264314555328
Rosenberg, D. E., Huang, D. L., Simonovich, S. D., & Belza, B. (2013). Outdoor built environment barriers and facilitators to activity among midlife and older adults with mobility disabilities. *The Gerontologist*, *53*(2), 268–279. https://doi.org/10.1093/geront/gns119
Sagaris, L. (2014). Citizen participation for sustainable transport: The case of 'living city' in Santiago, Chile (1997–2012). *Journal of Transport Geography*, *41*(dezembro), 74–83. https://doi.org/10.1016/j.jtrangeo.2014.08.011
Sawchuk, K. (2017). Impaired. In P. Adey, D. Bissell, K. Hannam, P. Merriman, & M. Sheller (Eds.), *The Routledge handbook of mobilities* (pp. 409–420). London: Routledge.
Schönfelder, S., & Axhausen, K. W. (2010). *Urban rhythms and travel behaviour: Spatial and temporal phenomena of daily travel*. Transport and Society. Farnham: Ashgate.
Seguí Pons, J. M., & Petrus Bey, J. M. (1991). *Geografía de redes y sistemas de transporte*. Colección Espacios y sociedades. Serie general, no. 16. Madrid: Editorial Síntesis.
Shakespeare, T., & Watson, N. (2001). The social model of disability: An outdated ideology? In B. M. Altman & S. N. Barnartt (Eds.), *Research in social science and disability* (Vol. 2, pp. 9–28). Bingley: Emerald (MCB UP).

Sheller, M. (2008). Mobility, freedom and public space. In S. Bergmann & T. Sager (Eds.), *The ethics of mobilities: Rethinking place, exclusion, freedom and environment* (pp. 25–38). Burlington, VT: Ashgate.

Sheller, M., & Urry, J. (2006). The new mobilities paradigm. *Environment and Planning A: Economy and Space, 38*(2), 207–226. https://doi.org/10.1068/a37268

Sze, N. N., & Christensen, K. M. (2017). Access to urban transportation system for individuals with disabilities. *IATSS Research, 41*(2), 66–73. https://doi.org/10.1016/j.iatssr.2017.05.002

Urry, J. (2007). *Mobilities*. Cambridge: Polity Press.

Van Wee, B., & Geurs, K. T., 2011. Discussing equity and social exclusion in accessibility evaluations. *European Journal of Transport and Infrastructure Research, 11*(4), 350–367. https://doi.org/10.18757/ejtir.2011.11.4.2940

Velho, R., Holloway, C., Symonds, A., & Balmer, B. (2016). The effect of transport accessibility on the social inclusion of wheelchair users: A mixed method analysis. *Social Inclusion, 4*(3), 24.

Wachs, M., & Kumagai, T. G. (1973). Physical accessibility as a social indicator. *Socio-Economic Planning Sciences, 7*(5), 437–456. https://doi.org/10.1016/0038-0121(73)90041-4

Wahl, H.-W., Iwarsson, S., & Oswald, F. (2012). Aging well and the environment: Toward an integrative model and research agenda for the future. *The Gerontologist, 52*(3), 306–316. https://doi.org/10.1093/geront/gnr154

Wasfi, R., Levinson, D., & El-Geneidy, A. (2012). Measuring the transportation needs of seniors. *Journal of Transport Literature, 6*(2), 08–32. https://doi.org/10.1590/S2238-10312012000200002

Webber, S. C., Porter, M. M., and Menec, V. H. (2010). Mobility in older adults: A comprehensive framework. *The Gerontologist, 50*(4), 443–450. https://doi.org/10.1093/geront/gnq013

Yen, I. H., Michael, Y. L., & Perdue, L. (2009). Neighborhood environment in studies of health of older adults. *American Journal of Preventive Medicine, 37*(5), 455–463. https://doi.org/10.1016/j.amepre.2009.06.022

EPILOGUE

URBAN MOBILITY AND SOCIAL EQUITY IN LATIN AMERICAN CITIES: EVIDENCE, CONCEPTS AND METHODS FOR MORE INCLUSIVE CITIES

Julio D. Dávila

As I write, the world is struggling with the novel Covid-19 respiratory virus pandemic, the most difficult challenge faced by humanity in generations. As infected individuals unwittingly continued to travel in a world more interconnected than ever before, the virus rapidly spread from China to parts of Asia, Europe, North and South America, and is making its way to the Middle East and Sub-Saharan Africa. The measures taken around the world to contain it[1] have placed a huge fiscal and monetary burden on their governments – and on future generations. This initially involved a range of measures to contain the spread of the deadly virus by tracing and isolating infected cases, and subsequently deal with the high levels of morbidity and mortality that risk overwhelming even the most advanced health systems. More importantly, it has also involved temporarily stopping most forms of face-to-face interactions other than with household members through variations on 'lockdown' measures, thus effectively bringing entire national and city economies to a screeching halt for a few weeks. In cities for which there is reliable data, by early May 2020, this had resulted in mobility being reduced to less than 10% of their usual patterns, as reported by Google[2] and Citymapper.[3]

What has the current pandemic got to do with urban mobility and social equity, the topics of this book? The key lies in all of these concepts: urban, mobility and social equity. Scientists are still trying to model the behaviour of Covid-19. The virus can be lethal for some vulnerable individuals; it spreads rapidly and easily through direct contact or in close proximity to an infected person, but it also survives for hours or even days on different surfaces. More worryingly, it would seem to persist in the form of microparticles suspended in the air many minutes after an infected person has sneezed, coughed or even spoken. All of this has extremely worrying consequences for cities. The quality that makes cities so unique as one of humankind's best inventions is their ability to facilitate the exchange of goods, services and ideas often through personal contact with others. Over the past 10,000 years or so, cities have been at the core of all forms of cultural and economic advances. The stringent lockdown and 'social distancing' measures imposed by governments the world over, desperate to reduce the speed at which the virus spreads while a long-term solution is found (such as a vaccine), conspire against this very quality of cities. At present, no amount of communications technology, however sophisticated, offers a substitute for face-to-face interactions, a feature so central to human society for thousands of generations.

The pandemic has also struck at the core of the issue of mobility and potentially threatens some of the policy gains made in the past few decades. Mindful of the heavy carbon and health cost of car-centric urban plans implemented in the richer nations in the 1950s and 1960s and subsequently copied elsewhere, in recent years progressive policy prescriptions have sought to avoid the need to travel, shift essential transport towards non-motorised or efficient public transport modes, and improve the fuel-efficiency and lower the emissions of all forms of transport (the 'avoid-shift-improve' model).[4] Urban and transport planners have sought to align more closely their plans to make cities more compact with diverse activities closer to each other so the need to travel is reduced.

If well thought out, these policies can potentially contribute towards more equitable cities, as poorer citizens who tend to travel longer distances and spend a higher share of their income on transport can instead devote more time to their personal development and the well-being of their families. In the rare case of an epidemic such as Covid-19, or some threat to street life such as a terrorist attack on public transport systems, unless stringent measures are taken to make public transport safe for all, people will take matters into their own hands by, for example, shifting to private cars or motorbikes if they can afford them, or else spend even longer time walking to work. This would reverse any social and economic gains sought by a succession of progressive policies. It is also likely to leave a very large hole in municipal finances as much-needed revenues from public transport fares are drastically reduced.

The pandemic is exacerbating socio-economic inequalities around the world. In both middle and high-income countries, only some white-collar workers are able to continue working from home while those employed in factories, retail, hospitality, personal services and as street traders who must travel to work risk being infected or deprived of an income during a lockdown.[5] As research from the UK shows,[6] those with lowest household incomes are less able to work from home, a result echoed in preliminary results from research on Colombian cities.[7] Evidence from the UK and the US points to ethnic minorities being much more likely to die from the disease.[8]

As those able to work from home using the internet will also tend to earn higher incomes than those in manual occupations, such measures are likely to further exacerbate already wide income inequalities, at least in the short term. Once the data become available, evidence from the large-scale experiments that lockdowns embody is likely to show that the ability to travel safely and efficiently is essential to generate wealth, reduce income inequalities and, therefore, improve social equity, the central theme of this book.

The unprecedented situation in which most of humanity finds itself offers policymakers valuable lessons. Before Covid-19, and largely due to the effects of the SARS epidemic in 2003, only a handful of countries such as Taiwan, Singapore, China and Hong Kong had adopted preventive epidemic plans. It is very likely that many countries will add the threat of new epidemics to the planning of new urban transport infrastructure.

As the highly engaging chapters in this book make abundantly clear, scholars and policymakers have learned much from applying social, environmental and spatial lenses to the study of transport. The current global emergency should help remind us of these extremely valuable advances. The challenge remains to make cities and urban transport safe, more equitable and less environmentally damaging for present and future generations, so that it continues to provide a lifeline to city economies, to communities and to individuals' own development.

NOTES

1. IMF. (2020). Policy responses to Covid-19. Retrieved from https://www.imf.org/en/Topics/imf-and-covid19/Policy-Responses-to-COVID-19. Accessed on May 4, 2020.

2. https://www.google.com/covid19/mobility/

3. https://citymapper.com/cmi

4. GIZ. (n.d.). Sustainable urban transport: Avoid-shift-improve. Retrieved from https://ledsgp.org/wp-content/uploads/2016/01/SUTP_GIZ_FS_Avoid-Shift-Improve_EN.pdf. Accessed on May 4 2020.

5. *The Guardian*. (2020). Lockdowns leave poor Latin Americans with impossible choice: Stay home or feed families. *The Guardian,* April 21. Retrieved from https://www.theguardian.com/world/2020/apr/21/latin-america-coronavirus-lockdowns-low-income. Accessed on May 4, 2020.

6. Atchison, C. J., Bowman, L., Vrinten, C., Redd, R., Pristera, P., Eaton, J. W., & Ward, H. (2020). Perceptions and behavioural responses of the general public during the COVID-19 pandemic: A cross-sectional survey of UK Adults. Retrieved from https://www.medrxiv.org/content/10.1101/2020.04.01.20050039v1. Accessed on May 4, 2020.

7. Oviedo, D., Arellana, J., Guzmán, L. A., & Moncada, C. (2020). Efectos de las medidas para mitigar la propagación del COVID-19 en los patrones de actividad y movilidad en Colombia: Primeros hallazgos. Retrieved from https://intalinc-lac.com/covid19/reporte_1. Accessed on May 4, 2020.

8. *BBC*. (2020). Coronavirus: Black African deaths three times higher than white Britons (May 1, 2020); APMResearchLab. (2020). The color of coronavirus: Covid-19 deaths by race and ethnicity in the US. Retrieved from https://www.apmresearchlab.org/covid/deaths-by-race. Accessed on May 4, 2020.

INDEX

Abnormality, 216
Access, 16–17, 60–63, 89
   in RTS, 200–203
   at Transitory Hospital, 197–200
Accessibility, 12–14, 60–61, 210
   Bogotá and unequal distribution, 17–26
   challenging, 6–7
   to destinations, 106
   local, 5–6
   as measure of urban (in) equality, 15–17
   mesoscale, 16
   reflections for policy and practice in Latin America, 26–28
   structural dimensions of, 3–4
Active commuting, 150
Active travel, 5–6
Activity-based approach, 44–53
Adolescents, 154
After-school programmes, 176–177
Age, 155
Annual average of daily traffic (AADT), 181
Anti-asylum movement, 192
Appropriation, 88–89
Asylums, 193
Atlas. ti software, 197
'Automobility', 105, 108
Autonomy, 142

Belo Horizonte, 60, 207, 210
   mobility experiences of people with disabilities in, 224–228
   urban accessibility in, 210–218
Belo Horizonte Metropolitan Region (BHMR), 217
BHTrans Plan of Accessibility for Urban Mobility in Belo Horizonte, 211

Bicimachismos, 143
Bicycle, 136, 139
Biking, 150
Body mass index (BMI), 157
Bogotá, 101
   household employees, transportation and socio-spatial stratification in, 91–97
   public transportation system, 89–91
   and unequal distribution of accessibility, 17–26
Brazil's Federal legal framework, 210
Brazilian Law for Inclusion of People with Disabilities, 210
Bus rapid transit system (BRT system), 17, 90, 225

Calibration factor, 65
Capetillo, 180
Care, 193
   crisis, 35
   mobility, 4, 38, 42–43
   role, 141
   trips, 71
Center for Disease Control and Prevention (CDC), 153, 156
Chained journeys, 63
Chi-square test, $55n4$
Child Friendly City movement, 173
Children/childhood, 60, 63, 66, 170
   activities, 184
   mobility disadvantages, 171–172
   obesity, 154
   playability, 171–173, 177–181
   social disadvantages of children's capability to play outside in neighbourhood, 176–177
   subvert time and space structure in favour of greater playability, 182–183

City planning, 36
City spaces
   methodology, 195–197
   research problem, 194–195
   theoretical discussion, 192–194
Class position, 87
Collective taxis, 123
Competence, 89
Complete streets concept, 185
Complex survey data analysis, 159
Comunas, 111–116, 121
Congress for the New Urbanism ('CNU'), 174
Covid-19 pandemic, 235–237
Crime perception in poor neighbourhood, 181–182
Culture, 155
Cycle taxis, 121
Cycling, 106, 108, 116, 121, 123, 136, 147. (*see also* Walking)
   analysis, 140–144
   linking to well-being, 139
   methodology, 140
   modal share by women, 138
   woman cyclists in Latin America, 137–138
   for women, 136

Daily mobility, 34
Daily travelling practices of people with disabilities, 219–224
Daily trips, 138
Democracy, symbol of, 144
Domestic labour, 87

Ecologies of modes, 123
Economic necessity, 87
Ella se mueve segura (ESMS), 118
Emotive factors, 135. (*see also* Social factors)
   freedom and autonomy, 142
   happiness, 142–143
   self-esteem and empowerment, 142
Empleadas Domésticas in Colombia, 87–88
Empowerment, 142

Encuesta de Movilidad Domiciliaria, 138
Equality, 193
Equity, 12
   in sustainable transport, 104–105
Ethnicity, 155
Everyday life, 34
Exercise, 155, 159
Expansion factor, 65

Family mobility patterns, 60
   methodology, 63–65
   mobility, access and gender, 61–63
   results, 65–79
Family pressure, 87
Fear, 96
Female household employees, 86
   Bogotá's public transportation system, 89–91
   household employees, transportation and socio-spatial stratification in Bogotá, 91–97
   household labour, space and mobility, 87–89
Financial access, 61
Freedom, 142
   of mobility, 192–193
Gender, 61–63, 105–109, 137
   relations, 36
   roles, 87
   in Santiago, 128–129
   in sustainable transport, 104–105

Gender-neutral transport, 104
Gendered mobility patterns, 39–42
Gini indices, 29
Gross domestic product (GDP), 60

Happiness, 142–143
Health, 153–156
Hispanic high school students, 150, 152
   data source, 156
   descriptive statistics of survey responses, 157–158
   method, 156–157
   participants, 157
   physical activity and health, 153–156

Index   241

policy recommendations, 162–164
race/ethnicity differences, 159–162
results, 157–162
statistical analysis, 156
study measures, 157
in United States, 152–153
Home-based care and work trips, 45
Horizontal accessibility, 214
Household
  employees, 86–87, 91–97
  labour, 87–89

Immobility, 65–66, 223
Impairments, 215
Insecurity, 96
Institute for Transportation and Development Policy (ITDP), 137
Instrumental factors
  care role and labour market, 141
  security and sexual harassment, 140–141
  technical skills, 141–142
Integrated Public Transport System (SITP), 90, 93–94
Interlocutors, 92–93, 95–96, 102
International Network for Transport and Accessibility in Low Income Communities (INTALInC LAC), 8

Labour market, 141
Latin America, 1, 12–13, 34
  cities in, 8
  reflections for policy and practice in, 26–28
  urban mobility and transport policies in, 3
  woman cyclists in, 137–138
Livable cities, 174
Liveability, 17
Local accessibility, 5–6

Men differential itineraries, 44–53
Mental health policies, 193
Meso accessibility, 28

Mesoscale of accessibility, 16
Metro underground train system, 116
Metropolitan Santiago, 120
Micro accessibility, 28
Micromachismos, 143
Mistrust, 96
Mobility, 4, 36, 61–64, 66, 87–89, 170
  disadvantages of children, 171–172
  experiences of people with disabilities in Belo Horizonte, 224–228
  general mobility statistics and patterns, 101–102
  mode of transport, 72–77
  motivation, 67–72
  patterns, 34, 63
  poverty, 6, 170
  practices, 211, 214
  ratio of trips per journey, 77–79
  in RTS, 200–203
  to school, 150
  in social sciences, 192
  at Transitory Hospital, 197–200
  turn perspective, 215
Modal share, 111–116
  evolution and investment by transport mode, 109–111
Model of Mental Health Care, 192
Montevideo
  case study, 37
  conceptual framework, 35–37
  data and methods, 37–38
  gender differences in, 34
  results, 38–53
Montevideo Metropolitan Region (MMR), 35
Motherhood practices, 36
'Motility', 88–89
'Move' system, 225
Multitasking, 63–64

National Youth Physical Activity and Nutrition Study (NYPANS), 152, 156–157
Neighbourhood of Río Piedras
  children's mobility, 171
  children's playability, 177–181

findings, 181–184
literature review, 173–177
mobility disadvantages of children, 171–172
playability of children, 172–173
Neighbourhood perception, 151
Neo-traditional cities and neighbourhoods, 174
Non-governmental organisations (NGOs), 136
Non-mandatory accessibility, 24–25

Organisational access, 61
Orientation, 170
Origin–Destination Survey (O–D Survey), 60, 63–64, 67, 211

Palma ratios, 29
Parents' perception of traffic, 151
People with disabilities, 216, 227
Perceptions and experiences of safety, 96–97
Permanent Accessibility Commission of Belo Horizonte, 211
Personal safety, 138
Physical
  access, 61
  activity, 153–156
Planning, 120–122
Play, 171
  opportunities to play in city, 174–176
  and relationship to children's mobility in neighbourhood, 173–174
  social disadvantages of children's capability to play outside in neighbourhood, 176–177
Playability, 171, 184
  of children, 172–173, 177–181
  study area, 178–181
Population growth, 150
Poverty, 111–116, 176
Project for Public Spaces ('PPS'), 174–175
Psychiatric Reform Policy, 193

Psychosocial
  attention network, 193
  factors, 155
Public policies, 192
Public spaces, 7
Public transport, 21–22
  subsidies, 27
Public transportation system (Bogotá), 89–91, 101
Puerto Rico State Highway System, 178

Quasi-Poisson regression, 152, 156

Race/ethnicity differences in effects of active commuting and physical activity behaviours, 155, 159–162
Residential Therapeutic Services (RTS), 194
  mobility and access in, 200–203
Río Piedras, 178–181
Road PR-27, 181
Road safety, 138
Rural-to-urban migration, 87

Safety
  perception and sexual harassment in Santiago's public transport system, 118–120
  perceptions and experiences of, 96–97
Santiago de Chile
  modal share evolution and investment by transport mode, 109–111
  origin–destination data revealing about women's travel in, 109–118
  poverty and modal share, 111–116
  safety perception and sexual harassment in, 118–120
  trip purpose, 117–118
Security, 140–141
Self-esteem, 142
Serra Verde Clinic (SVC), 194

'Sex', 105
Sexual
  division of labour, 35
  harassment, 140–141
Shadowing, 197
Single-use residential subs, 175
SIU-Mobile application, 228
Social equity, 1–2, 152, 193
Social factors, 143
  bicimachismos, 143
  socialisation with others, 143
  symbol of democracy, 144
Social inclusion, 170
Social justice, 15
Social mobility, 141
Social sustainability, 106
Socialisation with others, 143
Socio-geographical stratification, 89
  in Bogotá, 91–97
Socioeconomic status, 155
Space, 87–89
  space-time constraints, 36, 62
Spatial segregation, 95–96
'Splintering Urbanism', 19
State Department of Metropolitan
  Management (SEGEM),
  217
Stratification, 86
Structural dimensions of accessibility,
  3–4
Subjective well-being (SWB), 139
'Subjectivity', 139
*Subsecretaria de Movilidad Sustentable
  y Segura*, 138
Superintendence of Urban Trains of
  Belo Horizonte (STU-BH),
  218
Sustainable transport
  challenges and opportunities for,
    120–123
  gender and equity in, 104–105

Tactile paving, 226
Technical skills, 141–142
Temporal access, 61
Time geography, 36

Time-structured and place-determined
  'play' in neighbourhood,
  183–184
Traditional city, 175
Transitory Hospital, 194
  mobility and access at, 197–200
Transmilenio, 17–18, 23, 90, 93
Transport, 3–4. (*see also* Sustainable
  transport)
  in Chile, 105
  corridors, 17
  deficiency, 14
  planners, 136
  projects, 136
  in Santiago, 128–129
  services, 15
'Transport justice', 104–109
Transport of Contagem (TransCon),
  218
Transportation, 91–97
  means of, 93–95
  planning, 170
Travel
  behaviour, 34, 40
  motivations, 67–72
  satisfaction, 139
Trip, 64–65, 69
  chaining, 117, 123
  purpose, 117–118
  trip-based analysis of gendered
    mobility patterns, 44
Two-trip itineraries, 45

United Nations (UN), 150, 164
United Nations' Sustainable
  Development Goals
  (SDGs), 13
United States, Hispanics in, 152–153
Universal design, 210
Urban (in) equality, accessibility as
  measure of, 15–17
Urban accessibility in Belo Horizonte,
  210
  conceptual framework, 216–217
  data collection and systematization,
    217–218

frameworks and methods, 216–218
literature review, 212–216
results, 218–228
Urban design-models, 174
Urban development, 15
Urban environments, 14
  and services, 214
Urban geography, 89
Urban mobility, 1–2, 60–62, 66, 152, 206. (*see also* Mobility)
Urban planning, 174
Urban policies, 211
Urban transport planning process, 12
  limitations of traditional approaches to, 13
Urbanisation, 150
Uruguay, 37

Vertical accessibility, 213–214

Walking, 88, 94, 106, 108–109, 122, 150–151. (*see also* Cycling)
  to school, 150–151
  trips, 104, 116
Well-being, 14
  cycling linking to, 139
Women
  cyclists in Latin America, 1 37–138
  differential itineraries, 44–53
  mobility, 91, 93
Work
  schedules, 91–93
  trips, 71
  work-related activities, 48
  work-related mobility, 68

Zoning ordinances, 175